DAVID C. RAPOPORT

WAVES OF GLOBAL TERRORISM

From 1879 to the Present

Columbia University Press / New York

Columbia University Press
Publishers Since 1893
New York   Chichester, West Sussex
cup.columbia.edu
Copyright © 2022 Columbia University Press

Library of Congress Cataloging-in-Publication Data
Names: Rapoport, David C., author.
Title: Waves of global terrorism : from 1879 to the present / David C. Rapoport.
Description: New York : Columbia University Press, [2022] |
Includes bibliographical references and index.
Identifiers: LCCN 2021046718 (print) | LCCN 2021046719 (ebook) |
ISBN 9780231133029 (hardback ; alk. paper) | ISBN 9780231133036 (paperback ;
alk. paper) | ISBN 9780231507844 (ebook)
Subjects: LCSH: Terrorism—History.
Classification: LCC HV6431 .R367 2022 (print) | LCC HV6431 (ebook) |
DDC 363.325—dc23
LC record available at https://lccn.loc.gov/2021046718
LC ebook record available at https://lccn.loc.gov/2021046719

Columbia University Press books are printed on permanent
and durable acid-free paper.
Printed in the United States of America

Cover design: Avivah Rapoport
Cover images: Shutterstock and VectorStock

WAVES OF GLOBAL TERRORISM

This book is dedicated to my lovely wife, Barbara,

whose intense commitment made it possible.

CONTENTS

INTRODUCTION

Shirked by our historians, the subject has been repressed in the national consciousness. We have been victims of what members of the National Commission on the Causes and Prevention of Violence have called a "historical amnesia"!. . . For the long span from about 1938 to the mid-1960s . . . the internal life of the country was unusually free of violent episodes. Americans who came of age during and after the 1930s found it easy to forget how violent a people their forebears had been.

—RICHARD HOFSTADTER, "REFLECTIONS ON VIOLENCE IN THE UNITED STATES"

Unlike crime, terrorism is not a permanent feature of our societies. Intermittent political events inspire terrorist activity. Global terrorism emerged in the 1880s, but terrorism with a more limited geographic base had been a significant feature of political life long before. It was largely confined to individual states, and terrorist groups in one state made no effort to cooperate with terrorist groups in other states. Earlier terrorist groups often survived much longer than their more recent global counterparts. Some states never experienced terrorist activity, and those that did had long periods of time when they did not.

The term "global terror" has been part of our political vocabulary since the late twentieth century, and it is usually linked to the invention of the computer and the internet. But the term should also be used to explain the evolution of rebel terror in the late 1880s, a development associated with important changes in politics and technology. The French Revolution transformed European politics dramatically in ways that became particularly visible after Napoleon's forces were crushed. Many insurrections, inspired by the desire to succeed where the French Revolution had failed, then materialized throughout Europe, creating nation-states as secular and egalitarian societies. An uprising in one state generated comparable efforts elsewhere, producing four different cycles in the nineteenth century. Passports were not needed at the time, and individuals crossed European borders frequently to become deeply involved in uprisings elsewhere, intensifying the international character of these events and creating what Alexis de Tocqueville called the "professional revolutionary," who spent their life participating in revolutions in different states.

While the French Revolution transformed the politics of the European continent, it was not until the terrorism of the 1880s that revolutionary activity transcended Europe and became global.[1] The technological changes contributing to the global character of terrorism were quite conspicuous. The telegraph transmitted information across the world in moments, and the new daily mass newspapers spread that information quickly to large numbers of people. The railroad and the steamship made international travel easy, quick, and inexpensive. In subsequent periods, the telephone, radio, television, airplane, and internet further reduced the time necessary for communication, made it possible to describe incidents and plans more graphically, and increased the numbers of residents of other countries that could be involved in a plot.

Another major technological change with enormous international impact materialized after Alfred Nobel in 1867 invented dynamite for mining purposes. Others quickly discovered that dynamite could be used to construct, conceal, and transport bombs. These new bombs made it possible for small groups and even individuals to attack large numbers. This was also the first bomb that could be detonated by a timer, enabling the attacker to escape from the scene before it exploded. The first global terrorists "worshipped" the bomb, and it has remained the major weapon of terrorist groups. Infuriated by the effect his invention would have on how he would be remembered, Nobel gave his fortune to establish the annual Nobel Prizes and made the Nobel Peace Prize the most important one.[2]

Terror is violence employed for a religious or political objective and is not limited by the accepted moral norms that limit violence. Both governments and rebels may use terror. The Reign of Terror of the French revolutionary government made the term part of our political vocabulary.[3] The revolutionary government distinguished two types of persons: "citizens" and "enemies of the people." Citizens had legal rights and obligations. When accused of violating the law, they were entitled to accepted judicial procedures to determine guilt and innocence. Enemies of the people were considered dangerous to the Revolution because of who they were and what they would eventually do. Since their character could not be altered, they had to be destroyed. Rebels using violence to achieve a political or religious end are terrorists when they operate unfettered by military rules governing violence.[4]

The discussion about global terror focuses on rebel terrorist groups attempting a *revolution*, defined as a dramatic reconstruction of the principle of legitimacy cementing the existing system. I will avoid terrorist groups concerned with a single issue, like animal liberation, environmental movements, etc. The only time single-issue groups will be discussed is when they are connected to a "wave" of terrorist activity. Antiabortion groups, for example, identify with the Christian Religious Right, a feature of the Fourth Wave. In all waves there are some terrorist groups that fight to protect the dominant system, but these groups will not be discussed much. I will give some attention to groups who were not rebels but who operated through terrorism in the service of a dominant power, such as the medieval Crusaders.

The First Wave of global terror was followed by three different waves that spread across six continents during the twentieth and twenty-first centuries. The aspirations of the French Revolution influenced each wave. First Wave groups sought egalitarianism and often aimed to achieve national self-determination. The French Revolution's principle of self-determination was foremost in the Second Wave, which began in Ireland in 1920. The Irish effort was followed by a series of anticolonial campaigns that ended forty-two years later in 1962, when Algeria emerged as an independent state. Then in the 1960s the Third (New Left) Wave generated a variety of terrorist groups, each again reflecting the egalitarian aspects of the French Revolution. The Third Wave reached its high point in the 1980s, and a few organizations are still functioning, for example, the Kurdistan Worker's Party (PKK), which arose in 1984 in the Middle East and was a major player in the struggle against the Islamic State (ISIS) in Syria and Iraq, which was a byproduct of the Arab Spring in 2011. The most recently founded group of the Third Wave is the Communist Party of Nepal–Maoist (CPNM). Established in 1996, its activities have increased tensions between India and China.[5]

The Fourth Wave, consisting of terrorist groups with religious ideologies, emerged in 1979, when New Left groups were ascendant around the globe. Virtually all Fourth Wave groups had religious agendas, which made them hostile to the French Revolution's aim to produce a secular world. For the first time, two waves significantly overlapped. Earlier waves had overlapped briefly, but the successors did not emerge in full force until the predecessors were virtually depleted. However, in the 1980s organizations from two different waves fought against each other, something that had never happened before. If the lifecycles of its three predecessors are relevant (and three examples are not many instances for confident predictions), the Fourth Wave will dissipate in the twenty-first century's third decade. If that does happen, and *if* history repeats itself, we will then experience a Fifth Wave.

Each wave had distinctive features and employed different tactics. The Second Wave largely abandoned its predecessor's commitment to assassinating prominent government figures and concentrated on eliminating the police. Third Wave groups introduced hostage taking and hijacking airplanes, and the Fourth Wave was committed to suicide bombing. Each wave had its own geography. The First Wave spread to six continents, although Europe and the Americas were preeminent. Second Wave groups limited themselves to the overseas empires of European states, largely those in Asia and Africa. The Third Wave was most significant in the developing world but was present on all six continents. Fourth Wave activity occurred on all the continents but was most significant in Asia.

The persistence of the wave pattern suggests that terrorism is deeply rooted in modern culture.[6] The public, however, does not seem to have absorbed this lesson. Certainly, in the past, when a wave dissipated, the assumption seemed to be that terrorism would never again be a serious major problem. In the academic world, this was made clear by J. B. S. Hardman's article "Terrorism," published in 1930 in the first edition of the *Encyclopaedia of the Social Sciences*.[7] Hardman concludes that terrorism had reached its high point at the beginning of the twentieth century but that now "modern technology" has made the world so complex that only classes and masses mattered.

One important reason that Hardman came to his conclusion was that the anticolonial Wave seemed over. The Irish revolution of 1920 was not followed by any other, and before Hardman published his article, the number of campaigns had greatly diminished. Despite Hardman's estimate, by the 1950s, two decades after he wrote, terrorist activity had become significant again, albeit with a vastly different geography. Europe and the Americas no longer were significant locations for terrorist attacks even though the Second Wave aimed to make Western states relinquish their colonial territories. Attacks occurred in the Western overseas colonial territories: the Palestine Mandate, Cyprus, Malaya, Kenya, Aden, Vietnam, and Algeria. Only Algerians made strikes on the European homeland of their colonizer, France, and those strikes occurred only during a brief period. Significantly, terrorist movements did not threaten Russia. Russia did not have overseas territories, and in 1922 the Union of Soviet Socialist Republics (Soviet Union) was established because the communists became convinced that they had to recognize the self-determination principle established by the Versailles Treaty if they wanted to survive.

Oddly, the second edition of the *Encyclopedia of the Social Sciences* in 1967 had no article on terrorism. Perhaps Hardman's conclusion had convinced the new editors, or maybe they believed that since the era of empires was over, terrorism had disappeared too.[8] The Third Wave was just beginning but was still comparatively insignificant. The editors of the second edition did not explain why the subject was no longer important.[9]

The absence of terrorism in the second edition was consistent with the editors' decision to eliminate other subjects, which suggests they viewed the world very differently from how their predecessors had in 1930. The first edition also published articles on violence, assassination, and praetorianism, subjects the second edition omitted. The first edition's articles on elections and succession noted that elections and successions sometimes could be violent. But the second edition's election article does not recognize the fact that elections sometimes breed violence, and it does not contain an article on succession, because succession is impossible to discuss in a meaningful way without dealing with the violence issue. The decision to exclude considerations of violence in so many contexts suggests that the best social scientists can sometimes be misled by their immediate experiences.

Richard Hofstadter's insightful quotation on historical amnesia that serves as this introduction's epigraph indicates that the amnesia of academics reflects the experience of a whole generation. "For the long span from about 1938 to the mid-1960s . . . the internal life of the country was unusually free of violent episodes. Americans who came of age during and after the 1930s found it easy to forget how violent a people their forebears had been."[10] Historical amnesia was especially pronounced in the 1990s, when various decisions by the U.S. government revealed that it did not understand the nature of terrorism's wave pattern. When the Soviet Union collapsed and so many terrorist groups disappeared, the United States decided that since terrorism had been primarily linked to the Cold War it was no longer important. Scott Stewart, a Diplomatic Security Service special agent who participated in hundreds of terrorism investigations, said the State Department "abolished my office . . . since terrorism was over."[11] The government ended its program of subsidizing terrorist research even though a number of religious terrorist groups had emerged.[12]

The 1999 Crowe Commission report *Confronting Terrorist Threats* examined attacks on embassies and blamed the government for greatly reducing intelligence resources. And in 2004, *The 9/11 Commission Report* found that same "indifference" had made the 9/11 strike easier to pull off. Clearly, as these examples indicate, we cannot deal with terrorism without understanding its history, a lesson Carl von Clausewitz, the founder of the science of war, emphasized was crucial for understanding military combat. Examples from history make everything clear and furnish the best description of proof in the empirical sciences. This applies with more force to the art of war than to any other.[13]

THE "GENERATION" AND THE "WAVE"

Our historical amnesia is partly attributable to the inadequacy of our analytical tools. Using the concept of "generation" compels one to recognize that when a generation gets older, its energy dissipates. In that respect, "generation" is different from more commonly used concepts like "class," "interest," "ethnic identity," etc. Energies inspiring those entities may dissipate in time, too, but that process is not associated with a specific time period. Because few analysts use the idea of the generation to explain important political developments, it is not surprising that when that development dissipates, they believe it has disappeared.

The generation as an important political concept has an unusual and often forgotten history. Plato, the founder of the Western political theory, discussed the transformation of governments from one political form to another—from aristocracy to oligarchy to democracy to tyranny—as generational processes. But his successors thought social status, class, and ethnicity were more useful than time was for explaining change.

Plato did not specify the number of years a generation consumed. The English language does not designate a fixed number of years to the word "generation." The *Oxford English Dictionary* indicates that a generation usually means thirty years. In some instances, the term can refer to twenty or forty years. Those familiar with the Bible knows it uses the idea of the generation to signify major change. The number forty or multiples thereof indicate the amount of time necessary for a significant transformation. The Israelites spent forty years in the desert before they overcame the slave mentality they had developed in Egypt. Moses lived 120 years and in the process experienced three different lives: an Egyptian noble, a nomad, and finally Israel's leader. While these examples indicate that a generation lasted forty years, it is also true that the Bible uses the number forty to designate important changes. It rained for forty days before a new world came into existence for Noah's return. It is perhaps pertinent, too, that pregnancy requires forty weeks to produce a new human life.

The concept of generation as essential for understanding political change revived in the nineteenth century when democracy became significant. The democratic form was constructed so that citizens could change governments regularly, but Alexis de Tocqueville's classic study of American politics states that the major changes occurred only when a new generation emerged. "Among democratic nations each generation is a new people" that provokes a "struggle between public and private concerns."[14] Two other prominent figures in Tocqueville's generation made similar points. Auguste Comte, the founder of modern sociology, emphasized that generations had an important role in determining "the velocity of human evolution," and John Stuart Mill refined Comte's concept, arguing that in each successive age the "principal phenomena" of society are different, changing only when a "new set" of individuals reaches maturity and takes possession of society.[15] Important early twentieth-century scholars also became committed to the notion. Karl Mannheim published "The Problem of Generations" in 1927,[16] and José Ortega y Gasset argued that the generation is "the pivot responsible for the movements of historical evolution. Its members come into the world endowed with certain typical characteristics which bind them in a common physiogeny distinguishing them from the previous generation."[17]

In the 1960s, the public in the West became aware of the generation issue. Large numbers of young adults, especially university students, got involved in different political efforts to change the status quo, for example, via the Civil Rights Movement and the feminist movement of the 1970s. During the Vietnam War, the radical New Left was created, and significant terrorist activity again emerged in the Third Wave across the globe. The European New Left appeared "first in West Germany and became a prototype for European student radicals."[18] German students protesting against the Vietnam War often wore discarded U.S. military uniforms and made influential contacts with dissident GIs—draftees also hostile to the war.[19]

Beyond the New Left, the 1960s generation developed a striking counterculture throughout the West. The hippie movement and other alternative lifestyles emerged. Widespread social tensions developed regarding women's rights, traditional modes of authority, and experimentation with drugs, and these tended to break along generational lines. A "sexual revolution" occurred that included an increased acceptance of premarital sex, homosexuality, transgender people, and abortion. The generational difference was expressed in new fashion and hairstyle trends. Men and women in the hippie movement wore jeans, long hair, and sandals or moccasins. Men often grew beards; women eschewed makeup. Popular music was also revolutionary. The American folk music revival grew into a major movement, using traditional music and new compositions pioneered by artists like Woody Guthrie, Pete Seeger, and Bob Dylan, who identified with left-wing politics and turned the folk music revival into an anti–Vietnam War movement. Finally, this generation raised environmental concerns about the ongoing damage industrialization was causing and the pollution generated by the misguided use of chemicals. Communes gained popularity as a revolt against capitalism and were efforts to return to the land and live free of interference from outside influences.

The strikingly visible and important differences between the generations alive in the 1960s stimulated academics to get more involved in generational analysis, and in 1986 the prominent historian Arthur Schlesinger Jr. produced the first systematic, detailed study of political generations in his illuminating *The Cycles of American History*, which developed Tocqueville's argument to describe the character of American politics from the eighteenth century to the present day. The country, since its birth, had been experiencing forty-year political cycles, Schlesinger argued. The initial generation, consumed with "political activism and social egalitarianism," was then followed by a forty-year period of "quiet conservatism and personal acquisition," a process repeated frequently: "Each new phase flows out of the conditions and contradictions of the phase before and then itself prepares the way for the next recurrence. A true cycle . . . is self-generating. It cannot be determined short of catastrophe by external events. Wars, depressions, inflations, may heighten or complicate moods, but the cycle itself rolls on, self-contained, self-sufficient and autonomous."[20]

While linking generations to cycles is useful for studying politics in democracies, which are systems organized to promote change, international terrorism cannot be viewed in the same way. Unlike the cycles Schlesinger describes, each wave of global terror was generated by political events that had global resonance and provided a new generation with the hope that the world could be changed dramatically.[21] The precipitating political event shapes the character of each period with respect to purposes and tactics, and each period produces texts to explain the change in tactics. Although each period, or wave, of terrorism lasted around forty years, the rhythm of each was different. While the cycle in domestic democratic systems that Schlesinger discusses always recurs, our experience with global terror is too limited to be confident that such dramatic political events will also always recur. Thus, the term "wave" seems more appropriate. A cycle is "a set of events or actions that happen again and again in the same order," but a wave "involves a disturbance travelling through a medium by which energy is transferred from one particle of the medium to another without causing any permanent displacement of the medium itself."[22]

The principal concern of this volume is to discuss the dynamics of the four waves of global terror. A wave, which is stimulated by dramatic international political events, consists of the actions of many different organizations sharing similar tactics and/or objectives. Those organizations often fragment and generally dissipate before the wave that gave birth to them does, though a few organizations sometimes remain active after their wave disappears. In those special cases, the organization sometimes incorporates features of the next wave.

Surprise attacks are essential because small groups must find ways to publicize their actions. These surprise attacks often produce excessive counter-reactions, especially when it is believed that a state has used a terrorist group to help its international agenda. The most striking overreaction occurred in the First Wave. It was well known that Russia and Bulgaria were sponsoring nationalist groups seeking separation in the Ottoman Empire. When a Serbian terrorist killed Archduke Ferdinand and his wife, the Austro-Hungarian imperial government was convinced the Serbian government was involved. Though it had no evidence to support that belief, and its response triggered the "Great War": World War I. Ultimately, the Austro-Hungarian Empire was destroyed by its response, and Gavrilo Princip, the Serbian assassin, became a national hero.[23]

The terrorist experience stimulated major changes in police practices everywhere. The need to accumulate information that could prevent surprise attacks inspired governments to employ unusual interrogation techniques, ones not used in ordinary criminal investigations. European states officially abolished torture in the late eighteenth and early nineteenth centuries; in response to terrorism, torture was revived in most countries and has remained an important feature of every wave. Although torture often does not produce the information sought and frequently provokes public anger about the visible abuses, some feel the pain inflicted on suspected terrorists is an appropriate response, a view Donald Trump emphasized strongly in his 2016 presidential campaign. "Would I approve waterboarding? You bet your ass I would—in a heartbeat. . . . If it doesn't work, they deserve it anyway for what they are doing."[24]

Before the development of global terrorism, police forces wore uniforms to deter criminals from acting, give the public visible evidence it was being protected, and make it easier to identify police officers when they were needed. Criminals were supposedly dealt with only after they committed criminal acts. But in dealing with terrorism, it was crucial to stop criminal acts *before* they occurred, and special elements of the police took their uniforms off to gain access to or infiltrate terrorist groups. To gain a terrorist group's confidence, undercover police agents would sometimes organize terrorist actions themselves. In the First Wave, the Russian Okhrana, the British Special Branch, and the FBI were conspicuous examples of new police forces without uniforms that emerged in response to terrorism.

Governments generally claim that terrorists should be treated as criminals, but rules that designate appropriate responses to criminal deeds are often deemed useless. Terrorists, on the other hand, usually claim they should be treated as enemy soldiers, but they do not follow the accepted rules of war. Early in the First Wave, terrorists were frequently held in prison camps without trials for indefinite periods.

Terrorism has been a feature of our life long before the global waves, our principal concern here, emerged. To help us understand better the uniqueness of global terrorism, the next chapter discusses terrorism from the first to the nineteenth century, focusing on the Abrahamic religions and the Western world.

1

TERRORISM BEFORE THE GLOBAL FORM

From the First Century to the Twentieth

This chapter has three sections. The first deals with terror in the three Abrahamic religions: Judaism, Islam, and Christianity. Secular eighteenth- and nineteenth-century local mob terror is then examined. The final section discusses the political and technological transformations that made global terrorism possible.

ANCIENT RELIGIOUS EXAMPLES

Before the eighteenth century, religion was the primary motivator of every terror campaign. I will discuss important examples from the three Abrahamic religions, Judaism's Zealots and Sicarii, Islam's Assassins, and Christianity's Crusaders.[1] The Assassins and Zealots are two well-known examples of ancient sacred terror, and the terms "assassin" and "zealot" are often used to describe contemporary terrorists. These cases are also instructive because they are remarkably different from each other and demonstrate the wide range of activities associated with ancient sacred rebel terror.

The West does not associate the Crusades with terrorism. It is a synonym for a "good cause vigorously pursued," often through force. On the evening of D-Day in World War II, General Eisenhower stated:

> Soldiers, Sailors and Airmen of the Allied Expeditionary Force. You are about to embark upon the Great Crusade, toward which we have striven these many months. The eyes of the world are upon you. The hopes and prayers of liberty-loving people everywhere march with you. In company with our brave Allies and brothers-in-arms on other Fronts, you will bring about the destruction of the German war machine, the elimination of Nazi tyranny over the oppressed peoples of Europe, and security for ourselves in a free world.[2]

After an anarchist assassinated President William McKinley in 1901, his successor, Theodore Roosevelt, proclaimed he would organize a world-wide "Crusade" against anarchist terror. A century later, after the 9/11 attack, President George W. Bush launched a "crusade against global terrorism."[3]

But in the Islamic world, the term *ṣalībiyyūn* (crusader) is associated with the atrocities Christian Crusaders committed when they recaptured the "Holy Land," which had been under Muslim rule for over 450 years. Crusaders abandoned all restraint in their violence, with enormous political consequences. Scholars of Islam such as John Esposito ultimately blame the Crusades "for destroying the five centuries of peaceful coexistence between the Islamic and Christian worlds and [for] leaving an enduring legacy of misunderstanding and distrust."[4] It is no surprise that Fourth Wave Islamic terrorists like al-Qaeda's leaders Osama bin Laden and Ayman al-Zawahiri described their struggle as one against the "Crusader-Zionist."[5]

ZEALOTS AND SICARII

Messianic hopes inspired the Zealots and Sicarii. They interpreted important events in their religion's founding period as precedents for their tactics. Their struggles had an international character and believed that their participation would secure places for them in paradise. The Zealots and

Sicarii survived for only twenty-five years, but their influence was enormous. They generated a mass uprising against the large Greek population living under Roman rule in Judea. That revolt produced numerous disasters, including the destruction of the Temple, the desolation of the land, and a mass suicide at Masada. Zealot and Sicarii activities also inspired two more popular uprisings against Rome in successive generations, which led to the extermination of large Jewish centers in Egypt and Cyprus and the virtual depopulation of Judea. These events precipitated the final tragedy—the Exile—which had a traumatic effect on Jewish consciousness and became the central feature of the Jewish experience for two thousand years, altering virtually every existing Jewish institution. It would be difficult to find terrorist activity in any historical period that more decisively influenced the life of a community. Given the fact that sparking mass uprisings has been a major aim of global terror since the 1880s, the Zealots and Sicarii are interesting forebears. Few contemporary groups have successfully generated a mass uprising, and none have matched the scale of those of the Zealots and the Sicarii. What made these early terrorists unique?

Jewish messianic doctrines outlined terror's general objectives and permitted different methods to achieve them. Their prophecies claimed that the apocalypse would manifest itself as a series of massive catastrophes in which "the upsetting of all moral order to the point of dissolving the laws of the laws of nature" would occur.[6] This vision saturated the generation preceding that of the Zealots and Sicarii and created a state of feverish expectancy. "Almost every event was seized upon . . . to discover how and in what way it represented a Sign of the Times and threw light on the approach of the End of the Days. . . . The strongest tales and imaginings could find ready credence."[7] New messianic pretenders soon flourished everywhere because so many people saw signs of imminent messianic intervention everywhere, for example, Judea's occupation by an alien military power and prominent Jews desecrating God's name and accepting the conqueror's culture.

In all of these visions and predictions of apocalypse, God determines a date of redemption. Still, the visions often suggest that humans could speed the process. Prayer, repentance, and martyrdom are the most common methods of bringing forward the eschaton. When these actions fail to produce the desired results, it becomes only a matter of time before some believers will amplify their attempts to "force history." Jewish terrorist activity apparently had two aims: make oppression so intolerable that insurrection was inevitable and frustrate all efforts to reconcile the parties.

Zealots and Sicarii associated themselves with an early biblical hero, Phineas, a high priest under Moses. Phineas's zeal stopped a plague afflicting Israel when Moses ignored acts of apostasy and "whoring with Moabite women." He killed a tribal chief and his concubine who flaunted their contempt for God in a sacred site, and he is the only biblical hero to receive a reward directly from God, who promised the priesthood would remain in his family forever.[8] In purifying the community, Phineas prepared the way for the Holy War (*herem*) that God told Israel to wage to gain the Promised Land. The Bible repeatedly refers to the terror that the *herem* was supposed to produce and to Israel's obligation to destroy all persons remaining in the land lest they become corrupting influences. *Herem* designates a sacred sphere where ordinary standards do not apply. In a military context, a *herem* is a war without limits.[9]

The name "Sicarii" comes from the daggers (*sica*) the group used. Rabbinical commentary indicates that Phineas used the head of his spear as a dagger, and the Sicarii normally assassinated prominent Jews, especially priests accused of succumbing to Hellenistic culture or avoiding war.

The Sicarii committed murders in broad daylight in the heart of Jerusalem. The holy days were their special seasons when they would mingle with the crowd carrying short daggers concealed under their clothing which they used to stab their enemies. Thus, when they fell, the murderers joined in cries of indignation, and through this plausible behavior they were never discovered. The panic created was more alarming than the calamity itself; everyone . . . hourly expected death.[10]

But the Sicarii did not limit themselves to assassinations or using daggers. They engaged military forces openly and with military weapons, often slaughtering their prisoners after the battle. They took hostages to pressure priests and terrorized wealthy Jewish landowners in the hope of compelling the more equal distribution of land the Bible prescribed. Zealot patterns were different. Their name signified the righteous indignation Phineas personified. However, they rarely plotted assassinations, and their principal antagonists, unlike those of the Sicarii, were non-Jews. They would commit atrocities on holy days to exploit the publicity potential and demonstrate that not even the most sacred occasions could provide their targets with immunity. Josephus's description of how the Sicarii and Zealots massacred a Roman garrison after the Romans secured a covenant—the most inviolable pledge Jews could make—that guaranteed safe passage back to their garrisons is just one of many examples of this audacious behavior. The massacre commenced after the Romans had laid down their arms; they were "neither resisting nor suing for mercy, but merely appealing with loud cries to the covenant. . . . The whole city was a scene of dejection, and among the moderates there was not one who was not racked with the thought that he should personally have to suffer for the rebels' crime."[11]

In order to quickly generate a mass uprising and sustain ever-increasing polarizing pressures, the Zealots and Sicarii developed many different tactics. Participants were pulled into a constantly escalating series of struggles, with shock tactics that manipulated their fear, outrage, sympathy, and guilt. Sometimes, these emotional effects were provoked by terrorist atrocities that went well beyond the conventional norms governing violence. On other occasions, they were produced by provoking the enemy to commit atrocities against its better judgment. In different phases of the Jewish uprising, the Zealots and Sicarii also deployed strikingly different tactics strategically designed for specific contexts. In its initial stages, the rebellion began with the use of passive resistance in cities, possibly for the first time in history. In modern times, passive resistance has sometimes appeared as the initial stage of a conflict that later matured into a full-scale terrorist campaign. We have learned that throughout history, many who would have shrunk from violence, let alone terror, regularly embrace passive resistance as a legitimate method to rectify grievances, often times not fully understanding how the ensuing drama may simultaneously excite hopes and fan smoldering hostilities.

In the Jewish case, when Roman strength seemed overwhelming and antagonisms had yet to develop sufficiently, passive resistance might have been the only illegal form of political action that many Jews were willing to take. Initially, confrontations with the Romans involved Jewish demands for respect of their sacred symbols. This strategy was an attempt to force the Roman government into situations where it either had to tolerate flagrant contempt for the law or commit actions that seemed to threaten the Jewish religion, possibly the only behavior that could unite all Jews. More often than not, the Romans retreated in the face of this novel form of resistance. They admired the Jews' displays of courage, restraint, and intensity. They also learned how difficult and dangerous it was to break up demonstrations that included women and children. Ultimately, the Romans feared a rebellion could engulf the eastern portions of the empire, whose population was at least 20 percent Jewish and contained many Jewish sympathizers with connections to members of the Roman ruling circles.

In addition to their concerns about internal rebellion, the possibility of an international conflict troubled Rome. Parthia, the last remaining major power in the ancient world, bordered Judea and had intervened in previous conflicts. Even if Parthia wanted to avoid involvement, the government might have found it difficult to do so because its Jewish population was large. In fact, one Parthian client state had a Jewish dynasty with a special hatred for Rome.[12] Unsurprisingly, Parthian Jews were important in the rebellion's early stages. Parthian Jews and Judea maintained a bond akin to that of the one that knitted American Jews to the Zionist uprising against Britain some two thousand years later. The annual pilgrimages of Parthian Jews to Jerusalem and the massive flow of wealth they contributed to maintain the Temple there demonstrate the strength of these Judean ties.

But Rome's anxiousness to avoid a serious conflict made it more vulnerable to tactics aimed at producing outrage. Roman restraint encouraged reckless behavior and weakened the case of Jewish moderates who argued that although Rome might be conciliatory, it was determined to stay. Ultimately, large passive demonstrations against authority tend to produce violence if both sides do not exhibit discipline and foresight. When some on either side prefer violence, or when passive violence is viewed not as an end in itself but a tactic that can be discarded when others seem more productive, explosions will occur. In the case of the Jewish rebellion, tensions ignited when, for whatever reason, demonstrators would become abusive and bands of youths would start throwing rocks and forming breakaway crowds. Roman discipline would then dissolve when troops—who had discarded their uniforms in the hopes of appearing inconspicuous and exchanged their swords for wooden staves—would be attacked by demonstrators. Soon crowds would panic in response to the confrontations, and hundreds would be trampled to death in Jerusalem's narrow streets. This horrific pattern kept repeating itself, and each time the resulting atrocities seemed all the grimmer because they would typically occur during holy days in Jerusalem, and pilgrims, who were crowded together in religious services, would often be killed. The massive outrage these events generated sparked both Roman atrocities and a Sicarii assassination campaign. The Sicarii campaign, which focused on moderates, put immense pressure on priests to refuse Roman sacrifices at the Temple. However, Rome viewed the decision to refuse their sacrifices as a rejection of its sovereignty and a declaration of war. Ultimately, Rome's claims of sovereignty over the religious practices at the Temple allowed the rebels to make the case that the coming conflict was not just any war but a *herem*, or holy war.

When the war finally materialized, both sides hoped to resolve it quickly with a political settlement, but these hopes were given a severe jolt after the first military engagement, in which a Roman garrison that had laid down its arms after being promised safe passage was massacred. In response, Roman troops ran amok, engaging in a pattern of reprisal and counter-reprisal that quickly spread throughout the area. However, when Roman military discipline was eventually restored, their behavior was unexpectedly restrained. Roman military advantages were not used out of hope that the olive branch of peace they offered would be seized. Understanding that most Jews wanted peace, the government believed that the atrocities being committed against Jews by the Sicarii would eventually destroy the popular tolerance required for a full-blown rebellion. A significant Jewish desertion rate, including some important personalities, made Rome believe that it could deliver peace without strenuous military effort. However, continuing Jewish atrocities—which ultimately culminated in the assassination of Roman peace envoys—forced Rome to conclude that only total war would achieve peace.[13]

The Jewish strategy was singularly designed to provoke a massive uprising. Continued atrocities would narrow the prospects for a political solution by destroying the credibility of moderates while simultaneously expanding the conflict by involving new participants. However, despite the strategy's effectiveness, no master hand can be seen at work, and one can view its development as an "irrational" process. Jewish terrorists ultimately reflected a bewildering array of forces. During this period there were several Zealot groups, at least two Sicarii organizations, and a number of other unidentified groups participating in the rebellion. Multiplicity encouraged each element to prove the superiority of its commitments, and in time, the groups fought one another, too. As these extraordinary actions unfolded, the groups, like so many of their counterparts today, found it necessary to make even more fantastic claims about their enemies and even more radical promises about the societal reconstruction their victory would produce. Ferrero's comment on the French Reign of Terror's dynamics is quite pertinent in this regard: "The Jacobins did not spill all that blood because they believed in popular sovereignty as a religious truth; rather they tried to believe in popular sovereignty as a religious truth because their fear made them spill all that blood."[14]

Yet to focus on popular insurrection as the principal object of the Zealots and Sicarii misconstrues the reality of their views. Insurrection was only a sign of messianic intervention to these groups. Their sole concern was with the audience of the divine, and it drove them to act in ways those preoccupied with the audience of the living would only ever dream of. Their decision to burn their own food supplies in Jerusalem's long siege only becomes intelligible if one believes that God might see it as proof that the faithful had placed all the trust in his divine intervention. One would also have to understand that God, upon seeing this demonstration of faith, would be bound by his promises and have no choice but to rescue the "righteous remnant." Given that so many believed God would be moved by their sufferings, even the most profound disasters still gave rise to new hopes. When the Temple was burning and the war irretrievably lost, a messianic imposter persuaded new recruits that the fire signified that the time for deliverance had finally arrived. Compared to the Assassins, the Zealots and the Sicarii seemed free to choose among a range of preferred tactics, but when the vision of who needed to be influenced most appeared so limited, they could not effectively reach human audiences.

ASSASSINS

There are important resemblances between the Assassins (or Ismaili and Nizari) and the Jewish terrorists. Messianic hopes inspired both to seek maximum publicity. Both interpreted important events in the founding period of their religion as precedents for their tactics and believed those who died in this struggle secured their place in paradise. Like the Assassins, the Sicarii were identified with a particular weapon, the dagger, and both rebellions had an international character. But the Sicarii used other weapons against Jews, and the Assassins only used the dagger against Muslims.

Nonetheless, their differences are striking and derived from variations in their messianic and founding themes. The Assassins (active from 1090 through 1275) sought to fulfill a political instruction that Islamic religious doctrine dictated, namely, the purification of all religious and government institutions for the establishment of a worldwide Caliphate.[15] The Assassins inflicted few casualties but seriously threatened several governments. In particular, governments of the Turkish-Persian Seljuk Empire were put in serious jeopardy by Assassin attempts to arouse the Islamic population through publicity-evoking acts. Victims were prominent individuals murdered in venerated sites, often on holy days when many witnesses were present. They did not need mass media to reach their target audiences.

To be noticed is one thing, to be understood another. When the objective is to rouse the public's attention, those threatened will impose their own interpretations of the terrorist's message, especially if the terrorist breaks down or tries to evade arrest. The Assassin doctrine eliminates that possibility. An Assassin always used daggers, making it very likely he would be captured or killed. "When therefore, any of them have chosen to die in this way . . . [the Chief] hands them knives which are so to speak 'consecrated.'"[16]

Islamic millenarian movements have largely been associated with Shi'a Islam, a minority sect that believes that a Mahdi (Messiah) will emerge to lead a jihad, or holy war, against the existing religious establishment to cleanse Islam. The Jewish and Christian millenarian view sometimes calls for violence, but "an essential part of the Mahdist theory" is its view of jihad or "armed revolutionary struggle as the method whereby a perfect social order must be brought into being."[17] Ultimately, a believer must keep their faith until the Mahdi summons them. To protect a believer among hostile Muslims, Shi'a permits *taqiyya*, or pious dissimulation, until the Mahdi arrives. The pure are permitted to conceal their beliefs for the same reason that deception is condoned in a war. Should an opportunity materialize, Shi'a must "use their tongues" or preach their faith openly, but they cannot "draw the sword" until the Mahdi arrives.[18] The Assassins ultimately interpreted this injunction to mean that while a believer could not use swords against other Muslims, they could use other weapons to expedite the coming of the Mahdi. In this interpretation, the Assassins resemble other earlier Islamic millenarian groups that attached ritual significance to particular weapons. Some eighth-century groups strangled their victims or used weapons that eliminated the possibility of escape— one group actually clubbed their victims to death with wooden cudgels— because the attack had to be public in order to result in martyrdom.[19] As a result, other tactics, like the use of poison, were considered inappropriate. The use of the dagger, popularized by the Assassins, came much later and signaled that more efficient methods of violence were acceptable as long as they were consistent with religious precedent.

The Assassins emerged from the more active Shi'a elements, which organized "summoners" to persuade fellow Muslims about the true meaning of their faith. Their roots were in Persia, but many were educated in Egyptian seminaries that promoted millenarian doctrines. After the capabilities of the Shi'a state in Egypt to promote such ideas waned, the founder of the Assassins seized several mountain fortresses where refugees could congregate and develop a distinctive Gnostic theology. This theology promised the messianic fulfillment of history, at which time law would be abolished and human nature perfected.

The Assassins constantly shifted their scattered mountain bases and crossed state borders in their efforts to make Islam into a single community again. For the first time in history, an international terror campaign had materialized and was being waged by an organization that could recover from setbacks.[20] Previous millenarian sodalities had been too scattered and their bases too accessible to wage such a campaign. Isolation gave the Assassins the time and space needed to establish a quasi-monastic existence in which they would train leaders, summoners, and *fedayeen*. Although their popular support evaporated after fifty years, the Assassins would survive for another 150 years, until Mongol and Arab armies destroyed their "states."[21]

Assassin legends from this period, like those of any millenarian group, are revealing. One such legend centered on the victim-*fedayeen* relationship. Typically, the movement would place a youthful member in the service of a high official. Through devotion and skill over many years, he would gain his master's trust; then, at the appropriate time, he would plunge a dagger into his master's back. This degree of immunity from personal feelings seemed so preternatural to orthodox Muslims that they described the group as hashish eaters (*hashhashin*), the source of the word "assassin." While no evidence exists that drugs played any role in these legends, the fact that the Assassins' training began in childhood may explain their extraordinary ability to submerge "natural" feelings. Everywhere the Assassins went, they inspired shock and awe. Those favorably disposed to their cause found their dedication admirable, whereas opponents viewed it as hateful, repulsive, and inhuman fanaticism. In medieval Christian Europe, the word "assassin" initially signified devotion but later came to be associated with one who used treacherous means to kill.[22] The potential utility of an assassination campaign is obvious. Dramatically staged assassinations draw immense attention to a cause. In the Muslim world, such a campaign was even more effective given that the basis of power was manifestly personal. Typically, "when a sultan died his troops were automatically dispersed. When an Emir died, the lands were in disorder," making assassination the preferred political tool.[23]

Although a theoretically effective method, the problems created by assassination campaigns became clear in time. A series of assassinations provokes immense social antagonism. Given that there is usually some level of popular identification with leaders, assassinations entail treachery not only against the leader but also against their supporters. "There can be good faith in war but not in unannounced murder. Although Mahdist Muslims often used assassination as an expedient, the adoption of a regular and admitted assassination policy horrified [Muslims]."[24] A similar logic moved the philosopher Immanuel Kant to describe belligerents employing assassins as criminals. He argued that such a breach of faith could only intensify hatred and diminish the possibility for a peaceful settlement before one party exterminates the other.[25]

In response to the Assassins' campaign, Orthodox Muslims slaughtered those deemed sympathetic to the *fedayeen*.[26] Despite the bloodshed, the Assassins exhibited extraordinary restraint, eschewing many chances to reply in kind. Orthodox areas would occasionally be set on fire, but these episodes were rare. The Assassins believed that only other assassinations were a legitimate response to the initial reaction they provoked.[27] The Assassins' commitment to a single form of attack is puzzling. While most early millenarians found assassination attractive, they used other terror tactics as well. The Assassins had resources for other tactics yet chose not to diversify, despite having much less to lose by doing so. In fact, Assassin armies only protected bases and raided caravans: their doctrine made war and assassination mutually exclusive. Assassin encounters with Christians also reflected this line of thinking. For them, the dagger was reserved only for those who had betrayed the faith, while the sword was meant for those who had never accepted it. When the Assassins fought the Crusaders, they used their armies, not *fedayeen*.

It is unclear why the Assassins were so committed to their tactics or why they did not use their resources more efficiently. This behavior most likely had its origins in the reinterpretations of major precedents in the parent religion. In the case of the Assassins, the life of Mohammed prescribed the model for their strategy. By withdrawing to primitive places of refuge (*dar al-hijra*), the Assassins deliberately imitated Mohammed's flight to the remote but more receptive Medina after failing to convert his own people in Mecca. "Medina was the first *dar al-hijra* of Islam, the first place of refuge—whence to return in triumph to the unbelieving lands from which one had to flee persecuted."[28] Islam's calendar dates from this event, and the pattern of withdrawing in order to begin again became one that millenarian elements in Islam often followed. In fact, studies of Muslim terrorist group activity in Egypt and of al-Qaeda in Afghanistan demonstrate that they still do.[29]

Mohammed's unusual employment of assassins and military tactics is particularly revealing. Initially, his army had only two tasks: to defend the community against attacks and raid caravans for booty. Only later did he permit assassinations of prominent persons within or on the fringes of Islam. Those considered "hypocrites" (*munafiqun*) and persons who "provoked" attacks by showing contempt for Mohammed's teachings were the main targets.[30] This process of purifying or consolidating the original nucleus of the faith seemed to be a precondition for expansion of their religion's ranks. Only when Mohammed decided the community was ready to become universal did its army initiate offensive operations and end assassination practices. Another reason for Mohammed's assassination pattern was that such deeds were meant to compensate for or atone for deficiencies of ardor. The ability to overcome such normal inhibitions or personal attachments to their victims was viewed as a significant measure of commitment. In every case, the assassin and victim were kinsmen, and no bond was considered stronger at that time.[31] Victims were unlikely to defend themselves because they were often older men, females, or were asleep. Others may have been engaged in activities likely to evoke the assailant's compassion, such as playing with children or making love.

A major difference between earlier assassins and the *fedayeen* that came later is that the former returned directly to Mohammed for judgment, while the latter sought martyrdom. In explaining this key difference, one should remember that the origin of the *fedayeen* is in the Shi'a and Ismailia sects of Islam, which link themselves to Ali and Husain, whom they consider Mohammed's true heirs. Ali and Husain were martyred after authorizing assassinations, and as a result, their martyrdom became a guiding principle for their followers.

Although we lack primary sources to determine how Assassins justified their tactics, we know that they saw themselves in a struggle to purify Islam and made extraordinary efforts to demonstrate they acted only defensively. The *fedayeen* put themselves in situations where intimate bonds or personal feelings would be violated in order to demonstrate their conviction. Similar tactics to those of the Assassins were also a well-known part of Mohammed's life and the lives of other figures central to Shi'a. Can there be justifications more compelling for believers than those originating directly from the founders of their faith?

CRUSADERS

There were nine Crusades between 1099 and 1254. Their common objective was to eliminate the Muslim rule in the "Holy Land." Several Crusades in Europe came later, and in some instances, the European and Holy Land cases overlapped. The Crusaders were driven by expectations of an imminent apocalypse, but unlike their Assassin and Zealot and Sicarii counterparts, the Crusaders were not rebelling against the established order. Popes authorized Crusades, and prominent government figures led each campaign. Nobles led the First Crusade (1095–1099), which was the largest—anywhere from 9,700 to 35,000 members strong—and most committed and successful.[32] When Pope Urban authorized the First Crusade, he announced, "Whoever shall determine upon this holy pilgrimage and shall make his vow to God . . . shall wear the sign of the cross of the Lord on his forehead, or on his breast."[33] Initially participants were called "pilgrims," but after a few decades the French began using the term *croisade*, reflecting the fact that participants were obliged to wear crosses. Not until the eighteenth century did the word "crusade" emerge in the English-speaking world to mean a "good cause vigorously pursued."

Pope Urban II stressed that a crusade was a "holy war," not a "just war," a new distinction for Christians. Christians regarded all wars as evil, but a war could be "just" if it met four standards. A legitimate government had to authorize it; the cause had to be just; peace had to be a central motive, even in the midst of violence; and finally, the fighters had to be restrained in their actions by avoiding killing prisoners or enemy fighters, engaging in plundering, etc.[34] However, in the Roman Catholic Church's holy war, participants were urged to be unrestrained in their efforts to eliminate the enemy and its property. The Church's holy war clearly resembles the Old Testament concept of the *herem*, when God commanded Israel to transform Canaan into the "holy land."[35]

The First Crusade's initial task was to help the Christian Byzantine Empire regain territories Muslims had seized. Pope Urban II bolstered these efforts by declaring that those killed in the process would go to heaven.[36] After assisting the Byzantines, the Crusaders sought to free the Holy Land from Islamic rule. Ultimately, the expectation was that when the Holy Land was liberated, a "New World" would emerge, a paradise that would eliminate all governments, allowing liberty to prevail everywhere. It was only after the establishment of this "New World" that Christ would return to participate in the final days of violence.[37]

Crusaders, like their Jewish predecessors, believed that the end of the existing world was imminent and that humans were obliged to do everything possible to hasten the process. Imminence in the Jewish case was advanced by using violence to successfully provoke a massive uprising, thereby demonstrating a level of devotion that would induce God to intervene. For Christians, a thousand years had passed since Christ's crucifixion, suggesting his return was due. To complete the process, Christians had to retake and "purify" Jerusalem.

The Zealot and Sicarii atrocities were essential elements of a complicated campaign to change the views of different audiences at specific moments in time. The Crusader atrocities were much simpler. There were no complicated and changing audiences to persuade, and the atrocities were meant to destroy the enemy and demonstrate the Crusaders' determination. While Muslims in the Holy Land were the original enemy, Crusaders later used atrocities against pagans to expand the Catholic Church's constituency among other Christian groups and strengthen their political domains.[38]

The First Crusade was the most successful Crusade—and the one that committed the most vicious atrocities. In fact, it even involved numerous instances of cannibalism. The historian Philippe Buc describes those acts as "an unplanned activity but a theme present in Christian literature." In two or three cases, prisoners were eaten to show contempt for the enemy.

When "a starving army ate Muslims," it struck "divine fear in the Muslims . . . and purged the Christian army of lukewarm elements . . . cowardly men useless for war."[39] Norman Cohn's classic *The Pursuit of the Millennium* contends that Crusaders became cannibals to "signify superior commitment or to prove themselves free of sin."[40] All conventions governing violence were abandoned. The differences between belligerents and neutrals, combatants and noncombatants, or appropriate and inappropriate targets were completely ignored. Prisoners were normally massacred, and most were tortured to death, often by stoning. Captured women and children were often killed by bashing their heads against a wall.

The eight-month Siege of Antioch (1097–1098) and its aftermath illustrates these phenomena. Antioch was a strategic location on the route to Palestine. It had a large Christian—Greek and Armenian—population and was difficult to enter. Traitors in the city lowered ropes, enabling Crusaders to scale the walls and open a gate through which the army could enter. After the gates opened, the invading Crusaders began shouting their battle cry of "Deus vult" ("God wills it") and began to butcher all of Antioch's sleeping inhabitants, including Christians, women, children, and the elderly. Only later would they distinguish Christians from infidels. Approximately ten thousand were massacred. Shortly afterward, the Crusaders began the gruesome sport of mutilating the enemy's dead. "The heads of two thousand Turks . . . were cut off, some were exhibited as trophies, others were fixed on stakes round the camp, and others shot into the town. On another occasion, they dragged infidel corpses from their sepulchres and exposed fifteen hundred heads to the weeping Turks."[41]

When Jerusalem was finally retaken in 1099, Muslims and Jews were killed indiscriminately in massacres aimed at removing the "contamination of pagan superstition" in order to remake Jerusalem as a strictly Christian city.[42] Muslims and Jews who survived did so either by escaping the city or by being ransomed as prisoners. Fearing they might help the Crusaders, the city's Muslim governor expelled Christians before the siege, ironically saving them from also being victimized. The captured territories became the "Kingdom of Jerusalem," an area corresponding roughly in size to present-day Israel, southern Lebanon, and southwestern Jordan. The monarchy established a Catholic Church hierarchy that considered Eastern Orthodoxies schismatic.[43] It described Coptic Christians as heretics or atheists and eliminated their places of worship. Abyssinian Christians were forced to pay fees to visit Jerusalem's holy places. Islam's third-holiest site, the al-Aqsa Mosque, which was constructed on the ground that Muslims believed Mohammad used to visit heaven, was turned into a church. The site was also originally the home of Israel's Holy Temple.

Fifty years after the First Crusade, Muslims recaptured some of the territories they had lost east of the Euphrates River, provoking a Second Crusade (1147–1149), which ultimately failed to regain them. Then Saladin, the founder of Egypt's Ayyubid dynasty, retook Jerusalem in 1187, ending eighty-eight years of Christian rule. Saladin did not commit any massacres. Native Christians were allowed to remain in the city, but those of Crusader origin had to leave and pay a ransom that allowed them to take their goods with them. Seniors unable to pay a ransom were allowed to leave as well. Saladin's soldiers traveled with those who left in order to protect them. The 15,000 unable to pay the ransom became slaves. Eastern Orthodox, Coptic, and Abyssinian groups became recognized as Christians. The Church of the Holy Sepulcher was kept intact so that Christians from everywhere could visit it. The al-Aqsa Mosque was ritually purified with rose water. Christian furnishings were removed, and the mosque was fitted with oriental carpets. Its walls were illuminated with candelabras and texts from the Quran. Despite losing Jerusalem, the Crusaders were able to hold most of the neighboring territories, making Tyre the Kingdom of Jerusalem's new capital. The Byzantine emperor congratulated Saladin for taking the city, requesting that he return all the Orthodox churches taken. His request was granted, and rights of other sects were preserved. Local Christians could pray freely in their churches, and the Byzantine patriarchate took control of Christian affairs.[44]

The loss of Jerusalem provoked the Third Crusade. While the campaign recaptured the important cities of Acre and Jaffa, it did not recapture Jerusalem, inducing Pope Innocent III to authorize the Fourth Crusade (1202–1204), with a new strategy to retake Jerusalem and overthrow Saladin's regime in Egypt. However, this Crusade was forced into a slight detour.

Venice had built most of the ships used for the voyage and supplied many Crusaders with funds needed to pay for the ships. In lieu of payment, Venice asked the Crusaders to help recapture Zara, a territory that had seceded. Pope Innocent III forbade the action, but some Crusaders still helped take Zara. The pope excommunicated all Crusaders and Venetians who participated in the mission. Despite their transgressions, the pope later granted the army an absolution, enabling the Crusaders to continue their campaign.[45]

Despite their assistance to the Venetians, more funds were needed, and those promised by the Byzantine Empire were not received. Emperor Alexios III Angelo had previously pledged the funds but was murdered in an uprising. At the urging of the emperor's son, the Crusaders decided to conquer Constantinople after the usurpers also killed some Roman Catholic inhabitants.[46] The Crusaders saw the Byzantine preference for diplomacy and trade over war as duplicitous and degenerate. They also viewed Byzantine policies of tolerance and assimilation toward Muslims as a corrupt betrayal of the faith:

> The Crusaders subjected the greatest city in Europe to an indescribable sack. For three days they murdered, raped, looted, and destroyed on a scale which even the ancient Vandals and Goths would have found unbelievable. . . . [Crusaders] raped nuns and murdered Orthodox clerics. They desecrated the greatest Church in Christendom . . . placed a whore upon the patriarchal throne . . . who sang coarse songs as they drank wine from the Church's holy vessels. . . . The defeat of Byzantium, already in a state of decline, accelerated political degeneration so that the Byzantines eventually became an easy prey to the Turks. The Fourth Crusade and the crusading movement generally thus resulted, ultimately, in the victory of Islam, a result the exact opposite of its original intention.[47]

The attack intensified the schism between the Greek and Roman Christian churches and dealt an irrevocable blow to the weakened Byzantine Empire, paving the way for Muslim conquests in Anatolia and Balkan Europe later.

While the Fourth Crusade never implemented the new strategy to retake Jerusalem via the conquest of the powerful Ayyubid dynasty in Egypt, the Fifth Crusade (1217–1221) did. However, after arriving in Egypt in 1221, the sultan attacked the invaders and forced the Crusaders to surrender. The Sixth Crusade (1228–1229) employed the same strategy but engaged in very little fighting. The Holy Roman Emperor, Frederick II, negotiated with the Egyptian sultan to allow the Kingdom of Jerusalem to regain limited control over some parts of Jerusalem and other areas in the Holy Land. Fifteen years later, the Muslims retook Jerusalem and sparked the Seventh Crusade (1248–1254), led by the French king Louis IX. This campaign again centered around conquering Egypt on the way to Jerusalem. It too was defeated, and King Louis IX was captured. After paying a king's ransom, King Louis IX launched the Eighth Crusade in 1270. It lasted only a few months; the king died shortly after arriving in Africa. Upon his death, King Louis IX's disease-ridden army returned to Europe. The Ninth Crusade (1271–1272), the last, was led by the English prince Edward and managed to achieve several impressive victories over the Mamluks in the area now comprising Lebanon and Syria. Despite the victories, the Crusaders were ultimately forced to withdraw because of Prince Edward's pressing concerns back home. By this point in time, the Crusading spirit was "extinct." The last remaining Crusader strongholds located along the Mediterranean coast collapsed shortly after.

In Europe, after the First Crusade's success, popes were inspired to call for a Northern Crusade to Christianize the pagan regions of northern and northeastern Europe. Shortly after, the Albigensian Crusade (1209–1229) materialized to eliminate Catharism in southern France.[48] In reaction to the often scandalous lifestyles of the Catholic clergy, the Cathars called for a return to the Christian message of perfection, poverty, and preaching. Pope Innocent III's diplomatic attempts to roll back Catharism ultimately failed, and after one of his envoys was murdered, he declared a Crusade against the sect. The ensuing massacres were so horrible that Raphael Lemkin, the prominent lawyer who coined the term "genocide" and produced some important studies on the subject, described the Albigensian Crusade as "one of the most conclusive cases of genocide in religious history."[49] The historian Mark Gregory Pegg agreed, stating that "the Albigensian Crusade ushered genocide into the West by linking divine salvation to mass murder, by making slaughter as loving an act as His sacrifice on the cross."[50]

The Cathars' struggle also produced the Inquisition, designed to combat any public heresy of baptized Christians. In 1252, the Inquisition began using torture to gain information. While "the overwhelming majority of sentences consisted of penances like wearing a cross sewn on one's clothes, going on pilgrimage, etc.," if a person convicted of unrepentant heresy was handed over to secular authorities for sentencing, it would usually end with a burning at the stake.[51] In the late medieval period, torture became particularly atrocious, especially in the Iberian Peninsula, where the conversion of Jews and Muslims was prominent.[52] Shortly after the Albigensian Crusade, the Bosnian Crusade (1235–1241) commenced. It was led by the Hungarians and targeted the independent Bosnian Church, which had been accused of Catharism. Although the Hungarians hoped to use the Crusade to take control of the area, their efforts abruptly ended once the Tatars invaded Hungary. Despite the premature end of the Crusade, many atrocities were committed—including massive fires that were ignited to kill Bosnian prisoners—and served as a persistent source of Bosnian hatred toward Hungarians for centuries.[53]

European Jews also became a target of the Crusades. In 1096, numerous Jewish communities in France and Germany experienced massacres. One especially horrific example was at Mainz, in which some 1,100 were tortured and killed. The atrocities were so grotesque that a mother killed her four children to keep them from suffering that fate. Similar events took place in Worms, where at least eight hundred people who refused to be baptized were massacred. Regensburg Jews spared themselves from a similar fate by accepting a mass baptism after being forced into the Danube. After the failure of the Third Crusade, King Louis IX expelled all Jews from France; no Jew lived there for several centuries afterward. King Edward I in 1290 expelled all Jews from England; only 350 years later did Oliver Cromwell permit Jews to return. From the thirteenth to the sixteenth centuries, there were at least fifteen occasions in which Jewish populations were expelled. Some occurred even after the Crusades were over, and intense anti-Semitism remained a persistent feature of the West.[54] It is interesting to note that while Crusaders tried to convert Jews who lived in the Christian world, they refused to allow Jews in the Holy Land to convert.

Although some Catholic Church officials were involved in the initial anti-Semitic attacks, after the First Crusade the church tried to protect the Jews. In 1272, Pope Gregory X stated that Jews "are not capable of harming Christians." Subsequent popes kept reminding Christians that Jews were not the enemy. Pope Benedict XIII stated that "Jews are never . . . to be molested or to have their goods seized. . . . [Rather, they are to be treated] humanely with clemency."[55] Yet despite a number of Holy Fathers' wishes, the attacks continued.

SECULAR TERRORISM BEFORE THE GLOBAL FORM: THE MOBS

In the eighteenth and nineteenth centuries, secular justifications for rebel terror largely replaced religious ones. The United States provides two well-known examples. One was known as the Ku Klux Klan. It emerged in the decade after the Civil War (1867–1877) and became an indispensable ingredient in the ultimately successful efforts to resist the federal government's goal of giving freed slaves equal rights.[56] Another group, the Sons of Liberty, emerged a century earlier (1765–1776); unlike the Klan, it was rarely described as a terror entity. The reason for such starkly different reputations is, in part, attributable to the fact that their ultimate goals were radically different. However, the methods each group used had some striking similarities, and in the end, terrorist activity is defined by the methods employed, not the ultimate political goals sought. As such, it is justifiable to describe both as terrorist groups.[57]

Both used "mobs" that suddenly materialized and always greatly outnumbered their victims. The KKK normally struck at night, disguised in bizarre costumes to conceal identity and inspire fear. The Sons of Liberty were more visible, although they frequently blackened their faces, wore costumes, and were led by "strangers."[58] Both groups usually posted warnings, giving victims an opportunity to avoid being attacked so long as they complied. Neither group had an international dimension. The KKK at its inception functioned only in states that had tried to secede. The Sons of Liberty were confined to the American colonies and did not initially seek international help. However, after the Revolutionary War broke out and a legitimate government emerged, international support materialized.

Mobs, of course, were not unique to America, as Benjamin Franklin, who spent much time in England, noted: "I have seen within the year riots in the country about corn; riots about elections; riots about work-houses, riots of colliers . . . riots of smugglers in which customhouse officers and excise men have been murdered, and the King's armed vessels and troops fired at."[59] Yet there was a striking difference between American and English experiences with mobs. Americans organized campaigns that persisted for a decade, but the English experienced riots that typically lasted for only a few days. Americans usually attacked individuals, but the English generally targeted property.[60]

THE SONS OF LIBERTY, 1765–1776: INITIATING A REVOLUTION

Colonial legislatures fiercely opposed the Stamp Act of 1765, an unprecedented tax. When the Crown could not be persuaded to back down, a series of mobs and riots erupted. In response, the Crown developed an alternative tax policy more consistent with traditional practices. Yet despite the adjustments, mob violence continued for a decade, intensifying divisions between the Crown and the colonists. As tensions continued to escalate, new and unanticipated dimensions of the colonists' ultimate political objectives emerged. "When the troubles began some ten years before . . . virtually everyone believed that the difficulties could be and should be developed within the framework of the Empire. Hence, opinion had been divided even among patriots in the use of [mob] violence . . . as not only unworthy of the cause, but . . . far more likely to alienate England than induce concessions."[61] One important supporter of the protests, Gouverneur Morris, argued that in time the mobs began to "think and reason," moving resistance in ways that surprised everyone.[62] "Mob violence," an eighteenth-century term still used by some historians, has some connotations that do not fit the activities of the Sons of Liberty well. In the *Oxford English Dictionary*, a "mob" is described as a "disorderly crowd," and the first edition of *The Encyclopaedia of the Social Sciences* similarly states that "a mob is an angry crowd that attempts to inspire or destroy an object." A mob's activities do not involve "an implementation of a rational policy." "Mob spirit" simply refers to "highly emotional and poorly coordinated behavior and expression." *Webster's Dictionary* notes that the Latin origin of the term explains that a mob's moods change rapidly and that most participants come from the "lower classes of a community."[63] Initially, a number of colonial assemblies resisted the Stamp Act. Violence would not have materialized—and certainly would not have been successful—without continuing political support, but that support was conditional, which meant that the violence had to be planned carefully. Most Sons of Liberty participants were tradesmen and artisans, and its leaders came from the "better" classes of professionals, merchants, and local officials.[64] A hierarchy of mobs was established during Sam Adams' rule of Boston: the lowest classes—servants, negroes [*sic*] and sailors were placed under the command of a 'superior set consisting of the Master Masons carpenters of the town' above them were put the merchants' mob and the Sons of Liberty, known to the Tories as Adams's 'Mohawks,' upon whom the more delicate enterprises against the Tories and Crown devolved.[65] "The 'lower classes' were always more visible. When the resistance to the Stamp Act was at issue, the uprisings . . . demonstrated a remarkable political extremism on the part of colonial crowds. Everywhere 'followers' proved more ready than their 'leaders' to use force . . .'the better sort are defending [English liberties] by all lawful means in their power,' Thomas Hutchinson explained perceptively, and the most abandoned say they will do it . . . at any cost."[66]

The Loyal Nine, which later became the local Sons of Liberty, helped create a number of mobs. The organizers "kept their identity secret and wished it to be believed that the mobs they set in motion were really spontaneous outbreaks of violence from the 'lower sort.' . . . Boston was controlled by a 'trained mob' and Sam Adams was its keeper."[67] The Sons of Liberty had important features that conflict with our definitions of mobs—in particular, consistency. Their political purpose always remained the same, namely, "no taxation without representation," a principle that after eleven years of violence became the essential inspiration of the American Revolution. Typically, Sons of Liberty violence was carefully planned and exhibited considerable restraint. Sometimes, it seemed that every likely contingency had been considered in order to prevent the violence from getting out of hand, as demonstrated by one of the period's most well-known incidents, the Boston Tea Party of 1773. Several thousand colonists watched from the shore while 342 chests of tea were seized and thrown into the water. No one was hurt, and the sailors' property—as distinguished from the East India Company's—was respected. Even a broken padlock was replaced.

Is it appropriate to describe the Boston Tea Party as comparable to "mob violence"? Given that one cannot isolate the incident from the broader campaign in which it occurred, I would argue it is indeed an appropriate comparison. Ultimately, the Boston Tea Party took place during a series of violent riots—which lasted a decade—that were organized by the same individuals who put together the Boston Tea Party. One key reason the Boston Tea Party did not become violent was that the British did not use force to resist it. While the Sons of Liberty preferred peaceful demonstrations, the group did not reject violence.

Most "spontaneous" outbreaks during this period were restrained, especially with respect to committing fatalities. The mobs "trusted to horror rather than to homicide. Though occasionally brandishing cutlasses and muskets, they typically employed less lethal weapons like clubs, rocks, brickbats and clods of dung." "In truth," wrote the English historian Lecky in the 1880s, "although no people have indulged more largely than the Americans in violent, reckless, and unscrupulous language, no people have been more signally free from the thirst for blood which, in moments of great political excitement has been often shown both in England and France."[68] In order to force Lieutenant Governor Hutchinson of Massachusetts to resign as the stamp distributor, a mob burned his home and stole his personal papers. The attack "startled men accustomed to venerate and obey lawful authority and [made] them doubt the justice of the cause attended with such direful consequences."[69] The unanticipated event occurred after mob members got drunk on the rum they had discovered in the governor's cellar. Sam Adams, who had organized the mob, publicly expressed dismay. Fortunately, "Boston patriots deprived Hutchinson of the sweets of martyrdom by the circulation of a story that letters had been found in his house ... [that] proved him to be responsible for the Stamp Act." However, "Sam Adams never produced these incriminating letters."[70] A similar attack occurred in Newport, Rhode Island, shortly afterward. The close timing of the events made sympathizers apprehensive. Boston and New York newspapers published directives for "Leaders" of mobs, emphasizing their mission was to redress grievances, not create new ones. "No innocent Person, nor any upon bare Suspicion, with insufficient Evidence, should receive the least injury ... lest they disgrace their Power and the Cause which occasioned its Collection. ... The greatest care should be taken to keep an undisciplined Multitude from running into mischievous Extravagancies."[71]

The sheer number and geographic distribution of these mobs also suggest that tensions could have easily boiled over. Without sympathizers constantly reminding potential participants that they could go too far with their actions, such mobs would likely have gotten out of control. In the nine months the Stamp Act was in effect, over sixty riots occurred in twenty-five different locations. "During some of these months in port cities like Boston and New York, mobs were in the streets almost every night and government ground to a halt."[72] Despite the mobs, Parliament was ambivalent about the Stamp Act. Significant MPs like William Pitt and Edmund Burke were strongly opposed to it, but if the riots had produced many casualties, the outcome might have been different. It is important to note that the rebels originally argued that they were fighting for their traditional rights as Englishmen, not to establish a new order. However, the repeal of the Stamp Act gave the rebels enormous confidence. "The successful attack on the Act ... was of great importance in subsequent periods of agitation when the opposition was not so universal. The experience of working together, the ideas that were inculcated during the agitation, and the sense of accomplishment resulting from united efforts were indispensable."[73] It seems odd to describe this mob activity as terrorism, especially when self-imposed limits were so conspicuous. Still, Schlesinger describes the victims' emotions as "terror," "horror," and "fear."[74] A few contemporaries also spoke of such "terror." Why, then, did no one describe this activity as "terrorism"? One reason is that the word "terrorism" did not enter our vocabulary until after the French Revolution, two decades later. It would take two centuries before some academics referred to the Sons of Liberty as terrorists.[75]

Yet the question remains: If the mobs were so restrained, how could victims be terrorized? The fact that victims simply did not know what their fate was going to be and had not the slightest assurance they would not be killed or tortured meant that they were terrified.[76] Many examples make this point clear. Grotesque effigies of leading Stamp Act administrators were beaten or whipped and then carried through the streets to hastily constructed gallows to be hanged or to funeral pyres to be burned.[77] A mob confronted Lieutenant Governor Thomas Oliver of Massachusetts, demanding he resign and denounce the Stamp Act. He heard "voices swearing they would have my blood" and complied because his wife and children in the next room were "frantic with fear." Later, away from the scene, he thought he should renounce his acts because they were made under duress and had no moral or legal weight. However, a renunciation would have been very costly, he stated on the record. "A hard alternative 'tis true; but still, I had it in my power either to die or make the promise. I chose to live."[78] His subsequent history of the period described mobs as "volcanoes" and "hydras," words indicating victims saw them as uncontrollable.[79] A Connecticut mob "threatened to bury the distributor alive when he insisted on remaining in office. [They] put this stouthearted soul inside a coffin, nailed the lid shut, and lowered him into a grave. They then began shoveling dirt on the coffin. The official called for release and thereupon submitted his resignation."[80] "Mobs used whatever force necessary to produce resignations. In several cases, they scarcely had to flex their muscles to frighten distributors into sending in their resignations."[81]

One historian's description of Edward Stow's experience is interesting. Stow was a Boston merchant-captain who in 1770 reported that he had "been mobbed and libeled ever since the Stamp Act, [his] house bedaubed with excrement and feathers three times in two months." A mob of three hundred severely injured Stow because he "seized for His Majesty two Gun Carriages, a pair of Swivels, and a Cow Horn." Compared to other instances of violence, Stow's persecution was so trivial that newspapers did not even report it.[82] In 1771, a commissioner of customs' sister described an employee's experience during an extremely cold winter night. "In a body stript, covered all over with tar then with feathers, his arm dislocated by tearing off his cloaths he dragged in a cart with thousands attending, some beating him with clubs and throwing him out of the cart then in again. . . . The doctors say that it is impossible this poor creature can live. They say his flesh comes off his back in steaks [*sic*]."[83]

In describing rebel terror in the modern world, one always refers to the crucial importance of having audiences beyond the victims experiencing the violence. In the case of the Sons of Liberty, there were two very visible principal audiences. One "audience of potential supporters saw the government as being so contemptibly weak, and the people so superior to the royal authority that they [were] . . . elated upon their triumph over the defenseless officers of the Crown."[84] A second audience was composed of opponents who needed to be intimidated or provoked to react in ways that would enrage the community.[85] One attack could be orchestrated to affect both audiences simultaneously. "Whatever their origin, they [the mobs] furthered patriotic purposes, in several essential ways. They highlighted grievances as mere words could never have done; they struck terror into the hearts of British adherents; and, as notably in the case of the Boston Massacre, they fashioned folk heroes out of street loafers and hoodlums."[86]

One would think the consistency and discipline needed to craft such attacks—especially under dangerous conditions in a period that lasted over a decade—would require a formal organization. Oddly, that key ingredient is missing in this case. If such formal organization did exist, historians certainly have not found evidence of it. The leaders of the first American mobs in 1765 called their groups "Sons of Liberty," and some individual entities, like the ones organized by Sam Adams, had structure. But organizational connections between the groups did not exist, and most groups disappeared a year or so after the Stamp Act was repealed. The title "Sons of Liberty" survived and was used to describe other mobs with similar ends; it ultimately became a synonym for "patriot."[87]

The Sons of Liberty, an informal network of autonomous societies, flourished largely in seaport cities. Members in one colony established rudimentary communication between elements in other colonies, largely through letters sent by "Committees of Correspondence," which were essential parts of each independent unit. One unit could not make a unilateral decision binding other groups, as there was no way to enforce such decisions, a necessary condition for a formal organization. This decentralized structure on the national level was reproduced in each participating colony. The Sons of Liberty provided a model for resistance, one emulated later in various phases during the decade. We know little about how various activities were related. The records are incomplete, partly because many participants were ambivalent about their activities. Those indicted for participating in such actions claimed to be innocent and when arrested often escaped conviction. In fact, few mob participants "admitted complicity until more than a half century had elapsed."[88]

The Stamp Act was enacted because the Seven Years' War (French and Indian War) that ended in 1763 had exhausted the British treasury. Efforts to pay the debts stimulated significant British taxpayer protests. All newspapers, legal documents, and commercial papers were forced to bear a stamp, a rare commodity in the colonies. The British argued that the tax was just because it fell equally on all. The colonies had benefited greatly from the French defeat despite contributing very little to it, which led Parliament to believe they would accept a significant tax burden. Parliament even pledged that the generated tax revenue would be used exclusively to pay for military expenses necessary to defend the colonies. However, the colonies had only ever experienced taxes levied on foreign trade, and the novelty and universality of the new tax provoked widespread and unanticipated resistance. The British made little to no effort beforehand to consider what means would be necessary to enforce the law if armed resistance materialized, let alone resistance involving all thirteen colonies. Clear-sighted observers on both sides believed colonial unity impossible because of the great differences between the provinces in manners, religion, and economic interest. Nevertheless, when confronted by the Stamp Act, colonial particularism began to crumble: America was awakened, alarmed, restless, and disaffected.[89]

British resources for dealing with the violence were meager. There was no professional police force in the colonies—or in Britain, for that matter.[90] If a mob emerged in Britain, the army could be called out to subdue it, which typically ended with British troops killing many. But there were few troops available in the colonies for such purposes. One prominent historian argued that the government's inability to mobilize forces gave the colonial riots their special flavor. It "was apparently more the restraint and timidity of the British authorities, and less the moderation of American crowds, that prevented a serious loss of lives during the American rioting."[91]

Normally a *posse comitatus* or colonial militia could be called on, but because those bodies were so deeply rooted in the local community and hostile to the Stamp Act, they usually refused to respond, and even if they did, they would not obey orders. It is also worth noting that a mob often consisted of persons from a *posse comitatus* or a colonial militia, giving it a semilegitimate status as embodying the people:

> The few British troops available thus caused more problems than they solved. After it was seen that stamps could be forced upon the colonists only at the bayonet's point, the weakness of the British government naturally made it contemptible in the Americans' eyes. . . . At Fort Johnson, North Carolina a garrison of two hundred British troops were besieged by five hundred heavily armed Sons of Liberty, and in New York, the headquarters of British military authority in the provinces, the troops could not keep order in the town. General Gage informed royal governors who clamored for military aid . . . it would be at the expense of strategic posts [along the frontier] which would be seriously weakened if their garrisons were removed.[92]

The tiny military detachments unexpectedly became a government "boomerang," John Adams emphasized. "Soldiers are wretched conservators of the peace."[93] Insults and beatings provoked British troops in America "beyond endurance." Juries consistently refused to convict rioters. Considering the repeated provocations, "the wonder is that the troops did not kill much more often, but this fact naturally failed to impress the colonists."[94] However, it was impotent British military forces that helped provoke the notorious Boston Massacre.

> On the icy cobbled square . . . a lone British sentry was being taunted by a small band of men and boys. [Suddenly] crowds came pouring into the streets . . . brandishing sticks and clubs. . . . The lone guard was reinforced by eight British soldiers with loaded muskets and fixed bayonets . . . the crowds pelted the despised redcoats with snowballs, chunks of ice, oyster shells and stones.[95]

In response, the soldiers abruptly opened fire, killing five. The soldiers were arrested and asked John Adams—who also happened to be Sam Adams's cousin—to defend them in court, creating ironies that reflected the public's conflicting emotions. While John Adams originally believed that the soldiers were guilty, he became convinced they acted in self-defense and organized a brilliant and successful defense in court.[96] Ironically, though the court believed the soldiers acted in self-defense and did not need to be punished, the incident was publicly described everywhere as the Boston Massacre. The moniker clearly implied those killed were not responsible for any misdeeds and deserved to be celebrated as heroes or martyrs.

> On each anniversary the bells of the town tolled intervals during the day, and at night lighted transparencies near the site of the bloodshed displayed tableaux of the "murderers" and the dead perhaps with a symbolic America trampling a supine redcoat. . . . The yearly orations continued . . . until the town authorities in 1783 substituted the celebration of the Fourth of July.[97]

The unintended "victims" electrified opposition to British policy, and those most immediately assaulted were persons directly responsible for administering the law. General Gage reported that the "officers of the Crown grew more timid, and more fearful of doing their Duty every day."[98] Lieutenant Governor Hutchinson of Massachusetts also observed that there was "not a justice of peace, sheriff, constable or peace officer in the province . . . [that] would venture to take cognizance of any breach of law against the general bent of the people."[99] The English government tried to reestablish its authority by passing the Townsend Acts to tax foreign trade, a traditional source of income.[100] Resistance materialized again, but this time the victims were different. It was not government representatives that were the main targets but private parties engaged in international trade. Those believed to be loyal to the Crown's policies were also targeted. Very late in their campaign, mobs also began preventing Tories from taking their seats in the legislatures.

Ultimately, the Crown decided that it needed a significant troop presence to cope with the mobs. Yet by the time those troops arrived, the colonists were able to cement their political union, organize their own military forces, and begin a revolution. Although the mobs' significance quickly diminished, during the war they drove many loyalists, or supporters of the Crown, to Canada, where as refugees they found a new home.

THE KU KLUX KLAN, 1867–1877: LOSING A WAR
BUT WINNING A PEACE

The Ku Klux Klan (KKK) emerged between 1867 and 1877 in a climate very different from the one that nourished the Sons of Liberty. When the bloody and bitterly fought U.S. Civil War ended, both parties had to establish the conditions for lasting peace and determine the most appropriate governments for the Southern states. What must new state governments do to prevent a renewal of civil war and resolve the political conflicts that would emerge from the liberation of the slaves? Deep differences in opinion divided the North from the South on these questions, a problem that was complicated by the fact that a deep ambivalence on these matters existed both within the North and South. Ultimately, it was this combination of deep division and dispassionate ambivalence that sparked the "most violent and nastiest rioting in American history."[101]

After President Lincoln's assassination, his successor was Andrew Johnson, a Southern Democrat chosen as Lincoln's running mate to ease reconciliation efforts with the South. Johnson believed the country would be brought together again if the two sides agreed that no state had the legal power to leave the Union. While every state's constitution would remain valid, they would all also accept President Lincoln's Emancipation Proclamation, which abolished slavery. These reconciliation efforts enabled most rebel leaders to participate in politics. White Southerners accepted these conditions, and fifty-eight former Confederate congressmen, nine Confederate generals and admirals, six Confederate Cabinet members, and the Confederacy's vice president won congressional seats in the first national election after the Civil War.[102] Confederate leaders also returned to dominate some state governments.

The North did not anticipate that the reinstatement of the old constitutions would deny freed slaves voting rights. Several months before the 1866 election, two very bloody riots occurred. "In both instances the riots opened with blacks aggressively advancing their claims to equality in the face of opposition by local officials and white police."[103] In Memphis, white residents and the police killed forty-six Black people in a hideous display of barbarism. In New Orleans, Unionists and Republicans called a political convention of "dubious legality" to enfranchise Blacks and allow them to seek office. White rioters exploded in response, igniting three days of rioting that killed around fifty supporters.[104] The event "created a unity among Republicans that had not existed even during the war."[105] Many Northerners felt the atrocities in New Orleans "proved" Johnson's plan did little justice to the enormous sacrifices made to win the Civil War. As a Democrat, he had little credibility among Republicans. Instead of reconciling the North and South, the 1866 election gave "Radical Republicans" in the North a powerful campaign issue. They ultimately dominated Congress and aimed to "reconstruct" the South or, at the very least, make it "democratic."

Congress moved to exclude members from the South by annulling their state constitutions, divided the South into military districts, and, to the great dismay of many white Southerners, established Black militias. Strenuous efforts were made to make Blacks a major political force, partly in the hopes that it would eventually give the Republican Party a clear national majority. When Johnson resisted Congress' efforts, Radical Republicans organized mobs to compel compliance. Johnson's vitriolic responses motivated Congress to impeach the president for the first time in history, although he avoided a conviction.[106]

Reconstruction made Southern whites feel they had been forced into an occupation, not a reconciliation. In the words of one Southerner, "the South [was] no more a real partner in the so-called Union than Poland [was] part of Russia or India of England or Cuba of Spain. Why should this country be called a Union? The very term signifies equality of parts. Let it be called 'Yankeeland.'"[107] At first, many refused to participate in the Southern elections for fear of legitimizing them. However, their refusal simply handed many Southern state governments to Republicans, who were dependent on Black voters. At the same time, Congress mustered the two-thirds majority needed to add the Fourteenth and Fifteenth Amendments to the Constitution, both designed to guarantee Black people equal rights.

While many Southerners chose not to engage in the political process, eventually mobs emerged in response to these efforts, reminding Southerners that there was another way to resist the North, one that had proved successful in dealing with abolitionist demands before the Civil War began.[108] The KKK was the first and most important of these mob groups. Other similar groups, such as the Knights of the White Camellias, Red Jackets, Native Sons of the South, Society of the White Roses, White Liners, White Man's Party, White Leaguers, White Brotherhood, and the Seventy-Six Association, emerged later. Ultimately, popular imagination "lumped those groups all together . . . as the Klan. Their costumes, rituals, tactics, and purposes were so similar, there is no practical way to distinguish them," and thus they "must be treated as part of a generic Klux movement."[109] During Reconstruction (1865–1876), at least 375 riots occurred; the KKK organized nearly all of them.[110]

Over time, KKK groups in various states merged,[111] and the former Confederate lieutenant general Nathan Bedford Forrest, the South's most distinguished cavalry officer, became the Klan's "Grand Wizard."[112] The aim was to make sure President Johnson's original reconciliation plan was revived, and KKK members normally identified with the Democratic Party. "Although the mystic syllables Ku Klux Klan were on people's lips everywhere, most night riders were unwilling to concede that they went by any other name than 'The Young Men's Democratic Clubs.'"[113] On paper, the KKK had an elaborate formal hierarchy headed by a Grand Wizard presiding over an Empire divided into Realms, Dominions, Provinces, and Dens headed respectively by Grand Dragons, Titans, Giants, and Cyclops. However, this structure never functioned as designed. The den, a basic unit established in the local areas of all relevant states, operated with little or no central direction. "A group of young men would form a den after hearing of the organization elsewhere."[114]

The KKK claimed to be restoring order out of the dreadful chaos sweeping the South since its catastrophic military defeat, chaos in which courts and police rarely functioned and considerable corruption prevailed.[115] Yet the ultimate objective was to bring down the "democracy" the Reconstruction policies aimed to create. KKK terror was intimately linked to reshaping electoral processes to keep Black people from voting and to force their "friends," "scalawags," and "carpetbaggers" to flee.[116] To make it impossible for Republicans to campaign in the South, the KKK decimated black militias and Republican secret societies like the Lincoln Brotherhood in Florida, which existed to protect the candidates.

The KKK was most vigorous in the Piedmont and Appalachian highlands of Georgia, Alabama, Mississippi, and North and South Carolina, where elections were most competitive.[117] In states like Virginia, where the Democratic Party was firmly in control, the KKK did not function. "Armed with the ballot . . . many blacks found that the privilege in fact jeopardized their lives and their livelihoods. When the blacks were slaves, they were mistreated but rarely killed because they were property; but when they were free, they became more vulnerable to a new form of violence."[118]

The campaign against Black suffrage quickly became effective, as clearly demonstrated by the voting statistics in Georgia after the KKK emerged. In Oglethorpe County in 1869, the Republicans got 116 votes; eight months earlier, they had received ten times as many votes. In Columbia County, the difference in the same period was even starker. Republicans got only one vote, even though they had 1,122 in a previous election that same year.[119] This campaign of voter suppression was ultimately a large and time-consuming one, given that so many voting districts in so many different states were involved. President Grant's election in 1868 further complicated this effort; ultimately the federal government intermittently used its military and legal powers to protect the electoral process.[120]

> As Election Day drew near, violence and intimidation reached epidemic proportions in another reign of terror. The whites, with guns in their hands and murder in their hearts, were intent on control. . . . Republican nominations were often not made, the candidates didn't campaign, and some Republican nominees and officials even fled their homes. . . . Economic coercion was added to physical intimidation as the whites refused to lease land, give jobs, or provide credit to blacks. . . . In some towns, graves were dug for those Negroes who might vote Republican. . . . Many blacks, fearing for their lives, did not dare to vote, and most of those who tried either did not receive ballots or were driven from the polls.[121]

Even though the army occasionally was called in to guarantee fair elections, the violence had an extraordinary effect on Republican voting statistics. In Yazoo County, Mississippi, the Republicans only received seven votes in 1875; several years earlier, when most Blacks had voted, the Republican majority was over a thousand.[122] Before the 1875 election, Mississippi's Governor Ames, a Republican, asked President Grant to send federal troops because on "election day [we] may find our voters fleeing before rebel bullets rather than balloting for their rights." When troops did not arrive, he proclaimed "a revolution has taken place—by force of arms—and a race are disfranchised. They are to be returned to a condition of serfdom, an era of second slavery."[123]

The next year, South Carolina's governor asked President Grant for troops to police an election. Soldiers were sent both to avoid another disgraceful scene and because this election was a national referendum with the fate of the Republican Party in Congress and the presidency at stake. Violence was reduced, and the local population seemed largely hospitable. Nonetheless, the force of one thousand was still too small to cover the entire state, and an effective terror campaign had already started against potential Black voters even before troops arrived.[124] Federal officials subsequently discovered that the voter rolls were fraudulent, a problem the army had neither the authority nor the skill to rectify.[125] As these examples indicate, one surprisingly important and usually neglected reason for the KKK's success was its restraint. Conspicuous atrocities, comparable to the New Orleans riot in 1866, most likely would have renewed fierce concerns in the North. The logic of the campaign was to "foment just enough terror in the strong Republican counties to demoralize and defeat the black Republicans, but not enough to provoke federal reaction."[126] Striking targets in the North would have been a political disaster. In the Northern state of Indiana in 1869, a group with views similar to the KKK, also called the Sons of Liberty, surfaced, whereupon the KKK quickly shut it down.[127] Republicans, aware of the North's ambivalence, generally exaggerated the reports of outrages to increase support for Reconstruction policies. But the "policy" backfired. More and more Northerners believed most stories recounting the atrocities were manufactured for partisan advantage.[128] The federal government found it too costly to create the tools apparently necessary to enforce the Constitution in the South. A shortage of Southern judges created excessive delays in adjudicating claims, delays that exposed potential witnesses to extraordinary abuse. Few federal marshals were available; most were employed in Northern and "border" states where serious problems of electoral corruption prevailed—and where Republicans were more likely to win elections.

Ultimately, federal election enforcement had much more significance as a campaign tool than as a genuine effort to do something. In other words, it was a "salvage operation [rather] than a permanent reform."[129] Everything depended on military forces, but there were never enough soldiers. The troops also used martial law and other measures to curtail civil liberties and suspend habeas corpus. Suspects were frequently thrown into jail for long periods of time without receiving a trial because juries would not convict them. "Excessive vengeance by lawlessness was . . . replaced by excessive vengeance by law."[130] These activities provoked serious national discontent and devastated military morale.

> Most officers detested service below the Mason-Dixon Line. Conserva-tive generals . . . disliked interfering with civil government and their inevitable entanglement in southern politics. . . . The army's effectiveness was further limited because its superiors in Washington discounted reports of southern outrages and favored a restrained use of military force. After struggling with maddening complexities of Georgia politics, Gen-eral Alfred Taylor informed General William T. Sherman "I would not again go through with a job of this kind even if it would make me a Mar-shal of France." The common soldiers shared many of their command-ers' prejudices, were often hostile to the government's Reconstruction policies, and were seldom radical egalitarians. . . . Commanders moved slowly against the Klan and opposed military trials for these outlays.[131]

In 1876, the KKK largely accomplished its mission when the House of Rep-resentatives resolved a disputed presidential election in favor of the Repub-lican candidate, Rutherford B. Hayes, after he agreed to withdraw federal troops from the South.

COMPARING TWO MOB TERROR EXPERIENCES

Both the Sons of Liberty and the KKK were successful. The Sons of Lib-erty played a vital role in fomenting anger toward the Crown and uniting the colonies in a common revolutionary cause to create an independent nation. The KKK's achievement was less durable. It demolished the Recon-struction program and made sure that Blacks would be "second-class" citizens. Only a century later did the nonviolent Civil Rights Movement in the 1960s finally change the situation.[132]

In both cases, potential sympathizers and opposition elements were ambivalent. The British government had opposition at home and was unclear about what the situation in the colonies required to be resolved. It had few troops in the region. The colonies initially lacked resolve, unity, confidence, and had an uneasy feeling that the mobs would get out of control, demolishing all respect for the law in the process. In the KKK case, white Southerners feared they might spark another war, and the North was unwilling to keep troops in the South for an indefinite period of time. Northern reluctance was partly because the North also harbored a serious hostility to Blacks, particularly among immigrants competing with them economically. Blacks were allowed to vote only in a few Northern states. It took time to dissolve commitments and exploit existing ambivalences.

Another key similarity that improved the groups' survival chances was their structure. Sons of Liberty and KKK groups were autonomous and informally connected, which made it very difficult for governments to get the leverage needed to break up groups deeply embedded in local populations. The original Sons of Liberty groups lasted around a year, and the KKK was officially disbanded after four. But both remained a model for successive groups, and the public rarely distinguished successors from their models. All members of both groups denied involvement; the KKK even made recruits swear oaths not to reveal any organization information.[133] Courts found it difficult to convict group members because juries were too sympathetic or too frightened to do so. These mob activities were also carefully orchestrated and planned. The KKK and Sons of Liberty mobs never intentionally destroyed the lives and property of potential supporters.[134] Nonetheless, some KKK members were involved in ordinary criminal activity, and the Sons of Liberty occasionally engaged in counterproductive criminal abuses, but only against those they had previously identified as political enemies.

Mobs always outnumbered their victims, but KKK mobs were much smaller than Sons of Liberty ones. KKK mobs typically numbered several dozen in size; a small Klan mob might consist of only six or seven men.[135] The KKK's decision to operate under the cover of darkness greatly reduced the need for larger forces. Nighttime attacks were more frightening and increased the likelihood of evading capture. The KKK was much more deeply implanted in rural areas, locations that complicated the army's mission.[136] Although it is impossible to establish the number of KKK victims, some estimates suggest there could have been more than twenty thousand. A Senate investigation found that in nine rural counties over a period of six months, the Klan lynched "35 men, whipped 262 men and women, outraged, shot, mutilated, raped and burned out 103 other people."[137]

The Sons of Liberty mobs were largely urban and usually numbered several hundred. Occasionally, a mob contained over a thousand people, and in one or two cases the number of participants is cited as being close to ten thousand people. The Sons of Liberty mobs also had many observers, and as the years passed the number of spectators kept increasing.[138] Since Boston's, New York's, and Philadelphia's populations were fifteen, thirty, and fifty-five thousand, respectively, the reported turnouts were enormous. Commenting on Boston mobs, one historian noted, "If the reported numbers are correct [they] would have consisted of half the city's adult males."[139] Large turnouts helped convince interested parties the mobs truly commanded popular support.

The disguises each group used give some indication of their anticipated audiences. KKK costumes were terrifying. The KKK wanted Blacks to see them as ghosts returning from another world, carrying the bones, coffins, and skulls of Confederate soldiers. They wore long robes and masks with "horns, beards, and long red flannel tongues." Their horses were covered to their lower legs and their hooves muffled. These disguises reflected the KKK's beliefs about ex-slaves being excessively superstitious and easily terrified. Victims were typically described as criminals and members of political or militia organizations.[140]

The Sons of Liberty disguises were more varied and often unnecessary. Nevertheless, the need to have a profound psychological effect sometimes made everyone dress alike. In the Boston Tea Party, for example, participants appeared as Native Americans. Leaders, however, were always disguised.

Initially they blackened their faces and later were "strangers," or persons not known in the local community. "Crowds repeatedly selected strangers to act as ad hoc leaders for direct confrontations with other members or sectors of the community. This facilitated subsequent reunification of the community while making prosecution more difficult."[141]

Unlike the Sons of Liberty, KKK activities were designed to kill as well as intimidate, a difference illustrated by the transformation of the "lynch law" practices both groups used. Charles Lynch, a member of Virginia's House of Burgess, established the precedent in 1774. There were not many victims of Sons of Liberty lynchings. During the Reconstruction period, the practice changed dramatically. Lynch mobs normally hanged their victims. As a result of this behavior, the term "lynching" has come to mean less "the seizing of a person in the custody of a police officer" and more to mean "the infliction of the death penalty in summary fashion, usually by hanging." The number of victims in the period is unknown, but it may have been near a thousand.[142] Even though whites controlled the legal machinery, the number of lynches grew yearly. Ida B. Wells's explanation for this increase is that lynching was "an excuse to get rid of Negroes . . . acquiring wealth and property, and thus keep the race terrorized and 'keep the nigger down.'"[143] Knowing this history, one would not expect restraint to be a subject that arises when discussing the KKK. Still, in some critical contexts, the KKK's restraint manifested itself in three key ways: an unwillingness to compel Union troops to produce casualties, an aversion to conspicuous atrocities during an election period, and forbidding members and sympathizers from using similar tactics in the North.

While both groups restrained their behaviors, their attitudes toward their victims could not have been more different. The KKK aimed to keep Black people "in their place" by enhancing their fear of the consequences if they tried to resist or assert their rights. The rituals of the Sons of Liberty suggest a different view of their victims, something much more complex, namely, a desire to transform or purify them. "Most commonly victims were tarred and feathered. Tar was known for its curative effects. Victims, too, were often dunked in water, and sometimes transferred under the keel of a ship from side to side, practices suggesting religious baptism or symbolic purification. Significantly, if a potential victim confessed and recanted, he would be 're-admitted' to the community."[144] The impurity theme also manifested itself in other ways. "Fumigation used in colonial Massachusetts against smallpox and against Tories, was supposed to have cleansing effects. . . . Noises and fires were designed to exorcise evil spirits. Public exhibition of offenders, usually explained by its deterrent effects, had a parallel in the belief that evil spirits, once brought into the open, lose their powers."[145] Doctors suspected of Tory sentiments were occasionally, especially during the 1775–1776 epidemic, accused of spreading smallpox. Rumors prevailed at Roxbury in 1775 that Boston's Loyalist inhabitants infected with smallpox were deliberately spreading it.[146]

As British policies changed, the Sons of Liberty sought new victims. Private persons engaged in foreign trade or those consuming their products began to replace administrators. Tories increasingly became targets as the years went on, and when the war broke out, mobs pushed many loyalist colonists into Canada. In the very last phase of the conflict before the war began—and even afterward—mobs struck at the electoral process, albeit in an unsystematic manner. Their aim was to diminish the Tory voice in the colonial legislatures by keeping certain elements from voting and preventing elected Tories from taking their seats.[147] In stark contrast, Klan tactics did not vary much. Blacks and their Southern white supporters were almost always the victims. Elections produced the most attacks, and the military forces available could not protect the enormous number of voting locations, which were spread over a wide geographic area.

MARTYRDOM

Before the Civil War, an important and very unusual case of martyrdom occurred when John Brown became convinced that the two decades of peaceful efforts by abolitionists to abolish slavery had not worked. He declared, "These men [abolitionists] are all talk. What we need is action—action!" In 1837, after the prayer service at a local church memorializing the famous abolitionist editor Elijah P. Lovejoy, who was murdered by Southerners, Brown publicly proclaimed his mission. "Here, before God, in the presence of these witnesses, from this time, I consecrate my life to the destruction of slavery."[148]

Unlike the Sons of Liberty or the KKK, Brown's efforts did not involve a steady campaign of attacks over a decade, instead producing four major violent encounters in a three-year period. The first three occurred in the territory of Kansas, an area where many violent political confrontations involving antislavery and proslavery groups had occurred since the passage of the Kansas-Nebraska Act in 1854, which stated that residents would determine whether Kansas would enter the Union as a free or as a slave state. Many persons from the South and North went to Kansas to promote their causes. In 1856, John Brown's family, including eleven sons, arrived and precipitated the Pottawatomie Massacre, in which a small group broke into the homes of proslavery settlers and murdered five in knife attacks. The victims apparently had been involved in sacking Lawrence, Kansas, destroying two abolitionist newspaper offices and the hotel where the Free State government group was located. Brown was outraged by both the violence of the proslavery forces and the "weak cowardly response" of the antislavery partisans.[149] The Pottawatomie Massacre drove a force of proslavery Missourians to attack the Brown family homestead, killing ten and capturing two of Brown's sons in the process. Soon afterward, Missouri forces attacked a Free State settlement in Palmyra, Kansas. John Brown helped defend the settlement and took twenty-two prisoners, who were later exchanged for his two sons. Shortly after, some three hundred Missourians crossed into Kansas and headed toward Osawatomie, intending to destroy the Free State settlements there. They ended up killing Brown's son Frederick, among others. Outnumbered more than seven to one, Brown killed at least twenty Missourians.[150] Brown's small group fled across the Marais des Cygnes River, and the remaining Missourians looted and burned Osawatomie to the ground. After Brown's escape, another 2,700 proslavery Missourians invaded Kansas. Brown had prepared for battle, but fortunately any serious conflict was averted after Kansas's new governor, John Geary, ordered the warring parties to disarm, offering clemency to all. Ultimately, Brown's bravery and military shrewdness in the face of over-whelming odds brought him national attention and made him a hero of Northern abolitionists.[151] When it became clear Kansas would not legalize slavery, Brown and his other sons returned to the North to raise money for his plan to abolish slavery. Although Brown was deeply religious, the argu-ments he made for abolition were political and secular.

In October 1859, Brown led an attack with twenty-one abolitionists on the U.S. military arsenal at Harpers Ferry, Virginia, with the hopes of seiz-ing one hundred thousand muskets and rifles thought to be stored there. The raid was intended to be the first stage in an elaborate plan to establish an independent armed stronghold of freed slaves in the mountains of Mary-land and Virginia. Ultimately, the attack failed, and Brown was wounded and captured. Ten other members of the attacking force, including two of Brown's sons, were killed. Virginia put the participants on trial and exe-cuted them. Unlike captured members of the Sons of Liberty or KKK, Brown proudly accepted responsibility for his actions, believing one could achieve a conquest by becoming a martyr, an assumption mob organizers rejected. Brown's trial electrified many onlookers, and Ralph Waldo Emer-son described his courtroom performance as "That new saint, whom none purer or braver was ever led by love of men into conflict and death—the new saint awaiting his martyrdom, and who, if he shall suffer, will make the gal-lows glorious like the cross."[152]

Following Brown's trial, memorial services were held throughout the North in his honor. The country soon became gripped by fear. Many South-erners felt that other abolitionists would try to emulate Brown and spark massive slave rebellions throughout the region. Many Northerners who had hoped that the widening division between North and South could be resolved with some type of compromise became concerned that such a res-olution was no longer possible. Two months after Brown was hanged, Abraham Lincoln, who at the time was running for president, made a famous address at the Cooper Institute in February 1860 denouncing

Brown's actions as "peculiar" and "absurd." The speech was a important in assuaging those with fears of an impending civil war to vote for Lincoln, handing him the Republican nomination for president.[153]

Despite Lincoln's efforts, the South withdrew from the Union, and the Civil War began.[154] Ironically, even after Lincoln's comments at the Cooper Institute, soldiers in the Union's army began using the newly composed "John Brown's Body" as their marching song. Within a year, the song's words were changed, and the new version, "The Battle Hymn of the Republic," portrayed Brown as a martyr and compared him with Christ.

> In the beauty of the lilies, Christ was born across the Sea,
> With a glory in His bosom that transfigures you and me;
> As He died to make men holy, let us die to make men free,
> While God is marching on.

Harriet Tubman, a key figure in the Underground Railroad's efforts to free slaves, described Brown as "done more in dying, than 100 men would in living."[155] As we will see in the next chapter, in the First Wave, which emerged two decades after Brown's martyrdom, the courtroom became an important arena for spreading a message and gaining recruits. While one could argue that the Sons of Liberty and the KKK did not need the courtroom to supply martyrs, given their large numbers, it would certainly still have been an effective way to create them. Although it was decades before members acknowledged their role, John Brown's trial shows how significant such behavior can be. Many subsequent U.S. terrorists admired Brown. Third Wave 1960s student groups and Malcolm X praised him.[156] In the Fourth Wave, Timothy McVeigh, the Oklahoma City bomber, and Eric Rudolph, a Christian terrorist who bombed the Atlanta Olympics and various abortion clinics, both cited him as an inspiration.[157] However, neither emulated his behavior in their own trials. Brown remains a controversial figure, both memorialized as a heroic martyr and vilified as a madman.

THE ORIGINS OF GLOBAL TERRORISM

To explain the origins of global terror, one must focus on the political transformations that took nearly a century to complete. The French Revolution transformed nineteenth-century European politics by making insurrections with international connections prominent. In the 1820s, rebels in several states emerged, hoping to realize the French Revolution's unfulfilled promises. Uprisings then erupted in 1830 and in 1848. The 1830 rebellions were brief, lasting a few months at most. The 1848 uprisings occurred mostly in those same states.[158]

Two different kinds of uprisings emerged. The first intended to break away from a multiethnic empire and create a separate state. Some of those, like the Polish uprisings, were especially complicated because the Polish community was spread across neighboring states and the Russian and Austrian empires. Only one successful nationalist rebellion occurred, the 1830 uprising against the Dutch, which produced Belgium. That insurrection nearly generated another continental war, as states anxious to preserve the international order began mobilizing troops.[159] When it seemed that the Austrian Empire might be destroyed, Russia's czar sent troops to save his fellow monarch. Although the insurrection aims were local, they generated sympathy and hope throughout Europe. "In the German states student enthusiasm was aroused by news from Paris, [and] there were also . . . riots in Bremen, Breslau, Aachen, Chemnitz, Cologne, Krefeldt, Nuremberg, Schwerin, and several Silesian towns. In Warsaw there were labor disturbances . . . and the Channel and the Irish Sea proved to be poor insulators."[160] The second type of uprising occurred in nation-states (for example, France), with the aim of equalizing power and wealth.

The 1848 rebellions exhibited the same pattern. The first insurrection began in Palermo, Italy, in January. Paris was next in February, and within a month rebellions occurred in portions of the Austrian Empire: Vienna, Bohemia, Italy, Hungary, and Transylvania. "In Germany, too, the news from France stimulated political demands. Disorders were reported from western Germany at the end of February and had spread to Bavaria and East Prussia by the first week of March and then in the north German areas including Berlin."[161] Emperor Friedrich Wilhelm IV of Prussia told Queen Victoria that the revolution would "engulf his small throne and then her bigger one."[162]

Ironically, when revolutionaries succeeded in capturing a state, the new government did not attempt to spread the revolution. Thus, the Second French Republic (1848) refused to help Poles who revolted in 1848, even though many foreign revolutionaries in France immediately crossed borders to support the Poles. In the Paris uprising of 1848, foreign immigrants for the first time in European history were important and became a factor in later insurrections as well. The historian William L. Langer notes that "Berlin like other big cities was experiencing a large and constant flux. Ten thousand workers . . . have come to Berlin in 1847, and many . . . were desperate people in search of work [and] may have contributed significantly to the [1848] insurrection."[163]

Langer describes the insurrectionary process as "spontaneous manifestations of crowd emotion. There was no preconceived plan of action, and indeed their salient feature is the absence of any . . . competent revolutionary leadership."[164] This description seems odd when we realize that many international revolutionary organizations, "secret brotherhoods," and/or "conspiratorial organizations" like the Carbonari, Free Masons, Philadelphians, Blanquists, etc. were present. Members often left their native lands to aid kindred souls elsewhere and frequently went abroad to seek support for their own efforts back home. Many spent considerable time in Geneva, London, or Paris, cities where they could publish materials and plan actions for the next revolution. While the insurrections seemed spontaneous, governments declared that "secret brotherhoods" had instigated them. In the 1848 Berlin insurrection, the government insisted that French and Polish revolutionaries were responsible. "Emperor Francis and other Austrian conservatives including Metternich . . . were so convinced that the Carbonari and other secret societies were dangerous to the preservation of Hapsburg interests in Italy that they organized a secret spy network encompassing all Italy to ferret them out."[165]

How do we reconcile the description of these insurrections as being planned versus as being spontaneous? James Billington's impressive *Fire in the Minds of Men: Origins of the Revolutionary Faith* states: "The brotherhoods . . . preferred to have their organizations' existence remain unknown. . . . Occasionally, a brotherhood did emerge . . . in an insurrection, but the great majority of insurrections . . . were over in a few days or, at the most, a few weeks."[166] One reason it was difficult to perceive the brotherhoods' true significance was because insurrections frequently involved large numbers demonstrating against government acts, and neither the government nor the crowd anticipated an uprising was in the offing. Demonstrators were rarely secret society members; indeed, most were not even aware that a brotherhood might be somewhere in the neighborhood. Whatever the truth about their role, secret societies did not seek publicity or accept responsibility.

The insurrections created the "professional revolutionary," Alexis de Tocqueville declared. Intellectuals such as Karl Marx, Friedrich Engels, Filippo Buonarroti, Mikhail Bakunin, Pierre-Joseph Proudhon, and Peter Kropotkin moved from country to country hoping to learn methods most appropriate for bringing the French Revolution's most radical promises to fruition. "The 'professional revolutionary' was destined to play a prominent role in politics of the 19th and 20th centuries."[167] One reason that occurred was the change in extradition practices. Earlier, political offenders were always sent back to their home countries when those countries requested extradition.

But the French Revolution and its aftermath started the transformation of what was an extraditable offence par excellence to what has become the non-extraditable offence par excellence. Belgium in 1833 was the first country to enact a law on non-extradition of political offenders and [soon] almost every European treaty contained an exception of political offenses.[168]

In 1871, Paris experienced the century's largest urban insurrection, lasting seventy-two days. James Billington describes its unanticipated dramatic effect:

Beginning as a protest against the government's surrender to Prussia, it transformed Paris into a Commune or a proletarian and anarchist challenge to the modern bureaucratized and capitalized state. . . . In the eyes of revolutionaries, the Commune aspired to a fundamental transformation of the human condition on a large scale for the first time since 1792–94. The savage reaction of the . . . French government was the most bloody and indiscriminate European response to a revolution known up to that time. Some twenty thousand Communards were killed.[169]

That was higher than the number killed in the Franco-Prussian War or during Robespierre's Reign of Terror (1793–1794). "More than 7,500 were jailed or deported to distant places such as New Caledonia and Cayenne. Thousands fled to Belgium, England, Italy, Spain and the United States."[170] Many foreigners were there; indeed, the Commune's last commander-in-chief to die on the barricades was Polish, not French. The Commune left a legacy of legends and symbols significant for subsequent revolutionary movements throughout the nineteenth and twentieth centuries.[171]

The military's new role made successful insurrections more difficult. In the 1820s, military officers often helped begin rebellions in Portugal, Spain, Russia, various Italian states, and the Polish territories in the Russian Empire. In Russia, the Decembrists, a group composed of military officers, began an uprising in 1825 without attempting to secure popular support first. Rebel officers felt that merely announcing their objective would rally instant mass support, as no European insurrection professed a more egalitarian objective. The officers, aristocrats, declared they would free the serfs, which meant abolishing their own privileges.[172] "Hitherto revolutions had been made by peasants who wanted to be gentlemen," Count Rostopehin, a defender of the old order, said. "Now gentlemen tried to make a revolution . . . to become cobblers."[173] In 1830, the Dutch and French governments decided not to use armies to put revolts down, and in 1848 the French made the same decision. Armies could disintegrate when faced with conflicting claims or, even worse, side with rebels, who often made significant efforts to neutralize or even co-opt military elements.[174] The military's ambivalence intensified in cases when nationalist uprisings occurred in empires and military elements shared ethnic identities with the rebels. In the Austrian Empire, uprisings occurred in Budapest, Prague, and Milan. Although Hungarian, Bohemian, Italian, and Polish troops could not be trusted to support the imperial government when they had to fire on their own nationals, they could be used against the empire's other nationals. But by 1867 the situation had changed; Fenians in Ireland assumed that Irish elements in the British army would desert, but to the rebels' dismay, that did not happen.[175] The military reaction to the Paris Commune was particularly devastating. Revolutionaries became convinced they lacked the equipment, organization, and knowledge to deal with the army. A new method of insurrection was necessary. Russian students felt that small groups using terror to gain publicity was the answer, and they gained support in some democratic states such as Switzerland, France, and Belgium.

The Industrial Revolution played a crucial role in strengthening Europe's political transformation. Steamships and transcontinental railroads made travel much quicker and cheaper. Between 1850 and 1914, 55 million persons left their native lands to seek new homes and jobs in a world that at that point did not require passports or visas.[176] Those mass migrations created diasporas, which in later decades would become politically significant.[177]

Daily mass newspapers developed, and groups found they could publish their own papers cheaply, creating what Jeffrey Simon described as the equivalent of the "20th century . . . web site delivering it through the mail."[178] The telegraph was invented, and the first permanent underwater cable system linked Europe and America in 1866, making it possible for events in one continent to be known on the other in a day or so. Subsequent innovations continued to shrink time and space, and the cost of information dramatically decreased. Russian terrorists found they had a global audience, and two decades later, terrorist activity emerged on six continents.

For the terrorist, dynamite became crucial. Alfred Nobel had invented it for construction purposes, but in a few years, it had precipitated a revolutionary change in weapons technology, a change that has persisted as a cardinal feature in terrorism ever since. The new explosive was twenty times more powerful than the black gunpowder, the "industry standard" for the previous eight centuries. Armies used black gunpowder, but terrorists found the new bomb was much cheaper, more accessible, and easier to transport. Dynamite retains its usefulness even today, and it has been used in 40 to 50 percent of attacks ever since its invention.[179]

Nobel was a pacifist who established the Nobel Peace Prize partly because of dynamite's extraordinary and unanticipated human cost. Ironically, four former terrorists have received Nobel Peace Prizes for their efforts to make peace: Menachem Begin of Israel, Anwar Sadat of Egypt, Nelson Mandela of South Africa, and Yasser Arafat of Palestine.

Dynamite attracted potential users everywhere. It was invested with almost mystical powers and generated apocalyptic expectations. The German anarchist Johann Most wrote that just as gunpowder and the rifle had eliminated feudalism, so would dynamite destroy capitalism. Albert Parsons, an American anarchist executed for his role in the Haymarket Affair, an 1886 riot in Chicago between police and labor protestors, said "in giving dynamite to the downtrodden millions of the globe science has done its best work. The dear stuff can be carried in the pocket without danger. . . . Dynamite is democratic, it makes everyone equal . . . it is a peace-maker."[180] The Spanish anarchist Jose Pérez Guerrero wrote, "It seems that the spirit of Shiva, the god of destruction, the eternal destroyer of life resides in the depths of its strange composition. . . . It creates, and it destroys, it annihilates, and it gives life . . . it illuminates and darkens. From civilization's necessity, it becomes its chastiser . . . the dissident sects' weapon of terrorism."[181] Dynamite strengthened the hope of potential revolutionaries, who were now convinced that they could structure insurrections in a new way and induced them to develop a "science of terror." Those three characteristics, "hope," "structure," and "science," are conspicuous and necessary ingredients of the tradition revolutionary terrorists created.

Revolts occur when rebels are confident they have a good chance to succeed, and the initial belief that a successful and irreversible revolution was in the offing came initially from how anarchists understood history.[182] Albert Parsons wrote, "The economic forces are at work incessantly generating the forces of the social revolutions. We can neither retard nor hasten the result, but we can aid and direct its forces."[183] Dynamite intensified the anarchist belief in the direction history was headed. New weapons had transformed the past, and anarchists believed that they were witnessing that process. "One man armed with a dynamite bomb is equal to one regiment of militia. The discovery of gunpowder overthrew feudalism. . . . Dynamite is the emancipator! In the hand of the enslaved it cries aloud: 'Justice or—annihilation.'"[184]

2

THE FIRST WAVE: ANARCHIST, 1879–1920s

The heroes and heroines of the "People's Will" established terrorism as a noble activity in the eyes of later generations. They created the image of the virtuous assassin.

—PHILLIP POMPER

In 1879, the First Wave began in Russia and, after becoming a global phenomenon, largely receded by the mid-1920s. Two political events in Russia were crucial in generating the wave. In 1861, Czar Alexander II introduced extraordinary political reforms, in an attempt to make Russia more like Western Europe, but those reforms were only partially successful, inspiring some Russians to make more effective efforts. University students created the first terrorist group, Narodnaya Volya (People's Will). The wave persisted for over forty years, though individual groups rarely lasted more than five. The assassination of prominent public figures was the principal tactic. Efforts were always made to seek international support, for example, foreign bases, diasporas, etc.

Outside of Russia, anarchists were the wave's most conspicuous element; they produced the "Golden Age of Assassination" (1892 to 1901), in which more monarchs, presidents, and prime ministers were assassinated than ever before. The wave's high point was between 1890 and 1910, a time that also produced furious antiterror sentiment, prompting many anarchists to abandon terror and seek other methods for achieving their goals.

RUSSIA

The English political philosopher Thomas Hobbes argued that an effort to overthrow a government requires three conditions: discontent, hope for success, and the transfer of legitimacy. Discontent is common everywhere, but no matter how deeply embedded it is, those most directly affected will not take up arms without the hope that success is possible. This explains why slaves rarely revolt; they lack confidence or are overcome by the fear that they will only make their situation worse.[1] In those rare occasions when a slave revolt did materialize, it normally collapsed quickly. The only successful slave revolt in history occurred in Haiti between 1791 and 1804.[2]

The genesis of Russian terrorism confirms Hobbes's analysis. Recruits came from the middle and upper classes. They were young people; the young are more confident in their physical capacities and generally have more hope than the older generation. Very few terrorists came from the lower classes, where self-confidence is less common, a pattern we will see repeated in every subsequent wave. In the Russian case, no member of the executive committee of Narodnaya Volya (People's Will), the first terrorist organization, had reached the age of thirty. The children of gentry (the class immediately below the nobility) supplied over half of the recruits; the clergy and wealthy merchants produced 12 and 10 percent, respectively.[3]

Every wave is associated with important political events that demonstrate in a striking way to a new generation that the conventional political worldview is no longer relevant. Potential terrorists become convinced that those in power no longer have legitimacy, that they no longer inspire confidence in their right to rule (Hobbes's third requirement), and that revolutionaries now have a political strength they lacked before.

The Crimean War (1853–1856) transformed Russia.[4] Czar Nicholas I aimed to gain Ottoman territories. Russia's army, crucial in the Napoleonic Wars and afterward, was Europe's largest military force. But the British and French, who supported the Ottomans, humiliated Russia. Russian technology was outdated. Russian generals were old and incompetent, and colonels frequently sold the best equipment and pocketed their men's pay. "Russia had been beaten on the Crimean Peninsula, and the military feared that it would inevitably be beaten again unless steps were taken to surmount its military weakness."[5]

Czar Nicholas's successor, Alexander II, pressed for industrialization, believing Russia had to make itself more like the Western democracies to regain its strength. In 1861, he freed around 25 million serfs, one-third of Russia's population, with a stroke of the pen. By contrast, 4 million U.S. slaves were only freed after a four-year civil war costing hundreds of thousand deaths, the nineteenth century's most deadly war. Three years after abolishing serfdom, the czar established local self-governments, "Westernized" the judicial system, abolished capital punishment, and relaxed censorship.

Alexander II was described as "Czar Liberator" throughout the world. Hopes were aroused but could not be quickly fulfilled, as indicated by the fact that the government lacked the money to help the newly free serfs purchase land. In the wake of inevitable disappointments, populist movements aiming to transform the system more profoundly appeared. University students led the way. Various riots and arson attacks occurred. Sergei Nechaev's extraordinary *Revolutionary Catechism* (1869) analyzed the commitment revolutionaries must have.[6]

Mikhail Bakunin's vision that agrarian communes were destined to be the final social form inspired the populists; when he died in 1876, university students commemorated him by making a "mad rush" to live among the "people" to prepare them for their future in anarchist communes. But peasants seemed indifferent, and students sensed that their speeches and pamphlets merely made the peasants think they were "idle word spillers."

Peasants instead helped the police, and soon some 1,600 students were in preventative detention.

The group Land and Liberty was then created to further the student cause; its Disorganizing Section was charged with freeing comrades and deterring police spies. But the Disorganizing Section also assassinated several policemen, alienating the peasants more. Land and Liberty decided to return to the cities, which were now flooded with penniless former serfs more sympathetic to radical activities. The decision to retreat from the countryside was also shaped by the outcome of the St. Petersburg Trial of the 193 (1877–1878). "The jurors were impressed by the youthful idealism of the defendants; 153 defendants were acquitted and forty . . . given mild sentences."[7]

Then an extraordinary and wholly unanticipated event dramatically reinforced the belief that publicity in the city and the courtroom had enormous value. Vera Zasulich, a "lone wolf" (one acting solely on her own initiative), wounded General Trepov, the governor of St. Petersburg who in 1878 had flogged a political prisoner even though Alexander II had outlawed corporal punishment.[8]

The government was confident she would be convicted and decided to treat her as an "ordinary" criminal subject to a jury trial instead of the court-martial political criminals normally received. The minister of justice told the czar that "the jurors would deliver a guilty verdict and thereby teach a sobering lesson to the insane small coterie of revolutionaries [showing] that the Russian people bow before the Czar, revere him and are always ready to defend his faithful servants."[9]

The jurors were petty bureaucrats, a class believed most likely to support the prosecution.[10] Prominent government officials, including the foreign minister and minister of finance, were in attendance. But contrary to all expectations, the trial in effect quickly became that of the governor. Zasulich said her aim was to prevent similar abuses in the future. When asked why she had thrown her pistol to the ground instead of killing him, she responded that she was a "terrorist, *not* a killer."[11] In ten minutes the jury declared her "innocent." The court's president described the bizarre aftermath. "It is impossible for one who was not a witness to imagine either the outburst of sounds which drowned out the foreman's voice or the movement like an electrical shock [that] rushed past along the whole room. The cries of unrestrained joy, hysterical sobbing, desperate applause, the tread of feet, cries of 'Bravo! Hurrah! Good girl! Vera! Verochka!' all merged in one crash."[12] Jurors lifted her onto their shoulders, and outside the courthouse enormous crowds greeted her with thunderous applause. The next day, German newspapers predicted a revolution would soon occur.

Police, attempting to calm the crowd, killed one demonstrator and wounded another. The government then compromised its difficult situation further. The czar annulled the verdict, but police attempts to arrest Zasulich failed; she had fled to Switzerland. Perhaps the acquittal might have vindicated the legal system and helped sustain the government, but the subsequent hypocrisy and striking incompetence increased hopes that a necessary struggle against the system would succeed. The government "made Zasulich the martyr she would have been if convicted and imprinted the trial in [the] people's consciousness."[13] Her trial became "the most momentous in the history of Imperial Russia."[14] Lone wolves struck prominent officials in several cities, killing four. Stepniak, an émigré, returned from London to kill his victim. When he returned, he was feted by the prominent Americans Mark Twain and George Kennan.[15] Zasulich's act stimulated similar ones outside Russia. Within four months, four failed attempts against monarchs in Prussia, Spain, and Italy had taken place, stimulating a widely held belief that Europe was experiencing an international anarchist conspiracy.

An abortive attempt to assassinate Czar Alexander II occurred in April 1879. A few months later, Narodnaya Volya was created. Nikolai Morozov, a founder, noted that "Zasulich's shot was the starting point for the whole struggle that followed."[16] Vera Figner, an executive committee member, wrote, "It began to seem ridiculous to punish the servant . . . and leave the master untouched," inducing the group to become committed to assassinating the czar.

Assassination and secrecy are two necessary ingredients for success. Political assassination in the present circumstances, is the sole means of self-defense and one of the best means of agitation. By dealing a blow at the very center of governmental organization, its awful force will give a mighty shock to the whole regime . . . an electric current throughout the entire state and will cause disruption and confusion in all its activities.

Secrecy gives a small group the ability to fight against millions of organized, obvious and visible enemies making the group truly terrifying. . . . From this point onwards, the enemy will have no choice but to go always in fear of his life never knowing whence and when the avenging hand will strike. Political assassination is the carrying out of the revolution in the present.

Because publicity was crucial, Figner, originally committed to the countryside, became convinced that the city was the best place to function. "Terrorist acts in the countryside passed virtually unnoticed. You could not even judge what impression they created. . . . They did not excite the villager . . . who did not experience the fear, the dangers, and the joy of a struggle. When they occurred in the city acts of terror, like electric impulses . . . ran through the minds of the young and society and raised their spirits."[17] The city supplied facilities for printing and quick distribution; Narodnaya Volya established a press

capable of producing up to 3,000 copies in a single run of clean, professional-grade newsprint to create respect for the message giver. It is example that is needed . . . and not just in name alone, but in action. We need energetic, utterly dedicated people, prepared to gamble all and to sacrifice everything. We need martyrs whose legend is far greater than their real worth and their contributions to the work.[18]

Later, when Figner was a prisoner likely to receive a death sentence, she was confident that she would become a martyr. "My thought for some reason turned to the fate of revolutionary movements in general in the West and at home; to the continuity of our ideas and of their dissemination from one country to another. Pictures . . . of people who had died long ago awoke in my memory. My imagination worked as never before."[19]

Women did not participate in ancient religious terror groups or American mobs. But they were visible in many early nineteenth-century European crowds and became very prominent in Russia; some became "legends, surrounded by an aura of romance that defies critics."[20] Women constituted 21 percent of the group and one-third of the original executive committee, a pattern repeated in successive Russian terror groups. Over 25 percent of those arrested in the Going to the People movement were women. In the 1860s, Sergei Nechaev was the first to anticipate the importance of women, describing them as the "most priceless assets" a terrorist group could have. The number of women was especially impressive because most recruits came from the university, and women were not admitted to Russian universities. They went instead to Switzerland for university education; most studied engineering or medicine.

The executive committee had thirty people organized into five-person cells, to make police penetration more difficult.[21] Group numbers are unknown; estimates are around five hundred.[22] An effort to create additional cells among workers, students, and military officers was abandoned when the organization became obsessed with idea of assassinating the czar, a goal that forced it to become increasingly centralized.

Zasulich had used a pistol, and the four subsequent Russian assassins employed pistols or swords. Narodnaya Volya did not preclude those weapons but clearly preferred bombs,[23] encouraging members to throw them from a short distance, making it more likely that they would lose their lives in the effort.[24] Without the bomb, "the assassin would not have created the same impression [and not have] . . . expressed a new stage in the revolutionary movement." Criminals did not use bombs, and it was virtually inconceivable that they would; the risk of killing oneself was too high.[25] By insisting on the importance of throwing the bomb, the likelihood a terrorist group would ultimately become a criminal gang was reduced, although some Russian terrorists did become criminals later. Some cells prohibited women from throwing bombs because they could not throw as far as males and were thus more likely to be killed in the process, a decision that seemed to vitiate their status. Women employed other weapons and participated in manufacturing bombs, a dangerous occupation responsible for many fatalities.

One could throw a bomb in the excitement of the moment, but if that assailant was captured, the ordeal afterward would tax one's moral determination. Imprisonment could be a prolonged process, giving abused prisoners ample opportunities to save their lives or negotiate a lighter sentence by expressing regret or revealing valuable information. But prisoners could also reaffirm the deed in court and indict the regime. This form of martyrdom harked back to the initial Christian notion, though Christian martyrs did not kill anyone. When the Romans persecuted them, martyrs would affirm their commitment to Christ even though they were likely to be killed if they did. Over 12 percent of the Russian terrorists were children of the clergy, which helped link terrorism to notions of martyrdom. "Those who saw him pass say that he was not only calm and peaceful but that his pleasant smile played upon his lips when he addressed cheering words to his companion. At last, he could satisfy his ardent desire to sacrifice himself for his cause. It was perhaps the happiest moment of his unhappy life. . . . Lysohub was the Saint."[26] Stepniak described the Russian terrorist as "noble, terrible, irresistibly fascinating, uniting the two sublimities of human grandeur, the martyr and the hero."[27] The legend cultivated inspired future terrorists. Fifty years later, the Soviet dictator Josef Stalin said, "If we bring our children up on stories of the People's Will, we [will] make terrorists out of them."[28]

Narodnaya Volya made seven efforts to assassinate Alexander II before succeeding in 1881 in killing the "Greatest Liberator in History," the first czar killed in eighty years. The weapon was a hand-thrown bomb. Six participants were tried and hanged; four refused to ask for mercy, which gave the group a powerful mystique and generated a flood of new recruits. But the negative consequences were much more significant. The expectation that the deed would spark popular support was a total delusion; indeed, the public was outraged. Ironically, two hours before his assassination Alexander II had established a committee to make the constitution more democratic. Narodnaya Volya hoped the government would now negotiate and offered the new czar "immunity" in exchange for a general amnesty and a parliamentary constitutional government.[29] But Alexander

III reversed his father's decision. The five assailants were immediately executed, including the first woman in Russian history to die that way.

Mobs abused university students and launched pogroms against the Jewish population, ostensibly because Jews were important in the terrorist movement.[30] Those pogroms were greatly intensified later by the most infamous twentieth-century forgery, *The Protocols of Zion of the Elders of Zion* (1903), which depicted a (fictional) Jewish plot to take over the entire world. Russia at this time had by far the largest Jewish population in the world,[31] and its anti-Semitic policies were inspirational elsewhere. The pogroms stimulated a massive flow of immigration to the West, especially the United States, and inspired the Zionist movement to return to the "Holy Land." *The Protocols* was translated into many different languages and disseminated globally. The American auto manufacturer Henry Ford had five hundred thousand copies translated and distributed throughout the United States in the 1920s. A decade later, Hitler used the *Protocols* as a propaganda tool against Jews, which helped precipitate the Holocaust. Later, as Jews resettled in the "Holy Land," the *Protocols* became significant in the Arab world. The 1988 Covenant of Hamas, a Fourth Wave Palestinian terrorist group, states:

> Today it is Palestine, tomorrow it will be one country or another. The Zionist plan is limitless. After Palestine, the Zionists aspire to expand from the Nile to the Euphrates. When they will have digested the region they overtook, they will aspire to further expansion, and so on. Their plan is embodied in the "Protocols of the Elders of Zion," and their present conduct is the best proof of what we are saying.[32]

Russia created the Okhrana, a notorious underground police force, which used agents provocateurs to curb terrorism.[33] Women became crucial to Okhrana and were paid as well or better than their male counterparts, an unusual pattern then and now, too.[34] The Okhrana significantly diminished Narodnaya Volya's reputation and the hope inspiring its members, and the organization collapsed three years later. The immediate precipitating cause was its excessive centralization and a carelessness Morozov had warned against. The police arrested a member who had a list of all its participants—and their addresses. Several hundred were jailed, and the remnants left St. Petersburg, moving largely to rural areas, where they continued to assassinate minor officials.

In 1887, the Terrorist Faction of the People's Will was born, determined to assassinate the new czar, Alexander III. All of its members were apprehended in their first attempt. The incident over time became well known partly because of the identity of three conspirators, Alexander Ulanov and Branislaw and Josef Pilsudski. Ulanov was the older brother of Vladimir Lenin, the leader of the communist revolution in 1917. Branislaw and Josef Pilsudski organized the first major Polish terrorist party, and Josef became Poland's dictator after the Versailles Treaty ending World War I established Poland's independence.

The attempted assassination of Alexander III made the government even more determined to reduce publicity opportunities for terrorists. It eliminated jury trials and made executions private. Terrorism revived in 1902. The Socialist Revolutionaries Party, a populist group Bakunin influenced, established the Terrorist Brigade, which modified its tactics and strategy, hoping to avoid its predecessors' fate. As the public remained hostile to assassinating the czar, the Terrorist Brigade concluded that major officials would be much better victims; they were not well guarded and often seen as very abusive.

The city was abandoned as the principal focus of operations, as it was believed that a serious recent famine would make peasants more receptive, proving Bakunin right after all. But the peasants remained indifferent. The city kept supplying recruits, and university students once again produced the dominant leaders. Successful attacks on major officials increased greatly.

There was some dissatisfaction with the movement's new limits on possible activities. In 1903 Burtsev, the Terrorist Brigade's counterespionage director and labeled the "Sherlock Holmes of the Revolution" for his success in finding "double agents," recommended that hostages be taken from the "favorites of the bourgeoisie and authorities to redeem [as] prisoners. [It] is the only way we have of making the enemy treat the people as a belligerent party."[35] But the recommendation was rejected for several reasons. States originally had employed the practice,[36] and during the Franco-Prussian War Prussians placed hostages on train engines so that "it was understood [that] in every accident caused by the hostility of the inhabitants, their compatriots [would] be the first to suffer."[37] Paris Commune leaders condemned the action as a violation of the Geneva Convention and passed a "Law of Hostages" enabling the Commune to seize French government supporters.[38] But that did not change the Prussian policy. Angry Commune supporters took hostages in response and were ultimately massacred.[39] Another important reason for rejecting hostage taking was that it might obscure the distinction between criminal and terrorist activity, a distinction terrorists insisted on making clear. No noticeable hostage-taking incident occurred in Russia.[40]

Pressures to modify assassination tactics increased. In October 1905, the ongoing Russo-Japanese War and a serious peasant insurrection made the government believe that establishing a Duma (Parliament) would rally popular support. Narodnaya Volya had said it would cease operations if a Duma was established, and the Socialist Revolutionaries felt obliged to accept the czar's proposal. But the Terrorist Brigade disagreed, feeling that more crucial concessions were needed; it withdrew from the Socialist Revolutionary Party to continue terrorism.

The Terrorist Brigade was also deeply divided on whether to use assassination in new ways. Some left the Terrorist Brigade to develop a new group, the Maximalists (1905–1907), which felt that the policy of restricting activity solely to assassinating politically significant persons was inadequate; assassinating *all* government personnel would be more useful and disintegrate the state. By this time, it had become clear that Morozov's argument that separate groups would ultimately merge was not going to happen. Groups kept splitting and only in a few cases did they reunite.

As anarchists, the Maximalists refused to have a central directing body. Autonomous groups joined for operations and then disbanded until the next operation. It had some five thousand members.[41] Two other anarchist groups, Black Flag and the Absence of Authority, operated mainly in the Ukraine, Crimea, and the Caucasus, killing thousands of lower-level civil and military personnel in 1906 and 1907. The remainder lived in fear for their lives and their families, which adversely affected the way they performed their duties.[42] The Maximalists sought martyrdom in a different way, too. "If young rebels had to die, they were determined to go in their own way. . . . Thus, when cornered by the police, it was not unusual for the terrorists to turn the pistols on themselves or if captured to resort to the grim gesture of Russian fanatics since the Old Believers of the seventeenth century—self-immolation."[43]

The Terrorist Brigade and the Maximalists were destroyed in 1907. The first collapsed when it discovered, to its enormous shame, that its leader Azev for years was an agent provocateur, a member of the police force. The Maximalists were too amorphous for penetration, but ferocious government responses ultimately ended the attacks.

> The authorities developed counter-terror, employing the death-penalty on a scale never before imposed. . . . At the height of the troubles, terrorists were also made subject to trial by Field Courts Martial. . . . [It] functioned for less than a year but the number sentenced to death—often hanged or shot with twenty-four hours of sentence—may have been over a thousand.[44]

The terrorist problem seemed solved. A commission was established to investigate how agents provocateurs were used, and a British police historian summarized the startling details:

> For many years . . . Okhrana agents had organized assassinations, fomented strikes and printed stirring calls to bloody revolution. . . . A bonus was paid to Okhranniks who unearthed illegal secret printing presses, and it was not uncommon for a police official to found such a press himself—and on police money—as a preliminary to "detecting" it and claiming customary money from police funds. . . . The Okhrana had systematically undermined the legality it was charged to uphold—as the Commissioners lost no opportunity to point out. Some former Okhrana chiefs asked in reply what [other] effective means were available. No convincing answer could be given . . . a measure of the impasse in which the late Okhrana found itself.[45]

Despite their 1907 demise, the groups succeeded in "breaking the spine of Russian bureaucracy, wounding it both physically and in spirit, contributing to the general paralysis in the final crisis of the imperial regime in March of 1917."[46] Events in February 1917 during World War I set the stage for both the revival and final collapse of every terror group. When his army refused to put down a massive demonstration in the capital protesting food shortages and the war, Nicholas II abdicated, ending nearly four centuries of czarist rule. The transitional parliamentary government, led by the Socialist Revolutionary Alexander Kerensky, granted amnesty to all anarchist and Bolshevik prisoners, which convinced many anarchist émigrés to return.

The "honeymoon" was very short. Because the state had not been eliminated, one anarchist journal described the new situation as "Nothing special. In place of Nicholas the Bloody, Kerenskii [sic] the Bloody has ascended the throne."[47] Anarchists demanded the state be dismantled and private property eliminated, which the Bolsheviks proclaimed as one of their ultimate goals, too. They mounted a successful coup in October 1917, one many anarchists supported.

But the Brest-Litvosk Treaty (March 1918), requiring Russia to surrender much territory to Germany, induced many anarchists and the Terrorist Brigade to strike the new communist government.[48] Anarchists assassinated policemen, district attorneys, Cossacks, army officers, factory owners, watchmen, and more. The Terrorist Brigade struck major Bolshevik leaders. Fanya Kaplan tried to assassinate Lenin, giving him a serious permanent lung injury. Kaplan, whom the czar had jailed, said Lenin's decision to close the Duma had provoked the strike. The Bolsheviks responded more brutally than the czars ever had. Over eight hundred Terrorist Brigade members and anarchists were executed without trials in 1918, and some 6,300 others met the same fate over the next two years.

The decision to return to terror divided anarchists. Gregori Maksimov, a leading figure, condemned terror as outmoded and as dissipating "revolutionary energy while doing nothing to eliminate social injustice."[49] Many supported the Bolsheviks, especially when White Russian armies launched a civil war, recruiting many Socialist Revolutionaries in the process. But anarchist supporters of the Bolsheviks retained serious suspicions and worked hard to maintain their independence. The case of Nestor Makhno is particularly striking. He organized a military division in the Ukraine; all officers had peasant or factory-worker backgrounds. Incorporated into the Red Army, it kept its internal structure and black banner, the symbol of anarchism. Its independent military exploits were significant, but eventually Red Army leaders tried to assassinate Makhno, inducing him to wage an unsuccessful guerrilla campaign against Bolshevik military targets.

What role did dynamite play? Heinzen and Nechaev wrote before the bomb emerged, suggesting that revolutionary terrorism in any case could have moved in that direction. Also, the ancient Zealots and Sicarrii were able with primitive weapons to be profoundly indiscriminate in their killing. The example of the Islamic Assassins shows that limits could be maintained, one reason perhaps that Russian terrorists at the beginning of their struggle referred to the Assassins as models. Still, the bomb created enormous pressures to expand the field of terrorist operations. In one unsuccessful attempt to assassinate Alexander II, eleven were killed and fifty-six injured. Most Russian terrorists considered the unintended casualties as "collateral damage," that is, an inevitable result of the decision to use explosives, a tool no one suggested abandoning.

Ivan Kalieyev, a Terrorist Brigade member, provided a different model, one that gained international respect. He refused to kill Grand Duke Sergius when accompanied by his children. He waited for another opportunity and assassinated the grand duke when he traveled alone. (Kalieyev's concern for the innocent induced Albert Camus to make him the hero in his remarkable play *The Just Assassins*.)[50] That example was not followed much. Bombs were used whenever possible; the risk of waiting always seemed too great, and no one was demanding that they wait. Indeed, Kalieyev did not criticize those who acted differently. He made his decision and believed they were entitled to make theirs.

The Russians remained committed to assassination though there was never consensus over who should be assassinated. Narodnaya Volya began by killing major officials and then concluded it would be more appropriate to focus on the czar. The Terrorist Brigade abandoned that position and returned to the original policy, while anarchists decided to assassinate any person associated with political institutions.

The problem was exacerbated because Russian terror groups (unlike some religious and mob predecessors) were wracked with factional quarrels and divisions over appropriate tactics and ultimate purposes. Terrorist groups could lose members to other radical elements that did not use terror or even violence. Disagreements between older and newer members were significant, and police infiltration increased internal tensions.

No wonder groups had short lives. The Terrorist Brigade, the most durable organization, survived only seven years. Anarchist groups lasted two years and revived themselves a decade later for two more. The Terrorist Faction of the People's Will disappeared after one attempt.[51] Another cause of fragmentation and of the dissipation of moral limits related to the way groups raised money, that is, by robbery. The two populist groups and the Socialist Revolutionaries limited this activity, but anarchists expanded their number of robberies immensely. In a single year (1905–1906), they carried out "1,951 robberies,"[52] taking "money and valuables from banks, post offices, factories, stores, and the private residences of the nobility. Middle class businessmen, doctors, and lawyers were forced to 'contribute' money to the anarchist cause under the penalty of death."[53] Robbery attracted criminal elements to terrorist groups, making Vera Zasulich's insistence in her notorious trial on the crucial distinction between criminals and terrorists hard to maintain. Indeed, criminals were hired as "mercenaries" for special tasks, and sometimes terrorists sold weapons to criminals and worked with them on joint operations. Increasingly, money seized was used for personal amenities. Many "later lived luxurious lives and spent money without restraint," finally "retiring" to Switzerland to enjoy their new wealth. Leaders tried to control the practice, but Grigori Gershuni, the Terrorist Brigade's last leader, admitted that "nine-tenths of all expropriations were acts of common banditry."[54]

ANARCHISTS AND THE WEST

Alexander II's assassination aroused enormous interest abroad, creating opportunities Narodnaya Volya was determined to exploit. Vera Figner organized

the propaganda of its actual aims . . . and enlist[ed] the sympathies of European society by acquainting it with the domestic policy of our government. Thus, while shaking the throne by the explosion of our bombs within the Empire, we might discredit it from without and contribute . . . to the diplomatic interference of a few countries which had been enlightened as to the international affairs of our dark tsardom. For this purpose, we had at our disposal those revolutionary forces which had been lost to the movement in Russia . . . the emigrants.[55]

The government had to present its case abroad too, where Russia was seen as despotic. To counter government efforts, Figner sent agents.

[We] had attracted general attention, the journalistic world seized eagerly upon news concerning Russia, and the events listed in the Russian revolutionary chronicle formed the most absorbing news. In order to check the streams of false rumors and canards of every kind furnished to the European public through the daily press it was necessary systematically to supply foreign agents with correspondence from Russia covering all events in the Russian revolutionary world. I sent Hartman [the international propaganda head] . . . copies of letters, biographies of those . . . revolutionary publications, pictures of . . . condemned revolutionists in Russian magazines and newspapers. After the assassination of Alexander II . . . I sent him a report of the event including the letter of the Executive Committee to the new Czar Alexander III.[56]

The Russian diaspora provided printed materials, lectures, and funds.

Beyond seeking support from public opinion abroad, foreign revolutionaries were an essential audience. The Internationale meeting in London held after Alexander II's assassination enthusiastically approved "all illegal tactics including the use of chemistry to construct bombs for offensive and defensive purposes."[57] Western European anarchists welcomed the Russian uprising, but they were also a potential liability, because Marxists and anarchists hated each other. Nonetheless, efforts to gain support from both were successful, Vera Figner emphasizes.

> All the eminent figures in the socialistic world of Western Europe promised Hartman their cooperation in one form or another. With some of them, for instance Karl Marx and Rochefort, the Committee communicated by letter asking them to help their agent Hartman in the work of organizing propaganda against Russian despotism. . . . Marx sent the Committee his autographed portrait together with his expressed agreement to serve.[58]

Marx's response was especially surprising; he had said revolutionaries should not employ terror.[59]

Other political elements, especially Western liberals, had to be reconciled with radicals; the difficulties of this issue compelled Vera Figner to spend a week writing a letter to Alexander III explaining why his father had to be assassinated, a letter that tried to mask the organization's radical aspirations. Understanding her dilemma, Karl Marx praised the letter as displaying "cunning, moderation and tact, [which] won the sympathetic approval of all Russian society."[60] Figner described the letter's impact. "Upon its publication in the West, it produced a sensation throughout all the European press. The most moderate and conservative periodicals expressed their approval of the demands of the Russian Nihilists finding them reasonable, just and such as had in large measure been long ago realized in the daily life of Western Europe."[61] This dilemma of appealing to nonradical elements in the West continued to inspire Russian terrorists. In 1881, when U.S. president James Garfield was assassinated, Narodnaya Volya felt compelled to distinguish that act from the ones it committed. Figner wrote an eloquent letter of condolence to the United States, stating that her group aimed to establish parliamentary government and that terror was abhorrent in free societies. As she anticipated, the letter disturbed many Second Internationale members.

In 1904, the Central Committee of the Socialist Revolutionary Party, which maintained the Terrorist Brigade, was faced with a more painful situation. In the 1890s, anarchists crossed international borders to assassinate prominent figures, including leaders in democratic governments. The Central Committee, to retain sympathies, wrote a proclamation to all citizens.

> The compulsory severity of our methods . . . must not becloud the situation. More than any others, we condemn publicly as did our heroic predecessors the use of terror as a measure of systematic warfare in free countries. But in Russia where despotism precludes any open political struggle and knows only lawlessness, where there is no protection against irresponsible authority, absolutist in all spheres of its bureaucratic structure, we are compelled to interpose the law of revolution against the law of tyranny.[62]

As expected, the statement provoked intense opposition from radicals, and when anarchists in the West began exploding bombs in crowded places, the tension grew more intense. Then France's Francois-Claudius Ravachol, who had been involved earlier in criminal acts, proclaimed himself an anarchist during his 1892 trial. These tactics and attitudes were alien to the tradition the Russians hoped to develop. But the revolutionary bond was so sacred that Kalieyev, whose concern for the innocent had induced him to forgo his first opportunity to assassinate Grand Duke Sergius, said,

> I do not know what I would do had I been born a Frenchman, Englishman or German. In all probability I would not manufacture bombs, and most probably I would not be interested in politics at all. But why should the Party of Socialist Revolutionists [i.e., the party of terror] throw stones

at French and Italian terrorists? Why this hurry? Why this fear of European public opinion? It is not for us to fear. . . . We must be feared and respected. Terror is power. It is not for us to proclaim our lack of respect for it. I believe more in terror than in all the parliaments of the world. I will not throw a bomb into a crowded café, but it is not for me to judge Ravachol, [who] justified his act by saying there are "no innocents." He is more of a comrade to me than those to whom this proclamation is addressed.[63]

As Vera Figner foresaw, foreign states that accepted political refugees did so knowing they would severely provoke Russia's government. In the last phase of her life, roughly half of the executive committee lived abroad in safety; the others, except Figner, were in Russian prisons. The Russian government used its secret police force to shape the foreign scene, penetrating Russian groups and inducing them to commit self-destructive acts. "The most notorious provocation occurred in Paris in 1890, when Arkadiy Harting . . . organized a well-armed team of bomb throwers and then betrayed them to the Paris police. These heavily publicized arrests helped persuade the French public of the dangers posed by Russian revolutionaries in France."[64] Okhrana also subsidized journalists to write favorable articles for Russia's government in sympathetic periodicals and created societies in France to promote its views.

Nevertheless, Russian revolutionaries found foreign states useful. In the second phase of Russian terrorism, Terrorist Brigade members often moved over international borders to seek temporary refuge; except for Russia, no passports were needed at that time. When they entered Russia, they could secure new passports from the Russian government to move more freely in Russia itself.[65] The organization created major foreign bases. Its headquarters were in Switzerland, the safest state for foreign terrorists. Geneva and St. Petersburg were situated on different ends of the European continent, but three days after Count von Plehve was assassinated in St. Petersburg (1904), every surviving participant reconvened in Geneva to plan their next move. The Central Committee also moved frequently to Brussels, Paris, and other capitals of democratic states.[66]

The organization had a laboratory in Paris teaching people to make and use bombs, and this laboratory welcomed potential terrorists from different countries. Indian and Chinese students learned techniques they used in their own lands.[67] Paris also hosted the Terrorist Brigade's extended trial of Azev (1907), Okhrana's notorious agent provocateur who had become the Terrorist Brigade leader.[68]

European sympathizers helped establish foreign sanctuaries and strengthen their governments' resolve to refuse extradition. The Second Internationale waged a prolonged campaign of demonstrations that contributed to the Italian government's refusal to extradite Michael Gotz, the Terrorist Brigade leader. German Social Democrats provided "legal assistance when Russian radicals were tried in German courts for subversive and criminal activities."[69]

In 1907, the Terrorist Brigade organized attacks from Finland, a nation linked to Russia but with considerable legal autonomy.

> We chose Finland as the base of operations. . . . There could be no question at that time of our being extradited to the Russian government from Finland and should the question have been raised it would have been immediately delayed and the persons wanted would be given an opportunity to disappear. Members of the sympathetic Finnish Party of Active Resistance were present in all Finnish government institutions and even . . . the police. The Finns . . . gave us refuge, supplied us with arms and dynamite, transported supplies to Russia, provided . . . Finnish passports, etc. . . . It may be said without exaggeration that it was only due to the conditions prevailing in Finland that the re-establishment of the Terrorist Brigade was made possible with a minimum of sacrifices.[70]

The Internationalist's London Conference of 1881 electrified anarchists by "authorizing propaganda of the deed" and provoking newspapers and governments to speak of a "gigantic" international conspiracy. Abortive assassination attempts occurred in Germany and Austria-Hungary. Most incidents were isolated, individual-initiated episodes involving local issues and assailants. Many concerned labor disputes and robberies. Black Band

and Black Hand groups were active among French and Spanish miners, respectively.

The 1890s created a new situation, one making an international conspiracy idea more credible. Most assassins were foreigners who used daggers and pistols. The years 1892 to 1901 became the Decade of Regicide, during which more monarchs, presidents, and prime ministers of major world powers were assassinated than any other time in recorded history: President Sadi Carnot of France (1894); Prime Minister Antonio Canovas of Spain (1897); Austria's Empress Elizabeth, reputedly Europe's most beautiful woman (1898); Italy's King Humbert I (1900); and the president of the United States, William McKinley (1901). Aside from McKinley, Italian assassins were responsible for the other four deaths.[71]

Dynamite was used against crowds, too. "The 1893 bombing of the Barcelona Opera House . . . killed as many people [thirty or more] . . . as many as in all the incidents of the 1880s combined." Threats were made to use chemical and biological weapons; a British newspaper reported falsely that biological weapons were being used.[72] The assassinations, crowd attacks, and claims of weapons of mass destruction made anarchists seem like a bizarre breed unable to live in peace anywhere. The working classes, especially in Europe's Latin countries, favored anarchists initially, but that support waned as the campaign developed.

Bismarck called a conference of Western governments to create "an alliance against the Internationale."[73] While only the Austrians and Germans developed a common policy, some European states concluded bilateral agreements. As the number of attacks kept increasing, more states wanted to create international arrangements to cope with the problem. The Rome Conference (1898) aimed at comprehensive international police cooperation and much better border control. International concerns grew even more intense after a devastating international assassination occurred, one organized in the United States in 1900 by an Italian anarchist who returned to Italy to assassinate King Humbert I.[74] The United Kingdom, United States, and Switzerland refused to participate. Why were the Americans unwilling to attend? For one thing, Europeans had experienced much more anarchist terror. Only two major incidents had occurred in the

United States, the Chicago Haymarket bombing (1886) and Alexander Berkman's unsuccessful attempt in Pittsburgh to assassinate Henry Clay Frick (1892), the Carnegie Steel Corporation's general manager and a ruthless strikebreaker.

But the American atmosphere was transformed when an immigrant's son assassinated President William McKinley in 1901. His successor, Theodore Roosevelt, immediately made the first American call for an international effort to eliminate terrorism.

> Anarchy is a crime against the whole human race; and all mankind should band together against the Anarchist. His crime should be made an offense against the law of nations like piracy and . . . the slave trade, for it is of far blacker infamy than either. It should be so declared by treaties among all civilized powers. Such treaties would give to the federal government the power of dealing with the crime.[75]

Despite Roosevelt's vigorous proclamation, his commitment to international efforts did not last long.[76] In 1902, the German and Russian governments invited states to accept an agreement for "rigorous surveillance of the anarchists by the creation of central bureaus in the various countries," which would exchange information and create rules to expel foreign "anarchists from all countries." Thirteen states, mostly Central European, signed a secret protocol in 1904 in St. Petersburg. Most democratic Western states refused to sign,[77] an irony when we consider how often democratic states became terrorist targets during the Third Wave and Fourth Wave. Democracies refused for three reasons: they normally granted asylum to political refugees, especially Switzerland and the United Kingdom; had experienced less violence than states signing the treaty; and believed that terror could encourage more states to adopt parliamentary institutions.

Even though the assassination of Italy's King Humbert I precipitated the St. Petersburg meeting, Italy refused to sign the protocol. It mistrusted Russia, Germany, and Austria-Hungary (the major powers involved) and feared that thousands of Italian anarchists abroad might be extradited, making Italy's domestic troubles worse than its international ones. Italians were particularly active as international assassins, crossing borders to kill heads of state or principal political officeholders in different countries.

Beyond democratic ambivalence, the United States had special reasons for not signing the protocol. Secret treaties were unconstitutional. It did not want to get involved in European politics, especially since Germany and Russia had instigated international clashes with the United States. A German fleet during the Spanish-American War (1898) had sailed into the Philippines, an act Americans saw as hostile. In 1902–1903, the Germans bombarded Venezuela to collect debts owed, making Americans feel that Germany might trample on the Monroe Doctrine. Russia's pogroms against the Jews angered Americans, and its expansion in Asia led President Roosevelt to support Japan in the Russo-Japanese War. The federal government also had only one police force, the Secret Service, with just fifty agents very much consumed with other tasks, namely, dealing with counterfeiters and protecting the president. It was not easy to persuade Congress that the federal government needed more extensive police powers. Then there was the "Miss Stone Affair," in which American missionaries were allowed to supply funds to the Internal Macedonian Revolutionary Organization (IMRO), a terrorist group in the Ottoman Empire, making it clear Americans could not treat all terrorist groups alike.

The Russian Terrorist Brigade's experience abroad also illustrates international ambivalence. Support was strongest in states refusing to sign the protocol. When the Russo-Japanese War broke out, the Japanese offered the Terrorist Brigade funds laundered by American millionaires.[78] Japan did not sign the 1904 protocol, but the Ottoman Empire did, even though it supplied the Terrorist Brigade with money and weapons. Signing the protocol meant different things for the signatories; for one thing, the protocol suggested that terrorism and anarchism were synonymous, but many states distinguished between anarchists and other groups.

How effective was the 1904 protocol? It did not remain in force for long enough for a clear picture to emerge. The number of heads of state assassinated declined dramatically in the decade after 1904, but it is not clear the protocol was responsible. Russia was the only major state where a prominent political figure was assassinated: Prime Minister Stolypin was killed in 1911, but the assassin was a Russian and therefore not covered by the protocol.[79] The decline also was related to the fact that prominent persons in major states were now much better guarded than before, but it is not clear how much significance that fact has. Oddly, Stolypin refused to have bodyguards or wear a bulletproof vest the day he was killed by a double agent. Beyond the striking decline of prominent assassinations by foreigners, terrorist activity in general was dropping in Central Europe, where the protocol was most strongly supported.[80]

In 1914, the protocol was destroyed in the aftermath of "the shot heard round the world," when a Serbian nationalist assassinated Archduke Franz Ferdinand, the heir to the Austro-Hungarian Empire, and his wife. The act provoked World War I, the most devastating conflict the world had ever experienced, ending in the destruction of Europe's international structure established by the Congress of Vienna a century before.

The new status of Bosnia-Herzegovina provoked the assassination. Previously a part of the Ottoman Empire, Austro-Hungarian troops occupied it after the Russian-Ottoman War (1877–1878), and in 1908 the Austro-Hungarian government decided to incorporate it, a decision Serbia and Russia opposed. Several assassination plots materialized, organized largely by the Black Hand, which had been founded by Serbian military officers encouraged by Russia and was composed of Serbian, Bosnian, and Croatian students.[81] The Serbian government suppressed the Black Hand. Gavrilo Princip, a Black Hand member, assassinated the archduke and his wife, who had come to Bosnia to reduce the population's antagonism toward its new status.

The Austro-Hungarians insisted the Black Hand, which had organized an abortive attempt several years before, was responsible. A strong ultimatum, intended to be unacceptable, was delivered to Serbia, which acceded to all demands except one authorizing Austro-Hungarian police to operate on Serbian territory to apprehend suspects. Vienna refused to compromise or wait for the investigation to be completed, Germany gave Vienna a "blank check," Russia backed Serbia, and World War I began.[82] This pattern of a state being unwilling to wait in the wake of a terrorist atrocity until all facts emerge, thereby producing a much worse situation, appears again both in the Third Wave and Fourth Wave.

The trial of Princip and his associates later demonstrated that Serbia had not been involved. Princip testified, "I am a Yugoslav nationalist, aiming for the unification of all Yugoslavs, and I do not care what form of state, but it must be freed from Austria." When asked how he intended to realize his goal he responded, "By means of terror."[83] When World War I was over, Princip and his associates were buried beneath a chapel "built to commemorate for eternity our Serb Heroes."[84]

NATIONALIST EXPANSION IN EUROPE AND ASIA

Our principal concern has been on the areas where two major distinct objectives, radical reform and anarchism, often intertwined. But the First Wave had a more extensive geography and other objectives as well. Nationalism was important in shaping the wave's geography. Eastern Europe was the initial home for nationalist terrorists, but nationalist aspirations soon spread to Asia and the Middle East as well. In virtually all these cases, a radical dimension was quite evident. Only the Irish produced a separatist terror movement in Western Europe or the Americas without a radical dimension. Separatism had a strong base in Russia's experience; recruits came from different national elements (for example, Armenians and Poles) inside the Russian Empire and soon founded their own national groups, which former Russian comrades helped train and arm. Two separatist efforts in Scandinavia succeeded without violence. Norway gained independence from Sweden (1905); both states had a common monarch but separate legislatures. The Norwegian parliament unanimously voted for secession, and a Norwegian referendum showed that over 95 percent of the Norwegians favored separation, convincing Sweden that it was not worth resisting. Iceland decided to separate from Denmark in 1918, establishing a legislature but retaining the Danish monarch.[85]

But nationalist terror did not produce successes in the First Wave, because the Congress of Vienna prevented the dismantling of empires. The most serious nationalist terrorist efforts were in the Austro-Hungarian, Russian, and Ottoman empires, where territories were contiguous, creating obstacles to separation. Separatist terrorist groups then were often dependent on neighboring states for sanctuaries and material aid, but those states found it difficult to continue the process.

Armenian activities were particularly interesting. Most targets were in Ottoman Empire territories near Europe, aiming to induce major European powers to intervene and establish Armenia as an independent state.[86] This hope was inspired largely by Russia's invasion of the Ottoman Empire in 1877 and 1878, provoked by massacres of Bulgarian Christians after the Bulgarian uprising against the Ottomans. The Treaty of Berlin (1881) ended that war, establishing new Balkan states and strengthening existing ones. The treaty charged six major European states with protecting Armenians against government-encouraged atrocities.[87] But those states were reluctant to pursue their obligations. Armenian groups consequently decided to provoke incidents to illustrate the horrors of the Ottoman Empire and arouse Europe's conscience. The pattern reflected a very significant theme in Armenia's cultural tradition, beginning with St. Vartan's military effort in the fifth century against overwhelming odds to reclaim the right to be Christian.

> The depiction of suffering, daring, rare partial success, and heroic death constitute cultural narratives which serve to establish the willingness to act against very high odds and to accept violent deaths. [They] are essential element[s] of those who would honorably live out their lives that are socially approved because their paradigm is represented in projective narratives.[88]

Armenian terror persisted intermittently for several decades, and the groups frequently splintered, much like the Russian ones. Every member of the first group, Protectors of the Fatherland (1881), was a Russian Armenian initially trained and supported by Russian terrorists. The group functioned largely in the Anatolia area of the Ottoman Empire. An uprising that provoked foreign intervention there would disintegrate the Ottoman Empire, an outcome the Russian government wanted to promote; it therefore gave the organization valuable logistic and financial support despite its well-known ties with Russian revolutionaries.[89] But efforts to inflame the Armenian population were difficult. "Constituting six to eight per cent of the total population, Armenians were not a majority in any province of the empire. Of the six provinces of eastern Anatolia where, apart from Istanbul, most Ottoman Armenians lived, in only one . . . they comprise[d] more than a quarter of the population, according to Ottoman census figures."[90]

The Protectors only lasted two years, but other groups soon emerged. The most important were the Social Democrat Party (Hentchak), created by Russian Armenian students in Switzerland (1887), and the Armenian Revolutionary Federation (ARF; 1890). Hentchak, the smaller group, was more public about its radicalism, aiming to establish "a socialist Armenia as a beacon for world socialist revolution" based on "workers and peasants." In 1907, Hentchak joined the Second Internationale;[91] it was much more global than ARF. Its headquarters were in Switzerland, with units in the Ottoman Empire, France, the United Kingdom, the United States, and Russia, raising considerable funds from the Armenian diaspora. ARF publicly emphasized nationalism more than socialism as the best way to get Armenian support. Over time, ARF developed ties with a sympathetic Persia and its large Armenian community. But the Armenian clergy and wealthier Armenians, especially in the Ottoman Empire, resisted both groups and became ARF terror victims.

In 1893, Hentchak masqueraded as a Turkish group in the countryside calling Muslims to revolt against the sultan and establish constitutional government. The disguise was quickly revealed, infuriating Muslims; its object, the British ambassador said, was "to create a 'semblance of revolt' by cutting telegraph wires, bombing the odd government building, etc." The sultan would then panic and order local authorities to "act in a stupid or overzealous manner . . . arouse Turkish and Kurdish masses with religious fanaticism and a massacre would occur."[92]

Allegations of arbitrary arrest, torture, and punishment without trial infuriated Europeans and Armenians, and a series of massacres occurred in Armenian villages. Assassination attempts precipitated even more indiscriminate responses; entire populations were eliminated and women and children deliberately mutilated. Thousands died, and the "statistics" were circulated widely.[93]

The most sensational Armenian effort occurred in 1896, timed to occur when Gladstone and the Liberal Party (strong Armenian supporters) returned to power in the United Kingdom.[94] A team of twenty-six, led by a seventeen-year-old, seized the European Ottoman Bank and held European bank workers hostage. ARF made fourteen demands to the six European states the Berlin Treaty had made responsible for monitoring the Ottoman situation. If the demands were not met within two days, the bank, with the captors and captives inside, would be blown up. When Europeans agreed to talk, the terrorists surrendered their hostages.[95] Over the next four days, nearly six thousand Armenians were killed, apparently at the sultan's command, and around 75,000 Armenians fled Constantinople.[96] Because the city contained European diplomats and tourists, the sultan's reactions were much more visible to the outside world than they would have been in the countryside, where so many previous incidents occurred. Spectators "literally waded in blood . . . and saw with their own eyes some of the Sultan's elegant aides-de-camp stamping with their heels on the bodies of dying Armenians."[97] Despite enormous European outrage, conflicting interests divided European powers from doing anything beyond demanding the massacres cease immediately.

A few years later, Russia became reluctant to help, fearing that a decimated Ottoman Empire would entice European powers to incorporate Ottoman territories on Russia's borders. Separatist sentiments in Russia were a concern too, and the government made efforts to transform ethnic groups into "Russians." Armenian Church properties used to subsidize Armenian schools were seized in 1903, inducing ARF to extend its struggle and fight for Armenian independence from Russia as well.[98] "In a bloody reign of violence lasting two years, hundreds of Russian bureaucrats fell before the bullets, knives and bombs of 'Armenian terrorists.'"[99] But the warm bond between Russian and Armenian revolutionaries continued. It may have even strengthened, because in 1905 when the Terrorist Brigade was established, some Armenians left ARF to join the Terrorist Brigade, and ARF gave it arms.

A desperate ARF changed its policy of avoiding assassinating heads of state, and in 1905, with the assistance of IMRO, planned to assassinate Sultan Abdulhamid II.[100] ARF stated its purpose in a letter addressed to the six major European powers. It "hoped the outrage might force the [Ottoman] Government to adopt measures against the Armenian people so as to induce the European Powers to intervene on their behalf."[101] Three assassination attempts occurred; none were successful, but the last effort killed twenty-six Turks and injured fifty-eight. The Ottomans interned many of the Armenians said to be involved; this time, conspicuous atrocities did not occur, which helped European powers avoid serious involvement again.

In the "Young Turk" revolution (1908), military officers eliminated the sultan and his dynasty, establishing a constitutional government. Armenian groups helped and pledged allegiance to the new order, but a year later the Adana Massacre materialized, killing over 15,000 Armenians.[102] Armenian groups withdrew; ARF retreated to a sympathetic Persia. During World War I, ARF abandoned terrorist activity to organize a sizeable military force, which created the Republic of Armenia (1919). In its first parliamentary election ARF got eighty-two of eighty-six seats, but Bolsheviks and Muslim dissidents quickly incorporated the republic into the new Soviet Union.

Polish terrorists emerged to continue earlier nationalist and ideological struggles. But the division of the Polish community across three different states, Prussia, Austria-Hungary, and Russia, continued to doom terrorist efforts, just as the Armenian dispersion had.[103] The two cases had other parallels, as well. Participants initially were members of Russian terrorist groups, and when Poles and Armenians created their own organizations they remained in useful contact with subsequent Russian ones. Polish students in Russian universities were attracted to Narodnaya Volya, and one, Ignacy Hryniewiecki, helped assassinate Czar Alexander II in 1881. As discussed earlier, the Terrorist Faction, which had organized an abortive plot to assassinate Alexander III in 1887, contained two Poles, Bronislaw and Jozef Pilsudski, who were imprisoned for their roles. When released, they returned home, where they helped found the Polish Socialist Revolutionary Party (BPP) during the 1905 Russian Revolution, when Russia was aflame with domestic violence and an international war. It was modeled after the Russian Duma's Socialist Revolutionary Party, which had created the Terrorist Brigade. The BPP had a terrorist wing, too, which sprung into action when demonstrations were brutally repressed in Russian territories. Austria-Hungary and Japan subsidized the terrorists. Like the Armenians, the Poles now aimed to create a socialist community.[104] But the Poles struck only Russians in Russia "to destabilize Russian authority in Poland and to frighten all figures of the Czar's administration. Polish terrorists attacked, killing 790 military and police officers [and] exploding 120 bombs in a short time of two years from 1905 to 1906. The victims were mostly Russian . . . staff of the Czar's administration."[105]

All Polish terrorists remained publicly committed to promoting socialism in Russia until November 1906, when the party split, and one element of the Revolutionary Faction, led by Józef Pilsudski, insisted that an independent Polish state was the primary aim. But he soon discovered that Polish support for terror, no matter what the ultimate cause, was tepid, and in 1910 he organized a new group in Austria-Hungary, the Union of Active Combat, a paramilitary group that ultimately served in the Austro-Hungarian army during World War I. Poland eventually achieved independence after the Versailles Peace Treaty went into effect, because unlike the Armenians, most Poles, though scattered across states, were in a large, contiguous area.

The Balkan world, a seedbed of persistent hostilities, stimulated many groups beyond those that had provoked World War I. A major Balkan terrorist organization, IMRO, was established in 1892 by Macedonian students in Russian, German, and Swiss universities working with Russian and German anarchists.[106] It used the cellular structures the Russians had developed.[107] Like the Armenians, the radical leftist elements founding IMRO dissipated over time; what emerged was a more popular nationalism. The Treaty of Berlin obliged the Ottomans to give Macedonia an autonomous status. The problem was further complicated because three Balkan states (Serbia, Greece, and Bulgaria) had Macedonian populations, and they competed with one another to gain the community's loyalties. IMRO aimed to induce major foreign powers to intervene. It waged several different campaigns, employing strategies and tactics with unusual features. Muslim elements (Turks and Albanians) were the principal victims. Areas attracting European tourists were bombed, hoping to evoke political attention and disrupt trade between the Ottoman Empire and Christian states. But few assassinations occurred, and European states distinguished IMRO from other terrorist groups.

The Miss Stone Affair (1901) is one of the few hostage incidents to take place during this period and the only important one that was successful. IMRO kidnapped an American Protestant missionary, Ellen Stone, and her pregnant companion, demanding the United States pay $110,000 for their release. Negotiations dragged on for six months.[108] Stone's gender and her companion's pregnancy multiplied American concern. Roosevelt's response reflected the conventional view of gender.

> It is impossible not to feel differently about [women] than men. If a man goes out as a missionary, he has no . . . business to venture to wild lands with the expectation the government will protect him as well as when he stayed at home. If he is fit for his work he has no more right to complain of what may befall him than a soldier has in getting shot. But it is impossible to adopt this standard [for] women.[109]

First Wave terrorists were reluctant to take hostages, a practice associated with criminal activity. But IMRO made its decision to kidnap for two reasons. It was virtually bankrupt and knew the missionary community was sympathetic to its purpose of ending Turkish Muslim rule in Europe. Twenty students at the Collegiate Seminary in Bulgaria were IMRO members, and the seminary's head confessed, "I respected them, and my heart was with them."[110] IMRO believed missionaries would persuade the U.S. government the Turks were responsible and intervene with military force if a ransom had to be paid. When Stone's companion gave birth to her child,

IMRO provided the necessary medical help. Although the United States refused to negotiate, it endorsed the money-raising efforts of the Foreign Missions Board, which had sent Stone to the area. Major newspapers, Protestant churches, and the Macedonian diaspora helped raised funds. IMRO eventually accepted $66,000, much less than it originally demanded, but the money financed a 1903 uprising. When released, Stone became an IMRO supporter and began a strenuous campaign to raise additional money for IMRO from Christian congregations, dismaying the U.S. government greatly. Stone's activities might be seen as the first example of Stockholm Syndrome in the history of global terrorism, but she had been sympathetic to IMRO's cause before becoming a hostage.[111]

Clearly, the Macedonian struggle did not provoke the same hostility among Americans that the anarchists did. The 1904 protocol developed in St. Petersburg was concerned with anarchists and other groups using "anarchist methods." IMRO activity aroused attention, sympathy, and international support, but the organization was unable to stimulate serious intervention because the major powers were apprehensive a war with the Turks might transform the European balance of power and enhance possibilities of a major war between European states.

When major powers refused to intervene, some Balkan states acted on their own. Bulgaria, Greece, and Serbia went to war with the Turks (the Balkan War of 1913), forcing them to cede Macedonian territories to Serbia and Greece, an unexpected and infuriating result for Bulgaria and IMRO. Bulgaria decided to enter World War I on the Central Powers' side because Serbia and Greece were linked to the Allies, and if the Allies were defeated, Bulgaria believed it could incorporate Macedonia. But Bulgaria chose the losing side, and Macedonia remained divided. Bulgaria kept IMRO alive for fifteen more years, and IMRO struck other Balkan states, particularly Greece. But Bulgaria and IMRO had conflicting aims and drifted apart. This development intensified existing divisions within IMRO, resulting in an abandonment of its left-wing origins, so much so that Italy's fascist government later subsidized the group. Ultimately, IMRO became a criminal organization accepting "contracts" for various schemes. After a Bulgarian military coup in 1934, the First Wave's most durable terrorist organization collapsed; it had lasted forty-one years.[112]

Unlike other separatist uprisings, Indian terror occurred in an overseas and not a contiguous empire. Russian terrorists influenced two major uprisings in India, namely, those of 1907–1912 and 1914–1918.[113] Indian students in Paris in 1906 attended the Russian bomb-making school and returned home to teach others those techniques. In 1909, a British police raid on a cell found two Hindu documents assessing the utility of the Russian experience for India.

> The system of the Bengali revolutionaries does not of course fit exactly with the Russian scheme [because of] adaptation of differences of country and race, national customs and tendencies. . . . [Also] the dominant religious element is entirely absent from the Russian propaganda, but the underlying principles are the same.[114]

Indian terrorist groups sought aid from Japan, but as Britain had helped Japan in its victory over Russia, Japan refused to repeat the offer it had made to Russian and Polish terrorists. Nevertheless, the dramatic and quick Japanese victory in the Russo-Japanese War reverberated throughout the Asian world, demolishing a widespread view that the West's great military strength signified racial superiority.[115] "If the rice-eating Jap is capable of throwing the meat-eating Russian into utter rout, cannot the rice-eating Indian do the same to the British?" a Calcutta paper asked.[116] Indian newspapers followed the war's progress in detail, and pro-Japanese demonstrations took place. Mahatma Gandhi wrote: "The people of the East seemed to be waking up from their lethargy," and the teenaged Jawaharlal Nehru (destined to be India's first prime minister) wrote: "Japanese victories stirred up my enthusiasm and I waited eagerly for fresh news daily. . . . Nationalist ideas filled my mind. I dreamed of Indian freedom."[117]

A second catalyst was the British decision in 1905 to divide Bengal, India's largest and most populated province, into two, hoping to blunt the nationalist sentiment there. The Hindu minority in one portion, deeply worried about Muslim domination, launched demonstrations to boycott

British products and replace them with indigenous ones. But after three years, some became convinced mass agitation was insufficient and endorsed terror. The primary organization, Dacca Anushilan Samiti (Self-Culture Association),[118] operated under the guise of suburban fitness clubs, as did its principal offshoot, Jugantar (New Era), tied to the Indian diaspora. Indian students at the University of California–Berkeley supported the uprising and created Ghadar (Revolution). In World War I, it tried to ally with the Irish Sinn Fein, an arrangement Germany tried to aid with money and military supplies, but the United States and United Kingdom thwarted them.[119]

Initially, all Indian terrorists were Hindu; over 80 percent of them were students from the higher castes. A British civil servant described them as "misled idealists" but noted that "one should never forget this, the Bengali boys who became terrorists were the best boys in Bengal."[120] Muslims and the British were principal targets. Funds were gathered through gang robberies, which occasionally made Hindus victims if they were perceived as administration members or "traitors." Recruits were normally integrated into the organizations in a temple of Kali. "There before the image of the Goddess Kali, the members took the vow with a *gita* [a scripture urging them to fight a righteous war] on the head and a sword in the hand."[121] "At the inauguration ceremony a white goat resembling the Englishman was sacrificed before the Goddess."[122] A picture police found in the organization's headquarters shows "Kali dancing, and the several heads which form her garland and the various limbs and heads lying above receiving the attention of crows and jackals are white."[123] The Self-Culture Association adopted the First Wave's weapons, tactics, and strategy. Kali's central place made it difficult for Muslims to sympathize, but as the Self-Culture Association became more anti-British it began to attract Muslims as well.

The special influence of the Russo-Japanese War and the location of Self-Culture Association cells in fitness clubs show that Indians were obsessed with physical culture to demonstrate they could deal with the "martial races." The clubs featured wrestling with daggers and lathes (staves), boxing, jujitsu, and riding. But the uprising failed. The British had no reason to give up their tenure or believe the revolt might be justified. Many

Muslims, suspicious of the terrorists' ultimate intentions, helped the British, and the police infiltrated the group.[124] Little thought was given to the new state's character: "The revolutionaries often acted on impulse and emotion without proper plans or precautions and had only short-term goals. The link between specific acts of violence and the independence of India was at best hazy. Perhaps it is in the nature of revolutionary activity not to have well-formulated conceptions of the past and the future."[125]

Nationalism and anarchism inspired Chinese activities as well. Movements began in Paris and Tokyo; in 1906, Paris had over five hundred Chinese students, and ten thousand studied in Tokyo, where educational costs were considerably less.[126] Ironically, most students were sent overseas because the government thought they would return to help "modernize" the country and strengthen its ability to deal with foreign powers. Britain, Germany, Russia, France, Italy, Portugal, Japan, and other major powers had made considerable inroads into China's independence, forcing significant concessions, including of territory. Those concessions provoked the unsuccessful Boxer Uprising (1898–1900), a massive popular military effort to eliminate all foreign influences and presences. The Boxers used only traditional weapons, swords, lances, and daggers, believing that their "martial arts were magical, and they were invulnerable."[127] The ruling dynasty became convinced that China had to understand the importance of Western technology, but the Russian Terrorist Brigade in Paris taught the Chinese sent there how to use bombs.

The Chinese had an assassination tradition that transformed some assassins into popular heroes, similar to the celebration of Western tyrannicides, but the Chinese tradition granted honor only if the assassin died in the effort. But now Chinese revolutionaries emphasized assassination's relationship to revolution. It made overturning a government "extremely easy. The tactic did not require much money or many people or coordinating groups. There was no risk of foreign intervention. [It did not] implicate or frighten innocent people in the area where it was undertaken [and] was [effective] in terrifying the authorities."[128] Assassination efforts occurred in two short phases, namely, 1903 through 1907 and 1910 through 1912. Anarchists and nationalists cooperated to remove the Manchu dynasty, China's government for centuries. As the dynasty had originated in Manchuria, the rebels denounced it as a foreign imposition. A republic would increase China's unity, strength, and ability to prevent foreign interventions.

The Society for the Education of a Militant People, largely composed of anarchists, generated the initial 1903–1907 phase.[129] Eight separate plots were carried out, but only one victim died, a provincial governor. Individuals organized the attacks but made no effort to coordinate them with popular uprisings. The attack that killed the governor was intended to be linked with an uprising, but the uprising did not get off the ground. A woman was the designated leader of that anticipated uprising, the first time a woman was involved in such a task, an event the Russian terrorists had inspired.

Every assassin died in their attempt. Contemporaries reflecting on the pattern felt that the participants had been transfixed by the ancient Chinese tradition and misunderstood the new meaning of assassination. A Japanese journal at the time said, "Those who committed suicide out of anguish should instead carry out assassination for the revolution." A recent commentator adds, "The appeal of . . . heroic suicide may help to explain the incompetence with weapons that characterized almost all the attempts. . . . Many of these episodes can be interpreted as ritual suicides rather than calculated attempts at assassination."[130]

The next assassination campaign (1910–1912) was more effective. A variety of groups cooperated for the first time. In 1905, the Chinese Revolutionary Alliance under Sun Yat-sen's leadership "promised to overthrow the Manchu empire and thus restore China to the Chinese, establish a republic and distribute land equally among the people."[131] By 1910, the Revolutionary Alliance had many supporters who generated popular uprisings and general strikes in some provinces and had assembled administrative structures, including military elements. The assassination campaign this time frequently succeeded in killing or injuring intended victims (four times in six attempts) and was correctly timed to coincide with popular disturbances.

Clearly, assassins had learned from previous mistakes. The Revolutionary Alliance precluded solo attacks. The most successful operation was the

1911 assassination of General Feng-Shan, who had been sent to suppress the rebellion in Kwangtung. None of the twenty assassins involved was hurt, and over twenty members of the general's protection unit died. The event had a dramatic effect. The imperial government sent no one to replace the general, and within two weeks the province declared its independence. The assassination campaign continued in the rest of the country, and a republic was established in the following year. Success did not hinge on the assassination campaign, but it certainly helped.

Sun Yat-sen, China's new leader, was ambivalent about such tactics. He refused to endorse assassination publicly but gave assassins funds and allowed an important journal associated with the Revolutionary Alliance to describe them favorably.[132] Huang Hsing, the uprising's chief figure and recognized as the "Co-Founder of the Republic," struggled with Sun Yat-sen over the matter.[133] Anarchist activity continued until the early 1930s, at which point the Communist Party absorbed the anarchists.

Ironically, though Tokyo's atmosphere provided inspiration and assets to Chinese students, Japanese terrorists never got far. Anarchists organized demonstrations against the outbreak of the Russo-Japanese War in 1904. But later they joined riots against the Treaty of Portsmouth ending the war in 1905, which gave Japan much less than they demanded. The contradiction between agitating against starting the war and then insisting on continuing it perhaps can be explained by the belief that riots against the peace treaty seriously threatened the system.[134]

In 1907 anarchists and socialists created an alliance of around forty people in Denjiro Kotoku, a group deeply influenced by European anarchists. Recruits came from an unusual source, relatively poor families; most had only completed elementary school and were involved in construction and tradesman activities.[135] The first strike planned was the assassination of the emperor, a wholly unprecedented act; the Japanese considered their emperor divine, and no assassination attempt had ever been made. One conspirator explained, "Because there was the myth surrounding the imperial family, there was the desire on my part to talk about the making of a bomb and the utilization of this as an attack on the myth of the emperor to show that the blood of the emperor was no different from that of the common man."[136]

A series of general strikes, assassinations of wealthy capitalists, fires, and attacks on government, especially police, was to follow. But twenty-six were apprehended before any attack was made. No public protests of the trials occurred, and the movement's remnants did not acclaim the convicted as heroes or martyrs. Ira Plotkin's examination of the trial concludes, "Because of . . . the crime for which they were accused, conspiracy to assassinate the divine symbol of the state, Kotoku and his followers did not become martyrs to the socialist or anarchist cause. The socialists feared total loss of support if they identified with such criminals . . . and [the] anarchist movement came to an end."[137] "The next generation of protestors and agitators could not attack the imperial institution as a way to bring about change, but rather they could attack the politicians in the name of the emperor to influence change."[138]

In the Great Treason Conspiracy trial of 1911, every potentiality of Japanese revolutionary terror was destroyed. The trial taught Osugi Sakae, the leading figure, "a lesson he never forgot even though he never articulated it, a radical may do almost anything, but he must never directly oppose a policeman or execute any violent action against the government."[139] But his rejection of violence did not preserve his life. The great Kantu Earthquake of 1923, which destroyed over 60 percent of Tokyo and Yokohama, provided cover to some Japanese to murder Osugi and many other radicals.

DECLINE OF THE FIRST WAVE

The First Wave began declining before World War I, and by the mid-1920s, four decades after it began, it was basically over. At its high point (1890–1910), terror activity occurred on all six inhabited continents and in at least thirty-eight nation-states. After 1914, only ten states experienced terror; all were in Europe or the Americas: Italy, Spain, France, Russia, Portugal, Bulgaria, the United States, Argentina, Uruguay, and Brazil. Terrorism in Spain remained important in the early 1930s, and a few incidents occurred elsewhere. An anarchist tried to assassinate Franklin D. Roosevelt (1933) when shaking hands with Chicago's mayor, who was killed instead. A year later, an IMRO member trained and sheltered by Italy and Hungary assassinated King Alexander of Yugoslavia together with France's foreign minister, Louis Barthou, in Marseilles.

Ironically, the wave's bloodiest incidents occurred during the wave's decline. The 1920 Wall Street bombing was the First Wave's deadliest incident, killing thirty-eight and injuring 143; it remained the deadliest terrorist attack in American history until the Fourth Wave Oklahoma City bombing in 1995. Antianarchist immigration laws leading to the deportation of some five hundred immigrants, including Luigi Galleani, and the unfair treatment of Sacco and Vanzetti made anarchists argue that bombing Wall Street, the "center of capitalism," was an appropriate "act of revenge." In 1921, the Diana Theatre in Milan, Italy, was bombed; twenty-one were killed and 159 injured. The aim was to kill Milan's police chief, who had abused prisoners. He was unhurt. Not until 1980, during the Third Wave, did Italy experience a more deadly terrorist massacre, namely, the Bologna train station bombing by the neofascist organization Armed Revolutionary Nuclei that killed eighty-five and wounded over two hundred.

There were three major factors contributing to the wave's decline: the inability of organizations to achieve success, the decision of many anarchists to become syndicalists, and changing police practices. Since the hope of success is the stimulant for all terror groups, across all four waves, that hope evaporates when there are no successes, especially when many efforts are attempted. In the First Wave, failures everywhere made it more and more difficult after the first two decades to get new recruits or inspire the formation of new organizations, especially in areas where anarchists dominated. Some anarchist intellectuals who had supported assassination began doubting their views. As early as 1887, Peter Kropotkin wrote, "A structure based on centuries of history cannot be destroyed with a few kilos of dynamite."[140] In 1895, the Italian anarchist Errico Malatesta argued:

> Violence used to another's hurt, which is the most brutal form the strug-
> gle between men can assume, is eminently corrupting. It tends, by its
> very nature, to suffocate the best sentiments of man, and to develop

all the antisocial qualities, ferocity, hatred, revenge, the spirit of domination and tyranny, contempt of the weak, servility towards the strong. And this harmful tendency arises also when violence is used for a good end. . . . Anarchists who rebel against every sort of oppression and struggle for the integral liberty of each and who ought thus to shrink instinctively from all acts of violence which cease to be mere resistance to oppression and become oppressive in their turn are also liable to fall into the abyss of brutal force. . . . The excitement caused by some recent explosions and the admiration for the courage with which the bomb-throwers faced death, suffices to cause many anarchists to forget their program, and to enter on a path which is the most absolute negation of all anarchist ideas.[141]

The French anarchist Fernand Pelloutier in 1895 insisted anarchists abandon "the individual dynamiter" and get involved again in the labor movement.[142] Soon syndicalism, often called anarchosyndicalism, developed in France and spread to many countries in the West. In 1922, syndicalism established a global bond in the International Workers' Association, which had several million members.[143] A new version of Proudhon's views appeared; workers living in a confederation of small communes could abolish capitalism, eliminate "wage slavery," and destroy the state through "direct action" by individuals and masses. Acts to take human lives were abandoned; instead, individuals sabotaged property, especially machinery. The most useful act would be a general strike in which all workers would participate and reject the intervention of third parties like politicians.

Syndicalist numbers grew rapidly in Europe. By 1920, France had around 130,000; most European states had fifty thousand or fewer. Sabotage and strikes were common, but ironically workers soon used strikes to increase their wages and working conditions and hence stay within the system. But when the Communist Party's hostility to capitalism became a feature of Western political systems, syndicalists often joined them. But the experiences of Italy, Germany, and Spain were very different. Their governments used violence to eliminate the syndicalists, though the process was different in each case. The Italian Syndicalist Union (USI) had 820,000 members in 1921, the second-largest syndicalist group in Europe; at the same time, Mussolini's Fascist Party was a major element on the political scene. The deadly Diana Theatre bombing by anarchists that year outraged many Italians and helped Mussolini become prime minister next year. The Fascists blamed it on "red rabble," or the USI, who had nothing to do with the bombing, and street battles became a prominent feature of Italian life for several years.[144] In 1925, Mussolini became a dictator and eliminated the USI.[145] In Germany, the Free Workers Union had over one hundred thousand members in the early 1920s, but it began disintegrating and had only several hundred left when Hitler was appointed chancellor in 1933. He immediately ordered most surviving members killed.[146]

Spain produced the world's largest, strongest, and most durable syndicalist movement, the National Confederation of Labor (CNT), based in Catalonia and Basque areas, both of which demanded more local autonomy. When General Franco revolted against Spain's Second Republic, the CNT supported the Republic. Some members became cabinet ministers, and others managed all the factories in some areas, the most significant attempt ever made to put syndicalist ideas into practice. Nazi Germany and Fascist Italy supported Franco, and the Soviet communists aided the Second Republic. But the communists unexpectedly moved against the CNT, killing and imprisoning many members, inadvertently helping General Franco win the bloody three-year war. Afterward, he killed thousands of syndicalists and put the rest in internment camps.[147]

Remaking the police forces was a third factor in the wave's decline. When police were only concerned with criminals, they responded to illegal actions after they occurred. But preemption or efforts to make it impossible for certain acts to happen became crucial in dealing with terrorists. Some policemen took their uniforms off to observe activities without being identified. The UK Special Branch, U.S. FBI, and Russian Okhrana were all created to deal with terror groups.

Undercover agents joined terrorist groups, a practice Alexsei Lopukhin, the head of the Russian police from 1902 to 1904, described as the very "foundation of police operation." "Political crimes unlike ordinary ones were marked by long-term clandestine planning compelling the police to take steps . . . to expose them in advance."[148] Many terrorists became police agents because, one police official explained, terrorists "naturally suspect each other and from their ranks the police [could] easily recruit agents. Their suspicion of each other contributes far more to their helplessness than to their safety." By 1912, the Russian government had "26,000 agents provocateurs" and an antiterrorist network of two hundred thousand people. The provocateurs aimed to stimulate internal tensions and mutual suspicions among terrorists, which would help police shape rebel policies. "Provocateurs often carried out actions that [alienated the public] from the revolutionary cause by shaming it and disgracing it."[149] In some cases, provocateurs sought people apparently ready to participate in terror acts. Police provocateurs would then get involved in "sting operations," inducing terrorists to commit actions they might not have done otherwise.

Russian and French police funded anarchist newspapers at home and abroad, hoping to provide "telephone cable[s] from the world in which the conspiracies were being planned, straight to the office of the Chief of Police."[150] Ironically, because the public knew the police were involved in such activities, the police exploited that fact to discredit authentic anarchist pamphlets believed dangerous by describing them as police products. Russian penetration efforts were so successful that a police agent, Yevno Azef, became the leader of the Terrorist Brigade from 1903 to 1908. When the Terrorist Brigade discovered his identity, the exposure demoralized the organization, and it disintegrated.

The double role agents played made it difficult to understand their commitments. The police found themselves confronted by unanticipated issues because in giving agents such enormous freedom they made it possible for the agent's individual interests to become a factor.

In Europe, torturing prisoners to gain information was common in medieval and early modern times.[151] Abolished in the eighteenth century, torture was revived and even appeared in states that had never used it before, for example, the United States. Did torture help or hinder the fight against terror? Officials often disagreed, but revelations about torture practices provoked public anger and stimulated radicals to seek revenge. The 1886 tortures in Montjich, for example, ordered by Spain's Prime Minister Antonio

Cánovas del Castillo, induced an Italian anarchist to come to Spain and assassinate him.

It should be noted finally that although new police practices were necessary to deal with terrorism, some practices aided the terrorist cause by stirring imaginary fears among the public, enabling terrorists to have greater destructive impact. A British vice consul declared "much of the violence of the Spanish anarchist movement must be attributed to the cruelty of police repression."[152] In Spain, a Black Hand plot to assassinate all the landowners in Andalusia ended in thousands being arrested, three hundred imprisoned, and eight executed—but the plot's very existence has been doubted.[153] The British Special Branch was the most effective and successful police program because it used the new tactics with great restraint, a program one scholar described "as the wonder of the world for thirty years."[154]

CONCLUSION

Revolutionary uprisings became international in Europe after the French Revolution, but only after terrorist activity began in the 1880s did the violence become global. The term "global" became part of the twentieth-century vocabulary, linked to the rise of the internet. But it was relevant earlier.

Two principal themes inspired the First Wave, "equality" and "nationalism." These purposes were understood differently in various contexts, which generated conflicts between and within terrorist groups. The egalitarian ethos ranged from anarchism to populism, with democratic and sometimes socialist connotations. Nationalist groups were important, but there were not many. I labeled the First Wave anarchist largely because the public normally described all terrorists as anarchists. All terrorists called their tactics "propaganda of the deed," an anarchist term, and several anarchist theorists played crucial roles in the wave's development. Populist groups like the Russian Narodnaya Volya, for example, acknowledged their debt to Bakunin, a major anarchist theorist.

First Wave terrorist groups had short lives. We have no definitive statistics on this matter. But it does seem that a group surviving five years had a relatively long life. IMRO existed for forty-one years, the longest in the wave, but it survived so long partly because nationalist groups tended to survive longer, and IMRO was willing to become a tool of successive Bulgarian governments. Clearly, IMRO's transformations would have astonished and angered its founders. Multiple entities emerged in most states. Some, like Germany and the United States, experienced a small number of incidents produced by lone wolves or very small networks, but those two states did not produce organized groups. No Russian group lasted long, but Russia experienced an intermittent history of terrorism for forty-one years.

Assassination was the distinctive, most commonly used tactic, for obvious reasons. The deeply embedded tradition of tyrannicide was important. Assassinations provided enormous publicity. The strikes were emotionally satisfying to assailants because their victims were so closely identified with the system. Assassination provided a good occasion for martyrdom, a key theme of the First Wave; the assassins often died in the attempt or were captured and sometimes had opportunities to display their commitment in court. Finally, extensive organizations with significant assets were not required; lone individuals could commit assassinations.

Over time, however, the limitations of assassination became clear. The enormous publicity became counterproductive. As preferred victims became better protected, people with less symbolic significance were chosen. The switch enabled groups to survive longer but did not bring success. IMRO was the group most reluctant to assassinate, a reluctance that contributed to its longevity. Ironically, its last act was assassinating King Alexander and the French foreign minister in 1933. To expand the range of tactics, hostage taking was suggested, but few incidents occurred because the practice was associated with ordinary criminal activity and had a historic link to offensive state practices.

Different groups produced different international responses depending on the conflicting interests and views of states. In the wave's third decade, the first international "war on terrorism" began with the 1904 St. Petersburg protocol. But many states, especially democratic ones, did not participate and often gave refuge to foreign terrorists who belonged to populist and nationalist groups from Russia and the Ottoman Empire, which were seen as despotic systems. States contiguous to those in Eastern Europe and Asia Minor were inclined to help nationalist groups, even socialist ones, as the Bulgarian and Russian experiences demonstrate.

Terrorism helped precipitate at least two international wars. The Balkan War (1913) pitted Balkan Christian states against the Ottoman Empire, a response to IMRO activities. Then, of course, there was World War I. The Versailles Treaty ending World War I established a new international order, dividing the defeated empires on the European continent into nine nation-states: Austria, Hungary, Czechoslovakia, Yugoslavia, Estonia, Latvia, Lithuania, Poland, and Finland. The defeated empires had experienced much separatist terrorist activity, including the act precipitating World War I, but the creation of new states virtually extinguished those efforts.

First wave terrorism was a "youth movement," and most groups originated among university students, largely physical science majors. Japan provided the principal exception to this pattern; there, most participants came from poor families with little education. Women were especially significant in the Russian groups, a fact that inspired similar events elsewhere, even in places where women had no previous role in politics or violence. Surprisingly, India was the home of the first all-female group. But no country produced as many female terrorists as Russia. Students often went abroad for education to democratic states, where physical sciences were better developed and interaction with others was easy. Terrorist exiles provided instruction in foreign cities, especially Paris, and democratic countries made no serious efforts to stop the practices.

No group achieved its stated end or a mutual agreement. The Chinese seem to be an exception, in that assassinations helped overthrow the imperial dynasty, but the Chinese Revolutionary Alliance's military and political efforts were most crucial. Remember, too, that the number of attempted assassinations there was small; approximately fifteen in a seven-year period, and only a few were successful. More terror attacks might have produced more obstacles to success.

3

THE SECOND WAVE: ANTICOLONIAL, 1919–1960s

When . . . President [Wilson] talks of "self-determination," what unit has he in mind? Does he mean a race, a territorial area, or a community? Without a definite unit which is practical, application of this principle is dangerous to peace and stability. . . . The more I think about the President's declaration as the right of "self-determination," the more convinced I am of the danger of putting such ideas into the minds of certain races. It is bound to be the basis of impossible demands on the peace conference and create trouble in many lands.

—ROBERT LANSING, U.S. SECRETARY OF STATE, 1915–1920

After World War II, terrorist activity emerged again partly because the Atlantic Charter stated that the victorious powers would not extend their territories and that all peoples had a right to self-determination. The United Nations replaced the League of Nations and implemented those principles. When the war was over, some victorious powers dismantled portions of their overseas empires. Territories not released became the sites of many successful terrorist campaigns, and the wave ended when government energies, not those of terrorists, dissipated. Most terrorist successes were incomplete, however, partly because bloody ethnic divisions in colonial areas persisted in the new states.

DIFFERENCES BETWEEN THE FIRST AND SECOND WAVES

The Second Wave's precipitating event was the Versailles Treaty, which created a new world order, replacing the one created by the 1815 Congress of Vienna. "Self-determination" became the crucial principle of legitimacy and still largely "guides world politics today."[1] New European nation-states— Poland, Austria, Hungary, Czechoslovakia, Latvia, Lithuania, Estonia, Finland, and Yugoslavia—were created from the defeated European multiethnic empires, the scenes of many nineteenth-century nationalist uprisings and terrorist groups, as we saw in chapter 2. To eliminate Europe's nationalist problem, the Versailles Treaty also expanded the boundaries of some existing states—France, Italy, and Romania. The Ottoman Empire was dissolved, and new states emerged in its various territories.

Russia did, however, recognize the right of self-determination. Czarist Russia tolerated non-Russian communities, but after Narodnaya Volya assassinated Alexander II, Alexander III began a "Russification" policy, which his successor, Nicholas II, continued. Initially, Lenin embraced the *Communist Manifesto*'s statement "the Proletarians have no fatherland" and did not expect nationalism to survive capitalism. But dismayed by the antagonism to the czar's most recent nationalist policy, he recognized the significance of self-determination for ethnic communities and in 1922 created the Union of Soviet Socialist Republics (USSR), a "confederation" of Russia, Belorussia, Ukraine, and the Trans Caucasian Federation, which was later divided into Georgia, Azerbaijan, and Armenia.

The Versailles Treaty also created European nationalist problems. Millions of Germans became minorities in the new states. One-third of the Hungarian population now lived outside Hungary. Many "new" minorities found themselves in difficult situations because the new governments were intent on defining the national character of the countries, often at the expense of minority ethnic groups. In 1921, Yugoslavia began efforts to create a national state but never succeeded. No Armenian state was created from the Ottoman territories because European support was weak, and the new state of Turkey strongly resisted any such plans.[2]

Terrorism developed a new geography—the overseas empires of victorious states. There were a few exceptions; Yugoslavia and Italy, the geographic scene of some First Wave groups, were also responsible for homegrown Second Wave problems. The Second Wave's timing also differed. First Wave groups seemed to appear everywhere at once, giving the impression of being intimately connected, a view strengthened when immigrants employed terror in their new homes or when they returned to their old homes to seek targets. But in the Second Wave, considerable time often separated different campaigns. Immigrant attacks ceased, though diasporas did supply money and political support. Groups no longer trained one another; individuals did not leave one group to join a foreign one. The absence of direct ties between foreign terrorist groups enabled local ones to bond better with crucial domestic and diaspora constituencies. Foreign state sympathies expanded significantly, because there was no reason to think an "international conspiracy" existed, a view the public emphasized in the First Wave, and international attacks diminished greatly. And for the first time, terrorist groups used violence against each other.

President Wilson's first draft of the Covenant for the League of Nations suggests he believed that national self-determination would bring peace.[3] World War I's victors (France, Britain, Japan, Belgium, Australia, and New Zealand) were given Mandates to monitor defeated empires' territories in Asia and Africa until the native populations were able to govern themselves.[4] Self-determination-seeking rebels thus had sympathetic significant international audiences, a sympathy that grew immensely after World War II, when the United Nations replaced the League.

Terrorist groups were larger, more formally organized, and more centralized than those of the First Wave. The Second Wave had no Switzerland to provide sanctuary for all groups. Only states neighboring a colonial territory provided sanctuary, for example, Tunisia and Morocco for Algerians, Greece for Cypriots, etc. Raids were frequently launched from those sanctuaries. The two waves had different rhythms. In the First Wave, terrorist activity grew more intense in the first and second decades; in the third decade it began to dissipate, and it was gone by the end of the fourth decade. The Second Wave produced less activity in its first two decades but in the third and fourth decades, terrorism increased greatly, a process inspired by a second major political event: World War II. The Second Wave ended when governments agreed to leave their colonial territories.

The Irish, who emphasized nationalism above everything else, were the model for most groups. The nom de guerre of Yitzak Shamir, the leader of the Israeli group Lehi (Fighters for the Freedom of Israel) was "Michael", to honor the IRA leader Michael Collins.[5] (Shamir later became an Israeli prime minister.) The Hindustan Republican Army (HRA) took its name from the IRA, and every Indian group found the IRA's experience instructive. A police officer noted, "Terrorism in Bengal has altered its complexion since the early days. For years assassinations and dacoities [gang robberies] were as much as terrorists hoped to affect. Since then, they have studied the Irish Rebellion and have enlarged their ideas, which now include attacks on police armories, treasuries, and district headquarters."[6]

The belief that terrorists are elements of a global revolutionary tradition persisted. Menachem Begin, the Israeli Irgun (National Military Organization) leader, wrote, "All the world's fighters for freedom are one family," a sentiment echoed by Georgios Grivas, a former general in the Greek army in both world wars, who led EOKA (National Organization of Cypriot Fighters) and was committed to rejoining Cyprus with Greece.[7]

Despite the significance of the Irish model, Israelis, Cypriots, Indians, Algerians, etc. emphasized heroes in their own national traditions more.[8] Grivas's nom de guerre was "Dighenis," a Cypriot pre-Christian mythical hero who guarded Alexander the Great's empire.[9] EOKA recruits "swore a loyalty oath on the Bible in the presence of a [Greek Orthodox] priest."[10] Many more Second Wave groups linked nationalism and religion than First

Wave, for example, the Irish, Cypriots, Jews, Burmese, etc. The First Wave's radical egalitarian theme emerged very late and was limited to Aden and Portuguese territories.

Women were usually no longer visible as terrorists, which reflected their subsidiary political roles in the cultures of the populations under colonial rule. They were restricted to messenger, intelligence, and publicity roles, which they performed well. Michael Brennan wrote that the "flying columns" would have collapsed without the women's group Cumann na mban. "In dispatch carrying, scouting and intelligence work, all of which are highly dangerous, they did far more than the soldiers. . . . The more dangerous the work the more willing they were to do it."[11] They hid arms; provided safe houses for IRA members; helped run the Dail Courts and local authorities; produced the *Irish Bulletin*, the official newspaper; and paved the way for women to gain political influence in the Irish government. In Algeria, women had enormous advantages over men in getting through the French lines to transport explosives. Women were combatants only in India and Puerto Rico. The Indians created a female terrorist group, the Women's Society, with seventy-one members, the first such terrorist unit in history, which, far from being an egalitarian gesture, reflected Indian desires to segregate the sexes.[12] Earlier, women were crucial in Gandhi's nonviolent-resistance movement, which successfully competed with terrorist groups. Ironically, the Puerto Rican Nationalist Party, an all-woman group, became violent against the United States. Its Daughters of Freedom branch, largely devoted to political activities, occasionally led men in some important strikes. Women also had had roles in the nineteenth-century Puerto Rican uprisings against Spain.

Second Wave groups largely abandoned assassination and developed more effective strategies and novel tactics.[13] But efforts to create a nation-state frequently generated new social divisions and intensified existing ones, as President Wilson's secretary of state, John Lansing, predicted they would. Those tensions sometimes produced serious violent conflicts between terrorist groups for the first time.

TERRORISM BETWEEN THE WORLD WARS

In Europe after World War, I nationalism produced new problems. A defeated Germany was forced to cede territories containing many Germans to the new states of Czechoslovakia and Poland, an issue that inspired the Nazi Party to regain those territories. Italy, a victorious power, felt entitled to more territories than those it received, and the Fascist Party exploited that grievance. The Nazis and Fascists launched successful efforts to take over their governments.[14] When the Nazis and Fascists captured their states, each introduced a form of state terror, and the Nazi form became the most devastating the world had ever experienced. Before taking over their states, the Nazis and Fascists created large, violent organizations. In 1922, Mussolini had two hundred thousand Blackshirts, who got their name from the color of their uniforms. In 1933, Hitler insisted his five hundred thousand Stormtroopers[15] wear uniforms, so as to avoid being considered a secret organization.[16] Since our concern here is with underground groups, Nazi and Fascist activities will not be discussed.[17]

The Irish, who produced the first Second Wave uprising, had a long history of insurrections against the British. Inspired by the French Revolution, Wolfe Tone led a military uprising in 1798 that became the "inspiration" for subsequent Irish independence movements, to "unite the whole people of Ireland . . . abolish the memory of all past dissensions and . . . substitute the common name of Irishmen [for] Protestant, Catholic, and Dissenter."[18] But the disastrous Easter Uprising during World War I induced the Irish to attempt nonviolent means again. In the elections held a month after World War I ended, the Sinn Fein Party, committed to independence, gained an overwhelming majority of the Irish seats in the British Parliament. But the Irish MPs refused to go to London and instead established an Irish parliament, the Dáil Éireann, which issued a declaration of independence. In 1919, the Irish delegation at Versailles argued the self-determination principle justified Irish independence. But the treaty did not "include Ireland in its list of small nations with a right to self-determination," a "rejection severely hampering" Dáil members, who had

argued that Sinn Fein's majority was irresistible, making violence unnecessary and counterproductive. The United States, anxious to maintain the
British alliance, refused to recognize the Irish state, to the bitter anger of
the influential Irish-American community.[19] Only communist Russia recognized Ireland at that point, an act alienating other states—a response the
British exploited.[20]

Violent strikes began gradually, as the rebels did not want to alienate
the public. But by 1920, most believed that political means alone would
not work, and the Irish Republican Army (IRA) initiated a terror campaign. The principal target was the police (the Royal Irish Constabulary);
members were assassinated in ambushes and their facilities destroyed. To
reinforce the constabulary, the British created a poorly trained police
force known as the "Black and Tans," which committed many atrocities,
striking indiscriminately those thought to be aiding rebels.

> What [the IRA did] was to keep the country in an uproar, drain off a
> substantial portion of the British forces at great cost in time, nerves, and
> gold, and through a series of pinpricks, delight the Irish and enrage the
> British. Since the British now took their vengeance openly, every IRA
> action almost guaranteed . . . a further instance of British misconduct
> retailed to the world and an increasingly uneasy public in Britain. And
> each example of Tan terror renewed the determination of the Irish
> people to resist Saxon arrogance and brutality.[21]

In the end, a "unit in every parish and 21,000 Volunteers waited for the
call."[22] It is easier to kill policemen than prominent figures because there
are many more police and they cannot be as well protected, enabling attackers to escape.

But this advantage of dealing with the police also made it difficult for
Second Wave assassins to become martyrs like their First Wave forebears
when killed in their assaults or after sentencing in the courts. However,
Irish "hunger strikes" helped stimulate a similar outcome. In the First Wave,
Russians used hunger strikes to protest "unfair" prison conditions and
demand prisoner-of-war status. Irish hunger strikers were more effective

than the Russians. Thomas Ashe and forty others demanded "prisoner-of-war" status. After five days of fasting, he died when prison guards force fed him. The authorities then gave the hunger strikers the rights demanded, and the strike ceased. At the inquest, an Irish jury condemned the prison authorities for the "inhuman and dangerous operation . . . and other acts of unfeeling and barbaric conduct."[23] This technique "effectively destroyed the British policy of mass internment. The prisoner release demoralized the armed forces and contributed to the outbreak of extra-judicial killings and destruction which further escalated the war."[24] A year later, Terence Mac-Swiney, lord mayor of Cork, began a hunger strike after being arrested for sedition. He died after seventy-four days, and his death gained much international attention. After many Americans threatened to boycott British goods, the German and French conducted protests, and Latin American states asked the Pope to intervene, the United Kingdom negotiated a settlement.

The Anglo-Irish Peace Treaty (1921) created the Irish Free State, a dominion within the British Commonwealth, but the result did not fulfill Wolfe Tone's dream to "unite the whole people of Ireland." Those who refused to accept the treaty waged a nine-month disastrous campaign against their former comrades, now Irish government officials. It began as a conventional war; ultimately the Irish government was victorious, with British help. The IRA returned to rural areas, but a public tired of violence refused to support the rebels. Oddly, in its unsuccessful antitreaty campaign, the IRA inflicted more fatalities on Irish troops (about eight hundred over the nine-month civil war) than they had on the British, who lost six hundred over the three-year campaign.[25] After failing to change the treaty, the IRA mounted terror efforts in Northern Ireland and demanded that the Dominion of Ireland become the Irish Republic. In 1939, it mounted a two-year campaign largely in Britain. There were over two hundred attacks, mostly on symbolic targets with minimum casualties, but no political support materialized.

Revolts developed elsewhere in European overseas empires. Most did not involve terrorism, but looking at them helps underscore the conflicting internal tensions later associated with many Second Wave terrorist campaigns. The Versailles Treaty encouraged Egypt's 1919 revolution, a very different enterprise from the Irish uprising. Under British rule since 1882, the Egyptians sent a delegation to Versailles.[26] But the British interned the delegation's members, who in response organized illegal demonstrations and general strikes, in which some eight hundred Egyptians and thirty-one Europeans died. The violence subsided only when the delegates were allowed to proceed. The Egyptians achieved little at Versailles. But the next year, the Milner Report promised independence,[27] and in 1923 Egypt became "independent," though "the British maintained control over . . . foreign relations . . . minorities and relationship with Sudan, then part of Egypt." In 1937, the League welcomed Egypt as a member, where it appealed "improper" British behavior.

The Middle East, as part of the Ottoman Empire, experienced virtually no violence for centuries. The population was divided into religious subdivisions, or millets, to administer civil law. But the League divided the Arab population into three Mandates, which ultimately served the interests of two colonial powers. Britain governed Iraq and Palestine, while France administered Syria. Lebanon later separated from Syria to become a second French Mandate in 1926. Iraq devolved into a "state of anarchy" in 1920 as Sunni, Shi'a, Kurdish, and various tribal elements clashed. The British created an Iraqi army composed of Ottoman army veterans, hoping its special character would enable some semblance of Iraqi nationality to emerge and buttress a British-established monarchy.[28] The army ended the violence but later rebelled successfully against British policies, and Iraq became a League of Nations member. The effort to create a Syrian nationality produced a more violent picture. The Druze community tried to withdraw from Syria. Hostile ethnic elements tried to push the French out, and the 1925–1926 conflict provoked such indiscriminate French responses that the League threatened to revoke France's right to retain its Mandate. "This social fragmentation was by no means a recent phenomenon; it had existed for centuries . . . [and] to be successful required a form of cooperation with which the Syrians had no experience."[29]

Tensions in Palestine grew intense when the British foreign secretary issued the Balfour Declaration (1917), promising Jewish immigrants they could establish a homeland there. In response, an "Arab nationalism with a loyalty based on common race and creed rather than geography," embracing the entire Arab world, emerged.[30] Cyprus, a part of the British Empire since 1878, generated anticolonial violence initially in 1921. When the British refused to discuss union with Greece (*enosis*), an economic boycott was organized. A decade later, the Greek Orthodox Church, the major Cypriot political force for centuries under Ottoman rule, organized angry demonstrations when the United Kingdom abolished the church's right to tax.[31] Again *enosis* was demanded, but Cyprus's Turkish inhabitants used violence against the Greeks, and the riots ceased.

Southeast Asia had special features that bolstered the resistance of European imperial powers to self-determination movements. One was an anxiety that those movements would become associated with the newly created Soviet Union. In 1926, the Communist Party of Indonesia (PKI) began a violent assault against Dutch rule, the first Southeast Asian revolt after World War I. Members went to Moscow to enlist support but never got it, partly because the PKI was also associated with bourgeois nationalists.[32] The communist Vietnamese Nghệ Tinh produced a series of revolts, strikes, and demonstrations against the French and Vietnamese landlords in 1930 and 1931. Communist groups such as the Annam Communist Party, Indochinese Communist League, and Communist Party of Indochina had also already been mobilizing workers and peasants, fanning discontent in these areas.

A second anxiety was Japanese expansionism. The League of Nations gave Japan the former German Marianas and the Caroline and Marshall Islands, which Japan had seized in World War I. In 1931, Japan defied the League of Nations by invading Manchuria to set up a puppet state, Manchukuo, under the Chinese emperor, Puyi. In 1937, Japan created a similar Mongolian puppet state in Inner Mongolia and then invaded China, creating a three-way war between Japan, communists under Mao Tze-tung, and nationalists under Chiang Kai-shek.

The Philippines's status provoked a third anxiety. President Wilson had promised that this American territory would be given independence, but the Dutch, with colonies in the East Indies, feared that would stimulate movements in territories throughout the region and provoke Japan to become involved.[33] The United States remained in the Philippines.

Saya San, a former Buddhist monk, led the "Saya San Rebellion" of 1930–1932 in British Burma, promising supporters he would restore the Burmese monarchy and revitalize Buddhism. Religious elements, infuriated by the British policy of separating church and state, organized a series of riots, which has been regarded as one of Southeast Asia's quintessential anticolonial movements.[34] Thousands were killed. Since the British had incorporated Burma into India, the unrest also had an anti-India dimension, and the rebels insisted the British stop using Indians to administer Burma. The British then separated Burma from India.[35] In the Cypriot and Burmese cases, religion stimulated ethnic clashes.

India experienced two significant campaigns, the first from 1919 to 1925 and the second from 1930 to 1934. The better castes supplied most of the recruits, and the First Wave groups Samiti and Jugantar reappeared in new forms. The Samiti became the Hindustan Republican Army (HRA), but hostility to Muslims persisted partly because Muslims had vital administrative roles and supported British rule more. The Jugantar became the Marxist Hindustan Socialist Republican Association (HSRA), attracting new elements but alienating many potential sympathizers. The IRA became the model for these Second Wave Indian groups: as mentioned earlier, the HRA took its name from the IRA. Significant conflict between the HRA and HSRA emerged, and after a decade both violent campaigns failed.

HSRA changed its strategy dramatically. Two leaders "dropped bombs carefully designed not to kill" in the Central Legislative Assembly building in New Delhi.[36] They handed over their guns and did not resist arrest. In prison they went on a hunger strike to change their status from criminal inmates to political prisoners, citing the Irish martyr Terence MacSwiney, the mayor of Cork, as their model.[37] Twelve republican prisoners joined them; one died in the process, but after sixty-three days they achieved their purpose. During their trial they explained they would not take the life of an innocent person. "They could have wiped out a majority of the members of the Legislative Assembly and could have shot scattered police officers milling around the Assembly in confusion after the blast."[38] Though later executed for their early activities as terrorists, they became martyrs for many Indians, intensifying the longing for independence. HSRA gave up terror and became India's Communist Party.[39]

The Indian situation produced another important element. In 1883, to overcome deep caste, ethnic, and religious differences on the subcontinent that made it difficult to govern, the British organized the Indian National Congress. The first session had seventy-two delegates, representing each Indian province. In time, the Indian National Congress became radical, but it officially rejected Indian terrorist activity, which greatly divided the subcontinent. In 1915, when Mahatma Gandhi returned to India after twenty-one years in South Africa, the Congress Party greeted him as a hero for organizing a successful passive-resistance movement, Satyagraha (Devotion to the Truth), which had gained civil rights for South Africa's Indian immigrants. He argued Satyagraha's success in India would depend on getting the masses involved, especially the poor in rural areas, something the Congress Party had ignored. To attract the poor, one had to deal with their economic problems. Gandhi became committed to helping the Bihar farmers, who were forced to grow indigo and subjected to outrageous government violence if they refused. Many Indians joined the nonviolent protest movement, and the British changed their policy. Then floods devastated a village in Gujarat, and a signature campaign emerged; peasants pledged to cease paying taxes while the floods persisted, a pledge that all the area's ethnic and caste communities endorsed, forcing the government to waive taxes until the famine ended. Sikhs in 1919 organized a violent demonstration against conscription and heavy war taxes. The British outlawed demonstrations, but a few days later the Sikh Baisakhi festival occurred, attracting thousands. British troops fired on the crowd, killing 329.[40] Gandhi then became the Congress Party's leader and insisted that Satyagraha be employed in all protests. At the 1928 Congress meeting, Gandhi declared that the British must grant India dominion status and started a campaign against the salt tax, which gave the British a monopoly on the collection and manufacture of salt. Even though salt was freely available to those living on the coast via the evaporation of seawater, they were forced to purchase it from the colonial government. For Gandhi, the salt tax was deeply symbolic, since salt was used by nearly every Indian, to replace salt lost by sweating in India's tropical climate. The salt tax hurt the poorest Indians most. Gandhi said, "Next to air and water, salt is perhaps the greatest necessity of life." He marched 368 kilometers against the salt tax, and thousands joined him.[41] British cloth and goods were boycotted, and the British responded by censoring correspondence and declaring the Congress Party and associated organizations illegal.

The Salt March transformed the Congress into a mass organization, but it did not win any major immediate British concessions. Nonetheless, British and world opinion increasingly began to recognize the legitimacy of claims for self-rule, and Jawaharlal Nehru, who two decades later became India's first prime minister, considered the Salt March crucial in changing Indian attitudes.[42] Despite its success in India, Gandhi's form of resistance had no real influence on other colonial situations, partly because Satyagraha is very difficult to organize and partly because terrorism was more effective at generating popular support in other colonial territories than it was in India. But Gandhi influenced other political efforts later. He inspired Martin Luther King Jr.'s effort to gain civil rights for African Americans in the 1960s and helped Nelson Mandela, Gandhi's South African disciple, eliminate apartheid.

The Arab Revolt of 1936–1939 in Palestine was a serious uprising against the Balfour Declaration.[43] As Nazis began the Holocaust, the Jewish flow to Palestine greatly increased, infuriating Arabs, who demanded the British end immigration and create a sovereign Arab state. The uprising began with a six-month general strike, which failed because Arab and Jewish civil servants continued working. In the revolt's second phase, armed bands from neighboring countries attacked the Jews and the British administration. But the revolt "lacked the disciplining spine of a developed political underground" that could unite Arabs.[44] Groups often attacked one another, especially for loot. Deep divisions along family, clan, regional, class, and religious (Muslim and Christian) lines persisted. Arabs inflicted virtually as many casualties on Arabs as on Jews; 10 percent of the Arab population was killed, wounded, or exiled, a fact that astonished the British Peel Commission investigating the uprising. "The novelty . . . is attack by Arab on

Arab. For an Arab to be suspected of a lukewarm adherence to the nationalist cause is to invite a visit from a body of gunmen."[45] "Finally, Arabs organized 'Peace Bands' [which] willingly cooperated with troops in fighting the rebels. The rebels reacted by using more frightening methods, and thus alienated themselves further from the villagers and townsmen alike."[46]

British-trained Jews were crucial in putting down the revolt. Participants like Moshe Dayan, who became a famous Israeli general afterward, used their training to organize the Israeli army after independence. The Arab revolt was crushed months before World War II began, but the British, intent on keeping the Arab world's loyalty, issued a 1939 White Paper limiting annual Jewish immigration to 75,000 for the next five years and stating that Jewish immigration would be stopped in 1944. This set the stage for Israeli resistance.

In 1939, a radically new IRA strategy, the S-Plan (Sabotage Plan) to gain Northern Ireland, emerged; "Irish blood would not be spilled on Irish soil." After a "Formal Ultimatum" from the "Government of the Irish Republic," warning the British to withdraw from all of Ireland, the campaign began.[47] The British public was the target; the army and police were not attacked. The belief was that a continuous series of bombings against industrial and communication institutions would exhaust British patience and security resources, compelling negotiations.[48] A public relations campaign to win the support of the Irish "exiles" in the United States was planned to create more pressure on the British. In a fifteen-month campaign, three hundred explosions occurred in British cities, killing seven and injuring ninety-six. Ultimately, the IRA realized the campaign had virtually destroyed its organization; alienated potential sympathizers, including many deported Irish workers; and made the British more resolute. The Irish Free State, apprehensive that British tensions with Germany might induce Britain to secure its western borders by taking over the island, refused to provide sanctuaries and interned IRA members. The IRA contacted Nazi intelligence officers. The crucial Irish-American support evaporated when World War II began. The campaign "brought nothing but harm to Ireland and the IRA," the S-Plan's author, Seamus O'Donovan, admitted two decades later.[49]

The League of Nations' existence encouraged rebellion, but its actions did not. Its principal concern was with groups striking targets across international borders, which did not occur in the Irish, Indian, and Palestinian situations. When IMRO assassinated Alexander I of Yugoslavia and Foreign Minister Barthou of France, the League, inspired by memories of how World War I started, acted. It tried to pass rules that defined terrorism as the attack by foreigners on prominent political figures, such as heads of state, and established an international court to try terrorists. Liberal states (for example, the United Kingdom and Belgium) were opposed because they did not want to make it illegal to strike despotic governments. Also, two League members (Hungary and Italy) had encouraged the assassination, creating considerable anxieties that another European war would occur if responsible parties were tried in an international court.[50] Parenthetically, the effort to define all assassinations as terrorism indicates that this tactic had become politically repulsive, a lesson most Second Wave groups learned quickly.

WORLD WAR II AND ITS AFTERMATH

World War II dramatically increased the significance of self-determination. The Atlantic Charter between the United Kingdom and the United States, drafted before the United States entered the war and later accepted by the victors, defined the war's goals: no territorial aggrandizement, no territorial changes made against the wishes of the people, restoration of self-government to those deprived, free access to raw material, removal of many trade restrictions, global cooperation to secure better economic and social conditions for all, freedom from fear and want, freedom of the seas, and abandonment of the use of force. American and British populations greeted the Atlantic Charter enthusiastically.[51]

After World War II, no Mandates were created; overseas territories were recognized either as sovereign states (for example, Libya, Ethiopia, and Korea) or reunited with their national homelands (for example, Manchuria with China). The victorious Allies transformed their own overseas empires quickly; most were dismantled within twenty-five years. In 1946, Jordan (part of the Palestine Mandate) became a sovereign state. India became independent in 1947, but one of its territories withdrew to become Pakistan, a process in which some 12 million became displaced persons and perhaps half a million died.[52] Then Ceylon (Sri Lanka) became a dominion. Burma became a republic named Myanmar. France gave Lebanon and Syria independence in 1946. In Africa, the Gold Coast achieved independence as Ghana (1957) and Nigeria became independent (1960). By 1970, twenty-seven new African states had been created.

The United States had four major overseas territories. The Philippines became independent in 1947, and in 1959 Alaska and Hawaii became the forty-ninth and fiftieth states in the union. Puerto Rico was a more difficult case; in the 1930s it produced anticolonial riots and bombings. After World War II, the Puerto Rican Nationalist Party began its independence campaign. In 1950, various uprisings killed twenty-eight, and the Nationalist Party attempted to assassinate President Harry Truman, hoping to stimulate international attention.[53] In 1953, 82 percent of Puerto Rico's voters approved a commonwealth status for the island, but the campaign for independence continued. The Nationalist Party attacked the U.S. Capitol, wounding five congresspersons. Women terrorists were prominent. Blanca Canales was the chief figure in the Jayuaya Revolt (the most violent episode of 1950); she led her group to the town's plaza, where she raised the Puerto Rican flag, declaring Puerto Rico a republic. She killed a police officer and wounded three.[54] Lolita Lebrón, who led the assault on Congress in 1954, was sentenced to life imprisonment, but President Carter pardoned her twenty-five years later.[55] While the overwhelming number of Puerto Ricans never wanted independence, over time its commonwealth status generated some antagonism. A referendum in 2012 gave Puerto Ricans three choices. Sixty-one percent wanted to become a state in federal union, 33 percent wanted to remain a commonwealth, and only 5 percent wanted independence.[56] But the United States refused to allow Puerto Rico its first choice.

These postwar transformations were not always a direct consequence of violence against victorious colonial powers, though the likelihood that they would need to fight at some point if they did not withdraw was critical for governments still recovering from World War II and whose home populations had important self-determination sympathies.[57] Sometimes when a colonial power decided not to grant a territory independence, some other territories benefited. For example, when France decided to hold Algeria, it granted Tunisia and Morocco independence because it did not want to fight all three at the same time. Had France realized that those countries would later provide sanctuary to Algerian terrorists, would France have given them independence?

The United Nations pushed for self-determination much more than the League, partly because all former colonial territories became UN members.[58] The United States, which had not joined the League, was a major UN player and pushed hard for self-determination. When the British decided it no longer wanted to administer the Palestine Mandate, the United Nations was given authority to devise a solution for conflicting Jewish and Arab claims. The League could not end conquest, as the Italian success in Ethiopia (1935–1939) showed, but the new UN world did, a fact of enormous and often forgotten importance, clearly signifying that empires could no longer be created or expanded. Only two conquests became legitimate. Both involved colonial areas: India's 1961 conquest of Goa, a Portuguese colony on the Indian subcontinent, and Morocco's 1959 capture of a portion of Spain's Moroccan territory. East Timor, a former Portuguese colony that became independent, was conquered by Indonesia in 1975, but the United Nations intervened in 2002, and East Timor regained independence. Israel's 1981 effort to incorporate the Golan Heights, a Syrian territory, was not recognized as legitimate. But Israel did not withdraw, and President Reagan of the United States supported Israel.

The Cold War added a new and crucial international ingredient. The United States and the Soviet Union competed to gain credit for dissolving empires. The Soviet position concealed a paradox. It was not recognized as a colonial power because it had no overseas possessions, imperialism's most conspicuous feature. Lenin had made important nationalities "constituent republics" within the Soviet Union, "demonstrating Marxism-Leninism had solved the nationality problem."[59] Soviet republics had a "right to secede." The Soviets dominated Eastern European states differently; East Germany, Hungary, and Czechoslovakia were supposedly independent, but the Soviets subdued their brief insurrections in the 1950s and 1960s.

The Cold War shaped responses to colonial uprisings. President Truman became apprehensive that British Palestine policies created a "mood of desperation," driving Jewish terrorists into Moscow's arms. The Soviets subsidized Lehi, and the Irgun sought Moscow's support, leading Americans to pressure the British for a quick solution.[60] Algeria displayed a similar picture. Initially, the United States accepted France's view that the Algerian conflict was an "internal problem" because Algerians were French citizens and many Europeans lived there.[61] But when the Soviets began backing the FLN (National Liberation Front), the U.S. position changed. The French described the FLN as a "communist group," but the United States distanced itself from France, especially when Egypt, Libya, and Tunisia became deeply committed to the FLN. Senator John F. Kennedy introduced a Senate resolution in 1957 supporting Algerian independence, stating, "Western imperialism [*not* the Soviet Union] is the greatest challenge to American foreign policy." He accused Eisenhower's administration of retreating "from the principles of independence and anticolonialism, an accusation that provided powerful ammunition to Middle East and Asia anti-Western sentiments. No foreign affairs speech by Senator Kennedy ever attracted more attention."[62] Subsequently, the United States said that it could negotiate directly with the FLN to end the crisis, an offer France spurned. Despite strenuous French objections, the United States and United Kingdom gave arms to Tunisia, the most important FLN sanctuary, "without which the FLN would have been crushed."[63] When Kennedy became president in 1961, he established direct contact with the FLN and warmly welcomed Ben Bella, its "founding father," to America. But in Malaya and Aden, anxiety about communist involvement had a different effect. In these cases, the United States supported British resistance.

World War II's events suggested that terror tactics might provoke less antagonism than they had earlier. The Allies sometimes deliberately targeted civilians when bombing cities. Hiroshima and Nagasaki suffered atom bomb attacks. The Allies supported underground resistance movements with intelligence and military aid, including personnel (for example, in France, Poland, Yugoslavia, Greece, Norway, and Belgium). Underground resistance was not called terrorism partly because it was directed against the Nazis, and the targets were largely military ones, though when resistance fighters wore German uniforms, the rules of war were violated.[64] Former underground resistance members were also very active in postwar politics and more sympathetic to anticolonial groups.[65]

Most colonial territories secured independence peacefully or with minor violence.[66] Special circumstances explain how the ten terrorist campaigns we will discuss were fought and resolved. World War II also created conflicting moral obligations. Protestants in Northern Ireland strongly supported British war efforts, making it difficult to ignore their desire to remain in the United Kingdom. European settlers in Rhodesia and Kenya behaved similarly. In the Palestine Mandate, a Jewish legion fought alongside British forces, and Arabs did not aid the Allies. The Holocaust had a major effect too. UN Resolution 181, which finally allowed Israel to become a state, was the "Western civilization's gesture of repentance . . . by those nations that realized they might have done more to limit the scale of Jewish tragedy during World War II."[67]

But the United Kingdom had promised Arabs that Jewish immigration would be terminated in 1944. Even though World War II was still being fought, the agony of Holocaust refugees induced Zionist resistance to the United Kingdom. The Irgun and Lehi initiated the activity and were later joined by Haganah, linked to the Jewish Agency, an elected body recognized as the Jewish community's representative. Palestinians kept out of World War II, hoping the combatants would weaken one another. But Menachem Begin, Irgun's leader, said, "Until we found our own means of manufacturing substantial quantities of explosives—the main weapon in the struggle for liberation—and apart from what we 'borrowed' from the British themselves, the major part . . . was acquired from Arab supporters."

Begin prohibited the Irgun from hitting British targets in Arab areas. Irgun members only received weapons moments before an operation was authorized, reducing the possibility that individuals or units would choose their own targets. Begin argued one should not strike Arabs; otherwise, Arab states would intervene when the Jewish population was divided and weak. After a four-year struggle, the British returned the Mandate to the United Nations, which proposed the "Two State Solution" in 1948,[68] one Jews accepted but Arab residents refused, leading Arab states to invade the Jewish area to regain the entire territory. The new Israeli state repelled them. Seventy thousand Arabs left Palestine; many were forced out. The territorial issue remains unresolved.

Cyprus, the principal British base in the Middle East after the Suez Canal was lost, produced the next terrorist struggle (1951–1955). Cypriots demanded union with Greece, but one-fifth of the population was Turkish, and EOKA authorized strikes against them. Turkey, a neighbor, became very hostile, and since it was a crucial element in NATO, most NATO allies supported Turkey. After four years of terror, General Georgios Grivas's partner, Archbishop Makarios, "negotiated a solution with the British which Grivas . . . furiously opposed and . . . contained a provision for his exile. Cyprus would become an independent state and Britain would retain its base. But Grivas remained committed to unity with Greece and formed a new organization, EOKA B, which tried to overturn Cyprus' new government." Enraged Turks invaded the island, splitting it into two states, a situation that still exists despite repeated reunification efforts.[69]

Britain freed Ghana and Sudan in sub-Saharan Africa quickly, but Kenya was a more difficult case because many white settlers lived there. In 1952, elements of the Kikuyu, Kenya's largest tribe and one-third of the population, created the Mau-Mau,[70] which alienated all outsiders by swearing, "If I am ordered to kill I will no matter who it is. In the event of my killing anyone I will cut their heads off, extract the eyeballs, and drink the liquid from them."[71] The British understood Jewish and Cypriot terrorists to have rational, if politically unacceptable, goals. But Mau-Mau practices seemed so bizarre that one could not believe their ultimate end made sense. It "offered no alternative except anarchy. The Mau-Mau was collective hysteria and must be brought to hell without compromise. . . . The clamor from the Left that the Mau-Mau was a national liberation movement was viewed as either the foolishness of the ignorant or a political maneuver by callous men."[72] Mau-Mau terror was often directed against Kikuyu tribesmen, particularly Christian converts cooperating with the British. The most conspicuous atrocity occurred in the town of Lari (1953). All victims were civilians; eighty-four were killed, thirty-one of those horribly mutilated with knives. "This raid with its mutilated corpses and burned-out huts became the lynchpin of British propaganda to discredit the rebels and their cause."[73] The Mau-Mau uprising was the only one in this wave without international support.

Mau-Mau had around 12,000 fighters, but the organization had no clear strategy. After its most important leaders were captured in 1953, those who remained were an "almost uncoordinated collection of independent bands allied to face a common enemy . . . but incapable of joint action."[74] The British had time to create an effective police force. Mau-Mau casualties numbered 11,000, while the security forces only lost 167, including 101 Africans. But the British were not opposed to Kenya's independence in principle. Seven years later, they pushed the local government to expand its African base, and Kenya became a republic in 1963. After independence, former Mau-Mau members were honored as heroes, but only European-educated Africans who had not participated in the violence held government positions.[75]

In British Malaya, the MRLA (Malayan Races Liberation Army) was a communist organization. The struggle was a long one (1948–1960), but the British public supported staying, as did most Western states, especially when the state of Malaysia was established in 1957, which indigenous Malays—over half of the population—embraced. One-third of the population was Chinese; they supplied 90 percent of MRLA's recruits.[76] But many Chinese were anticommunist and, as the MLRA sought funds, were initial victims of terror. The strain of double loyalties was too great for the Chinese, and only Malays became policemen.[77] MLRA's initial advantages were considerable. A veteran organization, it originated in World War II, fighting the Japanese, with considerable success. It stayed in the jungle after the war, but this time isolation from the general population was a serious liability. Foreign support was weak. Thailand initially provided sanctuaries but later closed them.[78] China's aid was insignificant. The MLRA at its maximum had ten thousand armed persons; the British army had thirty thousand, supported by a police force twice as large.

Algeria's special circumstance was that so many Europeans lived there, nearly one-fifth of the population, largely because the French had been in Algeria since 1831. Algeria was geographically closer to France than any other part of France's empire, and Algerians were French citizens. Morocco and Tunisia, more recent additions, had small European populations. The FLN began its fight in 1954. In 1958, an Algerian government in exile was established in Egypt, with links in Morocco and Syria. When France said it would negotiate a solution, military elements threatened a parachute assault on Paris unless General Charles de Gaulle was put in charge to establish France's Fifth Republic (1958). The FLN continued to grow; by 1961 it had five thousand members in Algeria and twenty thousand waiting to infiltrate from Tunisia, facts that convinced de Gaulle to negotiate a solution. In response, the Secret Army Organization (OAS), composed of settlers and military sympathizers, attempted an abortive military coup, an assassination attempt against de Gaulle, and a terrorist campaign in France, the first time a government's colonial policy provoked violence at home. The FLN may have achieved the Second Wave's first complete success, but its initial manifesto stated it would establish a democratic state and include Europeans, a crucial economic element. But Europeans returned to Europe, and Algeria never became democratic.[79] French-Algerian relations remained difficult for decades.

A special circumstance in the Irish question was the British determination not to leave Northern Ireland as long as the majority wanted to remain in the United Kingdom. The IRA launched its fourth campaign in 1956, lasting five years and animated by a new strategy. All targets were military and police facilities in rural Northern Ireland; cities were not targeted, to avoid reprisals on Catholics. IRA forces divided into four "flying columns" of fifty men each. The IRA described the activity as guerrilla war and said it was complying with the Geneva Convention, making members wear identifying emblems and carry weapons openly; however, attacks on the police violated the rules of war.[80] In the 1955 Northern Ireland elections, most Catholics voted for the Sinn Fein, the IRA's political branch, convincing the IRA that it had the support needed. But four years later, reactions to the IRA's terrorist campaign brought the Sinn Fein vote down by more than half. Although Ireland relinquished its dominion status and became a republic in 1948, a crucial IRA objective, the relationship with Ireland remained tense. To avoid antagonizing the Republic of Ireland, IRA members were ordered to destroy their arms in Ireland and avoid *all* "defensive action." But that seemed to make no difference, and after the IRA began a new campaign in Northern Ireland, the Republic of Ireland interned all IRA leaders and major sympathizers. This campaign lasted longer than any previous IRA campaign; 341 attacks were launched in 1957. By 1960, that number had declined by over 87 percent, and only eighteen were killed, twelve IRA and six Royal Ulster Constabulary members. When the IRA abandoned its campaign, it stated, "Foremost among the factors motivating this course of action has been the attitude of the general public whose minds have been deliberately distracted from the supreme issue facing the Irish people, the unity and freedom of Ireland."[81]

Aden had been a base to secure the British hold on India and the Suez Canal, but when the British withdrew from those places, they wanted to leave Aden as well. But Aden's National Liberation Front (NLF) was communist, and the proximity of oil facilities made NATO allies pressure the British to stay.[82] Aden had no local ethnic element willing to fight the NLF. A British Conservative government tried to forge a federation between a part of Yemen and Aden to reduce Marxist influences, but when Labour returned to power it repudiated the agreement and handed Aden over to the United Nations, a decision Arab states and European socialist parties strongly endorsed. By the time the British left, they had lost fifty-five people, while Aden had lost over two thousand. The NLF usually numbered around two hundred and was based in North Yemen, an independent country at the time. Nasser's Egypt gave it significant military, economic, and political support. Tensions between the two quickly developed; Egypt withdrew its aid, yet the NLF survived. The British could not create an effective police force in Aden. Few natives wanted to serve, and those who did were frequently assassinated, particularly Special Branch members charged with penetrating the NLF.[83] The People's Republic of South Yemen was created in 1967, and in 1990 it merged with the pro-Western Republic of Yemen, which then survived a 1994 civil war led by secessionists.

Although the Second Wave basically ended in the mid-1960s, two special cases persisted. In the sixteenth century, Portugal became the first European country to occupy elements of Africa, and many Portuguese settlers lived in Africa. A right-wing Portuguese dictatorship was established in 1928 to hold the empire. In 1974, after thirteen years of terrorist activity in Africa, the Portuguese "Carnation Revolution" occurred, a successful, left-wing, bloodless military coup with the professed goals of eliminating "fascism," promoting "decolonization," and "maximum self-determination." The colonial problem was the major precipitating issue; never before had domestic antagonism overthrown a government determined to hang on.[84] Grivas in Cyprus had noted that all a rebel group needed to do to win was survive, and the Portuguese experience illustrates his argument best. The rebels won no important battles or made any significant strikes, but the Portuguese army could not eliminate them. "It was a case where the Portuguese had to lose—what the Portuguese did, of course was quit!. . . and the Portuguese did not turn over the government to anybody, they left."[85]

A major problem was that the Portuguese volunteer army in Africa began to need more personnel. Conscripts were sent, drafted for four years, the longest draft period in contemporary Europe. History shows that imperial wars require volunteer armies and that often foreign mercenaries are employed, for example, the French Foreign Legion.[86] It is not surprising that volunteer French forces in Algeria revolted against the government's decision to accept secession, but French conscripts, like their Portuguese counterparts, were much more favorable to the terrorists' aims.[87] When

Portugal left its colonial territories, civil wars ensued there. Over a million citizens, mostly Portuguese, fled Africa, one of the largest peaceful migrations in world history.[88] Portugal, Europe's poorest country, spent half of its national budget to maintain its empire and faced immense international hostility. "The United Nations provided a platform for anti-Portuguese movements unmatched by movements then and now."[89] When UNESCO denounced Portuguese efforts as "genocide," Portugal withdrew from UNESCO. Rebel groups often attended UN meetings, and Portugal's NATO allies provided harsh criticism. Portugal even broke diplomatic relations with Denmark over the issue. Neighboring African states gave rebel groups sanctuaries "most of the time."[90] The Organization of African Unity provided diplomatic and financial aid, and Cold War protagonists helped different terrorist groups. The Soviets and Cuba publicly supplied weapons and training to the Popular Movement for the Liberation of Angola (MPLA), while the United States covertly used third parties to aid the National Union for the Total Independence of Angola (UNITA).[91]

The other special case was South Africa, which held the League of Nations Mandate over neighboring German imperial territory.[92] The United Nations revoked the Mandate, but South Africa refused to comply. Uprisings began in 1973, and the United Nations recognized the SWAPO (Southwest Africa People's Organization) as the government. When the Cold War ended, South Africa yielded to a twenty-four-year terror campaign to create the state of Namibia.[93]

STRATEGIC CONCERNS

Before launching his campaign, General Georges Grivas wrote that one must arouse

international public opinion, especially among the allies of Greece by deeds of heroism and self-sacrifice which will focus attention on Cyprus until our aims are achieved. The British must be continuously harried and beset until they are obliged by international diplomacy exercised through the United Nations to examine the Cyprus problem and settle it in accordance with the desires of the Cypriot people and the whole Greek nation.[94]

"My resources were meager, and I could not hope to win a military victory; it was rather a question of raising a force and keeping it in being, no matter what the enemy did to destroy it."[95]

The FLN's view was similar. The manifesto opening its struggle said its chief external objective was "internationalism [*sic*] of the Algerian problem."[96]

Important FLN strategic decisions were calculated to involve the UN more deeply; the FLN, for example, stopped the "Battle of Algiers" to start a general strike in 1957, just as the UN General Assembly began a new session, to show in the most decisive manner, the total support of the whole Algerian people for the FLN. The object of this demonstration is to bestow incontestable authority upon our delegates at the United Nations in order to convince those rare diplomats still hesitant or possessing illusions about France's liberal policies.[97]

For Menachem Begin, international interest was clearly indispensable. While Begin acknowledges the Holocaust was extraordinarily helpful in generating publicity and sustaining beliefs that his cause was just, he was also clear that this special advantage could be undermined if his group did not realize that its language and activities had to be carefully monitored. Strategic restraint, a new vocabulary, and new tactics were necessary. Begin was not the first to note the significance of vocabulary. The Irish in the 1920s called themselves "soldiers,"[98] and Bhagat Singh, who placed bombs in the Indian Legislative Assembly (1929) to arouse attention, said, "I am not a terrorist; I am a revolutionary."[99] But governments kept calling all rebels "terrorists," a term that had accumulated enormous political liabilities during the First Wave.

Zionist groups discussed the matter intensely and in doing so made the issue clear to other parties. Lehi rejected Begin's suggestion and claimed it was necessary to use the First Wave's language.[100]

> If the question is: is it possible to start a revolution or bring about libera-
> tion by means of terror, the answer is: No! If the question is: do these
> actions help to bring revolution or liberation nearer? The answer is: Yes!
> Terror . . . is part of contemporary political warfare and [because] it plays
> a very large role in language that will be heard throughout the world,
> even by our wretched brothers beyond the borders of this land, it is proof
> of our war against the occupier.[101]

Begin responded that one had to use language highlighting the ultimate purpose of both participants. Irgun members were "freedom fighters," and since the British aimed "to intimidate the population," they were "terrorists."[102]

> Our enemies called us terrorists. . . . Our friends . . . called us by a sim-
> pler, though also a Latin name, "patriots." General McMillan . . . thought
> that the term "terrorist" was too good for us. . . . [He] ordered that they
> must not be called terrorist any longer, but "murderers" or "thugs." His
> order did not make any difference. The British Press and the British
> troops continued to call us by the name, which in their General's opin-
> ion suggested bravery on our part and fear on theirs.[103]

Virtually all Second Wave groups followed Begin's advice about lan-
guage, a practice that continued in the waves that followed.[104] Even though colonial governments continued to describe *all* groups as terrorist, many onlookers found the "new" language appealing. Sympathetic governments in UN debates described anticolonial groups as "freedom fighters" or "guerrillas."[105] Occasionally, an organization labeled itself an "army" and called its members "soldiers." When a group characterized itself as a "liberation movement," its members were "freedom fighters," for example, Algeria's FLN, Aden's NFL, South Yemen's FLOSY (South Yemen Liberation

Front), Mozambique's FRELIMO (National Liberation Front), and Angola's FLNA (National Front for the Liberation of Angola). Ironically, Lehi is a Hebrew acronym meaning "Fighters for the Freedom of Israel," and Irgun means "National Military Organization," but Lehi insisted on describing itself as terrorist and may be the last group in the history of global terrorism to do so; the term has become so obnoxious it is hard to imagine a group using it to describe itself.[106]

The media understood that employing either the language of colonial governments or rebels exclusively created serious problems for their readers and developed an unusual way to deal with the issue. Major American newspapers often described the same people alternatively as terrorists, guerrillas, and soldiers in the same story—a peculiar unexplained practice. Presumably, editors thought it demonstrated "objectivity" and offended interested parties less. Yet they did not use this practice to describe government action![107]

Strategic restraint explains why terrorists "spared" metropolitan homelands, making it easier for colonial powers to relinquish territories. In the successful IRA campaign, nearly all attacks were confined to Ireland. England was the main target in the IRA's 1939–1940 campaign, a strategic disaster for the IRA. Israeli groups and EOKA avoided targets in the United Kingdom. General Grivas felt that a campaign to kill informers who had taken refuge abroad should be organized, but Archbishop Makarios refused to finance or endorse the risky operation.[108]

Algeria's FLN was the only successful terrorist group to strike in the metropolitan homeland (1957). It was deeply divided on the issue but wanted to destroy its chief rival, the MNA (Algerian Nationalist Movement), supported by many Algerians in France. The MNA was eliminated in the "Café War." Significantly, the decision to go to France occurred after French torture during the "Battle of Algiers" received much hostile publicity in France and abroad. Indeed, the torture outraged some Frenchmen so much they gave the FLN money.[109]

An interesting feature of the FLN's international strategy was its deliberate avoidance of foreign victims. Martha Crenshaw Hutchinson notes,

"On one occasion, an American Methodist missionary was kidnapped and released five weeks later. Any terrorism on foreign soil (Belgium, for example) was directed against the Algerian emigrant population and not designed for international effect."[110] If Americans had been killed abroad, American support for the FLN at the very least probably would have been delayed. Assassination did not seem to work. An IRA element tried to undermine the treaty establishing an Irish state without Northern Ireland by assassinating in 1922 Field Marshall Sir Henry Wilson, a much-decorated British war hero, in London.[111] But the British did not change their minds. Then the IRA assassinated Michael Collins, the IRA's former leader, as a traitor for signing the treaty and because he was very effective in leading Ireland's army against the IRA. The assassination was counterproductive, contributing to a quick IRA defeat. The Irish government used Collins's assassination to justify a "long toll of IRA prisoner executions," which the public accepted.[112]

Assassination was first discussed publicly in the Zionist uprising because Lehi admired First Wave groups. Indeed, when the British killed Lehi's leader Avraham Stern in his office, they found Narodnaya Volya's platform on his desk. Begin noted that a major reason for avoiding assassination was that it was so closely associated with the word "terrorist":

> We were not terrorists. . . . In building our organization we created no group of assassins to lurk in wait for important victims. From foundation to attic, we set up our underground as an army which planned attacks on the most vital enemy targets, which shook the very foundations of the enemy's military establishment and his civil rule.[113]

Despite its preoccupation with assassinating prominent persons, Lehi killed only two.[114] In Cairo in 1944 it killed Lord Moyne, Britain's highest official in the Middle East and well known for provocative anti-Zionist speeches, and in 1948 it assassinated Count Folke Bernadotte, the UN representative attempting to negotiate a peace treaty between Israel and the Arab states to end the war after Israel's independence.[115] Most victims were policemen or Jews denounced as traitors.[116] In thirty-four attacks, it killed twenty-three people.[117] Begin wanted to assassinate General Evelyn Barker, who after the King David bombing said he would punish Jews "in a way the race dislikes, by striking at their pockets and showing our contempt."[118] But Begin changed his mind, fearing it would harm the Zionist cause.[119]

In subsequent Second Wave campaigns, few prominent individuals were assassinated, except in Aden.[120] Terrorist leaders did not discuss the issue publicly, but their restraint suggests they believed the tactic was counterproductive. A few exceptions occurred. In 1955, Grivas organized an abortive attempt on Cyprus's governor Robert Armitage. His next target was General Keightley, governor of Gibraltar, who was visiting the island, but Archbishop Makarios III "vetoed the plan." Two abortive attempts were made to assassinate Field Marshall Sir John Harding, but they were apparently local unit decisions that Grivas did not authorize.[121] Algeria experienced the wave's bloodiest struggle, but the "only assassination of an individual prominent enough to attract publicity was the 1957 shooting of Amedee Froger, the spokesman for European opposition to concessions to Algerian opinion. During the entire war, there were no assassinations of high-level government officials either civilian or military."[122]

The Mau-Mau committed one significant assassination, Chief Waruhiu, a Kikuyu Christian and government spokesman, in 1952, producing a "state of emergency" that gave the imperial government special powers to crush the uprising quickly.[123] Malaya witnessed one crucial counterproductive assassination, the murder of High Commissioner Sir Henry Gurney in 1951, which intensified the British commitment, and his replacement, Field Marshall Sir Gerald Templar, the "Tiger of Malaya," was very capable. A year earlier, the Puerto Rican Nationalist Party made its only effort to kill a head of state, President Harry Truman, which failed. Aden saw many successful assassinations. The NLF began its efforts with a spectacular attempt in 1963 against High Commissioner Sir Kennedy Travikas. He survived, but two aides and fifty others were wounded. The police superintendent and the speaker of the house were also assassinated.

Second Wave groups were reluctant to take hostages; when they did, the acts were justified as defensive measures to prevent governments from "mistreating" prisoners. The Irgun captured two soldiers, threatening to hang them if the British hanged three captives, whom the Irgun insisted were "prisoners of war." When the British hanged their prisoners, the Irgun hanged theirs and booby-trapped the bodies. Thirty British soldiers and policemen went on a retaliatory rampage in Tel Aviv, destroying shops and beating up Jews. Berserk security men sprayed pedestrians and shops with gunfire, killing five and injuring two.[124] The inability to restrain its colonial forces outraged the United Kingdom and other nations, inducing the decision to withdraw soon after.

Grivas had a similar hostage policy. In 1956, after two EOKA prisoners were hanged, two British soldiers were taken prisoner and killed. Later, the British hanged three more members; EOKA, unable to kidnap soldiers, took a retired civil servant prisoner instead but then decided it could not hang one so "elderly."[125] The FLN killed French military captives when the French executed FLN prisoners but did not kidnap hostages for other ends.

Before his terror campaign began, Grivas focused on developing political support, first with the church and then by organizing local demonstrations, to show that the British would always respond violently to legitimate protests. "I began the battle for the minds of the population in earnest; above all, I concentrated on the young. . . . [In] our first demonstration . . . some 700 pupils threw themselves into the struggle with such determination that the police bolted before them, pressed by a hail of stones, and the army had to be called out."[126]

EOKA planned school demonstrations as a regular campaign feature. "See that the Greek flag flies from elementary schools and is kept flying. This will certainly mean that the schools will be closed but it will also show an unshakeable will to fight to the final victory."[127] The anticipated reaction materialized. Many schools were shut down. "Soldiers wasted a great deal of time going around the villages removing flags: there were frequent clashes between armed troops and crowds of small children. . . . Thus, we showed the world at large that the whole of Cyprus from the smallest schoolgirl to the Archbishop himself was in the battle with EOKA."[128]

Then EOKA began its first armed attacks. "The aim will be to terrorize the police and to paralyze the administration. . . . Disillusionment will be spread through the Police Force. . . . Active intervention of the Army in security . . . will stretch them out. . . . In the face of our strength and persistence . . . it is very probable that the United Nations . . . will bring about a solution."[129]

When information about the Holocaust became public, the Irgun needed no demonstrations to justify sabotaging British immigration policies and attacking the police.[130] Begin gives three reasons for making the police a crucial early target.

On an August day in 1944, we attacked the police stations on the Jaffa–Tel Aviv border. . . . We simply wanted to take a few arms from the British police. . . . We had decided not to attack military installations so long as the war with Nazi Germany was in progress. . . . But the British police and their armories were always legitimate targets.[131]

Surprised and infuriated policemen often responded with atrocities, creating more political support for the rebels. In one case, "four Jews were killed and fifteen injured when a grenade was tossed in a café in Tel Aviv from a police armored car."[132] Finally, the police were the source for British intelligence.

The successful IRA campaign displayed the same pattern. Reprisals largely went in tandem with the pace of the IRA campaign: the bigger and the more elusive the rebel force became, the more provoked and frustrated were the targets.

After the assassination of a Head Constable several unidentified police broke into four public houses, killed two alleged Sinn Feiners and burned or damaged fifty other buildings. . . . As the sequence of reprisals went on . . . men . . . would inevitably break the frail bonds of discipline and strike out since the public would not assist them in pursuing and identifying the attackers.[133]

The Battle of Algiers, a film based on the memoirs of Yacev Saadi, the FLN leader (who played himself in the movie), illustrates this point, too. An effective campaign, killing many officers, led the police to plant a bomb in the Kasbah, inadvertently exploding an ammunition dump and killing women and children. A wild mob emerged, which the FLN restrained by promising revenge. It now had a "moral warrant" to attack French civilians and bombed them in crowded places.[134]

When Cypriot police families were targeted, most officers quit, and the soldiers replacing them needed extensive police training.[135] But they did not know the neighborhoods, and inexperience made counteratrocities more likely. Note the Irish experience. In 1919,

> the IRA had found a task: neutralize the RIC [Royal Irish Constabu-
> lary]. . . . The IRA had too few trained men, no heavy weapons, and the
> tolerance but not yet the support of the country. By necessity, the weap-
> ons used would be those of the weak: stealth, ambush, assassination,
> intimidation. To the British, those who shot policemen from behind
> walls were murderers and the IRA was a murder gang. . . . In Tipperary
> and Limerick no one cared very much what the British thought, as long
> as the lads were getting their own back.[136]

Order could not be restored. The British turned to counterterror. On March 20, a group of unknown "civilians" entered the home of Tomas Mac-Curtain, lord mayor of Cork and CO of the Cork IRA, and shot him dead in front of his family. Collins soon had several culprits shot.[137]

The film *The Battle of Algiers* provides another example of provoked government atrocities. A decimated, discredited police force was replaced by paratroopers, who embarked upon a campaign of torture that became widely publicized and reminded the French public of its own experiences under the Nazis a decade before, deeply troubling major administrative figures. Paul Teitgen, secretary-general of the Algiers Prefecture, resigned.

> If you once get into the torture business, you're lost. . . . All of our so-
> called civilization is covered with varnish. Scratch it and underneath
> you find fear. The French, even the Germans are not torturers by nature.
> But when you see the throats of your captains slit, then the varnish
> disappears.[138]

Torture increased international hostility, greatly alienating the United Kingdom, an important ally.[139] Support in France became more ambivalent.

The atrocity and counteratrocity process resembled a jujitsu struggle where the physical strength of one side is transformed into political weakness because of the ambivalence of other interested parties. French torture practices enabled them to win the battle for Algiers,[140] but in time it strengthened the enemy. Shortly afterward, Tunisia let the FLN move their "government-in-exile" from Cairo to Tunis, and many countries recognized it quickly. In 1958, the French bombed a Tunisian border village, Sakiet, an FLN sanctuary, hitting a hospital and school, killing over eighty. Tunisia accused France of aggression before the United Nations; UK and U.S. envoys tried to negotiate a solution.

Second Wave groups often employed "guerrilla-like" actions against troops. The attacks were still terrorist assaults because assailants concealed their weapons and had no identifying insignia. In some cases, like Algeria, terror was one aspect of a more comprehensive rebellion that included extensive guerrilla forces. Different views of tactics and/or ultimate purposes sometimes precipitated serious violence between competing groups. Irish differences after the peace treaty was signed led to a civil war and contributed to IRA failures in its next two campaigns to get control of Northern Ireland (1939 and 1952), as Ireland offered minimal support. The Algerian MLN, a more moderate element, entered the scene after the FLN had become dominant. The clash produced appalling atrocities. In the village of Melouza (1956), which had helped its rival, the FLN "rounded all males over the age of 15 from the surrounding area, herded them into houses and the mosque and slaughtered them with rifles, pickaxes and knives, a total of 301 in all."[141] Algerian and foreign opinion were horrified, inducing the FLN to say the French committed the act. But when the truth came out, it received little attention abroad. These different international responses reflect the fact that the rebels were seen as weak and without alternatives, a persuasive theme in a world privileging national self-determination.

In the Zionist case, tensions between groups appeared immediately. During World War II, the Irgun and Lehi felt Holocaust refugees had to be saved. But Haganah, the largest and most popular group, refused to take up arms, believing it essential to help the British defeat the Nazis first and that the United Kingdom would create a Jewish state afterward. The Irgun distinguished between the British war effort, which needed strong support, and the Mandate administration, which had to be seriously disrupted for the sake of the refugees. During World War II, the Irgun struck only facil-ities preventing immigration. It also issued warnings before striking to reduce casualties and potential outrage, a policy many groups in this Wave copied.

Lehi thought the Nazis would reward attacks on the British by releas-ing Jews from concentration camps. Lehi assassinated Lord Moyne in 1944, believing that would rally Jews and turn Arab populations against the British.[142] It could not have been more mistaken; Lord Moyne and Prime Minister Churchill were close friends, and Churchill changed his mind about partition, now insisting on a single state Arabs would govern. The assassination also intensified tension between the three Israeli groups, climaxing in the "*saison*" (the hunting season), when Haganah captured many Lehi and Irgun members, often torturing them before turning them over to the British.[143] The Irgun denounced the assassination and was enraged that Haganah had exploited the occasion to get rid of its rivals. Members demanded the "right" to strike back, but Begin refused, a difficult decision rarely taken by terrorists. He argued instead for patience; Haganah members would resist their leaders, and the public would force Haganah to back down.[144] Events showed him to be right.

When World War II ended, the British refused to establish a Jewish state, surprising and infuriating Haganah. Ben-Gurion, the Jewish Agen-cy's leader, concluded that a violent campaign had to be organized, to "pro-voke deep sympathetic international responses that would force Britain to alter its policies."[145] The three groups formed a Hebrew Resistance Move-ment, an alliance in which each retained its unity but where Haganah could veto particular actions. Haganah became responsible for bringing immi-grants in, a task it refused during the war for fear of killing British person-nel. From 1945 to 1948 Haganah hijacked boats, to bring seventy thousand

Holocaust survivors to the "Promised Land."[146] Irgun and Lehi struck communication facilities, railroads, bridges, patrol boats, and coastguard stations; military and police facilities were attacked to seize weapons.[147]

The cooperation lasted seventeen months, until the Irgun bombed the British military and administrative headquarters in the King David Hotel (1946), killing ninety-one. Begin argued that the British did not transmit evacuation warnings or take Irgun's warning seriously. Haganah denied responsibility for the event and dissolved the Hebrew Resistance Movement. Ironically, although the attack infuriated British public opinion, it also convinced the government that the Mandate's political status had to be reconsidered and a partition offered. Haganah resumed diplomacy. But Irgun and Lehi continued attacks to regain biblical Israel, that is, the entire Mandate, including the state of Jordan. Ultimately, however, Begin accepted partition. The alternative, he said, was a Jewish civil war, and the last one fought by the ancient Zealots resulted in losing the land for two millennia.[148] He also realized Haganah, a larger, better-trained group backed by most Jews, would win that war.[149] Irgun and Lehi pledged loyalty to the new government, but Lehi secretly continued its struggle, assassinating UN representative Count Bernadotte for negotiating a peace treaty between Israel and the Arab states. The assassination destroyed Lehi too: it was outlawed, most members were imprisoned, and the group collapsed.[150]

In dissolving Portugal's empire, Angola provided a striking picture; rival rebel groups could not end their struggle. The Popular Movement for the Liberation of Angola (MPLA) seized power a year after Portugal left, provoking a twenty-seven-year civil war. Beyond implacable tribal tensions, violence persisted because each side was receiving crucial assistance from opposing Cold War elements. The Soviet Union, Cuba, and Eastern European states supported the government, while the United States, South Africa, and the People's Republic of China, among others, helped the opposition. Over five hundred thousand were killed and 4,250,000 displaced, one-third of Angola's population. The conflict was primarily a guerrilla war, though many terrorist acts occurred. Some nine thousand children were forced to bear arms.[151] Several secessionist groups also complicated the conflict.

Diasporas were increasingly important. The Jewish-American diaspora became increasingly effective as Holocaust horror was revealed. Outside influences change when terrorist activity and the local context are perceived differently, as the Irish experiences illustrate. The early effort in the 1920s was seen simply as an anticolonial movement, and the Irish-American community had its most productive impact. But frequently the Irish situation was more complicated. Beginning with the French Revolution, Irish uprisings were often timed to occur when Britain was at war.[152] Diaspora responses depended on the identity of the enemy. During World War II, many Irish-Americans refused to support the campaign to bring Northern Ireland into the Republic, fearing it would help the Nazis.

CONCLUSION

The favorable attitudes of public opinion in foreign states and in the metropolitan homeland of colonial powers were crucial conditions for global terror's first successes. Terrorists understood they had to behave differently than those of the First Wave. Efforts to go abroad to seek targets or to cooperate with foreign terrorist groups were abandoned. Targets that provoked unnecessary international hostility were avoided. Assassination, the First Wave's most conspicuous tactic, was seen as invidious. Second Wave groups rarely used the tactic and identified themselves in a new way, emphasizing their purpose—for example, "freedom fighters"—and often described their enemies as terrorists. Initial targets now were largely the local police, a target the First Wave ignored. Governments then made soldiers do police work, but soldiers proved to be poor substitutes, and their provocative responses created more international sympathy for the rebels and intensified local support, enabling Second Wave terrorists to create larger groups with a more formal and better-organized structure.

The IRA provided a new strategy and tactics and became the first successful group in terrorist history, though it did not gain control of the whole island. There was no direct interactive activity between it and other groups, but the IRA became the Wave's inspiration and model, linking its origin to the French Revolution, which had fomented a number of Irish self-determination uprisings in the nineteenth century. IRA heroes were recognized by other groups, but those groups also reached back into their own cultural histories to find heroes more likely to resonate with local populations. The concern with cultural history is one reason that women's roles were so much more limited than they had been earlier.

Successful groups refused to operate in the metropolitan homeland of colonial empires. The Algerian FLN was a conspicuous exception. It had special reasons for the decision, which prevented furious response. The campaign was short and directed against Algerians in France supporting a rival terrorist group. Also, the attacks began after the French army tortures provoked deep anger in France and elsewhere.

"Self-determination," the goal of the Wave, evoked considerable international sympathy. The peace treaty ending World War I was formulated to construct a new international order based on self-determination, or nationalism, and after World War II the principle became much more firmly entrenched. The United Nations, unlike the League of Nations, helped those pushing for self-determination, and its activities became more and more significant as the number of states in the United Nations kept growing. Empires that tried to use conscripts to hold their territories found that impossible. In special cases, colonial governments resisted the self-determination demand, especially when several hostile ethnic elements existed in the territory seeking self-determination and independence might produce civil war. In some cases, for example, Algeria and Kenya, settlers from the metropolitan homelands were hostile to secession and more likely to get support from colonial governments.

In the First Wave, geography made prominent nationalist struggles serious potential threats to international peace, as the Polish, Armenian, and Macedonian cases illustrate. Ethnic populations transcended the borders of neighboring states, which often had significant military resources. Indeed, the Armenians and Macedonians created a strategy to provoke military intervention by major European powers into the Ottoman Empire, an intervention virtually everyone realized could produce a serious war engulfing major European powers. Terrorist activities played an important role in stimulating the Balkan War (1913) between minor Balkan states and the Ottomans. World War I was precipitated by the Austro-Hungarian Empire's reaction to the assassination of the archduke and his wife.

But Second Wave terrorist activity did not stimulate war between major states or produce an occasion when war seemed imminent, facts that help explain why the international world's anxieties about terrorist activity continued to dissipate. The multiethnic empires during the First Wave were contiguous entities. But in the Second Wave, the term "colonial empires" referred normally to states with overseas territory where ethnic bonds did not significantly transcend colonial territories into the metropolitan homelands. There were exceptions to this pattern. South Africa incorporated a German colony neighbor and was not part of an overseas empire, and it therefore endured the Second Wave's longest struggle. Algeria, Kenya, Angola, and Mozambique did have considerable European populations, which explains their long-drawn-out character too. Ethnic overlaps in Algerian, Angolan, and Mozambican struggles became tension points in the Cold War. But the Cold War did not become a "hot war" partly because whatever the outcomes of those anticolonial conflicts might be, they would not deeply affect the major Cold War protagonists. France was the only metropolitan homeland with many residents from a colonial territory, one reason the FLN opted for its brief campaign there. Ethnic ties, on the other hand, often did reach into bordering states in Africa and Asia. But those states were not strong enough to engage an imperial government on the battlefield, though they felt secure enough to give rebels sanctuaries and other forms of aid.

Various twists in the Cyprus conflict brought Turkey and Greece close to armed conflict, but both were NATO members, an alliance that helped prevent Cyprus from producing a war. After Jewish terror forced the British out of Palestine, the United Nations established a two-state solution. Enraged Arab states invaded the new state of Israel, and after that invasion failed, four more wars followed. But the major powers were not

- physically involved, and those wars were very short, as the Arabs had very little military power. First Wave terrorist groups rarely fought against each other but Second Wave groups did, and even if independence was achieved peacefully, violence in various forms emerged and continued in the Third and Fourth Waves.

4

THE THIRD WAVE: NEW LEFT, 1960s–1990s

Terrorism is theater. . . . Terrorists want a lot of people watching, not a lot of people dead.

—BRIAN M. JENKINS

n the 1960s, the international world changed dramatically. The Cold War got even frostier, and the Soviet Union tried to help radical groups in the Third World, an area that included virtually all former colonial territories. UN membership was also expanded to include a large number of newly created states. Two events taking place in the Third World were critical during this period: Castro's triumph in Cuba generated terrorist groups in the Third World, and the long Vietnam War was crucial in animating terrorist groups throughout the West.

As in the First Wave, university students provided most of the initial terrorist recruits for what would become the Third Wave, the wave primarily driven by the New Left. Women became important again, except among separatists. Foreign groups used Cuban and Palestine Liberation

Organization (PLO) training facilities, intensifying the wave's global character. The PLO became the wave's most conspicuous group because it conducted more assaults abroad than at home. Groups and individuals from different countries typically cooperated in attacks. At home, targets with international significance, like foreign embassies, were struck. Over seven hundred hijacked airlines intensified the wave's international character. As in the First Wave, publicity became a principal concern partly because television had become so important. Earlier waves produced more deaths. For the first time, hostage taking became preeminent and often very lucrative. Many hostages taken in the Third World were foreigners involved in commerce, and their firms quickly paid enormous ransoms. The Sandinista National Liberation Front held Nicaragua's Congress hostage in 1978, eventually sparking a successful insurrection.

The wave began ebbing in the 1980s. New groups stopped emerging, Israel destroyed PLO facilities for training terrorist groups, and international counterterrorist cooperation became effective. Terrorists now found the United Nations hostile to their purposes. Eight successes occurred, including six when the Cold War ended. Most successes, however, were limited. The PLO became so weak by the end of the Third Wave that it was allowed to return home and negotiate a two-state solution, one still not achieved. Only three of the wave's successes are arguably "complete" ones: Italy's South Tyrolean Liberation Committee (STLC), Nicaragua's Sandinistas, and South Africa's ANC. The STLC had a very limited autonomy objective, one that Italy had accepted in an international treaty but failed to implement. The Sandinistas overthrew a right-wing dictator and produced a democratic, left-wing state. The ANC's success was striking; it was allowed to participate in elections, which it won overwhelmingly. But in the Nicaraguan and South African cases, problems occurred later, which make one wonder about the durability of the successes achieved.

THE NEW INTERNATIONAL WORLD
AND ORIGIN OF THE THIRD WAVE

The New Left Wave emerged in the 1960s, and while its radical aspirations reminded one of the First Wave, the New Left described their members as freedom fighters and sometimes guerrillas, terms the Second Wave had introduced. Two important new features transformed the international scene. The "Third World" emerged from the dissolution of the West's colonial empires. As there were so many new states, UN membership expanded. Since the term "Third World" referred to underdeveloped countries, it also included Latin American states that had gained their independence in the early nineteenth century. Alfred Sauvy, a French demographer, invented the term in 1952, inspired by the French Revolution, where the Third Estate (the Commons) created a "nation" by eliminating the Clergy and Nobles, or First and Second Estates. "This Third World ignored, despised like the Third Estate, also wants to be something."[1] Many believed the Third World played the proletariat's role in traditional Marxist theory, a view Third Wave groups endorsed. The second important new feature is that the United States and the Soviet Union had now become bitter enemies. The United States organized NATO in 1949, a military alliance of Western states; the Soviets created the Warsaw Pact in 1955, linking seven Central and Eastern European states.[2] In 1956, Soviet leader Nikita Khrushchev in a "secret speech" said that since atomic bombs precluded a real war with the West, communist parties should work through the electoral systems of the Western states to create a world of peaceful coexistence.[3] At the same time, the Soviets endorsed many violent efforts in the Third World, intensifying the Cold War.

I label the Third Wave the "New Left Wave" because many groups were linked originally to New Left political movements of the late 1950s.[4] These movements shunned voting because existing parties were "dominated by wealth and bureaucracy." A "participatory democracy" was sought through direct action,[5] mass demonstrations, and nonviolent civil disobedience. University students were the main participants and normally associated themselves with significant domestic issues. In the United States, for example, the New Left was inspired by the African American Civil Rights Movement led by Martin Luther King Jr. and participated in its activities.

The Students for a Democratic Society (SDS), founded in 1959, was the most prominent New Left movement in the United States. It had a thousand members in nine universities and within a decade grew to fifty thousand across 150 universities.[6] In 1962, the SDS crafted the Port Huron Statement, a useful picture of the New Left's worldview. Stalinism, the statement argued, had perverted the Old Left's dreams, and therefore "a new agenda for this generation" must be created.

> Communist parties throughout the rest of the world are generally undemocratic in internal structure and mode of action. . . . [Communism] has failed, in every sense, to achieve its stated intentions of leading a worldwide movement for human emancipation. But the Cold War is largely the fault of the U.S., a consequence of capitalism, particularly its "military industrial complex." . . . We find violence to be abhorrent because it requires generally the transformation of the target, be it a human being or a community of people, into a depersonalized object of hate.[7]

Yet in June 1969, as the Vietnam War effects intensified, a SDS element, the Weathermen, produced a manifesto that attempted to transform the organization's view of violence. "You Don't Need a Weatherman to Know Which Way the Wind Blows" stated,

> The most important task for us toward making the revolution, and the work our collectives should engage in, is the creation of a mass revolutionary movement . . . different from the traditional revisionist mass base of sympathizers. It is like the Red Guard in China, based on the full participation of the masses in making revolution . . . in the violent and illegal struggle.[8]

Although the Weathermen failed to alter the SDS, it pursued more global aspirations by sending thirty members to Cuba to meet North Vietnamese representatives, who requested them to use violence to help stop the U.S. Vietnam War. The Weathermen then withdrew from the SDS and "accepted funding, training, recommendations on tactics and slogans from Cuba."[9]

As the example of the Weathermen shows, two crucial political events in the Third World precipitated the emergence of the New Left Wave. The first was the transformation of Cuba in 1959, when Fidel Castro's guerrilla force[10] overthrew Fulgencio Batista, a dictator who had seized power in a military coup in 1952 and received American support until the United States imposed an arms embargo on Batista, six months before Castro's triumph.[11] Castro's campaign intrigued the Soviets; it was the first successful uprising "against capitalism" without Soviet aid. Castro's radical redistribution of wealth generated immense enthusiasm throughout Latin America. Cuba was next door to the United States, which made the Soviets confident Cuba would be a valuable ally.

The United States was alarmed; the alliance threatened the Monroe Doctrine and utterly transformed the Cuban-U.S. relationship. Cuba had been a U.S. "protectorate" as a result of the 1898 Spanish-American War. The Spanish defeat induced the United States to claim sovereignty over Cuba, even though Cubans had been fighting for a long time for independence, a goal Americans cited as one major reason for declaring war on Spain. In the Treaty of Paris (1898), the United States gained control of the Spanish Empire in the Caribbean (Puerto Rico and Cuba) and the Pacific (the Philippines and Guam). The United States claimed sovereignty over Cuba because it feared a powerful European state like Germany might seize Cuba and threaten the Monroe Doctrine. But five years later, in the Treaty of Relations the United States withdrew from Cuba and was given the right to lease Guantanamo as a naval base, and Cuba agreed not to offer other powers naval base rights. If Cuba went into excessive debt or had a bad government, the United States had the right to intervene. The United States twice reoccupied Cuba, in 1906–1909 and 1912–1917. American investments also dominated Cuba's economy; before Castro came to power, Cuba was third among foreign states with the most U.S. investments.[12]

In 1960, Castro issued the First Declaration of Havana, which announced a fight against colonialism, capitalism, and American "neoimperialism."[13] The United States then trained Cuban exiles to invade Cuba's Bay of Pigs in 1961; they were disastrously defeated. Soon uprisings emerged in twelve Latin American states and persisted in Peru, Colombia, Bolivia, Guatemala, Venezuela, and Paraguay. Cuba aided all the uprisings. President Kennedy described the region as the "world's most dangerous area," and the U.S. trained and equipped Latin American military forces.

Yet everything changed with the Cuban Missile Crisis. The Soviets were disturbed by the fact that U.S. aircraft in Europe could easily reach them but that they could not strike the United States in return, lacking a long-range bomber fleet. The Soviet's problem was a consequence of World War II, when the USSR had focused on using short-range aircraft to assist ground operations. The United States had engaged Germany and Japan from considerable distances and developed long-range bombing capacities. U.S.-based aircraft in Europe and North America were able to attack the Soviet Union with nuclear weapons. Since the Soviets lacked bombers to retaliate against the United States, the balance of power completely favored the latter. In 1961, the United States secretly placed missiles in Italy and Turkey, but Soviet missiles could reach the United States only if they were launched from a much closer site.

The Soviets asked Castro if they could install missiles in Cuba. Castro was enthusiastic, convinced that if Soviet missiles were placed on the island, the United States could never invade Cuba again. But the Soviets were stopped before they completed their objective. An infuriated President Kennedy threatened to invade Cuba, and the Soviets were worried that he might order a nuclear attack on the Soviet Union, using the missiles in Italy and Turkey. The Soviets backed down and agreed to remove their missiles from Cuba; the United States declared it would never invade Cuba without direct provocation.[14]

The Vietnam War was the second Third World event stimulating the Third Wave. When a Vietnamese insurrection pushed France out, the country divided into two states, and the United States aided South Vietnam, which refused to merge with communist North Vietnam. The Viet

Cong, trained and subsidized by North Vietnam, fought to change South Vietnam's policies. Soviet-aided North Vietnam eventually invaded South Vietnam. The United States claimed that if South Vietnam fell, other states would succumb to communism in a "domino process." In 1964, the United States claimed North Vietnamese naval vessels had attacked U.S. military ships, and Congress passed the Gulf of Tonkin Resolution, giving the president power "for all necessary action to protect our Armed Forces."[15] Important allies (the United Kingdom, France, Canada, West Germany, and Japan) refused to help, fearing the operation would be seen as reviving colonial rule.

In 1966, the Soviets sponsored the Tricontinental Conference in Cuba, which was attended by 513 delegates largely from eighty-three Third World terrorist groups. Castro welcomed them: "All must pledge the most resolute support for the valiant people of Vietnam. A new 'imperialism was being created; the United States is behind every aggressive action committed by the other imperialists.' "[16] Mehdi Ben Barka, an exiled Moroccan socialist and conference organizer, said that "we blend the two great currents of world revolution . . . born in 1917 with the Russian Revolution, and that which represents the anti-imperialist and national liberation movements of today."[17]

Castro focused initially on Latin American insurgencies. But a year later, after his aide Che Guevara died in a futile Bolivian uprising, his priorities changed. Guerrillas who had received Cuban backing since the early 1960s were cut off, while Havana sought rapprochement with the governments those guerrillas had been trying to overthrow in Peru, Panama, and Argentina.[18] Cuba then got more involved in Africa, aiding seventeen African governments and three Second Wave insurgencies in former Portuguese territories.[19] In 1963, Cubans trained the People's Movement for the Liberation of Angola (MPLA), while the United States, South Africa, Rhodesia, Zaire, and China, among other nations, supported its rival, the National Union for the Total Independence of Angola (UNITA). The Soviets gave Cuba military aid and paid 90 percent of its expenses. Cuban forces in Angola numbered about 35,000.[20] Over half a million Angolans died in the conflict, and approximately a fifth of Angola's population, some

two million people, were displaced. Cuba lost some two thousand participants, and despite Soviet financial aid, Cuba's economic costs were devastating. When the Soviet Union began to weaken, a peace agreement (*the
New York Accords*, 1988) enabled Cubans to remain until 1991. But the war
began again in 1992 and continued for ten more bloody years, with aid from
neighboring states.

In January 1968, the Viet Cong and the North Vietnamese Army
launched the Tet Offensive, their largest campaign against South Vietnam
and U.S. forces. The operation resonated everywhere, both in the West and
the Third World. The year 1968 became the "Year of the Barricades." The
Vietnam War was the first war the U.S. lost—and the longest it ever fought
up to that time. A small Third World state had beaten a superpower, convincing many that a "New World" was in the offing.[21] The anticolonial reputation the United States had enjoyed in the Second Wave was turned
upside down.

The United States denounced Viet Cong terror but itself committed
many atrocities, bombing Viet Cong bases in Cambodia and Laos. In 1969,
information about the My Lai Massacre, "the most shocking episode of the
Vietnam War," became public. U.S. soldiers killed between 347 and 504
unarmed Vietnamese civilians, including men, women, and children.
Women were gang-raped and their bodies mutilated.[22] The United States
sent over 550,000 soldiers; over 59,000 died. The public's resistance to the
war intensified greatly as the draft continued, and it learned the government's account of the Gulf of Tonkin incident that precipitated the war was
untrue. By 1971, most Americans rejected the war, and there has been no
draft since.

In thirty Western and Third World countries, university demonstrations
occurred. Central American military forces suppressed the demonstrations.
Demonstrators often linked their dissatisfaction to local issues. Belgian students aimed to expand the political significance of Flanders. U.S. students
were consumed with racial relations. Mexicans were outraged their poor
country was spending so much money for the 1968 Olympic Games. The
protesters were peaceful, but in the Tlatelolco massacre, around three hundred were killed and over one thousand three hundred arrested.

Demonstrations continued into the early 1970s, embracing many causes. Most participants intended to be peaceful, but often inappropriate public responses dramatically transformed the situation. When Catholics in Northern Ireland, for example, organized a civil rights demonstration in 1968, Protestants responded with violence and interned demonstrators. On Bloody Sunday, in 1972, British soldiers killed twelve demonstrators protesting internment and wounded many others. The Provisional IRA (PIRA), which had broken away from the official IRA to get involved in the violence, was suddenly flooded with recruits.

In the Middle East, student demonstrations protested the inability of Arab armies to help Palestine. The Arab League then created the PLO in 1964; its members served as soldiers in various Arab armies. But in 1969, the PLO broke off and became an independent terrorist confederation, and the Popular Front for the Liberation of Palestine (PFLP), the second largest and most radical PLO group, named four units after Viet Cong leaders.

GROUP TYPES

During the Third Wave, academics compiled statistics on and taxonomies of terrorists for the first time. The wave contained 404 groups, 212 "separatists" and 192 "revolutionaries." There were two kinds of revolutionaries: 49 "transnational" and 143 "nationalist."[23] Transnationals, a product of the developed world, saw themselves as Third World agents. Nationalists and separatists aimed to remake their own states. Nationalists were consumed with equality, while separatists wanted to create a new state from an ethnic base transcending state borders.

Separatists were present everywhere except Latin America, where all groups were nationalist. Language, religion, and intermarriage explain Latin America's uniqueness. If residents speak different languages, the ethnic divide across states becomes more intense. All Latin Americans speak Spanish except Brazilians, who speak Portuguese. In the late nineteenth century, Latin American countries began "differentiating Spanish into

'Chilean,' 'Peruvian,' 'Mexican,' and so forth. . . . In most countries the incorporation of vocabulary, inflections, and rhythms from indigenous or from immigrant languages has also been significant in developing a sense of national distinctiveness."[24] Ethnic groups often have different religions. But in Latin America, Catholicism was dominant everywhere because natives had been converted when Spain and Portugal established their empires. A third factor was that the populations of most states were largely *mestizos*, or individuals with both European and indigenous ancestries. The current Mexican population, for example, is 93 percent mestizo.[25] Argentina and Uruguay are principal exceptions because they eliminated their indigenous populations in nineteenth-century wars. A subsequent flood of European immigrants and many marriages between Europeans of different nationalities then occurred. In a few states, such as Peru and Guatemala, some natives retained their identity, the poorest living in rural areas near national borders. They were prominent in some Third Wave uprisings but made no efforts to change borders or connect with ethnic compatriots elsewhere.[26]

In some cases, important Catholic Church members supported Latin American uprisings. In 1965, the Colombian priest Camilo Torres Restrepo, an Army of National Liberation (ELN) leader, was killed in battle and became a Latin American icon. He proposed a "United Front which would link together peasants, workers, slum dwellers, professional people, and others to pressure for basic change."[27] "Liberation Theology" was born, defining the church's main purpose as the elimination of poverty.[28] In the "Year of the Barricades," a council of Latin American bishops endorsed many liberation theology tenets in the movement's "Magna Carta."[29] Catholic study groups developed to liberate the poor; many foreigners participated and became revolutionary-nationalist group leaders. About half of the Sandinista leaders in Nicaragua participated in these study groups, and the same occurred in Brazil, Peru, and Chile. While the Latin American New Left was favorable to religion, Europe's New Left remained hostile. On that continent, liberation theology only influenced Italian groups.[30]

Guatemala's military accused the church of using "Marxist concepts," which justified military support for Protestant fundamentalist groups. In

1981, a Protestant government launched the "Silent Holocaust" against the Catholic Maya population in over six hundred villages. Torture, mutilation, and sexual violence against children became common. Over two hundred thousand died in what some scholars called "genocide."[31] The Vatican then repudiated liberation theology for describing the clergy as a "privileged class" that had oppressed indigenous populations for centuries.

The names groups chose are informative. Separatists normally included the name of the nation they intended to create, for example, Basque Fatherland and Liberty (ETA), Red Army for the Liberation of Catalonia, Quebec Liberation Front (FLQ), etc. The national-revolutionary pattern is more complicated. The PLO linked itself to a state in the offing. But when the state some national-revolutionary groups claimed to represent already existed, they frequently used a national hero's name. The Sandinistas in Nicaragua were named after Augusto Sandino, who led the fight against U.S. marines in the 1920s. Many others also included the word "revolutionary" in their names, for example, the Revolutionary Armed Forces of Colombia, the Guatemalan National Revolutionary Union, and the Nicaragua Revolutionary Democratic Alliance, and some did without referring to their national context, for example, the People's Revolutionary Army (Argentina) and the Revolutionary Party of the Central American Workers (El Salvador). Sometimes significant dates were used. The M-19 traced its origins to the allegedly fraudulent Colombian presidential elections of April 19, 1970 (the *M* stands for *movimiento*, "movement"). Black September's name came from the month Jordan pushed the PLO out. The Popular Forces of April 25 adopts the date of one of the military coups ending the Portuguese empire.

In stark contrast, transnationals rarely utilized national references in their names. Note the United States' Weather Underground, West Germany's 2 June, France's Direct Action, the United Kingdom's Angry Brigade, and Italy's Front Line. The Japanese Red Army was unusual in having a national identification. Transnationals rarely used the term "revolutionary" and preferred "red" or "communist," for example, West Germany's Red Army Faction and Belgium's Communist Combatant Cells. Jane Alpert, a Weather Underground leader, explained why: "I came to see all anti-establishment uprisings as aspects of the world revolution which in a slightly different form had been predicted by Marx. . . . I [identified] my own discontent with that of the rebels all around the globe."[32] The United States "holding the world under its foot" was the principal target. Americans were struck abroad 636 times, throughout the globe.[33] European and North American transnational revolutionaries usually had only several dozen members. Europe had some national-revolutionary groups also. Italy's Red Brigades had eight hundred members, a significant Italian constituency, and was the only European group that almost overthrew a government.

Beyond their desires for publicity, the First and Third Waves had other striking resemblances. First Wave individuals were very young; a study of eighteen Third Wave groups in Europe, the Americas, and Middle and Far East showed that all members were between twenty-two and twenty-five years old in fourteen groups; the members of three other groups were two or three years older, and those in the last very small group averaged thirty-one years. More than 65 percent came from the middle and upper classes, as did 90 percent of Uruguay's Tupamaros. In Northern Ireland, the picture was different; PIRA recruits came from the poorer Catholic population. Two-thirds of Third Wave terrorists had some university education. Separatists like the Basque ETA and PIRA were less highly educated. Middle Eastern students, like those in the First Wave, largely studied physical sciences, but in the West social sciences and humanity studies were more significant.[34]

Women became very important again. Female objections to "sexism" compelled the Weathermen to change their name to the Weather Underground. Ulrike Meinhoff was an initial Red Army Faction leader, and Fusako Shigenobu founded the Japanese Red Army. The best-known airline hijacker was Leila Khaled, of the PFLP. Norma Arrostito cofounded the Argentine Montoneros, and Margherita Cagol was important in the Italian Red Brigades. Half of Uruguay's Tupamaros and a third of West Germany's terrorists were women. The West German Revolutionary Cells had a woman's branch dedicated to gender issues, especially those of the Third World. But the branch left the Revolutionary Cells because it was too brutal and formed the Red Zora (1977–1995); it struck firms "exploiting women" in a series of forty-five bombing attacks, causing no casualties.[35] The importance of women reflected the fact that feminist movements were vigorous again, a connection a Swiss passenger emphasized on a plane Leila Khaled hijacked in 1972, "The Women's Lib Movement is really moving!"

In the Second Wave, separatist women were largely scouts and messengers. In the PIRA, "only a handful were women, reflecting the traditional nature of Irish society. Fighting is a male activity. Furthermore, working class Catholics marry young, get pregnant quickly and have large families . . . making it unlikely that Catholic women have time to spare for terrorist activities."[36] Spain had a feminist movement, but ETA "was not . . . really open to feminism. [ETA] . . . is based on a 'machoistic' mentality which is indifferent to the aspirations of women in the movement when they talk of reestablishing new relations with men."[37] This bias diminished over time, but ETA women remained unequal. The Corsican Liberation Front refused to accept women in any role.[38]

The Kurdistan Workers' Party (PKK) was the most conspicuous exception to the separatist gender pattern; a surprising fact because most Kurds are Muslims, a religion that greatly emphasizes gender differences.[39] Initially, very few women were involved, but in 1989 the PKK began to operate more in cities, where women were less restricted and often university students. After the Turks decimated the PKK by interning many males, its founder declared that "our basic responsibility is to liberate women treated like slaves." In 1993, one-third of PKK members were females, making the organization seem more revolutionary than separatist.[40] Another exception was the Eritrean People's Liberation Front: Thirty percent of its fighters were women.[41]

WEAPONS, TACTICS, AND TARGETS

The bomb remained the terrorist's most commonly used weapon.[42] From 1968 to 1997, there were 2,287 terrorist incidents, 65 percent of which involved the use of bombs.[43] Business firms were targeted 405 times, diplomatic posts 358 times, and airline facilities 175 times. Bombs were used so often because they were cheap, typically made by individuals, easily hidden, and could be easily moved to different locations. Their size varied from less than a pound to a ton or more, which meant that they were useful for both discriminate strikes involving as few victims as possible and massive casualty attacks involving hundreds. Still, the bomb was dangerous to employ, and although we have no conclusive statistics on the risk, PIRA casualty estimates are a useful indicator because they had very durable and efficient veterans. Over the 1969–1989 period, 117 PIRA members were killed in accidental or premature explosions, approximately 51 percent of its 227 members.[44] J. Bowyer Bell notes that "other than carelessness that comes from unfamiliarity and limited original training, the necessity for speed and the quality of the weapons are major reasons for premature explosions."[45] The "improvised explosive device," an odorless, almost undetectable, and very lethal terrorist weapon, was initially used in World War II, primarily in Eastern Europe. Semtex, created for industrial use, became a favorite explosive. It has an indefinite shelf life if stored properly, is easy to use, can be molded into any kind of shape, and cannot be detected by X-ray machines or sniffer dogs.[46] Investigators believed a few ounces packed in a cassette recorder were responsible for the midair destruction of Pan Am Flight 103 over Lockerbie, Scotland, in 1988, killing 270. Libya reportedly supplied between five and ten tons of Semtex to PIRA, Fatah, and the Red Brigades.

Most major Cuban and Viet Cong campaigns were fought in rural areas, like all Second Wave campaigns. But in 1969, two years after Che Guevara's death and the failure of his rural campaign in Bolivia, the Brazilian terrorist and founder of the Asção Libertadora Nacional (ALN) Carlos Marighella published the *Mini-Manual of the Urban Guerrilla*, insisting the city was the best place for terrorist activity because acts there generated much more public attention, an argument made in the First Wave as well. Gene Shanahan notes, "Translated into 20 some languages it became the standard handbook for urban terrorists in Latin America, Europe, Lebanon, and Japan."[47]

But four years before the *Mini-Manual* was published, the Tupamaros had begun an "urban guerrilla" campaign in Uruguay.[48] Composed largely of students and members of the upper classes, its violence was relatively discriminate, producing few casualties and generating much public support. A 1969 Gallup poll revealed most Uruguayans held the organization in high esteem.[49] European and American radicals admired the Tupamaros greatly and adopted some of its tactics. But they ignored one crucial effort, the Tupamaros' "Robin Hood" policy, distributing seized money, mostly from banks, to the poor. One Christmas, it hijacked a food truck to distribute groceries to Montevideo's poor. A casino was robbed, and a fund was set up for casino employees to reclaim their salaries. The Tupamaros were conscientious about explaining the intent behind their actions. Seized radio and TV stations transmitted news about government corruption, especially of major political officials, high-ranking military officers, etc. In the 1950s and 1960s, the Tupamaros tried to expand their Robin Hood policy by establishing a state within a state.[50] Beyond its "courts" and "prisons," it built a hospital and primary school, the first terrorist group to do so. It "levied taxes" to finance its activity.

The Tupamaros were the first to take hostages, a tactic that Marighella's *Mini-Manual* strongly endorsed and that became the Third Wave's distinguishing feature, even though the first two waves had generally prohibited it. The tactic spread rapidly to seventy different states. Between 1968 and 1982 there were 1,411 hostage incidents, including 409 international ones.[51] In Argentina in the early 1970s, one person was taken every eighteen months; by 1976, the average was over five every day.[52]

The enormous publicity hostage taking produced led Brian Jenkins to comment: "Terrorism is theater. . . . Terrorists want a lot of people watching, not a lot of people dead." His ten-year-period study shows that specific demands were rarely granted, that casualties were low, but that useful national and international publicity was gained. Jenkins labeled the tactic as a "new kind of warfare."[53] First Wave participants explicitly refused to take hostages, believing the publicity produced would eventually be disastrous. Apparently, the world had changed.

Most hostages were held for ransom, but the response depended on who received those demands. Families are willing to pay ransoms. Businesses may resist demands, although when executives are insured, ransoms are paid, making kidnapping very lucrative. The practice apparently "earned" $350 million,[54] replacing bank robbing as the best source of revenue.[55] There are always potential victims and not enough security to protect them all. Most efforts targeted wealthy businessmen. ETA has kidnapped over seventy people since the 1970s; none was a foreigner. Irish terrorists seized some foreigners and in 1983 even kidnapped a racehorse, but the owner refused to pay a ransom.[56]

Negotiating with governments is much more difficult than negotiating with private entities.[57] The hostage takers gained a semilegitimate status, and concessions were likely to stimulate more hostage taking. Governments cannot provide safety to every citizen, and negotiations sometimes required weeks or months to resolve, enabling the public to learn more about the hostage takers' cause, information that, when an incident is over quickly, as in bombings, often does not get a chance to be disseminated. Since democratic governments feel especially obliged to protect their citizens, conspicuous concessions occur often.[58] For example, Israel's deep concern for its soldiers enabled the PLO to make extraordinary disproportionate exchanges. Seventy-six convicted Palestinian prisoners were released for one Israeli soldier, and six Israelis were returned in 1983 for 4,700 Palestinians and Lebanese imprisoned during the 1982 Lebanon war.[59] In the 1985 Jibril Agreement, Israel released 1,150 prisoners for three soldiers. Among the released were Kozo Okamoto, a perpetrator of the Lod Airport massacre, and Ahmed Yasin, who later became a Hamas leader.[60]

The most difficult, important, and dramatic crises occurred in barricade situations. Hostages were held in a known, enclosed area, and any assault might kill them or prompt their captors to do so. The time for negotiations is very limited compared to the time available when dealing with hostages held in an unknown site. The tensions produced often generate different and unpredictable consequences, depending on the risks participants are willing to take. The most successful occurred in 1978, when twenty-three Sandinistas seized Nicaragua's Chamber of Deputies, taking nearly one thousand hostages. The sheer number and political significance of the hostages kept government forces from responding. After intense negotiations, the hostages were released in exchange for fifty-nine prisoners, five hundred thousand dollars, a radio broadcast telling Nicaraguans to organize an insurrection, and permission for the hostage takers to leave the country. The incident tarnished the government's image and electrified the opposition. It demoralized the army, inducing the government to dismiss many officers to forestall a coup d'état.

Inspired by this event, Colombia's April 19 Movement (M-19) seized the Dominican embassy in 1980, taking thirty-one hostages, including fifteen ambassadors. It demanded three hundred prisoners be freed, fifty million dollars, safe passage out of the country, and for their manifesto be released in the hostages' countries. The Organization of American States (OAS) agreed to monitor prisoner trials, and private sources raised a $2,500,000 ransom. Cuba welcomed the hostage takers, and all specified states published the manifesto. The success helped increase the group's size, and the M-19 in 1985 seized Columbia's Supreme Court. This time the government refused to yield, and one hundred people, including eleven justices, were killed, and no foreign party was involved. M-19 lost four prominent figures and negotiated a "solution," laying down its arms. It became a political party but did not attract many votes. Eventually M-19 returned to terror as a much weaker group.

The 1972 Munich massacre drew enormous international attention and illustrated publicity's potentially counterproductive consequences. Black September, a group secretly organized by the PLO, attacked Israel's Olympic compound in West Germany, killing two athletes and taking nine hostages. The group demanded that Israel release 234 prisoners and West Germany release four RAF members. The Germans promised to comply and allow the terrorists to leave the country with their hostages, but as the Palestinians were leaving, the Germans made a very clumsy attack, and all the athletes were murdered. Since no stated demands were achieved and all the hostage takers were killed or captured, the Palestinian effort seems a failure.[61] But Abu Iyad, the PLO intelligence chief, argued the aim was to put the Palestinian cause on the international map, "which it did." It was planned after Olympic officials had refused a PLO request to accept Palestinian athletes.[62] The PLO gained political benefits. Eighteen months after the event, the United Nations invited PLO chief Yasser Arafat to address it.[63]

Comparing international and domestic barricade results is interesting. International hostage takers were nearly ten times more likely to get demands met. But international situations were more than twice as likely to produce shootouts, which hostage takers almost always lose. Furthermore, international situations were three times as likely to produce situations where no negotiations occur—and where hostages do not survive.[64]

When hostages are in secret sites, governments feel less pressure to negotiate. But if kidnappers feel they cannot hold a hostage indefinitely, the result could be disastrous. When in 1970 Uruguay refused to release prisoners in exchange for the American security advisor Dan A. Mitrione, he was killed to maintain the Tupamaros' credibility. But members deserted, and a hitherto sympathetic public began turning against the Tupamaros.

In the same year, the FLQ produced the most devastating hostage failure. Aiming to separate French-speaking Quebec from Canada—a popular objective at the time—it kidnapped the British trade commissioner James Cross, demanding that its manifesto be published, much cash, the release of all FLQ prisoners, and free passage to Cuba. The government refused, and another cell murdered Quebec's vice premier, Pierre Laporte, alienating many FLQ supporters. The police then discovered the site where Cross was held, and the hostage takers were willing to release him if they could go to Cuba, a proposal the government accepted. Canada passed a War Measures Act to apprehend 250 persons believed connected with the FLQ, and the FLQ lost all support. Even Pierre Vallières, the FLQ's intellectual leader, denounced it as a "terrorist menace" and said violence could never solve Quebec's problems.[65]

Italy also produced a remarkable failure. Aldo Moro, a former prime minister, was kidnapped in 1978 on his way to the Chamber of Deputies to propose that the new government include the Communist Party. Moro's effort to put the "Old Left" into government infuriated the Red Brigades, who killed five bodyguards and a chauffeur during the kidnapping. It denounced his plan as a "crime" but said it would free him in exchange for fifteen imprisoned Red Brigade members. The government refused to negotiate. After fifty-seven dramatic days, a "People's Court" found Moro "guilty," "executed" him, and put his body in a truck parked in Rome halfway between the Christian Democratic Party's and Communist Party's headquarters, to symbolize Moro's "crime." The consequences were wholly unexpected. By 1984, imprisoned Red Brigade leaders had signed a declaration ending their campaign: the "international conditions that made the struggle possible no longer existed."[66] Previous Red Brigade sympathizers gave the police information, which led to the capture of many members.

Hostage taking sometimes happened despite a group's intentions. Nelson Mandela made South Africa's MK publicly pledge never to take hostages, but in 1980 police intercepted members "on their way to carry out a mission" who took refuge in a bank, detaining twenty-five people there. The MK decided to use them as hostages to release Mandela from prison. But the government refused, and eight deaths occurred: three kidnappers, three policemen, and two hostages.[67]

Over seven hundred international hijackings occurred during the first three decades of the Third Wave, producing over five hundred casualties.[68] Many were taken to secure hostages; this almost seemed like a revival of piracy, an ancient activity largely over by the mid-nineteenth century.[69] First and Second Wave terrorists did not attack commercial transportation because they did not want to be seen as pirates.[70] First Wave Russian terrorists attacked steamboats and trains but did not seize hostages or confiscate vehicles. Their goal was to take money from passengers.[71] Although airplanes had become a significant mode of transportation over the first half of the twentieth century, it was not until the Cold War that they were hijacked. Only two Second Wave hijackings occurred, both in Peru (1931), to distribute political leaflets. From 1947 to 1969, individuals fleeing the Soviet world hijacked twenty-six planes.[72] The process continued when Fidel Castro seized power in 1959; anti-Castro Cubans hijacked seventeen planes to the United States. After the Bay of Pigs fiasco, the United States became the scene of most efforts; seventy-nine planes were taken to Cuba from 1968 to 1972.[73] These hijackers had different purposes. American radicals wanted to join the Cuban Revolution, Cubans who had fled the previous regime wanted to return, and criminals wanted to escape prosecution. As before, there were few injuries; the United States told pilots not to resist, and Cuba returned all the planes. The United States experienced 137 hijacking attempts, "or one every 13.3 days."[74] All were domestic events, and half sought private gain, extorting money from passengers or demanding ransoms from those on the ground.

In 1958, Raul Castro organized the first hijacking "to coerce a government; a Cuban plane was seized to disrupt President Batista's internal communications before Cuba's presidential elections."[75] The PFLP seized an El Al plane in 1968 flying from Rome to Tel Aviv and took it to Algeria, demanding Israel release one thousand prisoners for twenty-two Israeli hostages.[76] The International Airline Pilots Association announced it would boycott Algeria if it did not help solve the problem. Algeria then convinced the PFLP to release ten hostages. Italy took over the negotiations, and Israel released sixteen instead of one thousand as a "gesture of gratitude" to Italy. Despite international outrage, Palestinians regarded the event as a great victory, believing it had immediately transformed the airline scene.[77] One hundred and eighty-nine hijackings occurred over the next four years (1968–1972), the "Golden Age of Hijacking," mostly to pressure states via hostage situations.[78] PLO groups were the most active, hijacking thirty international flights, often with foreign partners. Oddly, though the United States experienced over forty hijackings in its domestic air space, only two incidents had a political objective. The Black Panthers requested $1,500,000. When their demands were refused, the hijackers took both planes to Algeria to get political asylum.[79]

In September 1970, the PFLP "made the most spectacular attack in the history of aviation terrorism," trying to hijack four planes simultaneously. A U.S. and Swiss plane were brought to Jordan. Another U.S. plane was taken to Egypt. The fourth plane was Israeli, but the Israelis aborted the effort. Three days later, a British plane was hijacked to Jordan. The "American plot to liquidate the Palestinian cause" by supplying arms to Israel "justified" the seizures.[80] After releasing its passengers, the U.S. plane in Cairo was blown up to protest Egypt's role in Middle East peace negotiations.

Fifty-six hostages from five countries were held, to be released in exchange for prisoners in those countries. It took three weeks to negotiate a solution after Palestinians destroyed planes worth fifty million dollars. "When we hijack a plane," George Habash, PFLP's founder, said, "it has more effect than if we kill a hundred Israelis in battle. . . . For decades world public opinion . . . simply ignored us. At least the world is talking about us now."[81]

The 1968 El Al hijacking transformed the international scene, making hijacking hostages a major activity, but Israeli security precautions prevented all subsequent efforts to hijack Israeli planes. The PFLP damaged Israeli air traffic in other ways. It attacked planes on the ground in Athens (1968) and Zurich (1969) and planted bombs on planes to detonate in mid-flight.[82] Habash said, "We think killing one Jew far away from the field of battle is more effective than killing hundreds of Jews on the battlefield because it attracts more attention."[83] The PFLP often used foreign associates, who were more likely to evade Israeli security measures. The deadliest strike occurred when three Japanese Red Army passengers on a French plane landed in Israel and attacked the crowd in the arrival hall, killing twenty-five on the Six Day War's fifth anniversary. Anniversaries often inspire terrorist attacks.

While specific reasons were given for each El Al attack, the ultimate aim was to destroy the airline, whose economic and political significance kept growing. "By 1968, El Al, Israel's gateway to the world, was one of the largest international airlines, out of all proportion to the size of its home state. El Al was the symbol of Israel abroad, the flag carrier advertising the permanence of a state Arabs refused to recognize."[84] Habash thought striking El Al would significantly reduce Israel's foreign currency reserves, by making people afraid to use the airline and reducing tourist numbers greatly, a "smart" strategy, Habash boasted. "Would you really want to fly El Al?" Still, El Al "expanded at an impressive rate . . . in 1972–3 it had the highest load . . . of any airline on the North Atlantic route."[85] But Jordan also made it clear airline attacks could be disastrous. It attacked the PLO, forcing it to leave the country, its major base at that point. Arab states were infuriated about the hijackings, too, as they often involved Arab airlines and landing fields.

In 1974, the PLO declared hijacking counterproductive and said it would only attack Israelis in Israel. The timing was shaped by an impending Arab League meeting to determine who represented the Palestinians, since the 1967 Six Day War had forced Jordan and Egypt to relinquish their Palestinian territories. The declaration enabled the Arab League to recognize the PLO as Palestine's representative, and the United Nations gave the PLO "observer status."[86] In time, 134 states gave the PLO diplomatic recognition. Some PLO groups continued to hijack and left the PLO. Hijackings declined substantially, and Arab states did not experience any more.[87]

Other major nationalist groups (for example, PIRA, ETA, and PKK) refused to hijack, but some weaker ones continued the practice, including the Kashmiri Liberation Front, Arab Eritrean Liberation Front, and the Freedom Fighters of Croatia, who felt they had no other option. But the efforts were abortive. The Croatians produced a most odd incident in 1976 when their "bombs turned out to be fake . . . shortly before surrendering, they cut up pieces of the clay bombs and gave them to passengers as souvenirs!"[88] Weaker revolutionary groups also hijacked planes, including the Philippine Maoists, Iranian neo-Marxist groups, Turkish People's Liberation Front, and Japanese Red Army.

Significant airport security measures contributed to the decline. More states refused to let hijacked planes land and created special rescue forces to thwart attempts abroad. In 1976, a French plane with many Israelis aboard was taken to Uganda, and an Israeli rescue force invaded Uganda and managed to bring all the passengers back. In 1977, a West German force rescued passengers on a plane taken to Somalia. In 1985, the United Nations passed a resolution unanimously to "facilitate the prevention, prosecution and punishment of all acts of hostage-taking and abduction as a manifestation of international terrorism."[89]

As hijacking declined, a few planes were blown up in flight. In 1985, an IED exploded on an Air India plane over Canada, killing 329, the deadliest international terrorist air attack before 9/11. No credit was claimed, nor was anyone brought to trial in the Canadian and Colombian cases. As mentioned earlier, a 1986 explosion brought down a Pan Am plane over Lockerbie, Scotland, killing 271 people from twenty-one countries. In 1989, an IED brought a Colombian Avianca flight down, killing 110 people. In the Lockerbie case, Libya seemed responsible. Sanctions were applied, and fourteen years later a Libyan intelligence official was turned over to British authorities. Unwillingness to claim responsibility in the deadliest cases indicates they were counterproductive, another reason why so few instances occurred.

Several ships were also hijacked during this wav The most important was the PFLP seizure of the Italian cruise ship *Achille Lauro* in 1985, to make Israel release fifty Palestinian prisoners.[90] When Syria refused to let the ship dock, a disabled elderly Jewish American passenger, Leon Klinghoffer, was murdered and his body thrown overboard.[91] Hijackers gave up the ship for a flight on an Egyptian plane to Tunisia, but the U.S. Navy forced it to land in Italy, creating serious tensions between Italy, Egypt, and the United States over who had the right to prosecute the hijackers. The turmoil hurt the Mediterranean cruise industry. For several years, cruise lines "kept their ships out of the Mediterranean."[92] The South Moluccan Suicide Commandos (1975–1977) seized several trains in Holland for hostages to compel the Dutch to pressure Indonesia to let the South Moluccan Islands secede. South Moluccans were Christians who had supported the Dutch during the Indonesian insurrection and established a state in 1950 that Indonesia quickly destroyed.

As hijackings declined, foreign embassies became a favorite target. In the 1970s, individuals from 113 foreign countries became hostages or were killed.[93] In most cases, prisoner release demands were made. In Thailand in 1972, Black September stormed Israel's embassy, taking twelve hostages and demanding Israel release thirty-six prisoners.[94] After hours of negotiation with an Egyptian mediator, all hostages were released.[95] Then Black September, determined to revitalize its reputation, captured the Saudi embassy in Sudan, seizing five diplomats from different countries, including the U.S. ambassador. It demanded Jordan release sixty prisoners, Israel release all Arab women, Germany all RAF members, and the United States the assassin of Senator Robert Kennedy. Not one of these demands was met; the hope was that Black September would repeat its Thailand decision. But a Belgian and two U.S. diplomats were murdered. The terrorists eventually surrendered and got a seven-year sentence.[96] Sudan's president delegated punishment to the perpetrators' "compatriots." The prisoners were given to the PLO, which sent them to Egypt to serve their sentences. The United States broke diplomatic relations with Sudan.

The year 1975 witnessed a spectacular assault; a six-man PFLP group including Germans attacked OPEC's Vienna meeting. Its Venezuelan leader, "Carlos the Jackal," was trained in the Soviet Union and linked to Cuban secret services in Paris. Ninety-two hostages, including eleven oil ministers from Saudi Arabia, Venezuela, Colombia, and Iran, were taken. The group demanded Austria make its radio and television stations broadcast its manifesto advertising the Palestinian cause every other hour and provide safe passage out of Austria. Arab states were told to nationalize oil facilities and pay ransoms; Egypt was told to resume war against Israel. Austria agreed to publicize the manifesto and let the terrorists leave if they released fifty Austrian hostages. The kidnappers left with forty-two foreign hostages, who were later released for $25 million. OPEC held no summit for the next twenty-five years; Carlos became the subject of novels and films—the Third Wave's "best known" terrorist.[97]

In 1980, a Guatemalan siege became a disaster for everyone. The Guerrilla Army of the Poor occupied Spain's embassy, protesting assassinations and disappearances by Guatemala's government. Spain's ambassador, five staff members, and two Guatemalans became hostages. Despite the Spanish ambassador's plea that Guatemala negotiate, security forces assaulted the site, starting a fire that killed thirty-nine; only the Spanish ambassador and one hostage taker survived. Spain broke diplomatic relations with Guatemala. The apparent incompetence intensified domestic tensions and became "the signal event in the ongoing civil war," which lasted for sixteen more years. Debates about who was responsible for the fire never ended, and the autopsies required were never done.[98]

Peru's government in 1996 handled a similar situation much better. The Tupac Amaru Revolutionary Movement (MRTA), a declining group, made an effort to revive. Fourteen members seized about five hundred high-level diplomats, public officials, and business people at a party in the Japanese ambassador's residence, celebrating Emperor Akihito's birthday.

The demand was for the release of 450 MRTA prisoners. Japan's government insisted Peru do so immediately. But Peru's president said he would try to achieve a peaceful solution. Negotiations lasted four months, and most hostages were released, though no Peruvian prisoner was. Then the embassy was stormed, freeing all remaining hostages; one hostage and fourteen MRTA members were killed. Afterward, MRTA continued to decline.

The forty-one attacks on embassies during the Third Wave's first decade achieved the release of only forty prisoners, an unimpressive figure. Only two saw every prisoner released. Six got all their demands met, but in all but one of these cases, the only demand was for the terrorists to be allowed to leave the country. Five other attempts were partially successful. Palestinians made twelve embassy strikes in the 1970s, the highest number by any single nationality, and struck Egyptian embassies five times to compel Egypt to resume war with Israel but had no success.

Publicity stimulated these attacks despite failures to get demands met, but in time the failures became more significant. Over the next twenty years, only eleven sieges occurred, compared to forty-one in the first decade, an indication the wave was dissipating.[99] Palestinians, the most active and early participants, stopped making attacks. Attacks in El Salvador declined from eleven to one.

Publicity concerns revived assassination, but Third and First Wave patterns were different. Assassinations now occurred later in campaigns, as revival efforts. Victims were less prominent; heads of state were rarely attacked.[100] The victim was always deemed a "criminal." An Italian Red Brigades member said, "You single out someone who is responsible; it is not the state as before."[101] The German RAF agreed. "Attacking people in their capacities as functionaries of the state is a contradiction to the thoughts and feelings of all revolutionaries."[102] But hostages were sometimes assassinated to teach governments "lessons" for refusing to negotiate, for example, Uruguay's Mitrione, Canada's Laporte, and Italy's Moro.

The RAF and Red Brigades had their own special patterns. The RAF's high-profile targets showed the group's hostility to capitalism and imperialism. It killed fourteen. The first was the prosecutor general who had convicted RAF leaders. Six were prominent business executives, including Alfred Heerhausen (1989); under Heerhausen's leadership, Deutsche Bank [had] become the largest bank in Europe. The other seven were U.S. soldiers.[103] No political figures were struck.

The Italian Red Brigades, the deadliest revolutionary group, assassinated forty-seven people. In 1976, the Italian state attorney who had prosecuted Red Brigade members was its first victim. A series of judge assassinations followed, and judges went on strike in 1980, protesting inadequate security. Most other victims were police officers and businesspeople. There was a special antipathy to the Christian Democratic Party, a major partner in Italy's ruling coalition. Twenty-four members were killed, wounded, or kidnapped.[104] The most high-profile foreign victim was Leamon Hunt, the U.S. director of the Multi-National Force and Observers in the Sinai, when he came to Rome in 1984.

> Putting an end to the miserable existence of this dirty servant of imperialism has been an honor for our organization and at the same time a duty towards the international revolutionary process. . . . The function of this military force, in which an Italian contingent also participates . . . is safeguarding U.S. interests in the Middle East through an agreement between Egypt and Israel against the Palestinian people financed by billions of dollars.[105]

Armenian groups, unable to function at home, were a special case, and they made assassination their principal tactic. The first incident occurred in Santa Barbara, California, in 1973, where a seventy-seven-year-old U.S. citizen, a member of the Armenian diaspora, killed a Turkish consul and his assistant. The aim was to publicize the Armenian genocide in the Turkish world between 1915 and 1922, where somewhere between six hundred thousand and 1.5 million Armenians were killed. The assassination stimulated the Armenian diaspora to strike Turkish diplomats; between 1973 and 1986, thirty-one were killed in thirteen different states.[106] The aim was to provoke the international world to force Turkey to give Armenians compensation, but that did not happen.

Nationalists based in their own country focused on security forces. ETA's first target, in 1972, was the city of San Sebastian's police chief, who had killed an ETA leader. Then it assassinated the dictator Franco's successor, Prime Minister Luis Carrero Blanco, who was deemed "responsible" for killing nine ETA members. An explosion lifted Blanco's car over a five-story building and into the cathedral's courtyard where he had just attended mass. In its first six years, ETA also bombed police stations, military barracks, and institutional symbols of Franco's regime. No prominent political person was attacked afterward. From 1970 to 1983 it assassinated five generals and Basque officials serving Spain's government. Several hundred lower-ranked officials were victims. Franco's Civil Guard was a major target. Over 62 percent killed were security force members.

Irish targets during the wave initially resembled ETA's: policemen, soldiers, and civilians associated with security forces. In 1975, a ceasefire was declared to negotiate a political solution.[107] But negotiations failed, and prominent political figures became victims. The British ambassador to Ireland, Christopher Ewart-Biggs, was the first killed, as he arrived in 1976 in Dublin to establish an agreement on how to respond to PIRA's new campaign. Sir Richard Sykes, who was sent to investigate the assassination, was assassinated in 1979 in The Hague, after becoming the United Kingdom's ambassador to the Netherlands.

A week later, Airey Neave, the Conservative Party's spokesman on Irish issues and likely secretary for Northern Ireland if the Conservative Party won the impending election, was assassinated in London. The fourth and most prominent 1979 victim was the World War II hero Lord Mountbatten, a former viceroy of India and a member of the royal family. Although he was never involved in Northern Ireland politics, he and four others were assassinated on his yacht in 1979. No reason was given for the assassination, but when a New Zealand journalist asked a PIRA spokesman "why a harmless old man like Mountbatten had been killed," he was told that

killing this man had the aim of making the world understand—and first and foremost the British—that there is a state of war in this country. Given his personal importance there was inevitably going to be enormous publicity attached to this operation . . . we had no hatred for him as a person. It is the society, the military and political machine he symbolized that we are aiming at.[108]

The explanation infuriated Irish-Americans, inducing Gerry Adams, PIRA's leader, who originally applauded the statement, to condemn it.[109] In 1984, Prime Minister Margaret Thatcher and her cabinet were targeted, being held "responsible" for the death of Bobby Sands and nine other hunger strikers; five were killed, including an MP.[110] Six years later, the Conservative MP Ian Gow, Thatcher's close friend, "central to policy decisions in Northern Ireland," was assassinated.[111] The last attempt, an abortive mortar strike in 1991 against Prime Minister Major and his cabinet while discussing British participation in the first Gulf War, angered Irish-Americans and diminished their support.

The Palestinian group most inclined to assassinate was Black September, the PLO's secret creation. After Jordan pushed the PLO out of Jordan, Black September assassinated Jordan's prime minister, Wasfi al-Tal, in Egypt. To publicize their determination, the assassins "licked his blood on the lobby floor" while he lay dead. In their trial, they proudly stood by their deed, and the Egyptian jury did not convict them.

Black September also attempted several times to kill Jordan's King Hussein. Nearly one-third of its thirty-four operations involved assassinations; many victims were hostages. Sixty-four letter bombs were mailed in 1972 to Israeli officials, Jews in the West, and prominent Americans, including President Nixon and the U.S. secretaries of state and defense. Several people, mostly postal workers, were killed. Black September was disbanded in 1974 to enable the Arab League to recognize the PLO as Palestine's legitimate representative.

Assassination was the only tactic of the Greek organization 17 November (17N). The reason is unclear,[112] but since its unsuccessful predecessors had used other tactics, this might have been a factor. 17N had only several dozen members and perhaps thought there was no other way to gain publicity.[113] Yet unlike First Wave groups, no prominent political figures were victims. The aim was to punish individuals responsible for the military junta governing the country, a junta student demonstrations finally overturned. In fact, 17N was named for the day those demonstrations began. It claimed that the United States had organized the coup to turn Greece into a "Latin American Banana Republic"; its initial victim was the CIA head in Athens. U.S. military officers and NATO personnel were also singled out for their "participation."[114] Turkish officers were vulnerable because during the junta's reign Turkey invaded Cyprus to divide it into two states.[115] The most prominent Greek victims, a minister and an MP, had participated in a notorious corruption scandal. Other Greek victims "helped" the military. A third Greek category was "capitalists," businessmen, and newspaper owners.[116] Greek police finally eliminated 17N before the 2004 Olympics in Athens.[117]

Martyrdom, a major First Wave feature, was much less prominent in the Third Wave. The first significant case occurred when Holger Meins, a cinematographer who became a German RAF leader, led prisoners in a hunger strike protesting prison conditions. After two months, he died of starvation in November 1974, despite being force-fed. Violent demonstrations broke out in Hamburg, Frankfurt, Berlin, Cologne, Stuttgart, and other parts of Europe. To retaliate for Meins' treatment, the 2 June Movement tried to kidnap Superior Court Justice Von Drenkmann and use him as a hostage, but he was killed in the process.[118] Hans-Joachim Klein of the Revolutionary Cells kept a copy of Meins's autopsy photo with him at all times, to intensify his hatred for the West German "fascist" system. The German movie *Moses und Aron* was dedicated to Meins (partly because he was a cinematographer), and in 1975 an RAF group Meins besieged the West German embassy in Sweden.

In 1980, hunger strikes, a deeply embedded Irish tradition, were used to protest the British decision to change the political status of PIRA prisoners and treat them as criminals. Bobby Sands, the strike's leader, decided that other prisoners should participate at staggered intervals to maximize publicity by extending the process over time. When an MP from a Catholic district died, Sands was elected to take his seat.[119] Three weeks later, Sands died after sixty-six days of hunger striking. Nine other PIRA and Irish National Liberation Army (INLA) hunger strikers then perished. The process sparked a new surge of PIRA activity; the group obtained many recruits and greatly increased its fundraising capability. Nationalists and Protestant unionists became more extreme. Sands's parliamentary seat was filled by his election agent, with an increased Catholic majority. After Sands's death, riots occurred in Ireland, Italy, France, Belgium, and Norway. French cities named streets after Sands.[120] The *New York Times* wrote that by appearing "unfeeling and unresponsive," Prime Minister Thatcher had given Sands "the crown of martyrdom."[121]

DISSIPATION OF THE WAVE

Second and Third Wave trajectories provide starkly different pictures. The IRA's success after World War I initiated the Second Wave, but for the next twenty-five years all terrorist groups failed, and the hope for success seemed to be vanishing. World War II changed the situation dramatically. The principle of legitimate overseas Western empires dissolved, and the wave ended two decades later, with many successes. The Third Wave's event sequence was much more complicated and moved in a different direction. The Viet Cong produced the initial success in 1973. The second came in 1979, when the Sandinistas overthrew Nicaragua's government, and unlike the Viet Cong, they did not require the aid of military forces from a neighboring state. By the early 1980s, some fifteen years after the Third Wave began, many revolutionary, as opposed to nationalist, groups were defeated, especially in the developed world, where they had few members and little public support. Few new groups emerged because unlike the Second Wave no dramatic political event had revitalized terrorist confidence. The Vietnam War was over by 1973. The United States had been defeated, and public fury against the war no longer inspired terrorist groups.[122]

Other circumstances shaped the demise. President Nixon's visit to China in 1972 helped dissolve the Chinese-Soviet alliance, and in 1978 China began withdrawing its support for terrorist groups. In the next decade, the PLO displayed a growing weakness. Pushed out of Lebanon in 1982, it could not replace its training facilities for foreign groups and was unable to coordinate major international efforts. The international world became more effective in coping with hijacking and hostage taking.

Then the Soviet Union stopped supporting foreign terrorist groups. While most revolutionary groups always had reservations about the Soviet Union and were convinced one had to go much further in creating a "new world," the unexpected Soviet collapse in 1991 had a generally demoralizing effect. After 1991, it became easier to negotiate with many Third Wave groups.

As indicated earlier, nationalist groups survived longer than revolutionary ones, and a few are still around. The National Liberation Front of Corsica began in 1976 and gave up the struggle in 2016, but a number of splinter groups are still alive. The Basque ETA began in 1968 and negotiated a settlement with Spain in 2017. In India, the National Socialist Council of Nagaland, founded in 1979, is still fighting for a sovereign state. The Kurdish PKK began in 1984, signed a ceasefire with Turkey in 2014, but revived in 2015 to fight Islamic groups in Syria, prompting Turkey to abandon its ceasefire accord.

Few revolutionary groups are still alive. The Naxalites, a generic term for different Maoist groups, are intermittently active in India. They began in 1967; university students went to the countryside to mount an "annihilation campaign" against landlords, moneylenders, and local policemen, but the campaign collapsed in 1975. A revival began in 2004, and Naxalites are still somewhat active, though their strength has diminished greatly.[123] In Mexico, where drug cartel violence was prominent, a small Maoist group, the Popular Revolutionary Army (EPR), emerged in 1996, on the anniversary of the Aguas Blancas Massacre, in which government forces attacked a peaceful protest, resulting in the deaths of seventeen farmers. EPR's last significant attack was in 2007, but it is still functioning.[124]

The Third Wave began ebbing in the 1980s. Revolutionary terrorists were defeated in one country after another. Israel's 1982 invasion of Lebanon eliminated PLO facilities for training terrorist groups. International counterterrorist cooperation became more effective. But state differences remained. France refused to extradite PLO, Red Brigade, and ETA suspects to West Germany, Italy, and Spain. Italy spurned American requests to extradite a Palestinian suspect in the 1984 seizure of the *Achille Lauro* cruise ship and refused Turkish requests to extradite a Kurd in 1988 because Italy precludes capital punishment while Turkey does not. The United States also refused to extradite some PIRA suspects. Interstate disagreements of this sort will not stop until that unlikely day when all states have identical laws and interests.

The role of the United Nations changed greatly.[125] Its membership expanded dramatically from fifty-one states in 1945 to 128 in 1970. Second Wave terrorists often created the new states and received UN support, but now those states believed the Third Wave threatened their existence, especially when driven by secessionist aims. Twelve major UN conventions between 1963 and 1999 tried to eliminate international terrorist tactics and designated hijacking airplanes, hostage taking, attacks on senior government officials, bombing foreign embassies, and financing international terrorists as criminal offenses. This new UN attitude was reflected in its language. The term "freedom fighter" virtually disappeared from UN debates, except in the South African case.[126] In 1997, the United Nations used the word "terrorism" to name some documents, for example, "International Convention for the Suppression of Terrorist Bombings."[127] Yet the United Nations still manifested some ambiguities on the topic, because terror sometimes serves different ends. The PLO received official UN "observer status," and over one hundred states gave it diplomatic recognition after the Arab League recognized that the PLO represented Palestine. That said, the PLO had to denounce many terrorist tactics before the status was offered.

Support for international counterterrorism efforts, a First Wave feature (recall the St. Petersburg meeting in 1904), materialized again. After the 1972 Munich Olympics massacre, TREVI (Terrorisme, Radicalisme, Extrémisme et Violence Internationale)[128] was established in 1975 and enlarged when Europol was created in 1994. States cooperated to battle state sponsors. Libya was the most conspicuous state sponsor to be eliminated. After the La Belle Disco explosion in Berlin killed five and injured 230, including many U.S. soldiers, the United States, with British support, bombed Libya in 1986, and the European Community imposed an arms embargo. Evidence Libya was involved in the Pan Am Lockerbie crash stimulated a UN Security Council resolution in 1988 obliging Libya to extradite suspects. Then, in 1993 the United Nations imposed a variety of sanctions. It cut Libya's airline connections with other states and reduced diplomatic representation. It prevented Libya from buying military equipment and froze much of its foreign assets. The end of the Cold War made such multilateral sanctions easier and more effective,[129] and in 2003 Libya agreed to compensate the Pan Am Lockerbie crash victims' families.

The global counterterror efforts had more impact on revolutionary than on nationalist groups because revolutionaries were more interested in remaking the international world and more likely to violate international law. Nationalists were much more concerned with redefining territorial borders, so their involvement in international matters tended to focus on neighboring states than on the general international scene, a pattern especially common in the new states in the postcolonial world.

In the wave's first two decades, every revolutionary group failed. But terrorists in Latin America dramatically transformed the local political scene, stimulating right-wing military coups that overthrew elected governments in Uruguay, El Salvador, Honduras, Guatemala, Chile, Peru, Ecuador, Bolivia, Brazil, Argentina, the Dominican Republic, and others. The military had always been a crucial ingredient in Latin American politics, and since the United States now helped train Latin American militaries as part of their Cold War anticommunist efforts, anxieties that terrorist activity would be met with gruesome atrocities intensified, as the Argentine general Luciano Menendez made clear: "We will have to kill 50,000 people, 25,000 subversives, 20,000 sympathizers, and we will have to make 5,000 mistakes."[130] Many Latin American states had similar experiences. "The convulsion of the period illustrates the fundamental interdependence of left- and right-wing extremism."[131]

Argentine national revolutionaries described their struggle as a "war for the second independence. . . . Just as the Argentine people did not hesitate in expelling the Spaniard neither will they hesitate today in struggling against North America imperialism."[132] Most Latin American groups agreed. Still, European separatists regarded the United States differently.

ETA required members to read particular neo-Marxist texts that down-played the United States' importance: "[Our] movement is directed against Spanish and French imperialism. . . . The confrontation between the Basque people and American imperialism is secondary."[133] ETA made very few international strikes. It did not attack Americans. Foreign consuls were kidnapped in Spain to get prisoners released, but none were killed. Some-times it struck Spanish facilities elsewhere in Europe. It had bases in Portugal but refused to participate in joint operations with any other group, though it was in contact with separatists in Brittany and Corsica; had some members trained in Northern Ireland, Cuba, and Lebanon; and got cash from Libya. PIRA in Northern Ireland had similar restraints, especially with respect to the United States.

Separatists were plentiful in Asia and Africa, wherever the new decolo-nized states did not match earlier precolonial ethnic boundaries. Many new states had different ethnic entities striving for equality or trying to secede. Ethnic entities often transcended the newly drawn postcolonial borders, and the strife they created induced neighbors either to help rebel groups or work against them. The two major North American separatist groups did not attract any foreign supporters. Canada's FLQ was isolated partly because the continent contained no other French-speaking communities. Puerto Rico's Armed Forces of National Liberation (FALN) was mistaken in thinking that Latin American states would come to its aid after conduct-ing 120 bomb attacks against the United States between 1974 and 1983.

SUCCESSES

A successful group either overturns an existing government or gets the gov-ernment to accept and implement one of its major goals. A terrorist organiza-tion may change a political community in a direction that the organization would consider more desirable, even in cases when that organization has been destroyed. While such posthumous changes are rare, we should not treat them as indicators of successful terrorist activity, and the experience of the Tupamaros more clearly illustrates why. While the Tupamaros were destroyed in 1972 by military forces that went on to establish a dictatorship, in 1984 Uruguay's democracy was restored. The Broad Front political party emerged in the new democratic government, becoming a very left-wing party that filled its ranks with many former Tupamaros. One of its members included José Mujica, a founder of the Tupamaros who killed a police officer and spent fourteen years in jail, enduring extensive torture and solitary confinement in the process. Yet against all odds, he survived and was eventually elected as president of Uruguay, running the country from 2010 to 2015. He was described as "the world's 'humblest' president," given his austere lifestyle and willingness to donate 90 percent of his $12,000 monthly salary to charities benefiting the poor.[134] The Broad Front remained in political power in Uruguay until 2019.

Seth Jones and Martin Libicki provide a useful database on terrorist activity between 1968 and 2004 that also illustrates the patterns of success described in this chapter.[135] It contains 408 Third Wave groups, and only eight were found to be "successful" in achieving at least one important aim, a success rate of approximately 2 percent. Six of the eight groups were national-revolutionary groups, and the two remaining groups were separatists.

In the Second Wave, all successful efforts aside from one occurred during the two decades after World War II. In the Third Wave, the Soviet Union's role was a critical component of success. The national-revolutionary Sandinistas in Nicaragua produced the first success in 1979. The effort began in the early 1960s and was originally based in neighboring Honduras. Cuba trained its leader, Daniel Ortega, and the Soviets supported the campaign. A major turning point for the campaign occurred after a devastating earthquake in 1972 brought the corruption of the Somoza dynasty to the forefront. The Somozas appropriated foreign money that had been sent for earthquake victims, forcing President Carter to withdraw U.S. support for the government.

A year later, the Sandinistas led a successful uprising that "avoided [the] random killing of civilians."[136] After they took control of the government, the Sandinistas initiated an ambitious social reform program, redistributing five million acres of land to some hundred thousand families. They also launched a literacy drive and made health services more readily available, eliminating polio and reducing other diseases in the process. Initially, the Sandinistas refused to have national elections, arguing that their success demonstrated how deep their popular support was and that elections would only "waste scarce resources." Nonetheless, international and domestic pressures prevailed. In 1984, Daniel Ortega was elected president, and the Sandinistas won most of the legislature's seats. The government became very active in supporting Latin American terrorist groups, and elements of the US government, despite congressional prohibition in 1983, secretly trained and subsidized the Contras—an organization employing terrorist tactics—in the hopes they would overthrow the Sandinistas. Ironically, the Sandinistas' radical reform policies alienated the poorer indigenous border population, which filled the ranks of the Contras. They believed the Sandinistas were destroying their indigenous culture. Nicaragua's economy was soon devastated, and in 1989 the Berlin Wall fell along with the Soviet empire, and the bond between Ortega and the Soviet Union collapsed. Fourteen opposition parties allied to defeat Ortega in a 1990 UN-monitored election. The United States quickly dissolved the Contras and lifted its devastating embargo shortly after the election. However, the Sandinistas remained a major political party, and Ortega actually finished second in the next two presidential elections in 1996 and 2001. In fact, after his first two election losses, he went on to win the next three: the presidential elections of 2006, 2011, and 2016. He remained hostile to the United States, especially on the international scene. In 2007 he visited Iran, where he secured subsidies for Nicaragua and made a speech that would be music to any Marxist's ears: "[The] revolutions of Iran and Nicaragua are almost twins since both . . . are about justice, liberty, self-determination, and the struggle against imperialism!"[137] He also renewed ties with Venezuela, Bolivia, and Ecuador, countries also hostile to the United States. Nonetheless, Ortega's hostility to the United States at this point was largely verbal, and he gave no foreign body physical support, which meant that trade relations with the United States could continue. In 2008, when the FARC of Colombia lost its leader, Ortega affirmed his support for the group. One main reason Ortega was elected for a third consecutive term in 2016 was because he passed a law banning the main opposition candidate from running for office. He then appointed his wife as vice president. Soon opposition to Ortega began to grow, including among some former colleagues. In April 2018, student protests erupted when the government cut welfare spending programs such as social security. Tensions escalated quickly. Police used mustard gas canisters and rubber bullets to quell the protests, eventually using real bullets on unarmed student protesters, resulting in the deaths of dozens. Even though the government reversed its spending cuts, the protests continued, and many demanded the government resign. Amnesty International and the Organization of American States also denounced Ortega for his violent oppression campaign against protesters.[138]

A month later, on Mother's Day, May 30, 2018, some three hundred thousand people marched to honor the mothers of students killed in the protests. The demonstration was peaceful, attended by children, mothers, and retirees. Ortega ordered sharpshooters perched at the National Stadium to shoot the marchers. Fifteen died, including one child who was killed in the arms of his mother, inducing Nicaraguans to name the event the Mother's Day Massacre.[139] The violence continued. After one hundred days of protests, on July 27, 2018, a total of 448 people had been killed.[140] With no peaceful solution in sight, Ortega clung to power despite the growing unrest. Ortega's brother Humberto, the former head of Nicaragua's military, called on him to stop the progovernment paramilitaries that were to blame for months of deadly unrest.[141] In its second period of power, which lasted eleven years, the Sandinista government never overcame the economic problems it had inherited from the Somoza era. The war, policy missteps, natural disasters, and U.S. trade embargo had severely hindered economic development. "Hundreds of thousands of jobs" were lost. "Experts estimate[d] that 60,000 [had] fled and 23,000 of them [sought] refugee protection[s] in Costa Rica."[142] A dictatorship like Somoza's was created.

The little-known European separatist group South Tyrolean Committee (STLC) achieved the second success of the period when Italy accepted the autonomy of South Tyrol after decades of denial. Austria provided

STLC with limited political support. The largely German-speaking area, formerly part of the Austro-Hungarian Empire, was promised to Italy if it joined the Allies in World War I. While an Italian-Austrian treaty in 1972 gave the German-speaking majority in the area special autonomy, Italy spurned its obligations, and a terrorist campaign began as a result. Twenty-four years later, an agreement was signed, creating a "Euro-Region" entity linking the Italian and Austrian Tyrol territories.

The PLO reestablished itself in its home territories after its capacities for terror were greatly weakened. Israel invaded Lebanon in 1982, forcing the PLO to abandon training facilities there that had made it a significant destination for other terrorists. In Tunisia, its new home, it could not train other groups, and as a result some organizations left the PLO entirely, greatly reducing its size. The intifada, a spontaneous Palestinian uprising (1987–1991), further weakened the PLO because it was not active in the effort, driving even more Palestinians to believe that they could not be represented by them. Hamas emerged to fill the void, but it was committed to the development of an Islamic state, not a secular one. Finally, the PLO's support for Saddam Hussein's invasion of Kuwait in 1990 induced Saudi Arabia and the Gulf states to stop subsidizing the PLO. Kuwait expelled most of its four hundred thousand Palestinian residents, a principal source of PLO revenue, and Yasser Arafat proclaimed that "what Kuwait did to the Palestinian people is worse than what has been done by Israel in the occupied territories!"[143] He then "denounced terrorism in all its forms" and called for a "two-state solution," which made the PFLP, the PLO's second-largest group, withdraw from the organization, weakening the PLO even more. However, after the Soviet collapse, the United States, which sought to improve its relations with Arabs, pressed Israel into accepting the Oslo Accords of 1993. The PLO was able to return to Palestine, but a final answer to the Palestinian question remains unresolved.

There were a number of reasons why El Salvador's Farabundo Marti Liberation National Front (FMLF) chose to negotiate with the government. While it controlled a third of El Salvador, a bloody 1989 offensive failed to generate any public support, and residents in the occupied territories refused to help their cause. When the Cold War ended, all foreign states ended their support of FMLF. The United States, which had supported the military government, became receptive to a negotiated solution if the rebels decided to avoid causing U.S. casualties. In 1992, the Chapultepec Peace Accords materialized. The agreement called for a reduction in the army's size by 70 percent and the establishment of a democratic government that would punish officials of the previous regime who were found guilty of human rights violations. Although the FMNL could not achieve their socialist objectives via the agreement, they became a major political party. In 2003, it gained a National Assembly majority and elected the president in 2009 and 2014. In similar fashion to Nicaragua, a weak economy and serious criminal violence still prevailed in the country, stimulating continued migration.

South Africa produced the most important success of the Third Wave, surprising many in the process. The African National Congress (ANC) began as a political party in 1912, and after apartheid was established in 1948, it became committed to nonviolent resistance, a strategy that Mahatma Gandhi had devised when he lived there.[144] That strategy continued for thirteen years, but in 1960 the government responded in savage fashion. During a peaceful antiapartheid demonstration in Sharpeville, government forces killed seventy protesters, in what become known as the Sharpeville Massacre. The bloodshed drove the ANC to form the Spear of the Nation (MK), a separate organization that would be used to engage in violence. Still, the ANC continued its nonviolent campaign. Its competitor, the Pan Africanist Congress, insisted that all whites must leave South Africa, but the ANC, which had whites in its ranks, demanded equal rights for all. At his 1964 trial, ANC leader Nelson Mandela said the MK was not engaged in terror and that "an outbreak of terrorism would produce an intensity of bitterness and hostility between the various races not produced even by war." After Mandela was jailed, ANC leader Arthur Tambo went to Vietnam to see what could be learned, and the extensive decimation there convinced him South Africa had to be different. In 1980, he convinced the MK to sign the Geneva Convention on the "humanitarian conduct of war," the only rebel group ever to do so.[145] These activities made South Africa's white population less apprehensive about the antiapartheid movement, and virtually all studies of the uprising emphasize the crucial importance of this restraint.[146] In 1987, when a military force sent to Angola to eliminate MK sanctuaries was defeated, white conscripts refused to fight outside the country, imposing serious limitations on government forces. Instead of trying to rectify their errors, the South African government continued to make bad decisions. Some twenty thousand students participated in massive and peaceful demonstrations protesting a law requiring them to be taught in Afrikaans. The police responded to the demonstration by killing around 175 people and injuring over one thousand more. The government's response induced residents in neighboring states to join MK camps in their countries and alienated many whites of British ancestry. MK sympathizers also set gasoline-filled tire tubes on fire and hung them around the necks of black "informers." Although it was slow to do so, the MK condemned the practice, called "necklacing," and it was not employed again.

Ironically, the ANC's model was taken from that of the Second Wave Israeli group Irgun, which focused on targeting the military and police. It was also the first group to give warnings to civilians that might be injured in their attacks. The MK did not use some of the more popular Third Wave tactics, such as hostage taking and hijacking, and its initial attacks were limited to power pylons and commercial property. However, when South African Defense Forces killed hundreds of blacks, the MK bombed a few commercial establishments and civilian targets they saw as government collaborators.

Nonviolent ANC practices intensified international sympathies for the cause. Even though the U.S. government was anxious about the ANC's Marxist connections and still denounced it as a terrorist group, many Americans supported the ANC. International boycotts also deeply affected South Africa's economy. The Soviet Union, the ANC's strongest supporter, made South African whites apprehensive. However, the unexpected Soviet collapse changed the situation dramatically, enabling negotiations to be completed quickly. In 1994, the ANC, allied with the Communist Party and Trade Union Congress, participated in South Africa's first postapartheid election, winning nearly 63 percent of the vote. Nelson Mandela became South Africa's first black president.[147] The ANC won the next four

National Assembly elections by large margins, but in the twenty-first century, corruption scandals began to tarnish the ANC's reputation. In 2018, President Jacob Zuma was forced to resign, although he was ultimately acquitted of criminal charges.[148]

The Balkans produced the next "success" of the period. Civil wars engulfed Yugoslavia when the Communist Party, the unifying bond in the region, dissolved leaving national elements—Slovenia, Bosnia, Croatia, Macedonia, and others—to establish their own independent states. Since most residents of the autonomous region of Serbia known as Kosovo were Albanian, the Serbs limited Kosovo's autonomy, sparking a campaign of "nonviolent" resistance that included massive labor and hunger strikes. Serbia imposed martial law in the region, and thousands of Albanians that had lost their jobs decided to flee, giving Serbians economic incentives to move into the area.

The U.S.-brokered Dayton Accords of 1995 ended the civil wars but mostly ignored the issue of Kosovo. After Serbian forces shot students who were peacefully demonstrating to reform the education system, the Kosovo Liberation Army (KLA) was born. Its terror campaign prompted an "ethnic cleansing" and numerous massacres. Serbia refused to withdraw its troops from Kosovo, and NATO initiated an aerial bombing campaign that cleared the path for a UN peacekeeping mission and NATO protection force to enter the region. In 2006, international negotiations began to determine Kosovo's status. Kosovo declared its independence in 2008, which Serbia has refused to accept. As of July 2019, only 101 out of 193 UN members and twenty-three out of twenty-eight European Union members recognize Kosovo. In 2014, an EU investigative task force concluded that after the war KLA members, now important in Kosovo's government, had committed crimes against humanity in 1999 by targeting "minority populations with unlawful killings, abductions, enforced disappearances, illegal detentions . . . sexual violence, other forms of inhumane treatment . . . desecration and destruction of churches and other religious sites."[149]

When Italy conquered Ethiopia in 1936, it merged Ethiopia with another one of its colonial possessions, Eritrea. After World War II, a UN resolution linked Eritrea and Ethiopia as a dual community. Nonetheless,

Ethiopia ignored the resolutions and claimed sovereignty over Eritrea. A Cuban-supported Eritrean People's Liberation Front (EPLF) emerged from Sudan to challenge Ethiopian claims to Eritrea. In 1974, Ethiopian Marxists with strong Soviet support took over Ethiopia, and Cuba abandoned the EPLF. However, after the Soviet collapse, Arab states aided EPLF in order to establish a sovereign Eritrean state.[150]

The last "success" of the period occurred when the FARC signed a peace agreement with the Colombian government in 2017, a decade after the Third Wave ended. FARC, the oldest and largest group in Latin America, was founded in 1964. It had 11,000 to 18,000 members based in the rural areas, jungles, and mountains. As Latin America's wealthiest and best-equipped rebel force, it took over 1,200 hostages for ransom, conducted a multitude of bank robberies, and engaged in the drug trade to pay the PIRA to send trainers to Colombia. In its remote locations, the FARC acted as a government force, collecting taxes, reducing small-scale crime, and providing some social services. It sent fighters to Vietnam and the Soviet Union for military training. Venezuela, Cuba, the Soviet Union, and Ecuador also supported it. In the 1980s, members began wearing uniforms and establishing military ranks that they hoped would meet the requirements of the Geneva Conventions, which were necessary in order to be recognized as a legitimate military force. Approximately 20–30 percent of the recruits were "drafted" minors.[151] Most of its targets were military ones, but civilians were also killed. Policemen, political adversaries, journalists, local leaders, and individuals who refused to pay taxes were also targeted. In the first decade of the twenty-first century, a Colombian military offensive weakened the FARC, and states that had previously supported the group became eager for a settlement. Cuba hosted peace negotiations that began in 2016. In 2017, the finalized settlement shielded FARC members from prison time, forced the FARC to surrender its weapons to the United Nations, and allow the FARC to establish a communist political party, the Common Alternative Revolutionary Force, which would automatically be given ten seats in Congress through 2026. The Common Alternative Revolutionary Force began competing in national elections shortly after and could gain more seats if it gathers enough votes. Although President Juan

Manuel Santos of Colombia received a Nobel Peace Prize for signing the agreement, it unexpectedly destroyed his domestic support. Many Colombians were furious with the peace deal, insisting that the agreement was too soft on the FARC. Voters rejected the deal in a national referendum, but Santos negotiated a new one that would avoid another national referendum. Colombia's legislature approved the new agreement, but the public's fury helped elect a new president, Ivan Duque, who had manipulated the anger against the peace deal to propel him to the presidency.[152]

FARC's political party got less than a half of 1 percent of the 2018 vote and did not gain a single legislative seat.[153] However, during that election period, violent attacks against campaign staff and candidates, including its former commander, Rodrigo Londoño, forced the FARC to stop campaigning. Furthermore, around 1,200 FARC members refused to lay down their arms, and their continued involvement in drug trafficking remains a serious problem for Colombia's armed forces. Stimulated by the government's agreement with the FARC, the ELN, Colombia's liberation theology group that was founded in 1964, around the same time that the FARC was born, demanded peace talks. Presently, the ELN, which has between 1,800 and 3,000 members, is holding eleven police officers and soldiers hostage, hoping to use them to compel the Colombian government to come to the negotiating table. Pablo Beltrán, a major ELN leader, said the hostages would be released as a gesture of good will, increasing the chances of a peace agreement being reached. He added that the group's ambitions are far less sweeping today than they were previously. "We're not asking for socialism," he said, and he emphasized that his group is mainly looking for basic protections for peasants. He noted that many ELN members did not trust the government to make a good deal. "I spoke with the guerrillas, the commanders, the low-level recruits and everyone asked me the same thing: 'Is it true they will really hold up their end of the bargain?'"[154]

One consequence of the peace arrangement with FARC was that the ELN expanded its territory into FARC lands and dove even deeper into the cocaine trade. It would seem that the country's conflict, which has resulted in the deaths of more than two hundred thousand Colombians, is far from finished. Pablo Beltrán agreed that the ELN's influence is rising and that its goal is to protect towns from paramilitary groups and developers. He emphasized that such goals would make it difficult for the rebels to lay down their weapons. In January 2019, ELN bombed a truck at the National Police Academy in Bogotá, killing twenty-one and injuring sixty-eight, the deadliest attack in Colombia's capital in sixteen years.[155] It was justified as a "military response" to government bombings during the ceasefire. The government suspended peace talks and demanded that Cuba extradite the ten ELN leaders living there. Ultimately, Cuba refused, contending that the negotiation protocols obliged it to protect all parties.[156]

Seven of these successes were connected to the Cold War, and only South Tyrol could be considered an effort completely untouched by the conflict. The Sandinistas' "success" came during the height of the Cold War and was the only one with both Soviet and Cuban support. However, President Carter's refusal to support the Somoza dynasty was very pertinent in this case. Carter was ultimately influenced by the fact that the Sandinistas "avoided [the] random killing of civilians" in its final campaign and that virtually all other Latin American terror campaigns had failed.

Five such campaigns "succeeded" because the Cold War ended. El Salvador, Eritrea, Palestine, Colombia, and South Africa found it easier to negotiate a solution after the Soviet collapse. Terrorists accepted Soviet support partly because they were hostile to the West, yet that link could obviously become a liability. In some cases, groups benefited from cutting international ties and making local circumstances more critical. The Kosovo problem was also a result of the end of the Cold War. While FARC survived for twenty-eight years after the Soviets fell, Cuba's support for the group weakened, helping bring FARC to the negotiating table.[157] Restraints and weakness also helped. Eritreans avoided committing atrocities and largely waged a guerrilla war. They constructed underground hospitals and built schools in areas they captured, factors that kept the United Nations from getting involved. The PLO's weakness and renunciation of terrorism enabled international powers to get Israel to accept the Oslo Accords, even though those powers have yet to convince Israel and the Palestine Authority to implement them fully. The restraint of STLC was evident in its second campaign (1972–1988), where it conducted 360 attacks but killed only seventeen Italians. The El Salvadorian FMNLF's decision to avoid American casualties was also of critical important. The South African struggle provides the clearest example of how important restraint could be. The white South Africans had to be persuaded they would survive in the new state. Initially the ANC was committed to nonviolent resistance and only created the MK after the government massacred peaceful protestors. Nonetheless, the ANC simultaneously continued its nonviolent campaign, realizing that demonstrations were vital to generate support. The MK shared similar sentiments, as their unprecedented decision to sign the 1948 Geneva Convention demonstrates.

The size of terrorist forces was another significant indicator of whether a struggle could go for decades without a political solution. All of the successful efforts in the Third Wave except for that of STLC put thousands into the field of battle. However, since the population of South Tyrol is only five hundred thousand people, a group of two hundred terrorists is actually quite large. In the case of Kosovo, when contending parties could not reach an agreement, international elements imposed a solution, an event never seen before in the history of terrorism. This unprecedented action was mostly successful because, at the time, Russia was too weak to resist NATO's efforts.

5

THE FOURTH WAVE: RELIGIOUS, 1979–2020s?

All these crimes and sins committed by the Americans are a clear declaration of war on God, his messenger, and Muslims. . . . The ruling to kill the Americans and their allies—civilians and military—is an individual duty for every Muslim . . . to liberate the al-Aqsa Mosque [Jerusalem] and the holy mosque [Mecca] from their grip. . . . This is in accordance with the words of Almighty God, "fight the pagans all together as they fight you altogether" and "fight them until there is no more tumult or oppression, and there prevails justice and faith in God."

—OSAMA BIN LADEN

lthough time gaps separating the precipitating political events and the development of terrorist activity existed in the first three waves, in the Fourth Wave there was no such time gap because the three major precipitating events were directly associated with terrorism. All occurred in the Islamic world, where religion was used to justify terror. Very quickly afterward, Jewish, Sikh, and Christian terror groups emerged. But Islamic groups were larger, more durable, and had more global impact.

Furthermore, while Sikh, Jewish, and Christian terrorists came from national bases, Islamic terrorists often came from many countries to join a specific group. Two groups, al-Qaeda (Foundation or Base) and ISIS (Islamic State), aimed to establish a Caliphate embracing the Islamic world. As in other waves, diasporas provided financial support, but some Islamic immigrants, like First Wave anarchists, employed terror in their new homes and then left to seek targets elsewhere. "Suicide bombing," or "self- martyrdom," the Fourth Wave's distinguishing tactic, made it the most destructive wave. The only religious groups to embrace this tactic were Islamic, though, ironically, the secular Tamil Tigers used it more often than any Islamic group. Islamic groups and the Tamil Tigers also provided social services for their constituents.

Al-Qaeda was born in the resistance to the Soviet invasion of Afghanistan and eventually became the wave's most important group. After the Soviets withdrew from Afghanistan, al-Qaeda began to aid uprisings in the Islamic world in Asia and Africa, which were ultimately unproductive. Al-Qaeda then decided to strike U.S. targets, hoping that U.S. reactions would unify the Islamic world. 9/11 was the wave's high point and the most destructive terrorist act ever. In total, 2,996 people perished—an even bloodier tally than the 2,403 killed in the Japanese attack on Pearl Harbor to initiate World War II. The United States then invaded Afghanistan, forcing al-Qaeda to flee the country. But instead of completing the job, the United States decided to invade Iraq to prevent Saddam Hussein's regime from giving al-Qaeda weapons of mass destruction, weapons that Iraq did not have. The invasion outraged Muslims everywhere, enabling al-Qaeda to get more recruits and develop Iraqi resistance. One unexpected consequence of al-Qaeda's activity was gruesome atrocities against the Shi'a population, which stimulated Sunni and Shi'a conflicts throughout the Islamic world. Some of these conflicts persist and are more intense. However, the United States immensely weakened al-Qaeda's first franchise, al-Qaeda-in Iraq (AQI) and al-Qaeda Central (AQC), but AQI was later revived and became known during the Syrian Civil War as the Islamic State (ISIS). It was a very important enemy of AQC because ISIS's primary concern was remaking the Muslim world, even if it required horrific acts of violence against Muslims, especially the Shi'a. While al-Qaeda concluded that Islam's history demonstrated that the "Near Enemy" would disappear once the "Far Enemy" attacked, ISIS argued the opposite. They insisted that success rested on eliminating the Near Enemy before grappling with the Far Enemy, even if attacking the Near Enemy yielded enormous Islamic casualties. While AQC never regained its ground bases, it employed two methods to revitalize itself. The first was a "lone wolf strategy" previously developed by U.S. Christian terrorists, though it did not yield significant results. The second was the creation of various franchises, but these tended to focus on local activities and occasionally employed terror against Muslims, which greatly irritated AQC. Those franchises also provided little support to help AQC's efforts against the West and especially the United States.

DISTINCTIVE FEATURES

The first three waves aimed to achieve various goals the French Revolution had introduced. But the Fourth Wave was hostile to the French Revolution's aim of creating a world of secular nation-states. Religion was seen as the basis for government legitimacy. Hostility to secularism generated hostility between the Fourth and Third Wave, the first time significant bloody clashes between groups in different waves occurred. In the Fourth Wave, groups from different religions were hostile to each other, a hostility rooted in profound historical memories. Islamic groups precipitated the wave in 1979. They later employed self-martyrdom, which the states in the West labeled "suicide bombing," a tactic that made this wave the most destructive and indiscriminate. Soon, the wave expanded to include Sikhs in India, Jews in Israel, Tamils in Sri-Lanka, Aum Shinrikyo in Japan, and Christians in the United States, Africa, and Asia. Europe and Latin America, the major geographical sites for First and Third Wave attacks, did not generate religious terrorist groups, but foreign religious groups made a few strikes there. Lebanon's Hezbollah, aided by the Shi'a diaspora, bombed

Israeli targets twice in Argentina.[1] In Western Europe, foreign Islamic groups aided by Islamic immigrants made many attacks.

States created in the anticolonial Second Wave and those in Asia that emerged after the Soviet Union's collapse produced the most terrorist organizations partly because those states seemed "artificial" to many of their residents. Bitter violent conflicts between Third and Fourth Wave groups erupted in most Middle Eastern states, a new pattern, illustrating that the differences between principles of religious and secular legitimacy were far more profound than those between various secular principles. There was one case of an important Third Wave person who joined a Fourth Wave group: "Carlos the Jackal," the Venezuelan Marxist-Leninist who led the spectacular 1975 Palestinian raid on the OPEC headquarters in Vienna that took sixty hostages. After 9/11, he converted to Islam and pledged allegiance to Osama bin Laden. Carlos was in prison at the time, serving a life sentence that prevented him from joining al-Qaeda in any more than a notional capacity.[2]

The international system was reshaped profoundly. The Soviet collapse after its defeat in Afghanistan meant that the United States was the only remaining superpower. Aerial drones were used to cross the borders of other states to strike terrorists, weakening the principle of state sovereignty. Islamic groups wanted to eliminate many of the nation-states created during the Second Wave, using religion to establish new boundaries. The Palestinian conflict was different; Hamas (Islamic Resistance Movement) aimed to make Palestine a religious state but made few international attacks. Sikhs and Tamils were also concerned with their own states, but Sikhs struck Indian targets abroad, and Tamils occasionally struck targets in India. Christians in the United States, Africa, and Asia focused entirely on their countries, and Jews confined their activities to the "Holy Land."[3]

As in Third Wave, assassinations of prominent figures were infrequent and often described as punishments. However, the Tamil Tigers (LTTE) of Sri Lanka was a prominent exception; it undertook many assassinations, like First Wave groups. One hundred and six Sri Lankan officials were assassinated, including a president, a presidential candidate, cabinet members, thirty-seven members of parliament, and an Indian prime minister.[4]

Hijacking, the Third Wave's trademark, also declined greatly. Between 1968 and 1977, the annual average was forty-one. Yet between 2000 and 2011, when only Fourth Wave organizations were active, that average fell to 2.4, which reduced passenger scrutiny and helps explain why it was so easy to hijack the planes for the 9/11 attacks.

Planes and other modes of transportation were occasionally bombed simply to destroy them and their passengers. In 1985, Sikhs bombed an Air India plane over Canada, killing 329, the deadliest airplane explosion ever.[5] In Kyrgyzstan, suspected Muslim separatists seized a bus and killed everyone on board. For some Palestinians, Israeli buses became favorite bombing targets.

The Fourth Wave's first decade produced important kidnappings. The 1979 Iranian hostage crisis, when the U.S. embassy was taken, an act embraced by Iran's government, was the wave's first terrorist act. To release the captives, President Reagan agreed to sell weapons to Iran to use in its war against Iraq; money from the sales was used to secretly fund the Third Wave Nicaraguan Contras. Lebanon's Hezbollah also kidnapped 104 Western citizens between 1982 and 1992 to prevent retaliation by U.S. and French forces for being forced to withdraw. Islamic elements struggling to separate Chechnya from Russia also produced shocking hostage incidents. In 1995, after demanding the Russians leave Chechnya, separatists seized a hospital, taking around one thousand hostages. Russian efforts to retake the hospital produced hundreds of casualties and injuries. In 2002, Chechens stormed Moscow's Dubrovka Theater, taking over eight hundred hostages. The Russians pumped gas into the theater, killing 140 hostages and thirty terrorists.[6] Two years later, over 1,200 hostages were taken at a Russian school. After a three-day standoff, a chaotic rescue operation killed thirty-one terrorists and 331 hostages, including 176 children. The Lord's Resistance Army in Uganda kidnapped children to make boys terrorists and girls "sex slaves."[7] In 2006, Hamas released an Israeli soldier in exchange for 1,027 Palestinian terrorists and terrorist suspects. In 2008, Islamic groups in Mali gave Western hostages to a secessionist movement. When Iraq was invaded after 9/11, Iraqi terrorists kidnapped over two hundred foreigners and publicly beheaded dozens in an attempt to compel their governments and companies to withdraw from the area.[8] In one decade, Europeans gave $130 million to Islamic groups to free hostages.

In 1996, during the first Chechen War, a new kind of atrocity emerged when a Russian soldier was beheaded for refusing to convert to Islam.[9] A beheading organized by an al-Qaeda member in 2002 drew enormous international attention. In Pakistan, Daniel Pearl, a *Wall Street Journal* reporter, became a prisoner for four months after 9/11 on charges that he was a spy.[10] The United States was told it must meet many demands, including freeing all Pakistani terror detainees and permitting a halted U.S. shipment to Pakistan of F-16 Fighting Falcons to continue. Attached to the message were photos of Pearl handcuffed with a gun to his head as he held up a newspaper. He was the first victim to appear on video denouncing the United States and emphasizing his Jewish heritage and Israeli connections. Shortly afterward, his throat was slit and head severed on camera. The video warned that if all Guantanamo Bay prisoners were not released the act would be repeated "again and again." But the tactic had no impact on Guantanamo Bay prisoners and was not repeated "again and again."

Kidnapping patterns in the Third and Fourth Waves differed too, particularly for those seeking money.[11] "44.3 percent of all kidnap ransom cases took place between 1975 and 1984 . . . the watershed for left wing terrorism worldwide."[12] From 2008 to 2010, only 3.5 percent of hostage cases involved money requests, and most were carried out by the Communist Party in India, a Third Wave Maoist entity. Religious groups rarely took hostages for money. Lebanon's Hezbollah was the major exception during the 1980s turbulence, when the presence of Westerners made it especially profitable.

Though comparatively infrequent, hostage taking remained important for other reasons. A number of Third Wave disproportionate prisoner exchanges happened and were repeated in the Fourth Wave. The most dramatic occurred in 2011, when Hamas exchanged an Israeli soldier for 1,027 Palestinian terrorists and terrorist suspects. Enraged Israelis made angry protests.[13] Nonetheless, other "disproportionate" Israeli releases occurred.

Third Wave terrorists preferred to strike from a safe distance, and if captured, comrades took hostages to get them released. In the Fourth Wave, there was much less interest in attackers' safety. Hezbollah, influenced by the medieval Assassins (a Shi'a offshoot), reintroduced the "self-martyrdom" tactic, but now bombs replaced knives, producing far more casualties.[14] The West described the tactic as "suicide bombing," a term radical Muslims argue is "a construct of the Jews to discourage our brothers from such activities."[15] One study estimates that "conventional bomb attacks" since the 1980s have killed fewer than one person per incident, while self-martyrdom attacks killed twelve, and this striking difference does not include figures from 9/11.[16] Suicide bombers can better pinpoint their targets, make last-minute adjustments, and choose the moment that inflicts the greatest damage. "This tactical flexibility is rare in [other] terrorist attacks . . . even with the most expensive and technologically advanced conventional weaponry."[17] Because the bomber does not need much help, there are fewer on the scene with critical information if captured. No escape plan is necessary, and the bomber becomes a "martyr" who garners enormous attention and inspires many emulators.[18]

The Fourth Wave also stimulated a new anxiety: weapons of mass destruction (WMD). In 1991, the U.S. Office of Technology Assessment stated that sometimes it would be easier for terrorists to use chemical and biological weapons (WMDs) than bombs.[19] For the next two decades, the fear kept growing, and as Alex Schmid notes, 18.1 percent of recent terrorism articles dealt with WMD threats. In fact, no subject in the field gets as much attention.[20] It became an obsession in 1995 after Aum Shinrikyo, a Japanese religious group influenced by the book of Revelation and Nostradamus, a sixteenth-century French astrologist and physician who said the world would end in 1999, attempted to initiate the apocalypse via five chemical attacks on the Tokyo subway system, the world's busiest, killing thirteen and seriously injuring fifty.[21] The world then learned Aum Shinrikyo had previously made abortive attempts to use biological weapons. Soon afterward, U.S. Defense Secretary William Cohen said in 1997 that "our military superiority is so great, potential adversaries may feel compelled to use chemical and biological weapons." Holding up a five-pound bag of sugar, he announced, "This amount of anthrax spores could wipe out Washington, DC." Bruce Hoffman, a prominent terrorist specialist, agreed: "Guns were now outdated."[22]

In 1998, when asked if he was trying to obtain chemical and nuclear weapons, al-Qaeda's leader Osama bin Laden said, "Acquiring weapons for the defense of Muslims is a religious duty. . . . It would be a sin for Muslims not to try to possess the weapons that would prevent the infidels from inflicting harm on Muslims."[23] A Saudi cleric, Sheik al-Fahd, issued a fatwa in 2003, "A Legal Treatise on Using Weapons of Mass Destruction Against Infidels," that stated, "In a defensive war, Muslims must use all means at their disposal and must not recoil from using any method to hit 'the Crusaders.'"[24] Between 1999 and 2001, al-Qaeda instituted WMD training courses in Afghanistan,[25] and fears that Iraq would give al-Qaeda WMDs was the reason given by the Bush administration for why the United States invaded Iraq in 2003. In 2007, al-Qaeda in Iraq (AQI) made bombs with chlorine gas and used them in thirteen attacks.[26] Hundreds were injured, but the explosives, not the chlorine, were responsible for the few killed. However, panic intensified,[27] even though al-Qaeda's "own literature and manual reveal many flaws" that explain the gas bomb's failure.[28]

Hamas also made bombs with poisonous chemicals. In 2001, one containing nails and bolts covered with rat poison exploded in Jerusalem, but the explosion destroyed the poison, and the bomb did no damage. Several Palestinian bombers conducted suicide bombings hoping to spread hepatitis B, but again, the damage was minimal. Palestinian terrorists were imprisoned for planning to use cyanide in several attacks. Some American religious right groups used WMDs. Several Minnesota Patriots Council efforts to assassinate around one hundred government officials using ricin failed.[29] A cyanide gas plot was thwarted in Tyler, Texas in 2003.[30] Shortly after 9/11, Army of God sent letters containing a white, powdery substance falsely claimed to be anthrax to hundreds of health clinics and abortion rights groups.[31] A week after 9/11, the United States experienced its first deadly WMD assaults. Letters with anthrax spores killed five and infected seventeen others. The FBI investigation, "one of the largest and most complex in the history of law enforcement," focused on scientists in biodefense labs at Fort Detrick, Maryland, where Bruce Ivins, the chief suspect, ultimately committed suicide.

From 1968 to 2012, there were over one hundred thousand terrorist incidents, and only sixty involved WMDs, roughly one in two thousand. Furthermore, no WMD attack caused mass casualties. What lessons does this history suggest? WMD-related deaths occurred only when scientific personnel were involved, and even then the number killed was minute. The fact that most attempts were aborted means that it takes time to learn to use such weapons, making them much less practical than conventional ones. The moral of the story may be that the public's unjustified anxiety fueled most efforts.[32] Bombs remained the preferred weapon; they were used in 57 percent of incidents, and in the mid-1990s, the percentage rose to 70 percent. Gun attacks also remained significant, with annual percentages varying from 7 to 30 percent; the long Iraq and Afghanistan wars produced the highest figures.[33] ISIS recently revived anxieties about chemical weapons by using them fifty-two times in Syria and Iraq. But ISIS then had considerable territory in which to establish its chemical factory. Still, the damage from these efforts has been "rudimentary." Variations in the delivery systems suggest that no way has yet been found to make the weapons a significant threat.

Government overreactions to terrorism are common. World War I, the Israeli invasion of Lebanon, and the American invasion of Iraq are prime examples. Despite Friedrich Nietzsche's warning that "he who fights with monsters must take care lest he thereby becomes a monster," the mistreatment of prisoners prominent in the First Wave resurged in the Fourth Wave. Part of this revival can be explained by the fact that there are no acceptable rules for dealing with terrorists, who are considered neither criminals nor prisoners of war. The need for information to prevent surprise attacks induces governments to use torture. Americans described their prisoners as "illegal combatants" and kept them in overseas detention centers like Guantanamo Bay, Cuba; Abu Ghraib in Iraq; and the Parwan Detention Facility, part of Bagram Air Force Base in Afghanistan. The atrocities committed in these centers sparked considerable international and domestic hostility.[34] In 2015, Senator Dianne Feinstein stated, "Guantanamo is one of the best propaganda tools that terrorists have today. ISIS dresses its victims in the same orange prisoner suits used in Guantanamo before their ghastly beheadings. . . . It costs billions, more than $2.5 million per detainee . . . 779 people were placed there without charge. . . . Only ten have been convicted or charged."[35]

In the First and Third Waves, women played very important roles, as women's emancipation movements were significant in the West. But in the Fourth Wave, like the Second, terrorist groups placed a great deal of emphasis on traditional gender roles. Women were normally restricted to collecting information and providing logistical support. Bin Laden's first training manual was dedicated to protecting Muslim women.[36] Although it displays a paramount desire to learn from the experiences of friends and enemies, it ignores the past value of female terrorists and initially excluded women from campaigns.[37]

The Tamil Tigers' experience was different. Initially they restricted women to intelligence and logistic roles, but in 1983, a mass rape called Black July in Sri Lanka enraged women across the country. The Tamil Tigers, weakened by casualties, capitalized on the anger and began using women everywhere. The Freedom Birds, an all-female unit, began in 1984. Soon, over 20 percent of the Tamil Tigers were female, the largest proportion of any Fourth Wave group. The ten-member Tamil Tigers governing cell had three female members. In 1991, the first female suicide attack occurred, and eventually one-quarter of the Tamil Tigers' suicide bombers were women. Women carried out forty-six suicide bombings, more than any Fourth Wave group. But they lacked the freedom of their First and Third Wave counterparts; they were segregated, and the sexual activities of "armed virgins" were monitored. Three were actually hanged in 1994 for having sex outside the group.[38]

In 2002, a decade after the Tamil Tigers, two female Muslim martyrs appeared in Palestine. Islamic groups elsewhere began producing them, especially in Iraq, Russia, and Chechnya. Afghanistan, Pakistan, Jordan, Uzbekistan, and North Ossetia followed suit. The spread was rapid because "on average, a [suicide bomb] attack by a woman gets eight times as much press attention as a similar attack by a man."[39] These women were generally better educated and more successful in their careers than male suicide bombers, but many had been dishonored by sexual indiscretions and rapes. In one astounding case, Iraqi authorities in 2009 displayed a video where the "mother of believers" confessed to sending twenty-eight women on suicide attacks, after organizing the rape of eighty women and then persuading them that martyrdom would redeem their lost honor.[40] In 2003, al-Qaeda changed its view that women had symbolic value only. A female unit was formed led by Umm Osama. Al-Qaeda then established a women's magazine in 2004. "Our goal is Shahida [martyrdom] for the sake of Allah. . . . We stand shoulder to shoulder with our men . . . covered by our veils and wrapped in our robes, weapons in hand, our children in our laps."[41] But al-Qaeda Central never employed female bombers, though some associated groups such as al-Qaeda in Iraq did.

Lebanon produced the first female bomber in 1985, Sana'a Mehaidli, a seventeen-year-old member of the Syrian Social Nationalist Party, a Third Wave Christian-dominated group. She targeted Israeli forces in Lebanon and was described as "the progenitor of all female martyrs for the Palestinian cause."[42] Nine years later, after the first female Muslim attack in Chechnya, other female attacks occurred in Israel, Iraq, Dagestan, Jordan, Russia, Afghanistan, Pakistan, Uzbekistan, and North Ossetia. France in 2010 was the only Western state to experience a female suicide bomber attempt, but it was thwarted. Unlike the female Tamil Tigers, Islamic women and those in other Fourth Wave groups did not engage in other forms of violence; they got information and provided logistic support, as they had in the Second Wave. They still had advantages in being able to move about freely and were not searched closely; those advantages also explain why they were used for suicide bombing and assigned particular targets. Thus, although "women make up roughly 15 percent of the suicide bombers within groups that utilize females, they were responsible for 65 percent of assassinations."[43]

The Fourth Wave produced large groups, comparable to those in the Second Wave, but the Second Wave groups did not last as long and produced fewer casualties, because colonial powers are more likely than national states to yield territories. Algeria is the striking exception. It experienced several campaigns from 1991 to 2002, which killed between 150,000 and 200,000, a significant number but considerably fewer than the million killed during its Second Wave eight-year campaign waged against the French.

In the 1980s, there were some two hundred organizations, mostly Third Wave; a decade later, there were only forty Third Wave groups. They had greatly outnumbered Fourth Wave ones but now had largely disappeared.[44] Fourth Wave groups are much larger because there are fewer major religions than nations, and those religions have much larger constituencies. Some Third Wave groups with different aims cooperated, but the practice diminished greatly. Shi'a and Sunni Islamic groups frequently fought each other; conflict was rare in earlier waves.[45] This tension eventually engulfed the Middle East, with all major states participating in the ongoing Shi'a-versus-Sunni Syrian civil war that began in 2011. In similar fashion, the Tamil Tigers formed a union with six groups and eventually destroyed its five partners. The four major Sikh organizations also decimated one another.[46]

Islam is the heart of the Fourth Wave. Islamic groups have conducted the most frequent, significant, deadly, and profoundly international attacks. They are also the wave's most durable groups, outliving all their Third Wave counterparts. The four key events providing hope for the Fourth Wave in 1979 occurred in the Islamic world, and the consequences strongly influenced groups elsewhere.[47] The Sikhs in India, Jews in Israel, and Christians in the United States, Africa, and Asia began terror activities in the 1980s. In 1995, an odd new religious group, Aum Shinrikyo (Supreme Truth), which combined Buddhist, Hindu, and Christian themes, began attacks in Japan. Buddhism and Hinduism produced late minimal efforts; the DKBA (Democratic Karen Buddhist Army) became active in Myanmar (Burma) in the mid-1990s and was followed by a Hindu group, Abhinav Bharat (Young India), which bombed Muslims in 2008.[48]

The Fourth Wave appeared first in various Middle Eastern states, Afghanistan, and African countries: Algeria, Libya, Sudan, and Somalia. Later, other parts of Asia became engulfed as well, including India, Sri Lanka, the Philippines, Thailand, and Indonesia. When the Soviet Union broke up 1991, Russia and former parts of the Soviet Union, now states in Asia, experienced terrorist attacks for the first time since the First Wave.

Finally, although the West had always been seen as the root of the Islamic world's problems, it was not until the third decade of the wave that Islamic groups began targeting Western states like the United States, France, the United Kingdom, and Spain. In sub-Saharan Africa, Islamic groups frequently engaged in riots. Boko Haram (Western Education Is Sacrilege), founded in Nigeria in 2001, initially targeted Nigerian Christians but after 2009 turned their attention to international targets.

Secular states sometimes used religious groups against domestic opponents, but those efforts often dramatically backfired. Prime Minister Indira Gandhi encouraged a Sikh religious figure, Jarnail Singh Bhindranwale, to enter the political arena and divide the opposition party, but he ended up leading a Sikh terrorist uprising. The United States supported Arabs in fighting the Soviets in Afghanistan, but when the Soviets were driven out, those Arabs attacked the United States several times, culminating in 9/11. Egypt's President Anwar Sadat released religious terrorists from prison to help combat secular opposition to the Israel-Egypt Peace Treaty, but they assassinated him instead. Israel gave the Muslim Brotherhood of Palestine aid to help Israel against the PLO. However, the Brotherhood eventually created Hamas, Israel's major Fourth Wave terrorist foe.[49]

Groups from different religions rarely cooperated. The U.S. Christian radical right and al-Qaeda had common enemies—the United Nations, the United States, Israel, and Judaism—but never made contacts. William Pierce, a major American figure of the far right, "occasionally offered veiled praise for Islamic terrorists, especially Osama bin Laden," and admired Palestinian suicide bombers, whom he described as "paying a terrible price to liberate their land."[50] 9/11 changed his view. While he was pleased "a great many Jewish lawyers . . . [and] financial consultants . . . died . . . thousands of young White women who worked as receptionists, secretaries, and file clerks were killed, along with hundreds of passengers and crew members." The act also enabled "our Jewish dominated government" to gain enormous powers through the Patriot Act passed afterward. Pierce concluded that the act was evil and that his former hero Osama bin Laden should be killed.[51] In 2005, the Aryan Nations leader August Kreis pushed for an alliance with al-Qaeda but received no response: "You say they're terrorists, I say they're freedom fighters. And I want to instill the same jihadic feeling in our people's heart, in the Aryan race that they have for their father, who they call Allah."[52]

Nonetheless, special circumstances sometimes produced limited cooperation between groups from different religions. In India, some Sikhs had ties to Kashmiri Islamic groups with similar secessionist aims.[53] Pakistan offered Sikh terrorists its training facilities. Sudan's Islamic government aided the Lord's Resistance Army, a Christian millenarian group, in neighboring Uganda.

While Second and Third Wave groups normally emerged in states where they had constituencies and bases, al-Qaeda evolved differently. In the Afghan struggle against the Soviet Union, Arabs from sixty countries volunteered to fill al-Qaeda's ranks. Groups were excluded; only individuals were accepted. Al-Qaeda also trained and sent members to help Sunni groups in Asia, Africa, and Europe. But unlike the Third Wave, they were not members of a unit.

Sikhs initially operated in India, especially in the Punjab region, where Sikhs constituted a majority, but when that was no longer feasible, they struck a few Indian targets in Canada, the United Kingdom, Romania, Austria, and the United States, aided by the Sikh diaspora. Jewish terror campaigns were waged in Israel, with one exception, the Jewish Defense League, which operated in the United States before relocating to Israel. Christian terror was largely confined to the United States, Africa, and Asia, though Europe had a few incidents. Finally, Aum Shinrikyo never struck targets outside Japan, although it intended ultimately to destroy the United States.is widespread variety in religious affiliations is not surprising, because all major religions have engaged in wars. Christian wars have been the most frequent, intense, and internecine. Islam is in second place.[54]

When a religious justification is offered for a cause that might otherwise be justified in political or economic terms the struggle is intensified and complicated enormously for many reasons. Perhaps the most important is that religious conflict involves fundamental values, and struggles involving questions of identity notoriously are the most difficult to compromise because they release the greatest passions.[55]

Fourth Wave Muslim and Sikh activities reflected these qualities best, making the wave the most destructive and casualty ridden of all. Christian and Jewish groups were, generally speaking, far more restrained.

Beyond providing justifications, religions sanctify moments, sites, and objects, and ceremonies can attract large and passionate crowds susceptible to manipulation. Enemies deliberately focus on these special moments and sites to display contempt, as Natalie Davis's study of sixteenth-century Catholic and Protestant riots in France reveals. "The occasion for most religious violence was during the time of religious worship. . . . Much is timed to ritual, and violence often seems to be a continuation of the rite. A Catholic mass is the occasion for an attack on the host."[56] In the ancient world, most violence between Jews and Romans occurred during Passover, when Jews commemorated the exodus from Egypt. Christians in medieval Europe also attacked Jews during Passover, falsely accusing them of murdering children to use their blood to make matzos, an accusation termed "blood libel."[57]

Friday is Islam's holiest day, when all Muslims are obliged to pray in a mosque, and Friday is also the day when violence most often occurs. Fiery sermons often incite riots, and persons hostile to Islam or a particular Islamic sect were tempted to strike mosques on Fridays because they knew there would be many worshippers. Al-Qaeda used Fridays in a different way; there were fewer people on the streets, so attacks could be conducted with less risk to their supporters.

Holy sites are especially dangerous places in the "Holy Land." Since 1929, violent clashes between Jews and Muslims have occurred in Hebron's Cave of the Patriarchs, the tomb of Abraham revered by Jews and Muslims. The Temple Mount in Jerusalem also saw frequent violent events during religious holidays. Abraham intended to sacrifice Isaac there, and the site later was chosen for the Temple. When Muslims conquered Jerusalem, they built the al-Aqsa Mosque on the Temple's ruins to commemorate Muhammad's ascent to heaven. In 2000, the Israeli leader Ariel Sharon led a thousand policemen to the Temple Mount to demonstrate that Israelis had the "right" to be there. After Friday religious services, Muslim riots began, sparking the al-Aqsa intifada, which continued for five years.

Christian secessionists in India, for example, the National Liberation Front of Tripura, targeted Hindu temples and the families of Hindu priests.[58] Sri Lankan Buddhist mobs struck Hindu temples, though the Tamil Tigers were secular. During Ashura, the highest emotional Shi'a moment in the year, commemorating the martyrdom of Husayn Ibn Ali, Muhammad's grandson and considered his rightful successor and their community's founder, pilgrimages are made to Karbala, Iraq, his burial site. There, Shi'ites flagellate themselves to share in Husayn's agony. Sunnis loathe the intoxicating ceremony, which symbolizes the eternal Shi'ite struggle against oppression, and often punctuate it with violent incidents, including in Bahrain (1923 and 1953) and Iraq (1921 and 1974). After the United States invaded Iraq in 2003, Christian groups were often targeted on Easter and Christmas. Christians, 40 percent of Nigeria's population, are particularly victimized on holy days. A spokesman for Boko Haram said it would kill all Nigerian Christians in order to establish sharia (Islamic law). In 2011, it killed over five hundred Christians and destroyed around 350 Nigerian churches. Muslim governments elsewhere have organized riots and terrorist attacks against Christians. UN reports indicate that Sudan's government has displaced between fifty and seventy-five thousand Christians.[59]

Charity has also been a central feature of major religions. It is less prominent in Hinduism. Ancient Greek and Roman religions did not engage in charity. In Islam, zakat (charity) is the third of Islam's Five Pillars, obliging Muslims to donate a portion of their wealth from 2.5% and 20% to the poor or slaves.[60] In a somewhat unprecedented fashion, some Fourth Wave Islamic terrorist groups developed durable extensive social welfare programs that contributed to their longevity. Four Third Wave groups had initiated social welfare efforts. The PLO, subsidized by Islamic elements in the oil states, was the first terrorist organization to develop an important welfare program.[61] Three other Latin American Third Wave groups made similar efforts, the Tupamaros, Sendero Luminoso, and FARC. But most groups then were in urban areas, where their limited financial resources and small size made them less able to conduct the visible activities social welfare requires.

The Egyptian and Tunisian Muslim Brotherhood produced the earliest, albeit unimportant, programs. Hezbollah's social welfare was very impressive and helped make it the wave's most durable and successful organization. The civil wars and foreign interventions of the 1970s so weakened Lebanon's government that it could only provide "skeleton" social welfare services. In 1984, Hezbollah used Iranian funds to launch an "extremely sophisticated network of health and social services" that it described as a "social jihad," administering thirty-three hospitals, twelve health centers, twenty dental clinics, and numerous schools, libraries, relief centers, and agricultural co-ops. Seventy-two percent of the poor said they would go to Hezbollah before the government for help. Initially, services were limited to the Shi'a, the poorest Lebanese, a sixth of the population. Now it aids Sunnis and even Christians in Shi'a areas. It helped those in other areas affected by Israel's 2006 attacks, which "displaced people, with water, food, shelter . . . and promise[d] to pay compensation to people whose homes had been destroyed, offering $12,000 until their homes were reconstructed."[62] Social work enabled Hezbollah to become "a state within a state" and explains why it is not on the European Union's terrorist organization list and why some Europeans marched with Hezbollah members in Europe to raise money for its social welfare program. Hamas's 1988 charter stresses the crucial importance of charity.

> Social solidarity consists of extending help to all the needy, both materially and morally. . . . It is incumbent upon members of Hamas to look after the interests of the masses. . . . When this spirit reigns, congeniality will deepen, cooperation and compassion will prevail, unity will firm up, and the ranks will be strengthened in the confrontation with the enemy.[63]

Hamas-affiliated social welfare groups provide more welfare services than the Palestinian Authority, Palestine's nominal government. The Muslim diaspora supplies more funding for Hamas's social welfare than Iran and Syria do for Hezbollah. Some Americans feel this activity should change their country's view of Hamas. In 2003, the *Boston Globe* wrote, "To tag Hamas as a terrorist organization is to ignore its far more complex role in the Middle East drama."[64] While their social services are intended for all needy Palestinians, those involved in Hamas's terror campaigns receive more.[65]

Despite the benefits of these social welfare programs, charity was also used as a cloak of secrecy for terror campaigns. According to a 2008 FBI report, many charity board members were directly involved in planning, transferring materials, recruiting participants, and funding operations for terrorist attacks.[66] Charity funds provided safe houses for Hamas fugitives, paid to bring them back home, and provided funds for weapons. Hamas subsidizes schools to involve students in Hamas's activities. Kindergarten signs read "The Children of the Kindergarten Are the Martyrs of Tomorrow," and arms are buried on school playgrounds. Summer camps teach children the history of Islam with self-martyrdom pictures, and they work to instill "seeds of hate" against Israel.

Islamic charitable groups also financed violent activities after the Soviets invaded Afghanistan, and the U.S. Department of Justice estimated that al-Qaeda received 30 percent of its money from foreign donations.[67] These contributions, used in the struggle against the Soviets, were listed in charities' record books as expenses for building mosques, schools, and "feeding the poor." A 1996 CIA report alleged that "one third of Islamic charity NGOs support terrorist groups or employ individuals . . . suspected of having terrorist connections."[68] Al-Qaeda in the Arabian Peninsula (AQAP) was the first al-Qaeda group to create a welfare program.[69] The Tamil Tigers followed the Islamic pattern when it controlled large Sri Lankan areas, making commitments to education, housing, health, and vocational training. The diaspora supplied funding for these efforts until foreign governments imposed strong restrictions on financial spending.

While First Wave terrorists helped spark two international wars and Third Wave terrorists triggered one, Fourth Wave groups precipitated six wars, all of which took place in the Muslim world: the Soviet-Afghan War (1979–1989), Iran-Iraq War (1980–1988), U.S.-Afghan War (2001–2021), U.S.-Iraq War (2003–2011), Syrian Civil War (2011–), and the Yemen–Saudi Arabian War (2015–). Terrorists participated in all these wars; struggles between Shi'a and Sunni were absent in the second Afghan war. Yet, despite the Islamic Republic of Iran's principal aims to reunite the two sects, in four wars they were a crucial factor that intensified all sorts of hostilities.[70]

ORIGIN

The Fourth Wave was an offshoot of the late nineteenth-century revival of "fundamentalism" in Christianity, Judaism, and Islam, which aimed to reduce secular influences. Particular doctrines and practices from a "sacred past are refined, modified and sanctioned . . . to serve as a bulwark against the encroachment of outsiders."[71] Fundamentalism began among American Protestants and then became important elsewhere. Fundamentalists are uncomfortable with nationalism, but the Islamic form is the most hostile, seeing nationalism as a product of the French Revolution.

Early Christian and Jewish fundamentalist groups were peaceful, as were most Islamic groups, with two major exceptions. The Muslim Brotherhood in Egypt in 1928 aimed to bring Sunnis everywhere together. It waged an assassination campaign in British Egypt against officials and organized mass demonstrations. Their efforts continued after independence. It tried to assassinate Colonel Nasser for establishing a military government in 1954 and experienced severe consequences.[72] In the 1970s it renounced violence, confined its activities to Egypt, emphasized the necessity to embrace sharia, and became committed to social welfare, managing 14 percent of Egypt's welfare services and highlighting the state's inadequacies.[73] The Iranian Devotees of Islam was the second exception to the period's mostly peaceful fundamentalist groups. It mounted an assassination campaign between

1948 and 1960, killing two prime ministers, to prevent the shah from establishing a secular state.[74] Following the Brotherhood's lead, the Iranian Devotees of Islam tried to create a Pan-Islamic movement to connect Shia and Sunni sects, but its leaders were captured, and the organization disappeared. However, former members played a key role in the Iranian Revolution.

Events in 1979 in the Islamic world precipitated the Fourth Wave by demonstrating religion's new significance and the weakness of secular groups.[75] The first event was the Iranian Revolution. From 1963 to 1977, the shah's government battled futile efforts by Third Wave terror groups.[76] However, an economic downturn produced popular demonstrations that numbered between six and nine million by December 1978, inducing the shah to leave Iran for a "holiday." Discounting exaggerated figures, one historian noted that the demonstrations may be the "largest protest event in history." Ten percent of Iran's population participated; by contrast, only 1 percent of the population was involved in demonstrations precipitating both the French and Russian revolutions.[77]

Different networks organized the demonstrations, but the outside world considered left-wing elements to be the major force. Over time, the Shia clergy attracted the poor, the left's "natural constituency." When Ayatollah Khomeini, the clergy's leader, returned from exile in February 1979, huge crowds greeted him. He dismantled the provisional government, which Iran's army refused to defend.[78] Leftists seized the U.S. embassy and held every occupant hostage. But Khomeini freed the hostages and apologized to the United States, which seemed oblivious to the political significance of the Shi'a sect and never tried to establish contact with the clergy.[79]

The United States admitted the shah for cancer treatment, reigniting memories that, after he fled in 1953, the United States had helped overthrow a democratically elected government. Infuriated students and Revolutionary Guard members again seized the U.S. embassy, taking sixty-six hostages. Unable to free the hostages, Iran's government resigned, and its successor strongly supported the hostage takers. The new government's head, Ayatollah Khomeini, announced, "This has united our people. Our opponents dare not act against us. We can put our constitution to the people's vote without difficulty."[80] The seizure is "celebrated every year as foundational event of the Islamic Revolution," a day in which the American flag is burned.[81]

The United States was told the hostages would be released when the shah returned. But President Jimmy Carter responded, "The United States will not yield to terrorist blackmail."[82] A 444-day crisis ensued. After the shah died in July 1980, an agreement was made, partly because Iraq had invaded Iran, and Iran desperately needed its frozen international financial assets. The United States promised never to intervene in Iranian domestic affairs again, freed Iranian assets, abandoned trade sanctions, and prevented hostages from suing Iran for personal damages. U.S. humiliation during the hostage crisis greatly contributed to Ronald Reagan's victory over President Carter in the 1980 election, and Iran released the fifty-two remaining hostages moments after Reagan's speech at his inauguration ended.

While the crisis came to an end, Iran remained involved in international religious terror. The Islamic Republic's constitution states its religious purpose: "All Muslims form a single nation, and the government of the Islamic Republic of Iran . . . must constantly strive to bring about the political, economic, and cultural unity of the Islamic world."[83] The clergy-led Council of Guardians vetoes "un-Islamic" acts and requires all government officials have Islamic credentials. The council finances and coordinates Islamic uprisings elsewhere.[84] It organized assassinations of Iranian émigrés in the West. When Salman Rushdie, a British citizen, published *The Satanic Verses* in 1988, Khomeini denounced it as a despicable description of Muhammad and issued a fatwa urging Muslims to kill Rushdie, inducing the United Kingdom to sever diplomatic relations.[85] Furthermore, instead of bringing Sunni (88 percent of the world's Islamic population) and Shi'a (12 percent) together, the revolution aggravated tensions in Iraq, Saudi Arabia, Bahrain, Kuwait, and Lebanon, states where Shi'a had experienced discrimination.[86] Shi'a demonstrations in various Gulf States were brutally repressed.[87] Iran helped train and arm some terrorist groups, inducing the six Persian Gulf states to link their military forces. In 1987, Iranian pilgrims sparked riots in Saudi Arabia, claiming the Saudi government was an unworthy guardian of Islam's holiest site. Pakistan and Afghanistan also experienced serious sectarian clashes. Afghanistan "had been immensely tolerant to a variety of Muslim sects, as well as to other religions and modern lifestyles. However, the civil war following the Soviet defeat dissolved this tolerance."[88] The Taliban (Students) quickly tried to force all Shi'a out of Afghanistan and killed every Shi'a found in the city of Mazar-e-Sharif.

In 1980, Iran was still engulfed in revolutionary chaos and had yet to attract Iraqi Shi'a, the country's largest sect. Most Iraqi Shi'a supported Iraq, as did the United States and most Arab states. The seven-year war, in which over 1.5 million died, was the twentieth century's longest conventional war. Although Iraq used chemical weapons, no supporting state, including the United States, objected. The war ultimately ended in a deadlock, but Iran's persistence demonstrated religion's new political significance.

As Shi'a-Sunni tensions continued to expand, some Sunnis sought alliances with Iran. In 1989, a military coup in Sudan brought Hassan al-Turabi to power. Al-Turabi, a Sunni radical, used his newfound authority to urge Shi'a and Sunnis to join against the West. He also invited Iran's Revolutionary Guard to train his forces and funded Shi'a factions in Lebanon. His regime achieved relatively little and lasted only six years. Syria, governed by the Alawites, a Shi'a offshoot, also became a firm Iran ally. After Israel invaded Lebanon in 1982 to eliminate the PLO, Iran helped organize Hezbollah to handle factional disputes. Hezbollah carried out suicide bombing attacks on American and French peacekeeping forces in Lebanon, forcing them to leave for fear that they might stumble into another Vietnam-style catastrophe.

The Israel-Egypt Peace Treaty in March 1979 was the second crucial event ending thirty years of conflict ,including three wars, and seemed to prove that Egypt, the most secular, left-wing, and powerful Muslim state, had surrendered Palestine. Indeed, the Arab League then suspended Egypt from the league at the behest of Saddam Hussein,[89] who took over Iraq in

1979, aiming to use the Palestine issue to help Iraq become the major Arab state in the region.[90] A Sunni terrorist group, the Egyptian Islamic Jihad, assassinated Sadat for signing the treaty. Ironically, before the group assassinated Sadat, he had freed some of Islamic Jihad's imprisoned members to help him deal with his left-wing opponents. To emphasize Iran's enthusiasm for the assassination, a street in Tehran was named to honor its organizer, Lieutenant Khalid Isambouli.

Iran was interested in the Palestinian plight but hostile to the PLO's aim of creating a secular nation-state. "The Ummah [Islamic community] has been parceled into small nation-states. It is no exaggeration to say that the post-colonial independent nation-states of today are more dependent on the West than they were in the heyday of colonialism. The Palestine struggle must be anchored in Islamic ideology and waged by a united Islamic front."[91] When the Iran-Iraq War broke out, the PLO and every Third Wave Iranian group sided with Iraq.

The first two events precipitating the Fourth Wave were unanticipated, but some Muslims expected the third one, except for its geography. One Islamic tradition maintains that a Redeemer (Mahdi) will come when a new Islamic century begins, an expectation that often sparked uprisings.[92] On November 20, 1979, the Islamic year 1400, over two hundred Sunnis from twelve countries captured the Grand Mosque in Mecca, Islam's holiest site, proclaiming that the Mahdi had arrived, denouncing the government for alien practices, and demanding it expel all non-Muslims from the Arabian Peninsula and stop sending oil to the United States. A wholly surprised government evacuated Mecca, and a ferocious two-week siege ensued, killing 255 and injuring 560. Saudi troops and Pakistani commandos stormed the Grand Mosque. The decision to employ outside military force and accept limited French support raised serious doubts about the government's ability to protect Islam's holiest site.[93]

The fourth key event was the Soviet invasion of Afghanistan in December 1979, the first time troops had been sent outside the Soviet orbit since World War II. The aim was to rescue a Marxist government that had seized power six years before and was facing a popular uprising. Soviet anxiety about losing a client state intensified because the Israel-Egypt Treaty signaled that the Soviets' most important Middle Eastern ally had shifted toward the West. To aid the Afghan rebels, volunteers poured in from across the Arab world and the Muslim diaspora. Inspired by Sunni religious beliefs associated with Salafism, the volunteers were convinced Islam's fate would be decided in Afghanistan. Pakistan, the United States, and Saudi Arabia provided significant help.[94] Shaken by the Mecca attack, Saudi Arabia aimed to resuscitate the religious source of its legitimacy. Indeed, Saudi involvement helped the monarch change his title from "His Majesty" to "Custodian of the Two Holy Mosques." It is striking that no secular Muslim group went to Afghanistan and that Iran, despite its initial commitment to bringing Islam together, developed its own efforts. After ten years in Afghanistan, the Soviets pulled out, and two years later, the Soviet Union collapsed. This stunning and wholly unexpected collapse of one of the two secular global superpowers convinced Islamic believers that their cause was irresistible.[95]

Third Wave terrorism was a Cold War instrument, intensifying the existing system of international tensions without changing it. Now terrorism became a major factor in transforming the international system. When the Soviet Union could no longer fund terror campaigns, many Third Wave organizations declined, leading the United States to stop funding terrorism research and reduce security and counterterrorism efforts.[96] This decision, which seems odd in retrospect, was greatly influenced by the fact that the United States was now the only superpower left. The choice was also reinforced by the fact that it had aided Islamic forces in Afghanistan.

Nineteen years after Iran had designated the United States as the "Great Satan," al-Qaeda made its first strikes against the United States, which quickly became the chief foreign target of many Islamic groups.[97] Surprisingly, no other foreign Fourth Wave group at that time followed al-Qaeda's lead. Aum Shinrikyo aimed to strike the United States in order to initiate a catastrophe that would produce a perfect world. But it failed in the first step of its strategy: disabling Japan's government.[98]

EMERGENCE OF AL-QAEDA AND 9/11

A few years after its creation, al-Qaeda, an Afghan resistance product, became the wave's major entity. In the last phase of the Afghan struggle, it focused on reunifying the Islamic world under a Caliphate. In 1996, it made a "Declaration of War Against the Americans Occupying the Land of the Two Holy Places" (that is, Saudi Arabia). Two years later, bin Laden signed a fatwa, "Jihad Against Jews and Crusaders," listing the actions of Americans that conflict with "God's order" and stating that the "ruling to kill the Americans and their allies—civilians and military—is an individual duty for every Muslim who can do it in any country in which it is possible to do it."[99]

While the "Crusaders" (the Far Enemy) were al-Qaeda's principal focus, bin Laden felt he had to eliminate the Near Enemy first, that is, states in the Muslim world with different religious sects and competing tribal, ethnic, and national identities: Algeria, Syria, Tunisia, Morocco, Indonesia, etc. Most of those states had experienced religious uprisings during the Afghan-Soviet conflict, and al-Qaeda supported Afghan veterans returning home to join the resistance in their home countries. The Soviet collapse also produced some sovereign states like Chechnya, Uzbekistan, Tajikistan, and Azerbaijan, where Muslim uprisings materialized and welcomed Afghan veterans. But the Near Enemy problem proved insurmountable, partly because terrorist tactics were so indiscriminate. A 1993 example is illustrative. The Islamic Jihad in Egypt attacked the prime minister from a girl's school in Cairo, hurting twenty-three and killing one young girl. An outraged Egyptian public took to the streets carrying the child's coffin and crying, "Terrorism is the enemy of God." Ayman al-Zawahiri, the attack's organizer, offered to pay the girl's family "blood money" to rectify the injustice; nearly three hundred members of Islamic Jihad were arrested after the attack. Four years later, al-Zawahiri tried to devastate the Egyptian economy by attacking Western tourists, hoping the government's response would generate support. However, after the Luxor massacre in 1997, where sixty-two tourists died, spontaneous antiterrorist demonstrations broke out again and made it virtually impossible to continue operating in Egypt. In Algeria, a ten-year civil war in the 1990s killed over one hundred thousand. The indiscriminate atrocities outraged the Muslim world, and bin Laden abandoned his Near Enemy policy.

One reason bin Laden decided the Near Enemy had to be dealt with first was historical: their crucial role in the Crusades. Their divisions and rivalries had made it impossible for a cooperative effort to resist the First Crusade, which left a tremendous psychological scar on the Muslim world. Bin Laden used the term "Crusader" deliberately to incite. Because of their apocalyptic commitment, the original Crusaders would not accept limits on their violence, a matter discussed in chapter 2. Subsequent Crusades were never able to reestablish Christian dominance in the Holy Land because, bin Laden argued, the Near Enemy had been defeated.

When bin Laden realized that al-Qaeda lacked the resources to eliminate the Near Enemy in the contemporary world, he attempted to provoke the "Crusaders" into committing acts that would infuriate and unify Muslims. On the eighth anniversary of the American military's arrival in Saudi Arabia to counter Iraq's 1990 Kuwait invasion, al-Qaeda's first major attack occurred: U.S. embassies in Kenya and Tanzania were bombed, killing 223 and injuring over four thousand.[100] But only twelve Americans were killed; the others were Africans, including many Muslims who had nothing to do with the embassies. In response, the U.S. launched missiles at al-Qaeda targets in Sudan and Afghanistan. A pharmaceutical factory manufacturing 50 percent of Sudan's medications was destroyed, and U.S. claims that the factory produced chemical weapons proved false.[101] U.S. strikes in Afghanistan occasioned few Muslim casualties. But the strikes and futile reactions had the unexpected consequence of making the relatively unknown bin Laden prominent.

Al-Qaeda decided next to inflict serious American military casualties, and a suicide bomber struck the U.S. destroyer *Cole* in 2000, killing seventeen sailors and wounding thirty-nine. For the first time, al-Qaeda claimed responsibility for a strike on the United States, but the "paper tiger" did not respond, turning the event into great victory for bin Laden. Al-Qaeda camps were soon filled with "new recruits and contributors from the Gulf States arrived . . . with petrodollars."[102] Arab states, especially Egypt, Saudi Arabia, and Algeria, produced most of al-Qaeda's new volunteers, and the Afghan training camps received Sunni volunteers from at least sixty countries. The international nature of al-Qaeda's recruiting was unique. During the Second and Third Waves, every organization recruited members from a single national base.[103] The contrast between PLO and al-Qaeda training facilities reflects this fact. While the PLO trained units from other organizations, al-Qaeda accepted only individuals.

Then came 9/11, a desperate gamble: a strike against the enemy's homeland, something that virtually all successful groups in the past had avoided because of the inevitable furious reactions it would garner. However, al-Qaeda believed a furious response would unite Muslims, thereby eliminating the Near Enemy.[104] The al-Qaeda operation took two years to organize. Members were screened for special skills; some were sent to the United States for a year to take flying lessons at commercial schools. On September 11, 2001, al-Qaeda carried out its mission. Nineteen terrorists seized four filled passenger planes to use as suicide bombs. Two planes brought the World Trade Center in New York City down, and one hit the Pentagon in Washington, DC. The fourth plane was supposed to strike Congress, but passengers fought with the terrorists on board, and the plane crashed into a Pennsylvania field.

OUTSIDE THE ISLAMIC WORLD

Before discussing reactions to the Fourth Wave's high point, we examine events outside the Islamic world. The Camp David Peace Accords induced ultraorthodox religious Jews in West Bank settlements to start a terror campaign to reestablish the boundaries of ancient Israel.[105] Their two main targets were West Bank Palestinians, "illegitimate occupiers" of biblical territories, and Israelis who either aimed to establish a separate Palestinian state or keep Israel as a secular state. The Jewish Underground (1979–1984), the first group to emerge, sprang from Gush Emunim (Bloc of the Faithful), the pioneer of the West Bank settlement movement.

After Fatah, the PLO's principal organization, slaughtered six Jewish students returning from prayer in Hebron's Cave of the Patriarchs in 1980, the Jewish Underground began assassinating Palestinian mayors to teach "Arabs a lesson and force Israel to provide better security for the settlers."[106] Their next undertaking in 1982 was more ambitious, a plan to blow up al-Aqsa, Islam's most sacred shrine in the Holy Land. Those who devised the plan believed that their act would create a catastrophe reminding God of his promise to usher in the Messianic era, a key theme of first-century Jewish terror.[107] But no rabbi would endorse the effort, and it was abandoned. In 1984, the Lifta Gang tried to destroy al-Aqsa, but guards intercepted them just before they could reach the site.[108]

Afterward, tiny independent cells and individuals made intermittent attacks on Palestinians.[109] Doctor Baruch Goldstein, a Jewish settler acting alone, murdered twenty-nine Muslim worshippers and injured 125 in the Cave of the Patriarchs in 1994, the wave's most indiscriminate Jewish atrocity. Within an hour it had inspired a clash in Hebron, causing twenty more Palestinian deaths and injuring 120 others, mostly Palestinian. Then in 1995, Yigal Amir, an ultraorthodox Jew aided by his brother and friends, assassinated Prime Minister Yitzhak Rabin. No other Jewish religious terror act had as much political impact. Rabin and the PLO were negotiating the Oslo Accords for a two-state solution to the endless Palestinian-Israeli conflict, and there seemed to be a very good chance of success. U.S. President Clinton lamented, "If Rabin survived we would have had a comprehensive agreement."[110]

In 1981, Sikhs in India launched a wholly unexpected and deadly campaign. Sikhs fared well in India; most lived in Punjab, India's "breadbasket," where the average income was three times the national one. The British had depended greatly on Sikh soldiers, a pattern India continued after independence. Although Sikhs only composed about 2 percent of India's population, 40 percent of India's generals were Sikhs, and the Sikh Regiment was recognized as India's best. But in the late 1960s, the government began restricting the number of Sikh soldiers.[111] In the 1970s, peaceful Sikh demonstrations began for a more autonomous Punjab to preserve Sikh significance. The Sikh Akali Dal replaced the Indian National Congress as Punjab's dominant party, and its ties with the Bharatiya Janata Party threatened the Congress Party's national domination. Prime Minister Indira Gandhi decided to split Sikh voters by joining forces with Bhindranwale, a relatively unknown *sant* (holy man), who led a prestigious Sikh theological school that aimed to "purify" Sikhism by restoring it to its original form. He helped the Congress Party in the 1980 election but soon went his own way. In 1981, a newspaper owner furiously hostile to Sikh demands was assassinated. Hindu opposition became more intense; the police killed more than one hundred Sikhs and arrested over thirty thousand. Bhindranwale praised the assassins immensely and was arrested as the plot's organizer. A series of terrorist acts against Hindus and Sikhs hostile to Bhindranwale followed the arrest, inducing the government to release him. He emerged as a national hero that did not feel beholden to Delhi for his deliverance and made triumphal tours.[112]

Indira Gandhi's "creation" soon became Frankenstein's monster.[113] He led Sikhs who sought to reestablish Khalistan (Land of Pure), a state Britain made part of India in 1849.[114] Support for violence dramatically increased. Bhindranwale moved to the Golden Temple, "the Sikh version of the Vatican," transforming it into a fortified stronghold for four terrorist groups. By 1984, many Sikhs saw the Golden Temple as Punjab's new government. After six Hindu bus passengers were murdered, India declared a "state of emergency" and launched Operation Bluestar on a holy day commemorating when Guru Arjan, who built the Golden Temple in 1604, had become a martyr. The festival attracted pilgrim crowds. Over 4,700 pilgrims were killed in the Indian operation, including Bhindranwale. One thousand more visitors and some five hundred soldiers were also killed.[115] "Tanks and high explosives devastated the sacred site. There were no warnings, no attempts to save innocent pilgrims, indiscriminate killings ... perpetrating atrocities on the arrested Sikhs by ... killing those prisoners who begged for water [this being the hottest month of the year]."[116] Operation Bluestar infuriated Sikh soldiers. Some four thousand mutinied and fought large-scale battles in response. The Indian prime minister's Sikh bodyguards assassinated her. Indian mobs then invaded Sikh areas, killing over two thousand, burning most alive. Sikhs everywhere remember Bluestar and its aftermath, referring to it as "their own 9/11, their worst trauma in modern history."[117]A commission reported that some three-quarters of around 405 Sikh temples in Delhi were the objects of a "systematic attack." About fifty thousand Sikhs fled to Punjab from other parts of India, and refugee camps for approximately two thousand Sikhs were set up in Delhi.[118]

But Prime Minister Rajiv Gandhi, his mother's successor, understood that in spite of Bluestar, most Sikh demonstrators primarily wanted more autonomy for Punjab. The 1985 Rajiv-Longowal Accord legitimized those demands, forgave the mutineers, rehabilitated many deserters, promised to create a commission to punish those responsible for the pogroms, and allowed more Sikhs to join the military.[119] Most Sikhs accepted the accord, but the Akali Dal, the Sikh leader who signed the agreement, was assassinated. Although "peace" had been achieved, the Sikh terrorists could not be united. Continued terror attacks produced more Sikh than Hindu casualties, and many potential supporters came to see the Sikh terrorists as looters and extortionists deeply involved in the drug trade. Sikh groups did not engage in social welfare policies because the Sikh population was well off, and India's government helped the displaced. Terrorists eventually returned to the Golden Temple in 1988, knowing they could provoke another Indian attack. But the Indian army was excluded this time, and a police force organized a nine-day siege using rifles and guns only. After thirty fatalities, the terrorists surrendered. Special efforts were made by the police, who sustained no casualties during the siege, to protect the site's sanctity. The Sikh population reacted positively.[120] By the mid-1990s, Sikh support for terror evaporated. Sikhs since then have enhanced their role in India. Prime Minister Manmohan Singh, a Sikh, was reelected to a second term in 2009, the only person to have done so since Nehru, India's first prime minister. In 2002, the highest-ranking officer in the Indian Air Force was a Sikh, Marshal Arjan Singh. In 2012, General Bikram Singh was appointed to be the Indian Army's chief of staff, the second Sikh to hold that office.

The Tamil Tigers was the only Fourth Wave group without a stated religious agenda, but the group strongly opposed efforts to make Buddhism the state religion, and like many Fourth Wave groups, it was trained in Lebanon to use suicide bombers. Tamil problems stemmed from their advantages during colonial rule. The British used Tamils (Indian immigrants) for the civil service in Ceylon because they were typically better educated and more comfortable than native residents in using English. In 1948, Ceylon became the independent state of Sri Lanka, accepting a British-made constitution that protected minorities. However, Buddhists soon decided to reorganize the state, granting Tamils some regional autonomy but reducing their presence in the central government. Sinhalese became the only official state language, and peaceful Tamil protests were brutally suppressed. Buddhism became the official state religion, and many qualified Tamils could no longer pursue administrative careers. A Prevention of Terror Act enabled the government to hold detainees indefinitely, many of whom were innocent. The act eventually gave birth to the Tamil Tigers.[121] In 1981, soldiers destroyed the chief Tamil library in Jaffna, home to rare palm leaf manuscripts and historical materials, convincing Tamils that the Buddhists wanted to destroy their culture.[122]

In Black July 1983, the Tamil Tigers made its first major attack, killing thirteen soldiers in an ambush. That precipitated a series of Buddhist monk–led riots, which led to the burning of thousands of homes, rape of many Tamil women, and death of some two thousand Tamils.[123] The mass exodus of Tamils following Black July created diaspora communities around the world, which provided financial support for the Tamil Tigers' twenty-six-year campaign of terror. Seemingly overnight, rebel groups with a dozen or so members swelled to several hundred. After Black July, India helped Tamil terrorist groups with training, funds, and weapons; in 1987, India's air force dropped food parcels in Tamil areas.

However, India changed its view after the Tamil Tigers became associated with Tamil separatists in India and when Sri Lanka asked Pakistan, India's perennial enemy, for military advisors. In 1987, India and Sri Lanka agreed to end the Sri Lankan civil war, and an Indian peacekeeping force was sent to Sri Lanka to enforce the agreement. But the Tamil Tigers committed a number of atrocities after the peace deal, resulting in the deaths of approximately 1,200 Indian soldiers over three years. Ultimately, Sri Lanka's president asked India to leave because the island was suffering, and the Tamil Tigers seemed stronger than ever. While India had won three wars against Pakistan, the struggle with the Tamil Tigers was the first "war" India lost. Tamil Tigers everywhere advertised their "victory against the world's third-largest army." Two years later, India's prime minister, Rajiv Gandhi, who had sent military forces to Sri Lanka, was assassinated by a female Tamil Tiger suicide bomber. Fourteen others died in the attack.[124]

Despite India's withdrawal, the Tamil Tigers continued to fight. The large number involved, the focus on military targets, and 1988 promise to abide by the Geneva Conventions made the struggle seem more like a guerrilla war than a terrorist campaign. But the terror persisted. In 1990, six hundred police officers surrendered to the Tamil Tigers, having been given an explicit promise they would be left unharmed and released. But the police were taken to the jungle, blindfolded, made to lie on the ground, and shot. In 1985, the Tamil Tigers killed nuns, monks, and pilgrim worshippers at the Bodhi Tree Shrine, a sacred Buddhist site. In one village, 120 civilians were hacked to death with swords and axes in an effort to drive the Buddhist population from an eastern province. Sri Lanka's army behaved similarly, and its list of massacres may be as long as that of the Tamil Tigers.

It took time for the international world to label the Tamil Tigers a terrorist organization because it rarely attacked outside Sri Lanka. Furthermore, the military's forces disregard for the rules of war kept many states from viewing their actions as "counterterrorism" efforts. Nonetheless in 1992, India, provoked by Prime Minister Rajiv Gandhi's assassination, became the first foreign state to declare the Tamil Tigers a terrorist organization. This was followed by the United States and the United Kingdom. Soon, financial subsidies from the Tamil diaspora dried up, especially from English-speaking countries, where fury over 9/11 was most pronounced. In 2006, twenty-eight states listed the Tamil Tigers as a terrorist organization, and the FBI described "the Tamil Tigers [as] among the most dangerous and deadly extremists in the world."[125] In 2009, the UN Security Council condemned the organization as a terrorist group for using "civilians as human shields" and refusing to let civilians flee the conflict area.[126] The group was defeated finally in 2009, when 11,664 members, including 596 child soldiers, surrendered. The thirty-three-year struggle took over one hundred thousand lives, including 22,000 Tamil Tigers.[127]

In the United States during the 1980s, violent religious and secular racist groups emerged. The Christian Identity movement was the most important religious element, combining nationalist, racist, and millenarian themes, as the Order of the Silent Brotherhood; Covenant, Sword, and Arm of the Lord; and Aryan Nations illustrate. Antiabortion elements with millenarian commitments were also active. Important secular racist examples were the White Aryan Resistance; the Hammerskins, a collective of Skinhead rock music fans with neo-Nazi sympathies;[128] and the National Alliance, led by William Pierce, the author of *The Turner Diaries*, an extremely popular novel among the radical right.[129] While the groups were distinctly different, their views overlapped so much that the "radical right," Michael Barkun noted, was very "confusing and fractious, a place where groups emerge and split, cooperate and compete, emerge and dissolve. Hence for every generalization there is a contrary case."[130] Often a religious group member would become associated with a secular group, and vice-versa.

Like their medieval models, many millenarian groups lived with families in settlements, waiting for the Second Coming to produce the "war to end all wars."[131] Heavily armed, they refused to pay taxes. No true "permanent underground" entity emerged, but occasionally individuals left a compound to rob banks, kill someone, or strike at symbols, violence often described as "hate crimes," not terrorism.[132] The need to wait for the apocalypse helped minimize Christian terror. Christian Identity groups believed the impending apocalypse would spark a race war. The U.S. government, or "Zionist Occupation Government" (ZOG), would vanish, and Aryans would inherit the world. The first series of strikes occurred in 1984 when the Order of the Silent Brotherhood, named after a group in *The Turner Diaries*, conducted several robberies and racial attacks and assassinated the Jewish radio talk host Allen Berg.[133]

In addition to these groups' staunch commitment and wide-ranging goals, the geographical locations of their compounds posed problems for law enforcement. Residents had the constitutional right to possess guns, but they also held unauthorized military weapons, artillery, machine guns, and so on.[134] In 1985, a large government team with arrest warrants arrived at the Covenant, Sword, and Arm of the Lord Arkansas (CSA) compound. Members were suspected of committing terrorist acts, but the warrants were for illegal weapons possession. The CSA retreated behind the compound's fortifications. After two days of intense negotiations, the CSA surrendered. Numerous illegal weapons were recovered, but the CSA destroyed evidence that could point to terrorist activities. The CSA experience made government agents determined to avoid the loss of evidence and organized larger forces that could act more quickly. Their "solution" ironically caused more problems. Sieges were not shortened, and police forces on two occasions gravely violated the law, creating serious public revulsion. One such occasion took place in 1992, in Ruby Ridge, Idaho. Four hundred government agents arrived with aircraft and armored vehicles to arrest Randy Weaver, a Christian Identity member and military veteran accused of offering to sell sawed-off shotguns to federal agents. The siege lasted for fifteen days and resulted in four deaths: Weaver's fourteen-year-old son, his wife, a ten-month-old baby in her arms, and a federal marshal.[135] When Weaver was brought to trial, the jury found him innocent, and the surviving family members filed a wrongful death suit, winning $3,100,000.

During the Ruby Ridge trial in 1993, a much more horrifying event occurred at the Branch Davidian compound near Waco, Texas. Seventy-six officers in three helicopters arrived to serve warrants, prompting a gun battle ending in the deaths of four government agents and six Branch Davidians. A fifty-one-day siege followed the gun battle. The FBI denounced conversations with David Koresh, the Branch Davidian leader, as "bible babble."[136] Fearing a repeat of the 1978 Jonestown Massacre in Guyana, where a cult of over nine hundred people committed suicide at their leader's behest,[137] the FBI deployed tear gas to force Branch Davidians out of the compound. However, fire soon erupted, and seventy-five residents, including twenty-five children, two pregnant women, and David Koresh, were burned alive.[138]

The Branch Davidians and the Weaver family both became religious right "martyrs," an odd link, because the Branch Davidians rejected the religious right's nationalist and racial views. Branch Davidian members came from many different countries, and half were nonwhite. Strong supporters of Israel, they believed that the Jews and Branch Davidians were the only ones destined to survive the impending apocalypse. Nonetheless, the religious right ignored these differences, focusing instead on the fact that the government had slaughtered Branch Davidians because they were armed and lived in a religious compound.[139]

The outrage Ruby Ridge and Waco sparked generated an extraordinary explosion of militia groups in the 1990s. The radical right's anger intensified after U.S. congressional Democrats and President Bill Clinton implemented regulations on the use of guns, which "showed their intention to eliminate the 2nd Amendment" right to bear arms. Many were reminded that *The Turner Diaries* begins with a government seizure of all weapons. By the mid-1990s, militias appeared in thirty states.[140] They were small groups, often numbering fewer than a dozen members, located in rural areas and involved with military training and weapons stockpiling. Yet "while there were attempts to create an umbrella organization to unify the movement or at least create a means of coordination . . . none were successful, and the militia movement remained decentralized."[141]

The militias' concern with the right to bear arms linked them to the religious and secular right, whose racial views they did not share. Still, many militias thought the federal government would soon establish a UN-dominated "New World Order," a view *The Turner Diaries* described. In 1995, the Oklahoma City bombing demonstrated just how dangerous such groups could be. Timothy McVeigh and two associates, all military veterans, with links to a Michigan militia, made the attack on April 19, the second anniversary of Waco and the date of the first Revolutionary War battle.[142] The Alfred P. Murrah Federal Building, housing several law enforcement agencies, was the target: 168 were killed and seven hundred injured. The property damage was valued at over $650 million, the most destructive terrorist act on U.S. soil until 9/11. The attack was strikingly similar to one that played out in Pierce's *The Turner Diaries*, a book McVeigh left in his car before the bombing.

Before the Oklahoma City attack, FBI Director Louis J. Freeh stated in 1995 that "law enforcement overreacted" at Ruby Ridge and Waco and had "violated the constitution." Federal agents now had to have a reasonable belief of an "imminent" danger before using deadly force, and the FBI organized a highly trained Critical Incident Response Group to combat similar threats in the future. Embarrassed by characterizing the Branch Davidian leader's comments at Waco as "bible babble," the FBI now sought advice from religious scholars. If the FBI had consulted such experts in the Waco case, it would have been told that instead of striking on Sunday, they should attack the compound on Saturday, the Branch Davidian's holy day, when they would not be armed. The effectiveness of this new approach was immediately demonstrated in the 1996 Montana Freeman siege. The FBI arrived with arrest warrants, and the usual armed confrontations ensued, but the FBI withdrew to a safe distance to avoid violence. After eighty-one days of negotiations, the Montana Freemen surrendered, and seven received prison sentences. The FBI regained the confidence of the public and even of some militias. The "millennial hysteria" continued, yielding some astonishing acts as the year 2000 drew closer. The Swiss Order of the Solar Temple, founded in 1984, spread to France and Quebec. It saw itself as a revival of the Knights Templar, a twelfth-century Crusader order that believed a worldwide catastrophe would occur in the mid-1990s when Christ returned. In 1994, fifty-three Swiss members committed suicide by setting fire to their buildings, hoping to enter the "new world." In Quebec, sixteen members killed themselves in 1995, and five more did the same in 1998, followed by thirty-eight Heaven's Gate members in California, who "eliminated" their bodies so their souls could board a spacecraft trailing the comet Hale-Bopp.[143]

Individuals associated with Christian millenarian movements initiated three violent attacks in 1998 and 1999. John King murdered James Byrd Jr., an African American, by chaining him to a truck and dragging him through the streets of Texas, announcing, "We're going to start the *Turner Diaries* early." Benjamin Smith, a World Church of the Creator member, went on a three-day shooting spree in Illinois and Indiana, killing two African Americans and wounding nine. Investigators discovered in his apartment a folder containing documents about an impending race war. Finally, Buford Furrow, an Aryan Nations member, attacked children at a Los Angeles Jewish daycare center, proclaiming, "It's time for America to wake up and kill the Jews."[144]

There were also deep anxieties about the "Y2K Problem." Computers were designed to date years by the last two figures, and it was widely thought that many would designate January 1, 2000, as January 1, 1900. The resulting malfunctions would shut down a world now dependent on the internet, sparking widespread chaos and panic. As the century closed, the FBI circulated a study, Project Megiddo, warning all federal, state, and local agencies.[145] Foreign intelligence services produced comparable reports.[146] Project Megiddo focused on Christian elements who believed "the year 2000 would usher in the end of the world and are willing to perpetrate acts of violence to bring that end about with a fragmented leaderless structure where individuals or small groups act with autonomy." Unfortunately, leaders could not control their groups, and many individual acts of violence occurred to convince others the apocalypse had begun. Christian millenarians felt the American "government of Satan" had to be destroyed before it destroyed them. Y2K did not occur. Few computers malfunctioned on January 1, 2000, and the *Wall Street Journal* called Y2K the "hoax of the century."[147] Only one terrorist attempt was made when an al-Qaeda-trained person attempted to bomb the Los Angeles Airport on New Year's Eve. The would-be Y2K terrorist was apprehended at the Canadian border.[148]

EFFORTS TO REVITALIZE AL-QAEDA

After 9/11, the United States invaded Afghanistan, something al-Qaeda had not anticipated, clearly demonstrated by the fact that it remained a very visible force in that country, a mistake underground groups rarely make. Its training facilities, a crucial ingredient in al-Qaeda's global jihad, were destroyed. Under UN auspices, more than one hundred states, including Iran, aided the U.S. invasion. Still, no one expected the overthrow of the Taliban to be so quick and apparently decisive. Afghanistan had always been difficult for invaders. Even when counterterrorist forces are familiar with the area (this time they were not), history shows that entrenched terrorists have considerable staying power: for example, Cyprus, Algeria, Northern Ireland, and Sri Lanka.

Al-Zawahiri had warned "the victory . . . against the international alliance will not be accomplished without acquiring a . . . base in the heart of the Islamic world. The model is the hijra of the Prophet Muhammad to Medina in advance of the return to Mecca."[149] It is unclear why al-Qaeda failed to prepare for a U.S. invasion; had it been convinced by previous American reactions that the "paper tiger" would avoid difficult targets and stay out of Afghanistan? The loss transformed al-Qaeda's overseas operations dramatically. Its sleeper cells had remained inactive until the central leaders designated a moment to strike. Operations were planned from above and rehearsed several times in Afghanistan, a process that lengthened the time between strikes but increased the likelihood of success against difficult targets. If supervision from the top no longer existed, striking patterns would become more "normal"; local units have more freedom to strike quickly and often. Still, the numbers and resources available to a cell were constantly in flux, limiting them to softer, less protected targets. After the Afghan rout, successful strikes were against "softer" civilian targets, like the 2002 destruction of tourist sites, for example, an ancient synagogue in Tunisia and a resort club in Indonesia, attacks that displayed the organization's trademark by maximizing casualties.

While the invasion's quick "success" surprised everyone, the United States decided not to finish the job. The United States then invaded Iraq to prevent it from giving terrorists WMDs, weapons Iraq did not have. The invasion ignited considerable hostility in the Muslim world toward the United States, the primary purpose of the 9/11 attack. Many Muslims saw the invasion as a "war on Muslims for the sake of oil and to keep Israel safe from regional powers." Subsequently, some Muslims mounted major attacks in Spain, the United Kingdom, and Muslim states believed sympathetic to the West, such as Morocco, Algeria, Turkey, Indonesia, etc.[150] The Iraq decision greatly weakened the extraordinary alliance 9/11 had created for the Afghan invasion. France and Germany did not believe Iraq had WMDs. New Zealand and Canada refused to participate. Between January and April 2003, 36 million people produced over three thousand protests. In Rome, the largest-ever antiwar rally took place, involving three million people.[151] UN Secretary-General Kofi Annan said that "from the Charter point of view [the war] was illegal." Forty-nine countries supported the U.S. decision, but only six contributed troops: the United Kingdom, Spain, Australia, Poland, Portugal, and Denmark. The United Kingdom was the only state to supply a significant contingent of soldiers, and Spain withdrew its troops in April 2004 in response to the Madrid train bombings.[152]

Many Americans believed that invading Iraq would prevent more attacks on the homeland, a view the intelligence community strongly supported. "Virtually the entire intelligence community in the months after 9/11 believed that a second wave of even more devastating attacks was imminent."[153] In 2006, "79 percent of experts polled declared it certain or likely that 'a terrorist attack on the scale of 9/11' would occur in the United States by the end of 2011."[154] But nothing like 9/11 took place. There were some attacks outside Iraq, but after their high point in 2004, they declined by 90 percent. Saddam Hussein's incompetent army fell quickly, but an uprising developed that was much more difficult to handle.

In April 2003, after the United States invaded Iraq, a Jordanian known as al-Zarqawi, who had fought with al-Qaeda in Afghanistan, established his own terrorist organization in Jordan and brought it to Iraq, where he became obsessed with fighting the Near Enemy. Al-Zarqawi first focused on Shi'ites, "the evilest of mankind." In August, he bombed a Shi'ite mosque, killing 125 worshippers, including the most popular Iraqi politician, Ayatollah Muhammad Bakr al-Hakim, who probably would have become Iraq's first freely elected president. In a letter to bin Laden intercepted by U.S. intelligence in January 2004, Zarqawi explained that "if we succeed in dragging [the Shi'a] into the arena of sectarian war it will become possible to awaken the inattentive Sunnis [to] feel imminent danger." He said he would pledge allegiance to al-Qaeda if bin Laden endorsed his battle against the Shi'ites. Bin Laden told Zarqawi to "use the Shi'ite card" but hesitated to make a formal alliance partly because most senior al-Qaeda figures did not want to battle Iran. Nevertheless, Zarqawi quickly renamed his organization al-Qaeda in Iraq (AQI). Soon, volunteers from neighboring countries and the Islamic diaspora joined AQI, which dominated the Sunni uprising in the Anbar province to become the heart of Iraqi resistance. But its inability to restrain excesses, a perennial problem, occurred.[155] Al-Zawahiri, who knew from personal experiences in Egypt about the dangers of excessively violent tactics, sharply criticized AQI for strikes against Shi'ites and publicly beheading American hostages. Ultimately, AQI's excesses led to its downfall, but it revived later.

Al-Qaeda made two major efforts at revitalization. The first involved using the "leaderless resistance" strategy developed in 1992 by Louis Beam, a Vietnam War veteran and KKK and Aryan Nation leader who argued that because the internet enabled police to infiltrate underground groups, one must switch to "leaderless resistance," that is, independent individuals or small autonomous cells, to carry out attacks.[156] By ensuring that these cells were "never reporting to a central headquarters or single individual for instruction," they greatly increased the likelihood an organization could withstand police infiltrations. By employing this strategy, terrorist groups made sure their attacks could be responded to after they occurred and not before.[157]

However, Beam, who was unfamiliar with terrorism's history, did not realize that his "new" tactic had been important long before the internet was created. Previously described as "lone wolf" activity, it was the strike of an individual "neither initiated nor backed by any underground organization."[158] Indeed, as pointed out previously, lone wolves were common in the First Wave, and the history of global terrorism began when the lone wolf Vera Zasulich struck St. Petersburg's governor for abusing a political prisoner. Lone wolves were common in the First Wave. The Second Wave shunned the tactic, and although Third Wave groups did not encourage it, in the 1950s lone wolves began to emerge again. Most conducted serial attacks and proclaimed personal causes. Because they were not associated with a movement, they were described as "idiosyncratic lone wolves."[159] Fourth Wave lone wolves were thus very different from terrorists in organized groups, whose "outstanding characteristic," Martha Crenshaw emphasized, "is their normality."[160] Earlier lone wolves also seemed "normal," as they embraced a cause many others supported.[161]

Timothy McVeigh's Oklahoma City bombing was the deadliest lone wolf act ever, and he expected others to follow him. Nonetheless, many members of the religious right believed the violence had gotten out of control. Beam condemned the Oklahoma City bombing as a "horrendous . . . and senseless loss of life" that gave government more public support for drastic countermeasures. "If McVeigh did it," Beam wrote, it was because the government's refusal to investigate the Waco tragedy infuriated him, but Beam thought it was more likely the government planned the act. He advised his associates to abandon terror and use the electoral process to get their revenge. "We still have the power to take back America so long as free elections are held. Between now and the next annual election we must all arm ourselves with a voter registration slip and use it like a .308 sniper weapon to take out the infectious bought whores of the new world government . . . now proposing to rule us all with an Orwellian iron fist forever beating us into submission while claiming to protect us."[162] Beam "returned to family life," restricting himself to website comments about how the Zionist Occupied Government (ZOG) had accumulated powers.[163]

Americans continued leaderless resistance, largely confined to antiabortion, homophobic, and racial attacks.[164] Eric Rudolph became the best-known figure after he bombed two abortion clinics, killing one; a gay bar, killing two; and the 1996 Atlanta Summer Olympic Games, killing two and injuring 111 others. His written statement to the court explained that the Olympics were targeted for the enormous publicity it would produce. He is also said, "Abortion is murder. And when the regime in Washington legalized, sanctioned, and legitimized this practice they forfeited their legitimacy and moral authority to govern. . . . The plan was to force the cancellation of the Games, or at least create a state of insecurity to empty the streets around the venues and thereby eat into the vast amounts of money invested."[165] The destructive potential of the Olympic bombing was enormous, which evoked public anxieties that Rudolph would produce an Oklahoma City–like bombing. But Rudolph apologized for the "innocent" parties he hurt and provided information about the bombs' detonation times and locations to a 911 operator so that the area could be cleared of everyone except uniformed arms-carrying government personnel. Police received the information thirty minutes before the explosion but did not act for twenty minutes, and a bomb exploded while being removed. "Remorse" made Rudolph remove other bombs he'd planned to explode on successive days. But he did not mourn the victims of his abortion clinic and gay bar bombings, because he deemed them "immoral."[166]

Pro-life Christians were the most committed to leaderless resistance to prevent "killing babies," which they believed otherwise would provoke an apocalypse.[167] The Phineas Priests, a Christian Identity element espousing anti-Semitic, antimulticultural, and homophobic sentiments, is a prominent example. Phineas, the first known lone wolf in history, was a biblical figure, Aaron's grandson and a priest who killed an Israelite and a Midianite for having sex in a sacred sanctuary. The act terminated a plague God had sent to punish Israel for mingling with Midianites. Phineas's reward was that his "seed" would produce all of Israel's future high priests.[168] Phineas Priests is not an organization; there is no governing body and no gatherings. One simply becomes a Phineas Priest by adopting priesthood beliefs and acting accordingly. The Phineas Priests' symbol, 25, is the chapter in Numbers, a book of the Bible, where the original incident is described. Between 1994 and 2009, the Phineas Priests made thirteen bombings and sixty-one arsons, causing eight deaths.[169]

In 2007, there were 131 militias and other antigovernment groups. Their resurgence began in 2008, and by 2010 the number rose to 840.[170] A Department of Homeland Security Report in 2012 designated right-wing activity and its "leaderless resistance" strategy as the "worst domestic terrorist threat." Several factors contributed to its growth: the Great Recession, the election of an African American president, the receding trauma of the Oklahoma City bombing, and concerns over illegal immigration (even though, ironically, the numbers of illegal immigrants entering the United States dropped during the Obama administration). The movement attracted many military veterans from Iraq and Afghanistan. "Large numbers of potentially violent neo-Nazis, skinheads, and other white supremacists are now learning the art of warfare in the armed forces."[171] In 2013, a Department of Homeland Security report noted that the internet gave right-wing veterans enormous power: "The advent of the Internet and other information age technologies since the 1990s has given domestic extremists greater access to information related to bomb-making, weapons training, and tactics . . . making extremist individuals and groups more dangerous and the consequences of their violence more severe."[172]

The 2013 report enraged veterans and many others who thought the threat from Islamic groups was being underestimated, and Secretary of Homeland Security Janet Napolitano felt she had to say that "an apology is owed. . . . We greatly respect our veterans." She said she did not read the report before it was distributed, but after reading it, it "struck a nerve with her," and she withdrew it from the Department of Homeland Security's website only a week after it came out.[173] One important unmentioned factor in the report's assessment of the religious right's revival was its anxiety about gun control laws. The Assault Weapons Ban expired in 2004, and when Democrats regained power in 2008, many anticipated new restrictions.[174] But the right's fury diminished when the Democrats did not impose new limitations, and important 2010 Supreme Court decisions further limited the government's ability to regulate firearms.[175] Statistics on the radical right's violence reveal that 4,420 incidents occurred between 1990 and 2012; 670 were killed and 3,053 injured.[176] Property, the favorite target, accounted for 43 percent of these incidents.[177] Individuals were second, at 42 percent, and only 3 percent aimed to cause many casualties. Some attacks were against nonwhites, often involving persons passing by who were suddenly attacked with fists, knives, and rocks. Explosives were used in only 9 percent of the cases. Christian Identity groups diminished enormously during the twenty-first century. Only militias attacked government elements directly, and 70 percent of their strikes employed bombs.[178] Still, militias made far fewer attacks on minorities than other radical right organizations. Militia groups grew enormously during this period, from fifty in 2008 to 330 in 2012. The growth increased the movement's lethal potential, but fortunately annual attack numbers did not increase much.

The new leaderless resistance strategy also intrigued al-Qaeda elements in 2005, and Abu Misab al-Suri, a veteran leader, concluded that the centralized hierarchical structure employing sleeper cells dispersed over wide areas was no longer suitable because it had failed to attract enough Muslims to their cause. Al-Qaeda should employ "leaderless resistance" focusing on Afghanistan, Central Asia, Yemen, Morocco, and especially Iraq.[179] To broaden its base, al-Suri recommended that al-Qaeda develop more extensive media operations and realize that the Arabic alone was insufficient for jihadi purposes. The 2003 Global Islamic Media Front now distributes information in many different languages. English is the most common, but Albanian, Bosnian, Filipino, French, German, Italian, Pashtu, Spanish, Urdu, and Uighur translations are available as well. Leaderless resistance could exhaust Western economies, but it also produced inappropriate attacks.

Nonetheless, al-Qaeda in the Arabian Peninsula (AQAP) soon publicly endorsed such attacks in October 2009. Shortly afterward, a gruesome attack at a U.S. Army Base in Fort Hood, Texas, killed fourteen soldiers. Major Nidal Hasan was responsible. Email exchanges between Hasan and Anwar al-Awakli, an American cleric in Yemen, suggest that the AQAP endorsement and slaughter were related.[180] In 2009, the "underwear bomber," a Nigerian, contacted Awakli to help him achieve self-martyrdom. Fortunately, the plastic explosives in his underwear failed to detonate when he was an airplane passenger over Detroit on Christmas Eve.[181] A U.S. drone later killed Awakli in Yemen.

In March 2010, an al-Qaeda spokesman urged Muslims abroad to follow the Major Hasan model. In May, a Pakistani American trained abroad made a Times Square bomb attempt, citing Awakli as inspiration. An American soldier allegedly aimed to kill more Fort Hood personnel in July 2011. In November 2011, New York City police stopped an alleged attempt to avenge Awlaki's death by killing soldiers returning from Iraq. In February 2010, CIA Director Leon Panetta described al-Qaeda's "lone-wolf strategy . . . as the main threat to this country."[182] On the first anniversary of bin Laden's death, President Obama said, "the biggest concern we have right now . . . is the lone wolf terrorist."[183]

While al-Qaeda lone wolf attempts increased significantly, they had no major effect.[184] Thirty-eight homegrown violent jihadist plots in the United States have been launched since 9/11; twenty-one occurred after May 2009.[185] Lone wolves conducted nine, including six after May 2009; four caused casualties.[186] The deadliest lone wolves were Muslim American soldiers on military bases. Sergeant Akbar killed two in Kuwait in 2003, and Major Hasan killed fourteen at Fort Hood in 2009. The other Islamic lone wolves were civilians; in 2006, Taheri Azar drove a vehicle into a student gathering at the University of North Carolina, injuring nine, and in 2009, Abdul Hakim Muhammad killed a soldier on a base in Little Rock, Arkansas.[187] The four "successful" lone wolves did not use bombs or get weapon-making information from the internet. Only one plot, an aborted strike on the New York subway in 2010, was a suicide bombing effort.[188] Sting operations aborted two-thirds of the attempts. Contact was initially established through the internet, and police involvement may have increased alleged effort numbers greatly.[189]

Although it is difficult to generalize from so few cases, the new strategy illustrated al-Qaeda's growing weakness in the West, and that of related Islamic groups. The Phineas Priesthood limited its targets to abortion providers, killing eight over fifteen years. In comparison, Islamic lone wolves killed seventeen people in ten years. The outcomes of these groups' efforts are closer than one would have anticipated. Undercover agents were involved in twenty-five of the thirty-eight Islamic cases, so contrary to what Beam believed, leaderless resistance does not always provide the isolation needed to avoid the authorities. Between 1968 and 2007, there were seventy-two lone wolf incidents in fifteen countries, 1.28 percent of the 5,646 terrorist strikes that occurred. Over 42 percent occurred in the United States, where weapons are easily available.[190] Al-Qaeda also tried to revitalize by creating "franchises" in the Middle East, Africa, and South Asia. Originally it expanded only by recruiting individuals, and when it merged with the Egyptian Islamic Jihad (EIS) it made all EIS members accept al-Qaeda's global purpose and strategy. But the franchises developed were largely autonomous. They adopted al-Qaeda's name, reputation, and ideology, giving the impression that AQC had been reinvigorated. But franchises were consumed with local matters or the Near Enemy, while AQC's struggle against the Far Enemy involved large-scale attacks requiring considerable planning time.[191] Franchises' brutal attacks on Muslims often embarrassed AQC and weakened its global efforts to create a single religious entity.

A look at major franchises helps explain AQC's quandary. Al-Qaeda in Iraq (AQI), founded in 2004, was the first and most important franchise. It organized significant resistance to the American invasion of Iraq. AQI developed from al-Zarqawi's Jordanian group, which had over a thousand fighters from many countries. After much hesitation, AQC accepted the franchise, even though AQI continued committing gruesome atrocities against Shi'a and even some Sunnis. In November 2005, AQI organized simultaneous suicide bombings of three hotels in Jordan, including one hosting a wedding, where dozens of Jordanian men, women, and children were slaughtered. Many Palestinians were also killed, including the Palestinian Authority's head of intelligence and brother of the speaker of the Palestinian National Assembly. AQI's aim was to undermine King Abdullah's government, but support for the monarchy intensified, and the attacks enraged Muslims everywhere, making them even more staunchly opposed to suicide bombings against civilians in their states. AQC's and AQI's differences kept intensifying.

In Somalia, al-Shabaab (Movement of Striving Youth), originally a nationalist group that wed jihad against "enemies of Islam," linked itself to AQC and became a franchise in 2012.[192] Its leaders were Afghan and Iraqi veterans. Recruits from Africa, the Middle and Far East, and the Somali diaspora in the West made it the world's largest franchise in 2014, with between seven thousand and nine thousand members. Surprisingly, 25 percent of its forces were Kenyan Christians who had converted to Islam. Somalia's government and its Ethiopian ally were its main targets. Their operations focused on Somalia, but some occurred elsewhere; during the 2010 World Cup, seventy-four fans in Uganda were killed. African Union troops were sent to Somalia in 2007 to combat al-Shabaab and are still there. A U.S. drone strike killed the al-Shabaab leader Mukhtar Abu Zubair in 2014.

Al-Qaeda in the Islamic Maghreb (AQIM) has received little attention. It originated as the Salafist Group for Preaching and Combat (GSPC) largely in Algeria and became one of North Africa's wealthiest and best-armed groups from ransoms, which produced 90 percent of its money. In 2003, it pledged loyalty to AQC and became AQIM, declaring it would eliminate Westerners in the Maghreb, a North African area along the Mediterranean Sea and Atlantic Ocean that includes Algeria, Morocco, Mauritania, Tunisia, and Libya. The region was united in the early eighth century and became an entity again between 1159 and 1229. In 1989, states in the region established a trade agreement to bring together all Maghreb countries. AQIM intended to reunify the region. Algeria, Morocco, and Mali supplied recruits. Mali experienced most attacks, and its government invited French troops to come to their aid.

THE ARAB SPRING TRANSFORMS THE WAVE

While franchises kept AQC alive, they did not revitalize it much. In 2011, the Arab Spring occurred. Huge peaceful demonstrations erupted across the Islamic world aimed at removing dictators and establishing democracies. Western commentators used the term "Spring" to describe the process because it reminded them of the 1848 revolutions—the "Springtime of Nations" that spread to fifty countries in Europe and Latin America, making many believe a "new world" was emerging.[193] The Arab Spring completely surprised AQC, which described popular demonstrations as "treating cancer with aspirin" and argued that only violent jihad could transform the Islamic world. Six months after the Arab Spring began, the United States carried out a successful operation to kill Osama bin Laden, and many felt that AQC was finished.

Initially, peaceful demonstrators induced the governments of Tunisia and Egypt to resign immediately. But the Arab Spring's character soon began to change. Violence replaced peaceful demonstrations as governments in Libya, Yemen, and Kuwait were overthrown. Armies in Yemen, Bahrain, and Syria took to the streets to quell new demonstrations, sparking civil wars in the process. The secular justifications stimulating those demonstrations soon became religious ones, as armies and demonstrators from different religious sects began to take up arms against each other, leading some observers to rename the Arab Spring the "Salafi Spring.", return to early Islam.[194] Syria produced the deadliest and most difficult conflict, which seemed to reinvigorate the Fourth Wave. The Syrian government wanted to create a secular, Arab, socialist state that embraced the Middle East. Its members were largely Alawites, a Shiite offshoot and 12 percent of Syria's population. It dominated the army and supported Bashar al-Assad's dictatorship. Sunnis, 70 percent of Syria's population, engaged in largely peaceful demonstrations for democracy. But Assad's violent response made demonstrators take up arms, inciting many Sunnis from the Arab world to join them. Elements of Assad's army then defected to form the Free Syrian Army. Shi'ite Iran and Lebanon's Shi'ite Hezbollah, Assad's long-standing allies, sent forces to help him. The conflict grew more extensive and ultimately became a war between the Shi'a and Sunni worlds. For the first time, the Arab League and the Gulf Cooperation Council designated Hezbollah as a terrorist organization. As the civil war spiraled, the United States and Russia got involved. Syria under the Assad dynasty had become Russia's most important Middle East ally, after Egypt abandoned the Soviet Union in 1979. Syria's government had sponsored many terrorist groups, and the United States was sympathetic to some rebels, especially the Kurds, providing them with funds and weapons.

While AQC remained uninvolved for over a year, remnants of its local franchise, AQI, urged its partner to change its strategy. AQC complied with the request, even though it was infuriated with the franchise's indiscriminate violence during the U.S. invasion of Iraq. Now, the two cooperated to create the al-Nusra Front, a group that was filled with many Syrians who had been in AQI. By November 2012, the al-Nusra Front had between six thousand and ten thousand fighters, nearly 8 percent of the Free Syrian Army, and became its most aggressive and successful element.[195] But differences between the two al-Qaeda groups intensified again; AQI was more interested in creating its own domain than in fighting Assad and ultimately withdrew its forces from al-Nusra.[196] In June 2014, AQI shifted its forces away from Syria to capture Iraqi territories. Mosul, Iraq's second-largest city, was captured after 1,500 invaders defeated over thirty thousand Iraqi soldiers who fled without fighting. In their retreat, Iraqi forces left behind equipment the United States had given Iraq. Captured soldiers were either set on fire or crucified.[197]

The spectacular achievements made many Muslims believe that God had finally become involved. After Aleppo was captured, the Caliphate was established. Ibrahim Awad Ibrahim al-Badri, who was renamed Abu Bakr al-Baghdadi, became the caliph. Abu Bakr al-Baghdadi was the name of Muhammad's successor; he presided over Islam's first great expansion. The caliph in Syria now claimed legal jurisdiction over all Muslims and ordered them to migrate to his territory.[198] AQI then became the Islamic State of Iraq and Syria (ISIS). In the next six months, around 15,000 Muslims from sixty states arrived. The CIA estimated ISIS probably had 31,500 members. Males came to fight and women to have families. In 2015, ISIS governed over 8 million people, in a territory larger than the United Kingdom.[199] Gas and oil resources enabled it to provide food, transportation, housing, and schools and meet its charity obligations. Fighters received $1,000 a month, a sum much higher than the average income in Syria and Iraq. Al-Qaeda had always been inspired by the belief that the caliph would return only after the United States was pushed out of the Muslim world, but ISIS insisted that the caliph would appear when one controlled the territory that tradition had designated as the site of the apocalypse.

ISIS committed gruesome atrocities. After Mosul, Iraq, was taken in June 2014, major massacres occurred in nearby Shabak villages. Over 125,000 Christians fled from what had been their home for nearly two thousand years.[200] Christian children were beheaded for not converting. Yazidis, a Kurdish Islamic offshoot, were considered devil worshippers. Between two thousand and five thousand men who refused to convert were also killed. Women and children were abducted and sold as sex slaves. Over fifty thousand Kurdish Yazidis got trapped in the Sinjar Mountains, and the United

States and Western allies began an airstrike campaign to prevent genocide. The trauma the 2003 U.S. invasion of Iraq produced prevented the United States from sending troops again, but Kurdish forces came to the Yazidis' rescue and helped most to escape.

Nonetheless, ISIS atrocities continued. Closing the gates of an Iraqi dam in Fallujah, ISIS flooded the surrounding regions and cut the water supply to the Shi'a-dominated south. Around 12,000 families lost their homes, while villages and fields were either flooded or dried up. The region's economy suffered greatly from the destruction of croplands and electricity shortages.[201] ISIS killed Shi'ites and Alawite s "perverting" the Quran and those worshipping at the graves of imams. Sunnis were removed from Islam if they were caught selling alcohol or drugs, wearing Western clothes, shaving their beards, or voting in an election. ISIS proclaimed that the heads of state in every Muslim country who elevated manmade law above sharia "deserved" the same fate. Anjem Choudary, a radical UK Islamic leader, described these acts "as policies of mercy rather than of brutality." ISIS is obliged "to terrorize its enemies with beheadings, crucifixions, enslave women and children, because doing so hastens victory and avoids prolonged conflict."[202]

However, Muslim leaders everywhere insisted that Islam provided no justification for ISIS's actions, and even al-Nusra stated that ISIS was alienating Muslims. These groups felt that a gradual approach was necessary before more provocative aspects of sharia could be implemented, like throwing homosexuals off buildings, chopping people's limbs off, and public execution by stoning.[203] Al-Nusra's campaign contrasts vividly with its rival's, though it had the same ultimate objective.[204] In early 2015, al-Zawahiri, Bin Laden's successor, instructed al-Nusra to pursue five goals: integrate the movement with the Syrian revolution, cooperate more with other Islamic groups, establish a sharia judicial system, use strategic areas to build a sustainable al-Qaeda power base, and cease activity linked to attacking the West.[205] With respect to ISIS, one al-Nusra leader said, "They assault Muslims, and their ideology completely drifted from the ideology that we follow, so we have to fight them." Al-Nusra initiated attacks against ISIS near Aleppo, Syria, battles that apparently produced over three thousand casualties. Ironically, the battle led the former CIA director, David Petraeus, to suggest that the United States and "moderate" al-Qaeda groups could sometimes cooperate.[206] In July 2016, al-Nusra separated from ISIS and merged with four other groups, becoming Tahrir al-Sham (Levant Liberation Committee).

Despite growing regional and international resistance, ISIS got within seventy miles of capturing Bagdad before it was stopped. Iranian Shi'a and Kurdish forces, including the Third Wave PKK, played a significant role retaking Kirkuk after Iraqi forces abandoned their posts. Within a year, ISIS lost almost 40 percent of its territory, and foreign recruits dropped greatly after Turkey closed its borders with northern Syria. Before the closure, approximately 60 percent of ISIS's foreign recruits had come to the Caliphate via Turkey. Many foreigners left ISIS, and about one hundred deserters were beheaded. Many women also returned home. The United States bombed ISIS-controlled oil sites, greatly reducing their available cash, forcing ISIS to cut its fighters' salary in half. Kurdish forces intensified the economic problems by cutting principal supply lines and retaking the important Syrian city of Kobani in January 2015.

Fourteen months after ISIS lost 40 percent of its territory, its strategy changed again, and for the first time it struck targets in the West. Its first attack was in Paris, in November 2015, when nine coordinated strikes were made on a football stadium, concert hall, and several restaurants, targeting people congregated in sites designed for a "reprehensible lifestyle." One hundred and fifty people were killed and 367 injured, the worst one-day attack in France since World War II. Four months later, three coordinated suicide bombings occurred at the Brussels airport and a metro station, killing thirty-two and injuring over three hundred, the deadliest terrorist incidents in Belgian history. The government declared three days of national mourning. The terrorist cell that had participated in the previous Paris attacks also produced the Belgian attacks.[207] France was targeted again on Bastille Day in 2016, where enormous crowds had gathered to celebrate in Nice. Eighty-six people were killed and 458 injured after a Tunisian resident drove a cargo truck through the crowded streets. ISIS claimed responsibility.

Why did ISIS try to enlarge its list of enemies just when its weaknesses became so conspicuous? The decision makes sense if we remember ISIS's obsession with the apocalypse. The Hadith, a collection of Prophet Muhammad's sayings, designated Dabiq in Syria as the site where the final world battle would be fought.[208] ISIS captured Dabiq in August 2014 and named its monthly English magazine *Dabiq* to highlight the looming doomsday battle. Videos ISIS took there are illuminating. In 2014, one video showed European jihadists sitting on a cliff in Dabiq, daring the West to intervene. "We are waiting for you to come and will kill every single soldier." Another video showed "Jihadi John," speaking with an English accent, standing over the bloody, severed head of an American aid worker: "Here we are, burying the first American Crusader [and] eagerly waiting for the remainder of your armies to arrive. Ultimately the armies of Rome will mass to meet the armies of Islam in northern Syria. After that battle, eternal life in paradise will begin." "Jihadi John" then ordered his men to behead twenty-one Syrian soldiers and addresses President Obama, "To Obama, the dog of Rome, today we are slaughtering the soldiers of Bashar [al-Assad] and tomorrow, we will be slaughtering your soldiers and soon we will be slaughtering your people on your streets."[209] The videos indicate ISIS's ultimate goal is defeating the United States, which could only happen after American troops arrived. But the United States remembered its previous Iraq invasion and restricted itself largely to air strikes.

If the United States was the principal enemy, why were European targets attacked? The most obvious explanation is that they were easier to strike. One had to strike quickly, and Europe was much closer. Many more ISIS recruits came from Europe than from the United States. ISIS sent back around four hundred well-trained jihadists to Europe and created a significant and extensive network there.[210] Europe's Islamic population was also larger and less integrated than its American counterpart, making it a more hospitable operating area. ISIS claimed it had made two strikes in the United States in 2015 and 2016, but the attackers were radicalized before ISIS had emerged, and there was no evidence that they ever contacted ISIS. The first attack was made by a married couple at a Christmas party in San Bernardino, California, killing fourteen. In the second attack, a security guard killed forty-nine at a gay nightclub in Orlando, Florida.

Much to ISIS's surprise, its European attacks did not induce any government to send troops to fight the Caliphate on its home ground. Instead, France increased its air campaign against ISIS, and Belgium, which had stopped participating in that air campaign, resumed its role. Antagonism to Muslim immigrants grew with each terrorist attack, and it was revealed that ISIS members had infiltrated the European Union disguised as refugees. ISIS claimed it had smuggled four thousand members into Europe who would punish the West for airstrikes carried out against ISIS in Iraq and Syria. According to many experts, the claims were nothing more than an exaggerated attempt boost their stature and spread fear.[211]

In the Caliphate's territory, ISIS continued to experience disastrous defeats. After four years of fighting, Aleppo, Syria's largest city, was lost in December 2016, producing around 31,000 deaths. The Red Cross described it as one of the most devastating conflicts in modern times: "The human cost of the fighting in Aleppo is simply too high. We urge all parties to stop the destruction and indiscriminate attacks and stop the killing."[212] Nine months later, the U.S.-led coalition took Raqqa, the Caliphate's capital since 2014, in a gruesome attack that led Amnesty International to say, "When so many civilians are killed in attack after attack, something is clearly wrong, and to make this tragedy worse, so many months later the incidents have not been investigated. The victims deserve justice."[213] Finally, in 2015, intelligence agencies confirmed that the caliph, al-Baghdadi, had been seriously wounded in an airstrike that left him unable to resume his crucial role.[214] ISIS became decentralized,[215] and four years later, the caliph was killed in an airstrike.

ISIS still has forces in Syria and Iraq, but it remains very weak. Nonetheless, the decline opened the door for other elements to go abroad and establish "franchises" or "affiliates." By 2018, twenty-nine countries had experienced ISIS franchise attacks.[216] It is likely that some groups will attempt to return to the grounds that the Hadith prophesized the caliph would emerge from after foreign powers left the areas. But the devastation the first uprising created may make any future effort impossible. In addition, any campaign to create a central base requires considerable territory in a weak state with a dominant Muslim population plagued by civil conflict. Otherwise, it would repeat al-Qaeda's experience when it was forced to flee Afghanistan and change its organizational structure and strategy to become AQC with franchises more concerned with local concerns. A look at the most significant new ISIS elements in Libya, the Sinai Peninsula, Yemen, and Afghanistan exhibit both similarities and differences between ISIS and AQC.

After Colonel Qaddafi and his secular Libyan government were destroyed in the Arab Spring, two governments emerged out of the rubble: the self-declared General National Congress in Tripoli, backed by Libya Dawn and a range of Islamist and non-Islamist militias, and the Western-backed coalition in the city of Tobruk. A low-level civil war developed in which prime ministers were kidnapped and major officials were assassinated. An extensive UN effort to bring the dueling governments together failed. Islamic terrorist groups were also active in the struggle, including an al-Qaeda franchise, the Abu Salim Martyrs Brigade. Another group, Ansar al-Sharia, attacked the U.S. diplomatic compound in Benghazi on September 11, 2012, killing the ambassador and three officials.[217]

Before Qaddafi was overthrown, many Libyans went to Syria to fight Assad's government, and one group, the Battar Brigade, pledged loyalty to ISIS and eventually returned to Libya. Unlike AQC, which restrained its activity against Muslims, the ISIS offshoot continued the practices it employed in Syria. It captured Derna, a port city with important enclaves in the vast oil-rich country, and Sirte, a central Libyan coastal city and Qaddafi's hometown. Islamic dress and behavioral codes were brutally enforced with crucifixions and lashings. Judges, civic leaders, and local terrorists who rejected their authority were killed, often by slitting their throats. Then ISIS announced the revival of slavery as an institution. Women and children in Derna were sold to raise money. A video was released showing the beheading of twenty-one kidnapped Egyptian Christian construction workers,[218] provoking Egyptians to bomb ISIS training camps and weapons stockpiles. Libya also conducted airstrikes in Derna, occupied by ISIS elements since 2014. In December 2016, following a seven-month-long battle, Libyan forces, aided by U.S. airstrikes, cleared ISIS from Sirte. ISIS affiliates withdrew to desert areas south of Sirte and began low-intensity attacks on Libyan forces and local infrastructure.

ISIS's Libya branch numbered between six hundred and eight hundred fighters and tried to recruit fighters from Chad, Mali, and Sudan, some of Africa's poorest nations, with promises of generous salaries.[219] AQC's Libyan franchise organized various attacks against ISIS and has around five thousand members. An Austrian security specialist in Libya noted, "Their strategic objective is to use the southern part of Libya as a haven. What they are doing right now in Libya is rather small-scale. They have no intent to regain territorial control. . . . Ultimately, they want to regroup and launch attacks outside Libya."[220] To date, ISIS's Libyan affiliate has been tied to only one foreign attack: the 2017 Manchester Arena bombing, by a British citizen returning from Libya, which killed twenty-three and injured 139. ISIS claimed credit for the act, but since the bomber died in the attack, it remains unclear whether he acted on his own or not.

In Yemen, the Arab Spring produced a situation initially like Libya's: a secular government was eliminated, and two religious sects claiming to be the new government violently clashed with each other. The United Nations made several failed efforts to unite them. Since Yemen was divided between Shi'a and Sunnis, the conflict became comparable to those in Syria and Iraq. Yemen's sectarian conflict enticed neighbors to become more deeply involved than Libya's neighbors were. Still, Yemen's neighbors, Iran, and Saudi Arabia were not as involved as those in Syria and Iraq were. Iran gave Houthi rebels money, training, and arms but denied doing so, and its forces were not involved in the fighting. The Saudis organized a coalition of nine Middle Eastern and African nations to train and equip Yemen's forces. The Saudis soon imposed a naval blockade and initiated a series of airstrikes. However, unlike the Iranians, the Saudis also sent a limited number of troops to the area. It is also important to note that major outside powers also acted differently in Yemen than in Syria. Russia refused to get involved, and only two Western states, the United States and United Kingdom, backed the Saudi coalition by providing money and airstrikes. In further contrast to the Libyan case, ISIS members sent to Libya were returning home, which helps explain why they were initially effective, but most Yemenites who went to Syria served with al-Nusra as opposed to ISIS, and the ISIS units sent to Yemen were foreigners unfamiliar with the area. Although the ISIS affiliates focused on striking Houthis, the Shi'a community,[221] the ISIS affiliates soon split up and were confined to the desert.

Al-Qaeda in the Arabian Peninsula (AQAP), established in 2009, was Yemen's most important terrorist entity. All al-Qaeda franchises attacked Westerners on the local scene, but AQAP was the only one to strike the Far Enemy overseas. In 2010, AQAP announced Operation Hemorrhage, which was an endeavor to capitalize on the "security phobia that is sweeping America."[222] The attacks were largely lone wolf efforts aimed at weakening the U.S. economy. The United States responded with drone strikes killing major AQAP leaders. In 2015, the simmering unrest in Yemen gave AQAP a chance to revive itself by seizing weapons in a series of raids on ISIS's Yemeni headquarters. One important reason that AQAP retained the support it had cultivated in 2011 was that unlike ISIS, its Yemen attacks were discriminate. Civilian casualties were minimized, and when AQAP made a mistake, as it did with an attack on a military hospital, its leaders apologized and condemned a "rogue" element for "outrageous" acts. It also quickly capitalized on mistakes made by the Saudi coalition, such as a 2018 airstrike on a wedding party.[223] The acceptance of AQAP by the population of Yemen has essentially enabled it to create an emirate there.

In 2013, UN Secretary General Antonio Guterres said the struggle in Yemen had created "the world's worst humanitarian crisis. . . . More than 22 million people, three-quarters of the population, need humanitarian aid and protection. Some 18 million people are food insecure."[224] A 2019 UN research report found the overwhelming bulk of civilian casualties in Yemen were caused by the 18,000 airstrikes Saudi Arabia and the United Arab Emirates launched.[225] Residential areas, markets, funerals, weddings, jails, refugee camps, hospitals, and boats were struck. In stark contrast, the number of Houthi-committed atrocities was much smaller and unmentioned in the report.[226]

In December 2019, Mohammed Saeed Alshamrani, a twenty-one-year-old Saudi Air Force student studying aviation at the Naval Air Station in

Pensacola, Florida, murdered three U.S. Navy sailors and injured eight others in an unprovoked attack in a classroom.[227] Two months later, AQAP claimed responsibility for the shooting, stating that it had told Alshamrani to make the attack. It was later discovered that twenty-one other Saudi trainees at the station possessed "derogatory material," including jihadist and anti-American content on their social media profiles and were sent back to Saudi Arabia as a result. The incident was a timely reminder of the enduring threat of a seemingly bygone era. As the terrorism scholar Colin Clarke writes: "It is important to note that if this attack were directed, and not merely inspired by AQAP, it would be the first successful directed attack on U.S. soil by a foreign terrorist organization since 9/11."[228]

The Arab Spring also produced a significant ISIS franchise in Egypt. Massive demonstrations brought down General Mubarak's secular dictatorship, and in 2012 Mohamed Morsi, who was associated with the Muslim Brotherhood, became Egypt's first democratically elected president. But the following year, after significant demonstrations, Field Marshall Sisi's military coup removed Morsi. Sisi was soon "elected" president of Egypt. In the Sinai Peninsula, some indigenous Bedouin Salafi jihadist groups fighting Israel merged to form Ansar Bait al-Maqdis and began striking Egyptian targets. After Sisi's coup, Ansar Bait al-Maqdis dramatically limited its Israeli campaign in order to free up resources for mass-scale attacks throughout Egypt.

In 2014, Sinai terrorists went to ISIS in Syria to seek financial support, weapons, and tactical advice. Many swore allegiance to ISIS, and when they returned to the Sinai, they created a new ISIS branch, Wilayat Sinai. While Wilayat Sinai's attacks on Israel resumed, their most infamous strike came when a bomb placed on a Russian plane exploded over Egypt, killing 224, the deadliest air disaster in both Russia's and Egypt's histories. Wilayat Sinai continued pursuing religious targets. It bombed a Sufi mosque in the Sinai, killing 305 and wounding one hundred in November 2017. The bombing was the "deadliest terrorist attack in Egypt's history."[229] Christians in Egypt also experienced "unprecedented levels of persecution": 128 were killed, and over two hundred others were driven from their homes. Fifteen Christian girls were abducted and forced to marry Muslims. "Tens of thousands of armed soldiers patrolled streets around churches all over Egypt" to stem the violence.[230]

ISIS also generated some South Asian franchises.[231] The most significant was the Afghan ISIS Khorasan (ISIS-K) in 2015, but it did not have as much impact as the ISIS affiliates in Libya, Yemen, and Egypt. Their ineffectiveness mostly had to do with the fact that they had to fight the Pakistani and Afghan governments, the U.S.-led NATO Coalition, and the Taliban, which was largely supported by the Pashtuns, the world's largest tribal society, numbering 50 million and situated in Afghanistan and neighboring Pakistan.[232]

ISIS-K's first commander, Hafiz Saeed Khan, and his principal deputy, Abdul Rauf Aliza, a former Guantanamo Bay prisoner, had been leading figures in the Pakistani Taliban. Their past experiences created anxieties among U.S. policy makers that ISIS-K would be incorporated into the Afghan Taliban and make it a larger, more radical force. U.S. airstrikes killed both leaders quickly, and airstrikes continued to be the principal U.S. method of dealing with ISIS-K. In October 2017, the United States dropped 653 bombs on ISIS-K, the highest monthly total ever.[233] By May 2018, ISIS-K made twelve deadly strikes in Khorasan Province, each of which killed more than thirty people.[234] Claiming the Taliban had cooperated with the Shi'a, ISIS-K then killed fifty-six people inside a Shi'a mosque in Kabul during October 2017. The thirteenth issue of *Dabiq* (January 2016) explains how ISIS described the Shi'a: "Initiated by a sly Jew, [the Shia] are an apostate sect . . . spreading doubt on the very basis of the religion [the Qur'an and the Sunnah], . . . and preferring their "twelve" imams to the prophets and even to Allah. . . . Thus, the Rāfidah [rejecters] are *mushrik* [polytheist] apostates who must be killed wherever they are to be found."[235]

Since the first ISIS-K leaders had been Pakistani Taliban leaders, it was thought that ISIS-K and the Afghan Taliban would cooperate. However, that did not happen. ISIS-K struck Pakistani targets to gain support from the Pakistani Taliban, which was trying to overthrow Pakistan's government. Yet while they did not cooperate extensively, the Pakistani Taliban provided ISIS-K with many recruits. This was not unprecedented:

the Afghan Taliban had overturned the Afghan government in the 1990s and had many volunteers from Pakistan's Pashtun areas. Some were even Pakistani soldiers.[236]

However, ISIS-K attacks infuriated the Afghan Taliban: "We have rejected all affiliation with Pakistani Taliban fighters. . . . We have sympathy for them as Muslims, but beside that, there is nothing else between us."[237] The fact that the Afghan and Pakistani Taliban have the same name often confuses outsiders about their differences.[238] ISIS-K tried to demean the Afghan Taliban's legitimacy by noting it had a narrow nationalist base and governed via "tribal customs." The ISIS-K proudly proclaimed that unlike the Afghan Taliban, it encompassed the entire Muslim community and governed it by sharia.[239] Yet much to the dismay of ISIS-K, the argument antagonized the Afghan Taliban, sparking violence between the two groups. A provocative incident occurred in June 2018, when twenty-five Afghan Taliban members were killed while celebrating the end of Ramadan and a three-day truce with the Afghan government, the first truce ever between the two parties.[240]

ISIS-K's resources attracted defectors, who were given laptops, pickup trucks, and funds for their families. Others were attracted by its ideology.[241] Recruiters operated in at least eleven Afghan provinces.[242] During his visit to Washington in March 2015, President Ghani of Afghanistan warned Congress that ISIS posed a "terrible threat" to his country and that he was "sending advance guards to southern and western Afghanistan to test for vulnerabilities."[243] It even has some support among Afghanistan's conservative rural population. Seth G. Jones, an expert on Afghanistan, said, "ISIS-K, on the other hand, is shrinking in size, controls virtually no territory, has conducted far fewer attacks, and has virtually no support among Afghanistan's population."[244] ISIS-K claimed the Afghan Taliban government had been a secular one, but the Taliban in fact aimed to establish a pure Islamic society, one imposing a brutal version of sharia.

In 2011, a decade after the war against the Taliban began, the United States decided that it was too costly to eliminate the Taliban and began seeking a negotiated solution. Afghan President Hamid Karzai did not support the original efforts, but President Ghani encouraged subsequent negotiations, though they still did not succeed. In June 2018, General J. W. Nicolson, the coalition commander, was able to arrange the first truce with the Taliban, a short one during the final days of Ramadan. In July 2018, U.S. Secretary of State Mike Pompeo came to talk with Afghan officials about the Taliban negotiations. While the Taliban was eager to negotiate the withdrawal of the American forces, it did not want the "illegitimate" Afghan government present. Alice G. Wells, principal deputy assistant secretary for South and Central Asia, said, "There is nothing that precludes us from engaging with the Taliban. . . . What we are not prepared to do . . . is [exclude] the Afghan government. . . . We are doing everything we can to ensure that our actions help the Taliban and the Afghan government [come] to the same table."[245] A week later, U.S. and Taliban representatives began negotiating in the Middle East state of Qatar. Some mass Afghan demonstrations for peace convinced the Afghan government to let the United States negotiate without its presence.[246]

Bangladesh was the only other South Asian country with an active ISIS group. During the first six months of 2016, it made eleven attacks, mostly against people with other religious affiliations: Hindus, Christians, Buddhists, and moderate Muslims. On the last Friday of Ramadan, July 1, terrorists took over a bakery in Dhaka, Bangladesh's capital. Its occupants were held as hostages, and the attackers targeted foreigners or Muslims not deemed sufficiently devout. Twenty-two people were killed, and fifty were injured. Muslims unable to quote the Quran were executed.[247]

Although the extent of the threat is not yet understood, ISIS and its related affiliates certainly created anxiety in other South Asian states. South Asians who had been with ISIS in Syria returned and cooperated with militant groups in the area who claimed ISIS had inspired them to make attacks in its name largely in four states: Indonesia, Bangladesh, the Philippines, and Sri Lanka. The first attack occurred in January 2016 in Indonesia's capital, Jakarta. Six strikes were made on embassies and luxury hotels in the city. Eight were killed, including four attackers, and twenty-three were wounded.[248] Its organizer had returned from Syria, where he had fought with ISIS. The next successful ISIS Indonesian attacks occurred on

Sunday, May 13, 2018. In an unprecedented event, entire families of suicide bombers targeted three Christian churches, killing thirteen and wounding forty-one. One included a father and mother, two teenage sons, and two younger daughters.

In the Philippines, the ISIS flag flies over some southern islands, which ISIS considers its East Asian province. Filipinos returning from Syria helped establish the franchise in 2014, and four existing groups became affiliated with the franchise. They conducted many deadly attacks; one was on a Catholic cathedral in 2019 that killed twenty-three and received extensive international attention.[249]

The next series of South Asian terror attacks occurred in Sri Lanka on Easter Sunday, 2019, where suicide bombers struck three Christian churches and three luxury hotels and housing complexes. Two hundred and fifty-nine were killed, including forty-five foreign nationals, and around five hundred were injured.[250] These were the deadliest ever attacks in Sri Lanka, even taking into account the very bloody thirty-year Tamil Tigers campaign. According to the Sri Lankan government, every suicide bomber in the attacks was a Sri Lankan associated with National Thowheeth Jema'ah, a local group that attacked Buddhists and Sufi Muslims. The group is thought to be linked with ISIS in the digital sphere. One bomber had tried to travel to Syria to join ISIS but was unsuccessful.

The Arab Spring created a struggle between ISIS and Iran to gain control of the Muslim world, a struggle that ultimately changed Israel's place in the Middle East. Suddenly, Israel was no longer the only state that all its neighbors were united against because of the Palestinian problem. In fact, ISIS improved the Egyptian-Israeli relationship greatly. The ISIS franchise Wilayat Sinai, based in the Sinai Peninsula, made a number of terrorist attacks against Egypt. In response, President Sisi sent troops to the Sinai, even though the Camp David Peace Accords with Israel prohibited him from doing so.[251] However, Israel did not object and launched air attacks on Wilayat Sinai, which pleased Sisi greatly and generated a new attitude in their relations. The *Economist* described President Sisi as "the most pro-Israeli Egyptian leader ever."[252] Sisi said he supports the Palestinians and that "now is the time to end the conflict . . . so that prosperity prevails, so that we all can have peace and security." He blamed the Israeli-Palestinian conflict for the extremism and terrorism in the Middle East and promised Egypt would deploy observer forces in the West Bank and Gaza Strip to guarantee Israel that Palestinians would not violate the peace treaty.

Several years later, in August 2020, Israel established a good relationship with another Arab state. The Israel–United Arab Emirates (UAE) agreement, a U.S.-brokered deal, was called the Abraham Accord, in honor of the patriarch of Judaism, Islam, and Christianity. The UAE is the third Arab state after Egypt (1979) and Jordan (1994) to recognize Israel. But the Egyptian and Jordanian treaties were made to end wars; the Abraham Accord explicitly aims to establish normal relations via the economy, scientific cooperation, and diplomatic ties. The UAE had been involved in Yemen's struggle to eliminate Iran's presence and feels that Iran is a security threat. Israel and the UAE already had security ties, but the agreement brings them into the open.

In 2011, a decade after the war against the Taliban began, President Obama sought a negotiated solution but failed to get one. Afghanistan's President Karzai did not support the original efforts, but his successor Ashraf Ghani did. The Taliban was eager to negotiate an American withdrawal but did not want the "illegitimate" Afghan government present.

President Trump, convinced that ISIS was virtually defeated, turned his attention to Afghanistan. He said that while his "original instinct was to pull out" of Afghanistan completely, he first had to expand U.S. troop presence there to increase the Taliban's anxiety. By February 2020, approximately 13,000 U.S. forces were in Afghanistan.

Then the Taliban and the Afghan government signed a peace deal on February 28, 2020, which was to go into effect by the end of May 2021. The central themes are (1) the prevention of future threats against the United States and its allies from terror groups operating from Afghanistan, (2) withdrawal of all American and coalition forces from Afghanistan, and (3) a commitment from the Taliban toward an intra-Afghan negotiation that would include a permanent ceasefire.[253]

Other elements of the deal are that the United States will work toward lifting American and international sanctions against the Taliban and seek the UN Security Council's endorsement of the deal. Both the United States and the Taliban pledge to pursue positive relations in the future with each other and the new, expected postsettlement Afghanistan government. The United States will seek economic cooperation for reconstruction with the new postsettlement Afghan Islamic government as determined by the intra-Afghan dialogue.

President Biden was determined to follow the agreement signed, though his withdrawal began three months later. President Ghani came to Washington to discuss the American withdrawal and told Biden he must be "conservative" in granting visas to the interpreters and others and "low key" about their leaving the country, "so it would not look as if America had lost faith in his government." Otherwise, a mass evacuation of Afghans who aided the Americans would suggest that everyone believed the present Afghan government was too weak to survive. But Biden did not anticipate the collapse and felt that he had to fulfil promises made to those who had helped the United States, even if their reason for doing so was to aid the Afghan government. Around 79,000 Afghans (including families) were evacuated. The Afghan army immediately capitulated, believing the United States was convinced the government would not survive.

When the United States was organizing a massive withdrawal (August 27, 2021) with the Taliban's help at the Kabul airport, an ISIS-K suicide bomber killed 170 Afghan civilians and thirteen U.S. servicemen, the most Americans killed in Afghanistan since 2011 and the first U.S. casualties in eighteen months. The United States responded with a drone attack, killing persons described as planning to be suicide bombers. But two weeks later, the Pentagon acknowledged that the drone strike was a tragic mistake; it had killed ten civilians, including one who worked for the United States and seven children. General Kenneth F. McKenzie Jr., the head of U.S. Central Command, told reporters at a Pentagon news conference, "I offer my profound condolences to the family and friends of those who were killed."

President Biden did make some explicit mistakes on the withdrawal. In July, a month before the event, he said the Afghan military was "as well-equipped as any army in the world."[254] Afterwards, military leaders, testifying before Congress, stated that Biden had ignored their recommendation to avoid complete withdrawal all at once.[255]

END OF THE FOURTH WAVE?

When will the Fourth Wave end? If it follows the pattern of its predecessors, it should last a generation and end sometime in the late 2020s. If it lasts longer, it may be because religious communities, compared to secular ones, are extraordinarily durable and capable of inspiring lasting commitments. These qualities may also help explain why the three ancient religious terror groups we examined in chapter 1 survived for so long.

Ironically, Islamic terrorism, the Fourth Wave's most significant element, declined immensely by 2010, making it seem like the Fourth Wave would be shorter than its three predecessors. However, the Arab Spring unexpectedly reanimated the Islamic dimension, making violence between Islamic groups the wave's most conspicuous feature, replacing the original aims to eliminate outside secular influences and reunify Islam. Will this transformation of purpose help end the wave?

The changes the Arab Spring produced were most conspicuous. The Syrian civil war shows how outside powers should respond if they think they must get involved. The war pitted Shi'a against Sunni, and seven Middle Eastern states—Iran, Iraq, Saudi Arabia, Lebanon, Turkey, Jordan, and Qatar—participated on different sides of the religious divide. In 2021, the United Nations estimated the conflict produced at least 350, 000 deaths.[256] Two major secular states—Russia and the United States—also got involved, but unlike their previous ventures in the Middle East, this time they did not inspire hostility throughout the Islamic world. Their original invasions two decades before were massive and motivated solely by their own interests. In 1979, the Soviet Union invaded Afghanistan with 110,000 troops, to aid a struggling Marxist government. The Soviet campaign animated devout Muslims throughout the Islamic world to join the Afghan resistance, and Western powers aided the resistance. The Soviets withdrew after ten years after 13,310 conscripted Soviet soldiers were killed and 35,478 injured.[257] The invasion was a key event in precipitating the Fourth Wave, and the war, especially the conscription problem, played a major role in bringing about the wholly unanticipated collapse of the Soviet Union in 1991.[258] Russia reduced its conscription to one year and much of its army was composed of volunteers. The U.S. had a similar problem with conscription during the 3rd Wave in Vietnam and created a volunteer army using conscription only when the U.S. was directly attacked.

Russian involvement in Syria was very different from the Soviet Afgan experience; Russia aided Shi'a forces in more limited, gradual ways. In 2012, military advisers were sent to aid Shi'a forces and Assad's government, a Russian ally since 1956. Then Russia gave Assad new weapons—armored vehicles, surveillance equipment, and helicopters. In 2015, at Assad's request, Russia launched airstrikes against ISIS and the al-Nusra Front. Russia then sent troops, and as of 2018, despite having 63,012 Russians in Syria, only 112 had been killed.[259]

The American military involvement also had an unexpected outcome. Iraq was invaded in 2003 to prevent it from giving WMD to Islamic terrorists, weapons Iraq did not have. Muslims everywhere felt the invasion to be improper, and Muslim volunteers from around the Islamic world came to mount a significant resistance. The United States sent over 130,000 troops, and 4,424 were killed. In the Syrian civil war, the United States, like Russia, got involved gradually, aiming to help Sunni forces overthrow the Assad regime. In 2012, the CIA participated in covert operations along the Turkish-Syrian border to find which rebel groups should receive training, ultimately allocating $15 million for that purpose.[260] A nongovernmental organization called the Syrian Support Group was also granted a license to fund the Free Syrian Army.[261] About two thousand U.S. soldiers performed various duties, and as of April 28, 2019, only eight had been killed.[262] The CIA proposed a detailed covert plan to remove Assad from power, but President Obama refused to authorize it because it would require too many troops.

Despite their support for different sides in the war, both Russia and the United States aimed to eliminate ISIS, the group most hostile to the Shi'a population. The struggle between Shi'a and Sunni groups continues to rage in Syria, Iraq, Iran, Lebanon, Jordan, Nigeria, Pakistan, Afghanistan, Yemen, Bahrain, and Kuwait. Will President Obama's successors continue this policy of limited involvement? President Trump has certainly not done so. In his 2016 election campaign, he appealed to the isolationist tradition by promising to terminate U.S. involvement in "endless wars" all over the globe, wars in which the U.S. military aided counterterrorist operations in twenty-two states and trained military forces in fifty-four others.[263]In December 2018, President Trump declared that all U.S. troops would be withdrawn from Syria because their mission to "defeat ISIS" had been accomplished, and it was the "only reason for being there" in the first place.[264] However, the United States got involved in Syria well before ISIS became significant, and a quick and complete U.S. withdrawal would give both Russia and Iran more influence in Syria. It would also greatly weaken the Kurdish Syrian Democratic Forces (SDF), a major U.S. ally. Congressional and military anxieties about the consequences of a complete withdrawal convinced President Trump to withdraw only half of the American forces in the region. The decision, which resulted in the relocation of one thousand troops, prompted U.S. Secretary of Defense James Mattis to resign in protest. Three weeks later, Trump said the withdrawal would be gradual and not take place until two conditions were met: first, that ISIS was eliminated and, second, that Turkey agree not to attack the SDF and its elements, which included the PKK, a Third Wave Kurdish separatist group.[265]

But ten months later, in October 2019, Trump announced that U.S. troops near the Turkish border would be removed and that all American forces in Syria would soon be withdrawn. The declaration once again greatly angered leading figures in both American political parties. The U.S. House of Representatives immediately condemned the president's decision in resolutions passed with a 364-to-60 vote. Republican Senate Majority Leader Mitch McConnell said that Trump had increased the risk that ISIS and other terrorists would regroup.[266] Turkish President Recep Erdogan said that the American withdrawal would require Turkey to send troops into Syria to protect Turkey's borders from PKK attacks.[267] However, many prominent U.S. government officials believed that the Turks would try to eliminate Kurdish forces, essential U.S. allies in the fight against ISIS. In fact, Kurdish elements had decimated ISIS, and the camps they controlled in northern Syria and Iraq held approximately 11,000 ISIS prisoners. Though President Trump had said the United States should leave Syria when ISIS was no longer significant, he refused to recognize that the Turkish attacks on the Kurds could result in the release of thousands of imprisoned ISIS fighters. In a statement to President Erdogan, President Trump boldly proclaimed that "if Turkey does anything, [he] will totally destroy the economy of Turkey."[268]

Despite the wave of anxiety about the regeneration of ISIS in the absence of the Kurds, it appears that such fears were somewhat exaggerated. All the major parties in the conflict—Syria, Iran, Russia, and Iraq—are extremely hostile to ISIS and will most likely continue to work hard to prevent its resurgence. Turkey is also very hostile to ISIS because ISIS caused more Turkish casualties during the Syrian civil war than the Kurds did. Nonetheless, the U.S. betrayal of its Kurdish ally may make it more difficult for the United States to find new alliances or maintain their old ones in the region.

The 2021 Pew Report indicates that the number of religious terrorist attacks has decreased greatly every year since 2012, which suggests that the Fourth Wave is in its last phase and will not last longer than its three global predecessors.[269]

Since 2004, only forty-six countries have experienced more deaths as a result of terrorist activity. In that same period, ninety-four states have experienced fewer deaths as a result of terrorist activity, the highest number of countries ever to record a year-on-year reduction. However, contemporary terrorist violence is still high compared to that of other Fourth Wave periods. In the decade before the 9/11 attacks, for example, the frequency and lethality of terrorist violence each year was less than a third of what it was in 2017.[270] In fact, every region in the world recorded a higher average impact of terrorism in 2017 than it did in 2002. While the increase was greatest in the Middle East and northern and sub-Saharan Africa, the total number of terrorist attacks worldwide has decreased 50 percent between 2014 and 2019, and the total number of deaths has decreased 54 percent. Terrorist violence seemed to peak in 2014, with nearly 17,000 attacks and over 45,000 deaths. In 2018, the number of deaths decreased by 27 percent, with the large drops occurring in Iraq and Syria.[271] Furthermore, only eight Western European states recorded at least one death from terrorism in 2017, the lowest number in the past twenty years. Deaths in this region fell by 52 percent, from 168 in 2016 to eighty-one in 2017.[272] The decreased lethality of terrorist attacks in Western Europe is one key indication that the ability of ISIS to launch large-scale terrorist attacks has been greatly reduced. Bombings and armed assaults have been the most common form of terrorist attack every year for the past twenty years. Furthermore, over 99 percent of all deaths from terrorism have occurred in countries involved in a civil war. In 2019, while the Taliban was engaged in peace talks with the United States, Afghanistan experienced 21 percent of all terrorist attacks worldwide, and 41 percent of all people killed were located in Afghanistan. But since the Taliban became the Afghan government in September 2021, those statistics have diminished even more. Obviously, the five-year decline of terrorist activity between 2014 and 2019 may indicate the wave is dissipating, but the trend could be reversed. The history of the Fourth Wave is unusual in that it has so far produced four cycles. The first began in 1979 and was sparked largely by the Soviet invasion of Afghanistan. It began to dissipate in the 1990s and was rejuvenated by the 9/11 attacks. The *Global Terrorism Index* statistics, which begin in 2002, show that between 2002 and 2007 terrorist attacks increased yet again; most were associated with the reaction to the U.S. invasion of Iraq. After 2007, deaths dropped by 35 percent until the Arab Spring of 2011–2014, when fatalities increased once again, this time by more than 350 percent. Most of this increase can be attributed to the breakout of the Syrian civil war, which also helped give rise to ISIS. In Nigeria, Boko Haram reemerged and developed a connection with ISIS. However, since 2014, deaths have decreased substantially as the civil wars in Iraq and Syria wane and Nigeria becomes less violent.[273] This cyclical pattern suggests that we may not really be witnessing the wave's decline and that another dramatic event may increase the wave's intensity yet again. If an Islamic attack on an important state in the secular world produces another mass invasion, the cycle may reemerge, as it did in the U.S. and Soviet cases. However, if the dramatic event involves a struggle between Islamic elements, as it did in the Syrian case, support for terrorism could continue to falter.

The *Global Terrorism Index* also examines the ten states with the most fatalities: Iraq, Afghanistan, Nigeria, Syria, Pakistan, Somalia, India, Yemen, Egypt, and the Philippines.[274] While Islamic terror haunts them all, India is the only country where Islamic groups are not especially prominent, which is odd when one remembers the India-Pakistan rivalry and the Kashmir problem. Although Third Wave groups remain more significant in the Philippines, Islamic groups are still very much present. Given that states with large Islamic populations typically experienced the most terrorist activity during this Fourth Wave, one would think that outsiders should limit their involvements in such areas. Yet contemporary analysts interpret the implications of the global geography of terrorism during this period differently. A 2018 Center for Strategic and International Studies (CSIS) report argued that the West needed to be more involved in these areas.[275] CSIS contends that if the West does not do so, many terrorist groups will begin to use WMDs, as ISIS did in Syria when it used chemical weapons.[276] Still, the damage chemical weapons created in the conflict was insignificant relative to other kinds of weapons, and while terrorist groups for decades have been eager to make WMDs— especially nuclear ones—they have failed to achieve their objective every time. Despite so many claims to the contrary, the chief weapon of a terrorist is still the bomb, which was made possible by Nobel's invention of dynamite in the late 19th century.[277]

Other analysts understand the new geographic implications of the Fourth Wave differently than CSIS. John Mueller and Mark G. Stewart wrote that although the number of attacks against Western targets has declined immensely in the last decade, the trauma of 9/11 still makes policy makers exaggerate potential terrorist threats and spend too much money and energy on counterterrorism efforts that only undermine other important international political concerns.[278] While fighting terrorism should be a key foreign policy objective, "the pendulum has swung too far at the expense of other interests." In June 2018, *Foreign Affairs* conducted a survey of foreign policy experts on the importance of international terrorism.[279] Fifty-seven percent of those polled believed that U.S. foreign policy focuses too much on terrorism. Thirty-three percent of experts disagreed, and 10 percent were neutral on the issue. The large majority felt that more resources should be spent on threats that China and Russia pose. While the second group of experts clearly recognized that the first group exaggerated the threat global terrorism poses for the West, they all agree that global terrorism remains a real problem. Despite this consensus, they do not consider ways to deal with it. Does President Obama's policy of limited involvement remain the most sensible today? If so, when should we intervene, and under what circumstances should we be convinced that our involvement should end?

If the Fourth Wave disappears at the end of a generation, how would it compare with that of its predecessors? The demise of each of the first three waves was associated with important international events. The First Wave ended when the Versailles Treaty after World War I established a new international order that divided the defeated empires into nine independent European states. Although the remaining empires experienced much separatist-motivated terrorist activity, Yugoslavia was the only new state to experience terrorism, because it was home to multiple hostile ethnic groups. The Second Wave was sparked by anticolonial sentiments, which finally achieved its objectives after the victorious Allied Powers of World War II lost their will to maintain their colonial territories. The Cold War was a crucial element in fomenting the Third Wave, and when the Soviet Union collapsed in 1991, the wave was virtually over within a decade. The Arab Spring was an international event, but states did not bring it about, and this time the targets of the participating groups were changed, something that had never happened before. In the preceding waves, terrorists were either defeated or received enough of their original demands to stop fighting.

If the Fourth Wave ends in the late 2020s, it could yield three successes: the Taliban, Hezbollah, and Hamas. The Taliban governs Afghanistan. Hezbollah became an important party in Lebanon's parliament in 1982 and quickly became the major party. Hamas in 2006 entered the Palestine's legislature, became its largest party, took over the Gaza Strip, and has much international support. Each group is large. The Taliban numbered one hundred thousand when it became the government. Hezbollah has over twenty-five thousand members,[280] and Hamas between twenty and twenty-five thousand.[281] But Lebanon's government has become very weak and may collapse, Israel could end Hamas's rule, and the successes of Hezbollah and Hamas might dissipate before the wave ends. The Taliban has recaptured Afghanistan's government.

What will happen after the Fourth Wave dissipates? Will global terrorism disappear, or will a Fifth Wave emerge? The conclusion to this book attempts to answer this question.

CONCLUSION: THE FIFTH WAVE?

Migration trends are to intensify over the coming thirty years. . . . All developed countries will be affected, including East Asia and the former communist countries. There will be an overall mingling of cultures and civilisations that may lead, as far as France is concerned, to the emergence of a predominantly African population and to rapid Islamization.

—JEAN-CLAUDE CHESNAIS

After 9/11, President George W. Bush declared, "Our war on terror . . . will not end until every terrorist group of global reach has been . . . defeated."[1] When the Fourth Wave ends, many may believe Bush was right and think global terrorism no longer exists, a common view after each preceding wave has ended. However, this time, partly because the Four Waves analysis is well known, some argue that a Fifth Wave has already begun. Dipak Gupta, Eric Walls, Vincent Auger, and Amber Hart contend that far-right terror in the West is the Fifth Wave.[2] Auger's "Right-Wing Terror: A Fifth Global Wave?" is the most comprehensive analysis. Using the criteria I specified for a wave, he argues that Europe's far right in 2010 apparently initiated the Fifth Wave.[3] But he notes that far-right terrorism may be over soon, a "transient phenomenon based on local political conditions," and needs more examination.

This chapter will examine those political conditions. Right-wing activity is not a new global terror feature. In the Second and Third Waves, it was directed at revolutionaries and their constituencies, for example, the Northern Ireland Protestant Ulster Defence Association. The Fourth Wave produced some far-right secular groups, for example, the National Alliance and Aryan Nations. Is the explosion of far-right terror in the West part of the Fourth Wave, or is a Fifth Wave emerging?

To understand whether the rise of right-wing terrorism in recent years is the beginning of a global Fifth Wave, one must be clear about a wave's features. Each wave contains several hundred groups sharing goals and/or tactics. Groups within a wave normally last only a few years but are replaced by new groups. A group may transcend a wave and often adopt some new wave features. There have been four successive waves, the First Wave (Anarchist), Second Wave (Anticolonial), Third Wave (New Left), and Fourth Wave (Religious). The names of the Second, Third, and Fourth Waves reflect the aim of most groups in the wave, but the First Wave contained nationalist, leftist, and democratic as well as anarchist elements. The anarchists produced the "Golden Age of Assassination" (1892–1901), during which more monarchs, presidents, and prime ministers were assassinated than ever before, and soon the public called all First Wave participants anarchists.

In each wave, the primary purpose of the attacks was to gain publicity for the cause, which is why First Wave participants described their activity as "propaganda by the deed." The first three waves lasted a generation of forty some forty years, and it appears the recent diminishment of the Fourth Wave means that it will not last any longer than that. Waves overlap in the sense that during one's decline, a new one is emerging. Each wave employed different tactics, and each produced at least one text describing how groups should organize themselves and their tactics and suggesting how to become more efficient. Each wave has its own geography; waves cover at least four continents.

Crucial unexpected dramatic political events stimulated each wave. The efforts of Czar Alexander II attempted to strengthen Russia's military capacity by making Russia's political character more like its democratic enemies. He freed the serfs (one-third of Russia's population), established local self-governments, and abolished capital punishment. But when he ceased his efforts at modernization, the First Wave began. The Versailles Treaty ending World War I (precipitated by a First Wave nationalist attack) made national self-determination a fundamental principle for the international order, which inspired the Second Wave. Two left-wing Third World states, Cuba and Vietnam, stimulated the Third Wave early in the 1960s, which became linked to the Cold War. The Fourth Wave was generated by four 1979 events in the Islamic world, which reduced the importance of secular politics and increased religion's significance.

The waves had different rhythms. The Second Wave did not produce many groups until its last decades. The Fourth Wave began with many groups but in its third decade it declined until the Arab Spring, when it revived. The Third Wave rhythm was steady and declined dramatically when the Cold War ended.

Each wave had a different geography. The First Wave began in Europe and spread to every inhabited continent over the next two decades. But most activity took place in the West. European democracies initially understood terrorists to have democratic aspirations and provided important help. Switzerland encouraged them to use its territories to organize and for sanctuaries. France and Belgium enabled foreign groups to meet with other radicals, and Russian terrorists organized a laboratory in Paris to teach individuals from many foreign countries, including Asian nations, techniques to use when they returned home. The Second Wave occurred in the overseas territories of Western empires in Africa and Asia, especially the Middle East. Europe saw its first case when Irish Catholics tried to remove the island from the United Kingdom in 1922. They were only partially successful because Protestants dominated the north. All other terrorist groups failed until after World War II. The Third Wave spread throughout the globe, apart from areas in the Soviet world. It was most significant in the Third World, large portions of which received Soviet support. "New

Left" organizations in the developed West helped Third World rebel groups and made the United States a principal target. The Fourth Wave began in the Islamic world, especially the Middle East and Afghanistan. Then the Sikhs in India, Jews in Israel, and Christians in the United States and Africa became involved. The United States and Europe became targets, inducing NATO to become involved in Afghanistan and the United States to invade Iraq.

The First Wave produced a large number of groups initially, then gradually dissipated with no later successes. After the IRA produced the Second Wave's first partial success, terrorists failed in India, Burma, Palestine, Puerto Rico, and other places. After World War II, the victorious allies gave many colonial territories independence. But there was a reluctance to free some because, like Ireland, they contained hostile ethnic elements that would generate civil war. But the willingness of colonial powers to release territories inspired many new groups and made the Second Wave the most successful one. Second Wave groups did not cooperate with foreign groups. For first time, terrorist groups fought each other; those fights were between groups in the same territories. Some successes were partial; Israelis wanted to regain all the biblical territories, but Arab resistance, which the United Nations supported, prevented them from doing so. Cyprus aimed to unite with Greece, but the conflict ended with Cyprus divided into two independent states, one dominated by Greeks and the other by Turks. Algeria wanted to keep its European population for economic reasons but could not do so. Ethnic clashes were significant elsewhere, but single independent states were achieved in Aden, Indonesia, Angola, Namibia, Mozambique, etc.

In the Third Wave, the South Tyrolean Liberation Committee achieved the only success not related to the Cold War when Italy in 1996 recognized German-speaking South Tyrol as an autonomous community. Nicaragua's National-Revolutionary Sandinistas, which the Cubans and Soviets aided, took over the government in 1979. When the Cold War ended, other successes occurred. South Africa's ANC was the most important (1994). Whites accepted the ANC fully because its violent wing, MK, was so restrained.

The ANC has won all subsequent elections. The United States sought to improve relations with Arabs and pressed Israel into accepting the Oslo Accords (1993), enabling a weakened PLO to return to Palestine. The PLO got some territorial autonomy and negotiating rights. The United States stopped supporting El Salvador's military government, and the Farabundo Marti Liberation National Front accepted a democratic government, won a National Assembly plurality, and elected the president in 2009 and 2014. The Fourth Wave is not over yet, but the three organizations most likely to succeed are Islamic. Hezbollah is a major element in Lebanon's government, Hamas governs the Gaza Strip, and the Taliban has regained control of the Afghan government. They are large groups. Hezbollah and Hamas each have around twenty-five thousand members, and the Taliban has well over one hundred and sixty thousand.

Each wave had its own special tactics. The first used assassination to reduce casualties and provide publicity. The assassin always used bombs, which sometimes took the assassin's life, making him a martyr. If the assassin became a prisoner, he was expected to proclaim his cause in court and die as a martyr. Second Wave groups rejected assassination and aimed to destroy the police, then struck military forces trying to replace the police. Sometimes the rebels developed guerrilla forces to cope with armies, but the guerrillas did not follow the Geneva Conventions. The Third Wave took hostages and hijacked planes. The Fourth Wave, the bloodiest, introduced self-martyrdom, which the West branded "suicide bombing" because the bomber intended to die, murdering many in the process.

The history of global terrorism suggests that in the Fourth Wave's last decade, a Fifth Wave should begin. Syria's civil war produced a massive refugee flow to Europe (2015–2016), provoking a far-right white suprematist reaction, which may be the harbinger of a Fifth Wave. In the United States, significant white supremacist activity has emerged partly from former President Trump's encouragement. Participants are confined to the Western world, use few bombs, rely on guns, and have not yet produced a tactics text. A young generation visualizing a new world initiated each wave, but now a middle-aged generation acting to preserve a dissipating world is dominant.

Each wave was triggered by dramatic and unanticipated events that transformed the political world for a new generation. The parallel today may be developing. Germany's Chancellor Angela Merkel declared that Europe is experiencing serious divisions on immigration that "could make or break the European Union."[4] Immigrants have stimulated far-right populist movements and terrorists to leave or destroy the European Union if they cannot to force immigrants to leave.[5] Immigration has inspired terror elsewhere. But in the United States, far-right terror emerged largely because of President Donald Trump's administration.

EUROPE

IMMIGRATION

In 2008, Western Europe suffered its first economic crisis since the 1930s,[6] which transformed public attitudes toward immigrants, who previously had been welcomed as an economic asset but were now seen as taking jobs from Europeans or receiving government support without paying taxes. The 2011 Arab Spring produced a dramatic flow of Muslim refugees, which grew immensely as Syria's civil war intensified. In 2015 and 2016, Europe received over two million immigrants.[7] ISIS also made several significant attacks in Europe; it was losing much Syrian territory and believed those attacks would induce Europeans to send more troops to Syria, provoking the Islamic world to respond as it did to the U.S. invasion of Iraq, which had inspired ISIS's birth. But Europe did not send troops; instead it tried to reduce the immigrant flow, and Europeans violently attacked immigrants. Recently, immigration numbers have dropped by 80 percent, and immigration is currently at the level it was in 2014.[8] Nevertheless, strong anxieties over the topic remain.[9]

Migration rules complicated the problem. Freedom of movement is a cornerstone for the European Union's economic and political successes;[10] in 2012 it received a Nobel Prize because the European Union and its forerunners had contributed to peace, reconciliation, democracy, and human rights in Europe. Germany and France had fought three wars over seventy years, and two became world wars. Today war between them is unthinkable.[11]

Ironically, a year before the prize was awarded, a survey indicated 67 percent of the British believed free movement was a bad thing and passed the 2016 Brexit referendum because so many Eastern European EU citizens resided in the United Kingdom.[12] Polls showed three-quarters of the generation under twenty-five years of age voted to remain. Older voters, whose turnout was higher, wanted to leave and triumphed.[13] After four years of negotiations, an agreement was reached that went into effect in January 2021, but its impact is unclear. The United Kingdom's economy could be badly hurt, a possibility that explains why Brexit took so long to negotiate—and the negotiations continue. Scotland and Northern Ireland voted against Brexit and could leave the United Kingdom partly over this issue. This explains why those other states unhappy with the European Union find it difficult to leave.

The British were upset at the unrestricted mobility of EU citizens, but most other EU states became hostile to the European Union when they had to accept foreign refugees. A 1951 international agreement created an obligation to avoid repeating the shameful situation when most countries refused refugees from Nazi Germany.[14] The 1951 agreement dealt with European refugees, but in 1967 a UN protocol obliged states to accept all global refugees.[15]

After the EU "refugee crisis" began in 2011, seven states (Austria, Poland, Hungary, Germany, Denmark, Sweden, and Norway) created border controls to keep asylum seekers from moving from the state that had admitted them to other ones. The European Union enabled states to retain internal border controls for limited periods and required them to apply later to extend them.[16] Some European countries built thousand-kilometer-long anti-immigrant fences, which challenged the Schengen Agreement. That meant passing responsibility for asylum seekers to other states already hosting many refugees. Human rights organizations heavily criticized the border fences. In 2014, Spanish border guards, for example, killed fourteen

African refugees climbing over a border fence. The European Court of Human Rights made the Spanish practice illegal.[17]

In 2016, the European Union and Turkey agreed to limit foreign immigration. Migrants entering the European Union through Turkey, bypassing the Turkish asylum process, would be returned and placed at the end of the application line. Turkey received 6 billion euros; half was to be spent on supporting Syrian refugee communities in Turkey. Critics felt the arrangement violated the 1951 refugee agreement by prolonging the application process, forcing migrants to use dangerous routes like the sea journey between North Africa and Italy. Amnesty International accused the European Union of turning "its back on a global refugee crisis."[18]

A Chatham House 2017 study showed how deep European hostility toward Muslims is. Ten states were studied and each was very hostile: Hungary (72 percent), Austria (67 percent), Poland (66 percent), Greece (65 percent), Spain (50 percent), Netherlands (35 percent), Sweden (35 percent), France (29 percent), and Germany (29 percent). Only one in five respondents felt Muslim immigration should continue. The 2017 EU Minorities and Discrimination Survey found that 33 percent of Muslim respondents had faced discrimination in the previous year, and 27 percent had experienced a racist crime.[19] Muslims are often seen as wanting to separate from the rest of society. A majority of Greeks and at least 40 percent of Italians, Hungarians, and Poles think that having an increasing number of different races, ethnic groups, and nationalities makes their country a worse place to live. Some 50 percent in nine of ten EU countries surveyed believed Muslims do not adopt local ways of life. The right believes this more than the left by significant margins.[20]

Government policies have failed to ensure equal rights for all, forcing many Muslims to face unemployment, poverty, and limited political participation. In the United Kingdom, 18.9 percent of Muslims are currently in full-time employment, according to the Social Mobility Commission, significantly less than the 34.9 percent for the population overall.[21] The most hostile countries, except Poland, had accepted many refugees or experienced Islamic terrorist attacks. A 2016 Ipsos MORI poll found Europeans greatly overestimate the number of Muslims present in their countries, a misconception reflecting and inducing hostility to immigrants.[22]

Even if the European Union stopped all Muslim immigration, Muslim residents would still provoke anxiety. The Pew Research Center said that the Muslim population would still increase from 25.8 million in 2016 to 35.8 million in 2050, that is, from 5 percent of Europe's overall population to 7.4 percent. While the Muslim population grows, the non-Muslim population will decline by roughly 10 percent. "Muslims are younger (by 13 years, on average) and have higher fertility (one child more per woman) than other Europeans."[23]

FAR-RIGHT NATIONALIST POPULIST PARTIES

Twenty-first-century far-right movements are described frequently as populist, as fighting for "the people" against corrupt self-serving governing elites. Charismatic figures often lead populist parties, presenting themselves as the "voice of the people." When in office they often undermine independent institutions like the media or judiciary as hostile to the "will of the people."

"Euroskepticism" is critical in Europe today. It ranges from those who seek to reform some EU institutions and policies to populists who believe the European Union cannot be reformed and nations should become independent again. Populists are hostile to NATO because the Soviet Union, the reason NATO was created, no longer exists; they believe that nation-states now will survive better on their own. Euroskeptics emphasize the European Union lacks democratic legitimacy and transparency; it is too bureaucratic, and EU immigration policies are undermining the cohesion of all nation-states.[24]

Support for the European Union fell below 50 percent in 2008 when the economy deteriorated.[25] Since 2015, trust in the European Union has risen as the economy has grown.[26] But the immigrant flow enabled far-right populist parties to secure seats in thirty-nine parliaments, and some became very important. If they fail to get their programs realized, their states may secede from the European Union to recreate a Europe where nationalism dominates.

Far-right populist movements became very important first in Eastern Europe after the 1989 Soviet withdrawal. The long period of foreign rule produced anxieties about outsiders' presence. Refugees became the crucial issue in Europe in 2016, after two million came in. Hungary's Prime Minister Viktor Orban described them as "Muslim invaders" and that Muslim "rust" would change "democratic government into an autocratic one."[27] Before the refugee flood, Hungary had 5,600 Muslims; immigration made that number nearly forty times higher. Orban's mission is to create a "Christian democracy."[28]

In 2015, the right-wing Polish Law and Justice Party (PIS) won the election, insisting Poland "can't accept any refugees because they could spread infectious diseases."[29] PIS members often decorated their clothes with Celtic crosses and the slogan "Death to the Enemies of the Fatherland." The government closed the bureau constructed to eliminate racial discrimination as "useless." The tiny Polish Muslim population (0.1 percent, or 30,000 out of 38 million) has never initiated any sectarian violence.[30] The UP (United Patriots), a coalition of three far-right Bulgarian parties, was elected in 2016 to stop immigrants from entering Europe. A European Commission Against Racism and Intolerance report described IMRO and the National Front for the Salvation of Bulgaria, two UP parties, as "ultra-nationalist/fascist."[31] Two members were photographed giving Nazi salutes; the deputy interior minister called refugees "apes."[32] The third UP party's leader labeled "Gypsies" (the nonoffensive term is "Roma") as "ferocious apes" demanding a right to salary without labor, "sickness benefits without being ill, child care for children who wallow with pigs on the streets, and maternity benefits for women who have the instincts of street bitches."[33]

ANO (Action of Dissatisfied Citizens) won the 2017 Czech elections. Andrej Babis, the new prime minister, pledged to maintain good relations with the European Union but kept a strong anti-immigration stance. Right-wing demonstrators in Prague waved nooses for "all traitors" who defend immigrants. The police protected the demonstrators and arrested left-wing dissidents protesting the demonstration. A 2015 survey showed that 83 percent of Czechs are seriously worried about a possible refugee influx.[34]

Western European experiences were initially very different. In the 1960s, Austria, Italy, Switzerland, France, Germany, Belgium, Denmark, and the United Kingdom welcomed many Muslims, who were not refugees and came to find jobs, were economic assets, and often became citizens. Most French and UK immigrants came from those states' former colonies; they were familiar with the language and culture of their new country. Immigrants elsewhere came mostly from the Balkans and Turkey, states whose institutions were compatible with those of the West. But later the situation changed. The economy deteriorated, and the immigrant flow now contained Middle East refugees, a different political world. France has Europe's largest Muslim community, over 8.8 percent of the French population.[35] Norway's Muslim population, at 3 percent, is the smallest in Western Europe,[36] though it is three times the U.S. proportion.[37]

Only Portugal still welcomes immigrants. Prime Minister Antonio Costa was cheered at a 2018 party meeting when he said, "We need more immigration, and we won't tolerate any xenophobic rhetoric."[38] Portugal's far-right National Renovator Party obtained only 0.5 percent of the popular vote in the 2015 parliamentary election.[39] Portugal has few Muslims; most immigrants come from former colonial territories like Brazil and speak Portuguese. In 1974, after thirteen years of Second Wave terrorist activity in Portugal's African territories, soldiers initiated the Carnation Revolution, a left-wing bloodless military coup to eliminate "fascism" and promote "decolonization" and "maximum self-determination." Unlike the older generation elsewhere, Portugal's older generation is hostile to the past.

Spain's history paralleled Portugal's for a while. General Franco governed Spain from 1939 to 1975, and given that the government itself was a far-right movement with numerous extralegal aspects, no independent terrorist factions developed. During the country's decade-long economic boom, which began in the mid-1990s, around five million immigrants arrived, helping the economy grow. Most came from former Spanish African and Latin American colonies and spoke Spanish. Eastern Europe provided many immigrants as well. By 2018, 12.8 percent of Spain's population was foreign-born.[40] Spain's far-right party Vox emerged in a unique way. Catalonia, Spain's wealthiest province, pushed for secession with an illegal referendum in 2017; the result was 90 percent for independence, but only 43 percent of the Catalonian electorate voted because those opposing independence refused to participate. Vox's furious response to the secessionists enabled it to become the first populist party in the Spanish parliament; it won twenty-four seats in 2019. Nine referendum organizers were sent to prison, and in the next election Vox received fifty-two seats to become Spain's third-largest party. It proposed eliminating Spain's autonomous communities.[41] Vox also announced it will stop immigration from Muslim countries, which had not been a significant issue.[42] But Vox's Euroskepticism is limited.[43]

Austria (2017) and Italy (2018) developed populist coalition governments. Ex-Nazis founded Austria's smaller Freedom Party, which wanted to leave the European Union, as did Italy's government. Significant populist movements emerged in seven other Western European states—France, Switzerland, Denmark, Greece, Belgium, Denmark, and Sweden.[44] In Denmark's 2015 election, the anti-immigration People's Party finished second, with 21 percent of the vote, and cooperated with the Conservative-Liberal coalition government to restrain immigration.[45] The neo-Nazi Greek Golden Dawn party in 2012 won twenty-one seats in the Hellenic Parliament, the sixth-largest number. In 2018, Sweden's far-right Democrat Party, the country's third largest, secured sixty-two Riksdag seats.

The United Kingdom has less anti-Islamic sentiment than most Western European states, partly because many Muslims fought in the British Indian Army in both World Wars; some earned the Victoria Cross, Britain's highest military honor. After India was partitioned in 1947, many Muslims settled in the United Kingdom to become the largest British Muslim group.[46] Muslims are younger than other residents and produce more children. Between 2000 and 2010, the Muslim population increased almost ten times faster than the non-Muslim population.[47] Muslims participate vigorously in British politics; in 2017 there were fifteen Muslim MPs and twelve Muslims in the House of Lords. In 2016, Sadiq Khan became London's mayor, earning the largest number of votes in the city's history.[48] Earlier he had won three parliamentary elections and served in the Labour Party's shadow cabinet. Most Muslims vote for the Labour Party.[49] But there are some important Muslims in the Conservative Party; Sayeeda Marsi served in a Conservative cabinet.[50]

The United Kingdom has four small far-right parties. The National Party aims to restrict citizenship to whites. It gained many local council seats and two seats in the European Parliament but got none in the 2010 general election and soon became obscure. The English Defence League lasted two years, 2009 to 2011. Former members created the Britain First Party in 2011, which failed to elect anyone in numerous elections and disintegrated in 2017.[51] Three parties in 2018 organized demonstrations attacking immigrants in mosques. The Independence Party (commonly known as UKIP) confined itself to elections and achieved its ultimate objective of getting the United Kingdom to withdraw from the European Union.[52] In 2016, it received 3.8 million votes, mainly from dissatisfied members of the ruling Conservative Party, making the government feel it might lose the next election if it ignored the EU issue. It thereby agreed to have a referendum. Brexit was passed, and UKIP disappeared, although its leaders continue to revive it under different names, for example, the Brexit Party.

When the Cold War ended, most immigrants in Italy were Eastern European.[53] Around 10 percent of the Italian population has an immigrant background, and in 2008 Italy had around 670,000 illegal immigrants.[54] Sixty-nine percent of Italians view Muslims unfavorably.[55] Italy has had economic problems since 2005 and in 2018 developed a deep economic crisis. Its public debt is the European Union's second largest, and the country has had a double-digit unemployment rate since 2012. EU institutions hold much of that debt, intensifying Italian antagonism. In a 2008 European Parliament poll, just 44 percent said they would vote to stay in the European Union, the lowest percentage of all twenty-eight states.[56] Ironically, Italians were initially very enthusiastic about the European Union.[57] A populist coalition made up of the Five Star Movement (M5S) and the Northern League, won the 2018 election.

The Syrian War refugee flow did not transform the United Kingdom's view of Muslims. A Pew Research study shows that the United Kingdom has one of the lower levels of hostility toward those refugees; 33 percent see them as a major threat, compared to France's 39 percent, Spain's 42 percent, and Poland's 60 percent. Ironically, countries with lower refugee numbers were more likely to believe refugees were a threat.[58]

Middle Eastern refugees arrived in France when the unemployment rate was 10 percent. In the French 2017 election, Marine Le Pen's far-right National Rally Party was second, with 34 percent of the vote. But it lost the election; only 29 percent of the population was anti-Muslim. West German labor shortages in 1961 induced the government to sign a labor recruitment agreement with Turkey to help Turks emigrate. Many Turks thought they would eventually return home with funds for a better life. But life in Germany was very comfortable; many remained, became more secular, and were comfortable associating with the many Muslim immigrants from southeastern Europe, once part of the Ottoman Empire. When the Syrian war began, Germany welcomed around 1,500,000 refugees because it appreciated how immigrants had helped make Germany's economy Europe's most prosperous. German views changed greatly as Islamic terror emerged, but the outcome is still unclear. Chancellor Angela Merkel's coalition won the highest percentage of the vote, with 33 percent but lost 8 percent of its voters, and her party, the Christian Democratic Union, experienced its worst election result since 1966. She resigned as party leader, and her replacement said Germany would restrict immigration. Merkel then gave up he role as chancellor in December 2021, seven years after she became the longest-serving incumbent head of a European Union government. After she won her fourth term in 2017, *Forbes* named her the world's most powerful woman for a record fourteenth time.[59] But in the 2017 election, AfD (Alternative for Germany) got 12.6 percent of the vote and won ninety-four Bundestag seats, the first far-right party to enter the Bundestag since the Nazis ninety years earlier. In subsequent local elections, AfD broadened its base, especially in regions of the former East Germany. In 2020, when Thuringia's popular governor lost his position, he was replaced by an AfD-supported candidate aided by some of Chancellor Merkel's party members.

The surprise event produced intense anger and dark memories. Thuringia was the state where the Nazis had won their first legislative seats in 1930. Merkel said, "It was a bad day for democracy." The major parties did not cooperate with AfD. Jan Techau, director of the German Marshall Fund, said, "Deep down we Germans do not trust ourselves . . . one legacy of the Hitler era."[60] In 2020, Germany's domestic intelligence agency designated AfD's Wing as extremist and put some leaders under surveillance. With an estimated seven thousand followers, the Wing is one-fifth of AfD's party membership, and an intelligence agency estimated that 13,000 Wing members were ready to commit violence.[61]

Belgium is unusual in not having a Euroskeptic element, partly because Brussels is the European Union's de facto capital, and hosting EU institutions helps Belgium's economy. But in the 2018 municipal elections, the VB (Vlaams Belang), a right-wing party aiming to secede and establish the state of Flanders, gained over 13 percent of the Flemish vote.[62] In the 2019 national elections, it was the second-largest Flemish party.

Denmark's Muslim problem began before many immigrants arrived. Islam regards it blasphemous to portray Muhammad in visual images. In 2005, Muhammad appeared in a Danish newspaper's editorial cartoons, which stimulated violent riots in the Middle East and North Africa; a judicial complaint against the newspaper was dismissed. The government refused to intervene or discuss the matter with foreign diplomats.[63] In the 2015 election, the anti-immigration People's Party emerged to help the government reduce immigrant numbers greatly.[64] Refugee social benefits were cut by 30 to 40 percent in their first seven years. The aim was to improve integration by inducing refugees to work, but a People's Party spokesman was happy that the cuts had decreased refugee numbers greatly, showing "one does not find gold in the streets in Denmark as has been told out in the third world."[65] Muslims were infuriated when a ban to circumcise children got the fifty thousand signatures needed for a parliamentary vote. The ban was overruled after religious protests, and the People's Party suffered a major election defeat in 2019, losing twenty-one of its thirty-seven seats.

Norway and Sweden's cold climate discouraged immigrants initially, though they received generous permits and benefits. But Syria's civil war changed everything. In 2013, Sweden accepted more than twice as many immigrants per capita than any other country in the world. Over the next five years, it welcomed six hundred thousand, making 20 percent of Sweden's population immigrants.[66] Muslims are 8.1 percent of the population, and some got involved in grenade attacks and car bombings. Swedes responded with arson attacks on three mosques in one week. But afterward, to show solidarity with Muslims, Swedes hung paper hearts on firebombed mosques.[67] Security Service Director Anders Thornberg in 2017 stated that several thousand violent Islamic extremists resided in Sweden. The Swedish Defence University contends that most were affiliated with the Islamic State, with around three hundred people traveling to Syria and Iraq to join it and al-Qaeda-associated groups.[68]

Earlier immigrants often gained permanent residency, but after November 2015 most asylum seekers are only eligible for temporary permits and cannot bring their families. Sweden now is at the bottom of the European Union in welcoming refugees. In 2018, the far-right Sweden Democrat Party secured sixty-two Riksdag seats to become the third-largest party. A 2014 poll showed that 50 percent of Norwegians considered Islamic and Norwegian values incompatible.[69] The anti-Islamic Norwegian Defense League emerged in 2010, closely associated with the English and European Defense Leagues, to fight for the democracy they claim Islam threatens.[70]

A brief look at the far right's efforts to restrict Muslims through the law is interesting. Dr. Barbara Kolm said Austria's populist government was produced by "those people, who contribute to the economy, pay taxes and work hard are the ones that actually lose." Austria must change its policies or be "harmonized to death."[71] The new government reduced funding for integration and banned women from wearing the hijab, a ban twelve EU countries imposed. Austria's new chancellor, Sebastian Kurz, closed seven mosques and expelled sixty imams. But Austrian courts quickly annulled Kurz's decision. Austria retained 231 mosques; 4.2 percent of its population is Muslim.[72]

Europeans often regard mosques as a major source of Islamic terrorism and blame them for intensifying cultural differences preventing Muslims from becoming "true" Europeans. Populists exploit these anxieties for political gain and to stimulate Islamophobia. Demands for more mosques to accommodate many new Muslim refugees is an issue in many countries. France's Le Pen's National Rally and Germany's AfD are prominent opponents. The AfD threw a dead pig, which Muslims regard as an unclean animal, into a Leipzig mosque, a common practice now.[73] The location for new mosques is an issue. Many insist new mosques should be constructed in a city's outer edges.[74] In the outskirts of Mollet del Vallès, Spain, where a mosque was built, a member noted, "It's good because it's big, but no one comes. Only Friday because it is a long way. If you want to come three or five times a week, or it is raining, or you do not have a car, it's difficult." Far-right leaders from fifteen European cities met in Belgium to promote a ban on new mosques, and at their meeting Filip Dewinter, leader of a Flemish separatist party,[75] declared, "We already have more than 6,000 mosques in Europe, which are not only a place to worship but also a symbol of radicalization, some financed by extreme groups in Saudi Arabia or Iran."

Switzerland undermined its reputation for religious tolerance in 2009 by banning minaret (prayer tower) construction in a far-right referendum added to its constitution.[76] Denmark made children living in "ghettos" spend twenty-five hours apart from their parents every week to be taught "Danish values," including Christmas and Easter traditions and the Danish language.[77] Denmark has no Muslim cemeteries; Muslim bodies must be returned to their home countries for proper burial.

Italy compels Muslims to use Italian for mosque services. When Italy's populist government came to power, the country had only eight mosques for 2.6 million Muslims.[78] Sixty-nine percent of Italians viewed Muslims unfavorably, the highest percentage in Western Europe.[79] Islam is not formally recognized as a religion in Italy, despite Muslims being the country's largest religious minority. Religious holidays and weddings are not recognized; mosques cannot receive public funds. British, French, and German groups demand that mosques use national languages to help Muslims become more integrated and so security officers can more easily detect violent enterprises. But the British, France and German governments have not yet been convinced.

Europe's populist movements developed important ties with Putin's Russia, which seems surprising because the Soviet Union was linked to

Europe's left. But both governments aimed to dissolve NATO. "Far-right leaders pay regular visits to Russia, to meet Russian officials and often appear on state-owned Russian media, facts which boost their credibility at home."[80] That connection was very conspicuous in the first far-right Western European governments in Austria and Italy. In May 2019, the "Ibza Scandal" occurred when a video showed that two years earlier, when the far right came to power, Heinz-Christian Strache, Austria's vice chancellor and the far-right Freedom Party's head, offered government contracts and a stake in a large Austrian newspaper for Russian support. The revelation induced mass Vienna demonstrations demanding a snap election.[81] Strache was removed; Chancellor Kurz, leader of the Austrian People's Party, authorized a snap election, which he lost. Once perceived to be the leader of Europe's far right, he became the shortest-serving chancellor in Austria's post–World War II history, with 525 days in office. The Freedom Party and Putin's United Russia party had earlier ties,[82] and Austrians were "election observers" in Russia's fraudulent 2014 referendum, in which Crimea was annexed.[83]

Matteo Salvini, Italy's Northern League leader, frequently praised Putin and even wore a Putin T-shirt at a European Parliament meeting. In 2017, Salvini's party and Putin's United Russia Party signed a "cooperation agreement," fostering economic, legal, and cultural ties. Since then, Salvini has consistently defended Russia. In 2018, he pushed for lifting sanctions on Russia for annexing Crimea and allowing Russia to return to the G8, even though the annexation violated international law. In 2018, when Russian military intelligence poisoned a former Russian military officer and his daughter in the United Kingdom, the European Union supported efforts to apprehend those responsible.[84] Sixteen EU countries expelled thirty-three Russian diplomats.[85] Salvini condemned the EU response, displaying staunch support for Putin. Salvini met Donald Trump during the 2016 election campaign to endorse him.[86] Many news agencies felt their political views were identical.

Marine Le Pen's political party National Rally's racism and anti-Semitism prohibited it from getting loans from French banks, but it received 11 million euros in loans from Russian banks for supporting the Crimea annexation. Russia also financed Sweden's Democrats.[87] In Eastern Europe, many far-right parties had good ties with Russia. Hungary's Prime Minister Orban openly admires Vladimir Putin's "strongman" style of politics, rejected the European Union's denunciation of Russia's Crimea annexation, and entertained Putin in Budapest.

In the 2019 European Parliament election, the far right increased its vote from 20 percent to 25 percent, but the gain was much less than what pro-EU forces feared. Recent revelations about Russia and far-right ties angered many voters.[88] More young people voted, supporting Green parties concerned with climate change and strengthening the European Union. The coalition of center-left and center-right parties lost the majority they had held for decades. But far-right losses were smaller than expected; perhaps they can obstruct the European Parliament.

Immigration restraints materialized on other continents, too.[89] Australia's right-wing prime minister won the 2019 election because he "resembled the force that has upended politics in the United States, Britain and beyond."[90] In South America, Peru and Ecuador restricted Venezuelan refugees. In Africa, Tanzania precluded refugees from Burundi, and in Asia, Indonesia, Thailand, and Malaysia refused to accept Muslim refugees from Myanmar.

India's Prime Minister Narendra Modi and the BJP (Bharatiya Janata Party Indian People's Party) is hostile to immigrants, especially Muslims. The BJP is committed to making India a Hindu country by restricting the religious practices of Muslims,[91] who constitute 14 percent of the population.[92] The BJP replaced the left-wing secular Congress Party, which had led the 1947 independence struggle and dominated India for fifty-four years. Modi's early political record as chief minister of Gujarat reflected his hostility to Muslims, where many anti-Muslim atrocities occurred in 2002. Dexter Filkins noted, "According to eye-witnesses, rioters cut open the bellies of pregnant women and killed their babies; others gang-raped women and girls."[93] The United Kingdom and United States deemed Modi responsible for the anti-Muslim atrocities and denied him visas for nearly a decade. But India's Supreme Court cleared Modi of complicity in 2012.

Modi became prime minister of a coalition government in 2014, prom-ising to wage a "religious war." "Place names were changed—so, too, were textbooks—to de-emphasize Muslims' contribution to India and play up Hindu teachings."[94] In 2019, he was reelected with an enormous majority; no election in the world had ever produced more voters.[95] Religious hate crimes increased more than fivefold. At least forty-six Muslims were mur-dered, accused of slaughtering cows, which Hindus regard as holy. Modi suspended the Indian constitution's article granting Kashmir autonomy, India's only Muslim-majority state, and flooded it with troops. His party described Muslim immigrants from Bangladesh as "termites" who "throw bombs and kill innocent citizens."

After Modi became prime minister, President Obama granted him a visa to expand commercial relations.[96] But Donald Trump during his 2016 election campaign wanted to develop a close personal relationship with Modi, declaring "I love Hindu," when seeking Hindu votes in Houston, Texas. After Trump became president, he met Modi several times. During Modi's visit to Houston in 2019, they walked onto the stage holding hands before a crowd of around fifty thousand Indian-Americans at NRG Stadium.

Putin's Russia intervened in many foreign elections. Russian interven-tions began many decades ago, a practice other countries employed too, including the United States during the Cold War in Latin America.[97] But the advent of the internet age made interventions easier, cheaper, and more effective, especially where ballots are no longer handwritten. In 2014, cyberattacks were often employed to help far-right parties, who also made cyberattacks. Beyond extensive interventions in every East European state, Russia intervened in many elections in the West— Belgium, Cyprus, Denmark, France, Germany, Macedonia, Malta, Norway, Portugal, Spain, Sweden, the United Kingdom, and the United States.[98] While it is difficult to know whether cyberattacks changed voting outcomes, they make it difficult for losers to accept the results and could undermine the legitimacy of the voting process.[99]

The 84.6 percent turnout in the 2014 referendum for Scottish independence from the United Kingdom was the highest for a UK election or referendum since the 1911 Parliament election. 55.3 percent voted against independence. Russia ran a cybercampaign to discredit the result, alleging it was rigged. An Atlantic Council analyst noted, "Pro-Kremlin accounts . . . boosted those allegations. The anger and disappointment felt by many yes voters were entirely sincere [and] those sentiments were fanned by pro-Kremlin trolls."[100] Russia then intervened in the Brexit referendum, infuriating the UK government.[101] Democrats on the Foreign Relations Committee wrote a 2018 minority report stating, "The Russian government has sought to influence democracy in the United Kingdom through disinformation, cyber hacking, and corruption. While a complete picture of the scope and nature of interference in the UK's June 2016 referendum is still emerging, the "UK condemned the involvement, and various government entities, including the Electoral Commission and parliamentarians, launched investigations into different aspects of possible Russian government meddling."[102] British intelligence agencies examined Russia's efforts to make sure the Brexit referendum to leave the European Union passed. But the Tory government said it would not publish the report before the December election, prompting an uproar. The investigating committee chair said: "The protocols are quite clear. If the Prime Minister has a good reason for preventing publication, he should explain to the committee what it is, and do it within 10 days of him receiving the report. If not, it should be published." Prime Minister Boris Johnson was accused of a coverup.[103] After nine months, the Russia report came out and dammed the government for underestimating "the response required to the Russian threat and are still playing catch up. . . . Russian influence in the UK is the new normal . . . the UK is clearly a target for Russian disinformation."[104]

After the Brexit referendum, Russia got involved in the 2016 U.S. presidential election to help Donald Trump, who said the allegation was a "hoax" by Democrats to explain their defeat. But Russia infiltrated the email correspondence of candidate Hillary Clinton and disseminated it with fake documents to Wikileaks. The Mueller Report concluded Russian interference was "sweeping and systematic."[105] Russia targeted twenty-one U.S. state voter-registration systems and various ethnic groups, especially African Americans, whose voter turnout is crucial for Democrats.[106] Twenty-six Russian citizens and three Russian organizations were indicted.

In 2017, Russia's effort to intervene in France's presidential campaign against Emmanuel Macron failed. Two days before the first round, Russia leaked tens of thousands of emails from Macron's campaign team. Many false documents were attached to the emails, some "so absurd that they were hardly credible. Macron's campaign team reacted by denouncing the hack on social media and turning it into a complete farce."[107] Macron won the second round easily; news about Russia's efforts likely increased his votes. A senior CSIS figure said France's centralized supervisory body protects election integrity better than the United States, where elections are managed by each state. "Protection of critical infrastructure (such as election systems) is provided by the Department of Homeland Security but must be developed in cooperation with each state (which may have different approaches)."[108]

In the 2017 Bundestag election, a far-right AfD (Alternative for Germany) candidate said that only the Russian media outlets "show our points of view in full."[109] AfD became the first German far-right party after World War II, winning 13 percent of the 2017 vote and ninety-one of 631 seats. Ironically, AfD stated one-third of its support came from Russian-speaking voters had who immigrated to Germany after the Soviet Union collapsed, 5 percent of the population, with ties to Putin's Russia. In the 2019 local elections, AfD got 28 percent of the vote in Saxony and 24 percent in Brandenburg, gains of 18 percent.

In January 2021, the COVID-19 pandemic compelled all EU states to restrict mobility from other EU states. This is a serious blow to the European Union and its economy. If it is sustained much longer, the European Union might be dissolved, because the economic advantages it provides are a primary reason for sustaining public support.[110]

THE UNITED STATES

During the Fourth Wave's first two decades, far-right militias were very important, and two militia men committed the Oklahoma City bombing, killing 168, including nineteen children, and injuring 680. It was the most destructive terrorist act on U.S. soil until 9/11. Support for the far right dissipated, and militias seemed to disappear by 2000. Resurgence began in 2008; by 2010, the number rose to 840.[111] A 2012 Department of Homeland Security report designated right-wing activity and its "leaderless resistance" strategy as the "worst domestic terrorist threat." Several factors contributed to its growth: the Great Recession, the election of an African American president purportedly committed to gun control (even though he had not campaigned on the issue), the receding trauma of the Oklahoma City bombing, and a more liberal immigration policy. Sixty-five militia groups existed by 2016.[112] Retired military and police officers dominated many militias. In 2020, the SPLC listed 566 active extreme antigovernment groups, including 169 militias.[113] These included the Three Percenters (2008), Oath Keepers (2009), Proud Boys (2016), Stop the Steal (2016), QAnon (2017), The Base (2018), Boogaloo (2019), and Patriot Movement (1980, revived in 2009).[114] White supremacist groups are obsessed with declining white birth rates compared to those of other racial elements and believe that, especially if current immigration policies continue, whites will be replaced.

The far right's significance helped the populist Donald Trump win his 2016 election campaign. The two populist parties in Austria and Italy governed for a very short time, but Trump's government lasted four years. Anthony Gardner, a U.S. ambassador to the European Union, noted Trump "decided European integration is bad, and that the EU is in fact an enemy."[115] Trump tried to unify European populist groups opposed to the European Union. In 2017, Steve Bannon, his chief strategist, founded the Movement in Brussels to create a bloc that could win at least one-third of the 751 European Parliament seats.[116] But the Movement drew a mixed response. Hungarian Prime Minister Orban and Italy's Deputy Prime Minister Salvini joined immediately. But the Dutch Party for Freedom rejected "the Movement as a plan to foster American interests," a view German, Austrian, and UK far-right parties endorsed.[117]

Several incidents illustrated Trump's far-right character. In his 2016 election campaign, he made immigration restrictions a chief issue, calling for "a total and complete shutdown of Muslims entering the United States until our country's representatives can figure out what the hell is going on."[118] When elected, he tweeted, "Our country needs strong borders and extreme vetting. NOW. Look at what is happening all over Europe and, indeed, the rest of the world. A horrible mess."[119] Trump restricted Muslim immigrants from seven countries and refugees from four. He refused to accept refugees and declared a national emergency to get funds for a border wall to control immigration from Mexico; he had not completed the wall by the end of his administration.

In Charlottesville, Virginia, in August 2017, a legal decision to remove Confederate General Robert E. Lee's statue was resisted by Unite the Right Rally demonstrators carrying weapons, neo-Nazi symbols, Confederate battle flags, and anti-Muslim and anti-Semitic group symbols. Counterprotesters arrived, which led to some fighting, and thirty were injured. The next day, a white supremacist deliberately ran his car into the counterprotestors, killing one and injuring nineteen. President Trump's initial statement was that there were "very fine people on both sides," which suggested he was sympathetic to white supremacists.[120]

In 2018, Trump announced a family separation policy to control illegal immigration on the Mexican border, a practice implemented a year before its announcement. Adults were prosecuted and held in federal jails or deported and over five thousand children put under federal supervision.[121] The policy did not include measures to reunite separated families. Trump refused to finance the cost of reuniting families; private groups provided the cash and volunteers to find the parents. By November 2020, the parents of 666 children still had not been found.[122]

The SPLC (Southern Poverty Law Center) noted that in the 2016 election campaign, Trump's "demonizing statements about Latinos and Muslims electrified the radical right, leading to glowing endorsements from white nationalist leaders." Trump refused to accept the World Health Organization's warning not to link diseases with racial groups and in March 2020 called the coronavirus the "Chinese virus." Several harassment and violent attacks against Asians occurred that day, but he kept using the term. A reporter asked why he used a phrase that some considered racist; he responded, "It's not racist at all. It comes from China . . . I want to be accurate."[123] Asian Americans were targeted in nearly 3,800 hate incidents in the past year. Also, the House of Representatives held its first hearing on anti-Asian discrimination in three decades.

Far-right movements are highly decentralized, an array of autonomous groups that aim to achieve their objectives largely through demonstrations, protesting immigration, racial issues, and left-wing enterprises. Those demonstrations sometimes produce violence, especially during the Obama administration, when government forces resisted the demonstrators, who were often armed. This form of violence is not considered terrorism. When Trump became president, their violence was no longer directed against government. Demonstrations on other issues continued, aggravated by responses to the Black Lives Matter movement, born when a police officer murdered George Floyd in May 2020. The U.S. Political Violence Dataset, along with IEP estimates for political violence from 2010 to 2020, indicate political violence in the United States is now at a fifty-year high. There were an estimated 671 riots from May to October 2020, with seventeen causing at least one death. These riots occurred in the context of a much broader protest sentiment of "nearly 13,000 peaceful demonstrations."[124]

It is difficult to estimate the size of each movement. Oath Keepers is the largest; in 2016 it claimed to have 35,000 members, but in 2020 the Anti-Defamation League estimated "between 1,000 and 3,000 Oath Keepers, though the group's influence extends well beyond that number."[125] The problem is that the movement estimates its size by how many followers it has on social media platforms, but many followers are not members, which is why Oath Keepers' largest demonstrations have a few hundred.

In the first 2020 presidential election debate, the moderator asked Trump why his administration had ignored issues of right-wing violence. Trump responded that the problem "I see is from the left wing, not from the right wing."[126] Biden then asked, "What about the Proud Boys?" Trump declared that the "Proud Boys stand back and stand by." Proud Boys had endorsed Trump and been involved in a number of violent demonstrations.

In the debate, Trump kept repeating that "antifa" was causing all the violence the United States was experiencing. But antifa is not the left-wing body Trump described. It is a movement of autonomous groups aiming to achieve their objectives through demonstrations largely inspired by reactions to far-right groups, clashes that occasionally become violent. The first group to call itself antifa emerged in Oregon in 2007 and consisted of former Anti-Racist Action members. All other antifa groups have similar genealogies and identify themselves as anarchist or communist. But they are not terrorists as Trump kept claiming. Antifa became "a conservative catch-all" term Trump supporters applied to all sorts of left-leaning or liberal protest actions.[127]

Various recent events weakened the far right. Greece's Golden Dawn party lost its twenty-one seats, and in 2020 its officials were arrested for creating a "criminal organization" that struck immigrants and left-wing groups. Fifty-seven were convicted of murder, assault, and weapons possession.[128] Italy's Deputy Prime Minister Matteo Salvini lost his office in 2019, and in December 2020 he went on trial for violating international law by preventing 116 migrants from disembarking and stopping a coast guard ship from granting aid to starving migrants. He declared, "I am proud to have defended Italy . . . and I will do it again."[129]

Trump's 2020 election defeat was the most important event. But he claimed many votes were fraudulent and that he had really won the election, a view that most Republicans believed even though every effort to find evidence of vote tampering failed. On January 6, 2021, a mob Trump incited attacked the Capitol to prevent Congress from certifying the election result.

The attack killed five and wounded over 140, and over three hundred were charged with federal crimes.[130] At least 17 percent of those charged were members of far-right movements such as Oath Keepers, Three Percenters, Proud Boys, Boogaloo, Traditionalist Worker Party, QAnon, Nationalist Social Club, neo-Confederates, and Holocaust deniers. At least 15 percent had ties to the military or law enforcement.[131] The mob also included Republican Party officials, political donors, and evangelical Christians.[132] When Trump was impeached for inciting the riot, his lawyers falsely claimed that antifa had produced the violence, a view that many people, even Republican lawmakers, endorsed.[133]

The Capitol had experienced terrorist strikes before. During the Second Wave (1954), the Nationalist Party, seeking Puerto Rican independence, injured five congressmen, and the Third Wave Weather Underground (1971) exploded a bomb, which fortunately caused no injuries, to protest U.S. bombing Laos during the Vietnam War. But never before had a massive demonstration struck the Capitol; nevertheless its violence, like the violence of other far-right demonstrations in the United States during the same period, was not considered terrorism.[134]

To secure President Biden's inauguration, 25,000 National Guard forces "vetted for extremist views"[135] arrived, the largest since the Civil War.[136] Some four thousand law enforcement officers supplemented the troops, and seven-foot-high crowd-control barriers were installed around the Capitol. But it is expected that Biden's administration will experience some far-right violence, largely generated by demonstrations.

NEW WAVE?

In July 2011, Anders Breivik, a thirty-two-year-old Norwegian, made the first significant terror attacks against European immigration policies, targeting Norway's Labour government for encouraging Muslim immigration that would "destroy European culture." He bombed the prime minister's office, killing eight and injuring over 200. Then in a mass shooting, he killed sixty-nine and wounded over one hundred at the Labour Party's youth branch's summer camp.[137] Before the attacks, he produced a 1,518-page internet manifesto, *2083: A European Declaration of Independence*, declaring the attacks were made to publicize his manifesto.[138] Breivik chose the date 2083 for "European Independence" because it was five hundred years after the "Great Turkish War" began, that is, when the Holy Roman Empire stopped Ottoman advances in Europe. The manifesto insisted no Muslim should remain in Europe and blamed feminism for Europe's "cultural suicide."[139]

In his pretrial hearing, Breivik insisted he was a hero for his "pre-emptive attack against traitors" who were "committing or planning to commit . . . destruction of . . . Norwegian culture." He claimed to be a Crusader, who was acting for the reborn dynasty and insisting every Muslim immigrant must convert to Christianity and take a Christian name or be deported or executed.[140] But, ironically, he also condemned personal violence against Muslim immigrants. "Muslim . . . bashing is a sure way to hurt our cause as this is what the cultural Marxist elites WANT you to do. . . . They want the indigenous Europeans . . . fighting Muslims as that will guarantee their positions. We will never have a chance at overthrowing the cultural Marxist if we waste our energy and efforts on fighting Muslims."[141] But Breivik's advice about target priorities was ignored; far-right violence was indeed directed against Muslims. The Global Terrorism Index 2018 stated that in 2015 to 2018, eight-six terrorist operations occurred in Western Europe.[142] For right-wing terrorists, Muslims were the principal target, but other religions, ethnic groups, persons with certain political views, and those identified as lesbian, gay, bisexual, and transgender experienced violence as well.

Eight years after Breivik's strikes, two similar cases occurred, though the victims were immigrants. In 2019, Brenton Tarrant, a twenty-eight-year-old Australian, massacred fifty-one Muslims in two mosques in Christchurch, New Zealand, the first act of terrorism in New Zealand.[143] Tarrant's seventy-nine-page internet manifesto, "The Great Replacement," states his goal was to prevent Muslims from taking over Western society and ends with the phrase "Europa arises."[144] He emphasizes the crucial importance of European low birth rates. "If we were to deport all the non-Europeans from our land tomorrow the European people would still be spiralling into decay and eventual death." Tarrant donated money to Generation Identity, the Austrian Freedom Party's youth movement, which published a poem describing Muslim immigrants as "rats."[145] A week after Tarrant's attacks, UK anti-Muslim hate crimes increased by 593 percent, and eight-five incidents (89 percent of the total) contained direct references to the New Zealand attacks.[146] Tarrant said his visit to Europe in 2017 radicalized him. While he was in Sweden, a Muslim immigrant drove a truck into some Swedes, killing five, including an eleven-year-old girl. Tarrant became deeply depressed when Marine Le Pen, who wanted to end immigration, lost France's presidential election. Tarrant cited Anders Breivik as his "inspiration." Like Breivik, he claimed connection to the Knights Templar. Tarrant's manifesto was headlined "To Christians" and stated,

"Let our lives be stronger than death to fight against the enemies of the Christian people." But he did not explain why he rejected Breivik's declaration to strike those who encourage Muslim immigration and avoid violence against Muslims.

The next important terrorist act was against Hispanic immigrants, to protect "American culture." In August 2019, Patrick Crusius, a twenty-one-year-old Texan, killed twenty-three and injured twenty-four others in an El Paso shopping mall. His manifesto, "The Inconvenient Truth About Me," identifies his inspiration.

> In general, I support the Christchurch shooter. . . . This attack is a response to the Hispanic invasion of Texas. . . . Some people will think this statement is hypocritical because of the nearly complete ethnic and cultural destruction brought to the Native Americans by our European ancestors, but this just reinforces my point. The natives didn't take the invasion of Europeans seriously, and now what's left is just a shadow of what was.[147]

There are 56.5 million Hispanics in the United States, 18 percent of the population; the number has grown immensely since 1980, when it was 6 percent. Eighty percent of El Paso's population is Hispanic, one reason the city became the target.[148]

Three of the four attacks were mass shootings. Breivik bombed the prime minister's office in his first attack, but it produced far fewer fatalities than the other three strikes. Since 2011, armed assaults have outnumbered bombing attacks, and if a new wave is emerging, this will be its distinctive tactic. The bomb had been the principal weapon of every previous wave. Why has this commitment to armed assaults with guns replaced it now? Such guns had been available for nearly a century. The answer must be in the far right's ideology. The massive indiscriminate casualties experienced in the Oklahoma City bombing probably caused the change in weapons. In the West, far-right attacks have increased by 320 percent from 2014 to 2020, with deaths increasing by 709 percent.[149] There have been over thirty-five far-right terrorist incidents in the West every year for the past five years. Far-right terrorism tends to be more lethal than far-left terrorism but not as lethal as Islamist terrorism in the West. Deaths have been increasing every year for the past three years, from eleven in 2017 to twenty-six in 2018 to seventy-seven by the end of September 2019. But far-right terror remains a small fraction of the worldwide total because even though the Fourth Wave is deteriorating, it is producing many more incidents. Even in the West, historically nationalist or separatist, Islamist, and far-left terrorism has been much more common. Nearly 60 percent of far-right attacks from 1970 to 2019 were carried out by unaffiliated individuals, while far-left and separatist attacks were under 10 percent each. Far-right attacks are more than five times deadlier on average than far-left ones.

New figures released by the United Kingdom's Home Office confirm victims' reports of a dramatic increase in incidents motivated by attackers' hostility toward their race, nationality, religion, or ethnicity. "Police data from England and Wales showed there were almost 80,400 hate crimes recorded in the 2016–2017 financial year . . . a 29 percent rise from the previous year – the largest annual increase since records began six years ago."[150] Germany, with the largest number of refugees, experienced many right-wing attacks. In 2013, there were twenty-four hate crimes recorded, largely against refugee shelters, homes, and mosques. In 2016, the number was 1,578 and in 2017, 1,536.[151] Germany experienced eight far-right terror attacks in 2018, up from five between 2016 and 2017. The most publicized was the 2018 stabbing of Altena's mayor, who was honored for welcoming refugees.[152] In 2020, hundreds of far-right activists protesting pandemic restrictions stormed the German Parliament but were unable to get in. President Trump's "face was emblazoned on banners, T-shirts and even on Germany's pre-1918 imperial flag, popular with neo-Nazis."[153]

Unexpectedly in Germany, and probably throughout Europe, the overwhelming majority of hate crimes were made by people with no previous far-right connections. Most attackers are in their thirties,[154] a decade older than those who created earlier waves,[155] and since those in their twenties voted in the Brexit referendum overwhelmingly to remain in the European Union, these age facts suggest a new wave is not emerging. Previous wave participants were virtually all in their twenties and able to devote all their time to the enterprise because they lacked the social commitments that jobs and marriages impose.

European far-right hate crimes focus on Muslims.[156] But since 2014, Jews have also been victims.[157] "Almost 90 percent of Jews believe that anti-Semitism has increased in their country in the last five years, according to surveys by the European Union." In 2018, France reported five hundred violent anti-Semitic attacks, a 74 percent increase over the 2017 total. The German number went up 60 percent, to sixty-two violent strikes.[158] Over half of Germany's Jews "said they have directly experienced anti-Semitic harassment within the last five years," and 41 percent believed Muslims committed the worst incidents.[159] The most common German offense "was the use of the swastika and other illegal symbols; the rest ranged from online incitement . . . to arson, assault and murder."[160] After World War II, anti-Semitism was restricted to the political fringes; now important figures have gotten involved. Hungary's Prime Minister Orban described the "Jewish billionaire George Soros as a secret instigator of Muslim immigration."[161] Nine UK Labour MPs left their party because it had a prominent anti-Semitic element, including the party's leader.[162]

Most European far-right terrorist groups have only three or four members. Seventy-two percent do not last longer than a year, as members are killed, arrested, or decide to promote their cause in new ways. In 2014, four Germans founded a Munich-based terrorist group, Old School Society. It comprised thirty members with anti-Semitic and anti-Muslim views.[163] It stockpiled weapons to attack a refugee shelter, but the organizers were arrested before the attack. The German Freital Group made four attacks, injuring two people; eight members were convicted.[164] In 2018, German police arrested seven Revolution Chemnitz members, a neo-Nazi group aiming to attack foreign nationals.[165] Nordkreuz (Northern Cross), with forty to fifty members is preparing for an expected state collapse on "Day X."[166] It planned a 2017 mass killing of refugee-aid workers. Most members come from the East German military and police establishments and own weapons. Muslims and some left-Green politicians and bureaucrats were their principal targets. Many far-right German groups had their "enemy lists" seized; Nordkreuz data listed 25,000 names as "enemies of the people," probably the largest.[167]

A Swedish lone wolf in Malmo (2009–2010) made fifteen shootings, killing two and injuring thirteen.[168] Far-rightists attacked a 2013 antiracist demonstration in Stockholm. A lone wolf with a sword struck the 2015 Trollhättan school attack in an immigrant neighborhood, killing two teachers and a student, the deadliest school attack in Swedish history.[169] In 2017, thirty-nine Swedish mosques were attacked.[170] Three neo-Nazis were arrested for a homemade bomb attack on an asylum-seeker center.

The UK C18 (Combat 18), a neo-Nazi organization, has killed many immigrants, nonwhites, and other C18 members.[171] Between 1998 and 2000, dozens were arrested.[172] C18 immigrant attacks continued through 2009, when the police seized all its weapons.[173] National Action, founded in 2013 after the implosion of the British National Party and the English Defence League, was dedicated initially to rid the United Kingdom of the "disease of international Jewry," which it believed was responsible for the 9/11 attacks.[174] But it then decided to expel immigrants, especially nonwhites and Muslims. It had over one hundred members and functioned largely in the northwest of England. Often allied with the North West Infidels, its many demonstrations frequently precipitated violence. Its last demonstration, in January 2016, was in Dover, the most important immigrant entrance point, violently attacking those favoring immigration. Over eighty demonstrators were arrested, and many received significant sentences.[175]

In 2016 Thomas Mair assassinated MP Jo Cox, calling her a "traitor to her race" for defending immigrants. Though Mair was not a National Action member, the group praised the deed, stating, "Don't let this man's sacrifice go in vain." National Action also praised the man who committed the Orlando, Florida, massacre and claimed allegiance to the Islamic State.[176] The massacre occurred in a gay nightclub; forty-nine were killed and fifty-three injured, the deadliest violence against gays in U.S. history and the worst U.S. atrocity since 9/11. Praise for the two killers led the United Kingdom to proscribe the group as a terrorist organization, the first UK far-right organization proscribed since the 1940s.[177] Home Secretary Amber Rudd described National Action as "a racist, anti-Semitic and homophobic organization which stirs up hatred, glorifies violence and promotes a vile ideology."[178] In June 2018, Jack Renshaw, a National Action spokesperson, admitted in court that he had bought a sword, hoping to murder MP Rosie Cooper.[179] In March 2018, the UK counterterror police head said the far-right terror threat was "significant" and that the public should be "gravely concerned." He compared Anjem Choudary, an al-Muhajiroun leader aiming to establish an Islamic state in the United Kingdom, with the National Action leader Tommy Robinson[180] and revealed that every far-right terror plot had failed since the 2017 Islamic terrorist Westminster Bridge attack, which killed five.

In the United States, the Anti-Defamation League noted that the far right had committed 71 percent of extremist-related fatalities between 2008 and 2017; Islamic elements were responsible for 26 percent. The 2018 Global Terrorism Index shows that terror incidents more than tripled and the number of those killed quadrupled in the United States since 2013. In 2017, sixty-five incidents and ninety-five deaths occurred, and *Quartz* notes that far-right ideologies inspired 60 percent. Left-wing ideologies were responsible for eleven attacks. Jihadists committed just seven. These statistics raise questions about U.S. domestic counterterrorism strategy, which for nearly two decades focused almost exclusively on jihadists. A Stimson Center report noted the United States spent $2.8 trillion on counterterrorism between 2002 and 2017, when Muslim terrorists killed one hundred people. In 2017, the FBI reported 7,175 hate crimes, the highest number since 2008, continuing a three-year rise.[181] Hate crimes overall increased by 17 percent in 2017, while anti-Semitic crimes increased by 37 percent, according to a new FBI report.

Thirteen Wolverine Watchmen, including two Marine Corps veterans, were arrested in October 2020 for attempting to kidnap Gretchen Whitmer, Michigan's governor. It is not clear yet what their motive was. But Whitmer delivered the Democratic response to Trump's 2020 State of the Union Address. Michigan was considered crucial in the 2020 presidential election, and Republicans thought Whitmer would bolster the Democrats' chances of winning the state. Whitmer blamed Trump for refusing to condemn far-right groups.[182]

The 2020 Global Terrorism Index notes that the three Western countries that experienced the most far-right attacks since 2002 are the United States (167), Germany (48), and the United Kingdom (35). The United States also recorded the most deaths (113). Some U.S. far-right terror groups have become international. The Atomwaffen Division (Nuclear Weapons Division), a neo-Nazi network of sixty to eighty members founded in 2015, expanded into Canada and European countries, making many attacks.[183] Its U.S. targets have been minorities, gays, and Jews; it burned the U.S. Constitution and flag in propaganda videos. It was accused of planning to blow up nuclear plants, to cause nuclear meltdowns.[184] Strangely, the group's propaganda idolizes Osama bin Laden and considers al-Qaeda's and the Taliban's culture of martyrdom and insurgency as something to be emulated.[185] In the spring of 2018, Rise Above Movement members traveled to Ukraine to celebrate Hitler's birthday and train with Azov Battalion, a neo-Nazi Ukrainian National Guard unit.[186]

French police destroyed AFO (Operational Forces Action), a small far-right group, when it began testing explosives to kill veiled women, imams, and released Islamic prisoners. A former police officer led AFO strikes on mosques and halal grocery stores. A right-wing National Assembly member told the newspaper L'Opinion that "if groups are forming to defend themselves, it is first and foremost because the state is being soft on radical Islam. An AFO website said French security services are 'incapable of stopping the Islamic attacks.'" The U.S. radical right regularly agitates and holds noisy and visible rallies, but "in France they have very little visibility," said the far-right specialist Jean-Yves Camus. "It's very rare to have demonstrations by the ultra-right. Everything is very much underground." While the government targets radical Islamists, not Muslims as such, "vigilantes" believe the real problem is Islam and that taking up arms is the only way to solve it.[187] Stephane François, at the National Center for Scientific Research, also suggested the threat from such groups is minimal now. "These people are fairly clumsy and disorganized. For the moment, they are at an amateur level. The risk is that they organize themselves more seriously."[188] Italian far-right terrorists made thirteen attacks in 2018; one drew enormous publicity when a right-wing Northern League election candidate wounded six African migrants in Macerata.[189] The United Kingdom, Spain, Finland, Sweden, and Austria were the only Western European states to experience increases in terrorism deaths. Canada and the United States had increases as well.[190] Far-right groups and individuals caused sixty-six deaths and launched 127 strikes in the region between 2013 and 2017. Lone wolves were very prominent, as in the left-wing First Wave. Just two of the fifty-three attacks recorded in 2019 were attributed to a specific terrorist group.[191]

The Russian situation is rarely discussed, though Russia experienced much more far-right populist violence than Western Europe did during the 2000–2017 period.[192] The frequency per capita exceeded four times that of Germany and was twice Sweden's—the two deadliest states in Western Europe—and five times that of the United States. The experience seems odd because of Russia's close relationship with Western populist movements. The major Russian weapon was a knife. Most victims were legal immigrants who had entered from Asian parts of the former Soviet Union, but "no deadly attack has explicitly targeted Muslims." In 2010, the Russian Supreme Court banned the National Socialist Society, whose members were convicted for twenty-seven murders.[193]

Hate crimes increased dramatically in the United States against Blacks, religious groups, and Jews. More than 1,700 occurred in 2017.[194] In a church in Charleston, South Carolina, Dylann Roof, a twenty-one-year-old white supremacist, murdered nine African Americans, including the senior pastor and a state senator, during a prayer service in 2015. Roof said he hoped the shooting would ignite a "race war."[195] The American far right made at least thirty-nine reported physical assaults on Jews in 2018, a 105 percent increase over the previous year, according to the ADL.[196] In October 2018, eleven were killed in a Pittsburgh synagogue, the deadliest anti-Semitic strike in U.S. history. The forty-six-year-old assailant said he wanted "all Jews to die" partly because they aided immigrants. Two hours before the shooting he posted "a Jewish organization that aids refugees likes to bring invaders in to kill our people. I can't stand by and watch our people being slaughtered. Screw your optics. I'm going in."[197] Six months later, a far-right lone wolf attacked a California synagogue, killing one and wounding three, including the rabbi.[198] Several months earlier, he had made a failed effort to burn up a mosque. Hate crimes the FBI reported reached a sixteen-year high in 2018; the Latino proportion was much higher than previously, and Muslims were targeted less than before.[199] A Jersey City kosher market attack in 2019 killed six people.[200] A recent Bureau of Justice statistics report made the surprising discovery that 54 percent of the roughly 250,000 people who said they were victimized in recent years did not file a formal complaint.[201] After the clash between Israel and Hamas in May 2021, left-wing groups got involved in anti-Semitic attacks. There were 222 cases of anti-Semitic attacks two weeks after the clash, compared to 127 two weeks before.[202]

In Germany, three far-right lone wolf attacks occurred in the same period. Walter Lübcke, a politician, was assassinated in June 2019 for defending Chancellor Merkel's immigration policies. Then two atrocities occurred in 2020, apparently inspired by the attacks in New Zealand and El Paso.[203] The first occurred in February: a forty-five-year-old killed ten and wounded five in two Hanau shisha bars. The gunman returned to his apartment, killed his mother, and committed suicide. His internet manifesto accused Donald Trump of stealing his populist slogans.[204] In October, a twenty-seven-year-old went to a synagogue in Halle, Saxony-Anhalt, during Yom Kippur, the most sacred Jewish holiday. He could not enter the synagogue and killed two Germans he thought were Jews outside. At his trial he declared himself a "failure" for killing Germans.[205] His manifesto stated, "Kill as many anti-Whites as possible, Jews preferred."[206]

Germany has an additional vexing problem. A 2020 parliamentary inquiry concluded that far-right networks inspired by immigration anxieties had penetrated the country's security services extensively. In North Rhine–Westphalia, Germany's most populous state, 203 police officers were investigated for far-right incidents, and there have been seventy-seven cases of far-right extremism in its police force since 2015. "Thirty-one officers in a unit were suspended for sharing images of Hitler, memes of a refugee in a gas chamber and the shooting of a Black man." A unit in KSK, an elite military antiterrorist special force, was eliminated because it became infested with far-right extremism.[207] The rest of KSK has to overhaul its recruitment and training practices before being allowed to rejoin any international military exercises. Some officers disguised themselves as Muslim immigrants and committed acts, to infuriate Germans.[208] The German situation reminds one of the U.S. problem, which is still minor in comparison.

CONCLUSION

Far-right terror and its distinctive characteristics will certainly persist for a few more years, but will it last long enough to constitute a Fifth Wave? If it is linked only to the immigration problem and significant Islamic attacks, it may end soon. If the European Union cannot solve the issue, states can withdraw peacefully. The 2019 European Parliament election suggests that the far right's popularity is diminishing. Another reason for doubting that the current set of attacks is a Fifth Wave is that the generation today is unlike those that created previous waves. The youngest in each generation produced each wave, individuals in their teens and twenties who can give virtually all their time to the task because they do not have the commitments that jobs and marriages produce. There is a strong relationship between the number of political activists on the one hand and political violence and terrorism on the other, but the younger generation has fewer politically active members than did preceding waves. The youngest members of far-right terrorist groups are in their thirties. Polls cited clearly indicate that anti-Muslim and anti-immigration sentiment is much more intense and widespread in older segments of the population. Also, most of the violent deeds taking place in Europe are hate crimes, not terrorist acts. Finally, the new terror in Europe emerged during the Fourth Wave's last decade, a process that has never produced a new wave before.

On the other hand, it is clear that in the United States immigration and Islamic attacks are only part of the problem. White supremacy, the belief that whites could soon become a minority, dominates the scene. If that anxiety persists after the immigration and Islamic issues fade, we may be seeing a Fifth Wave. White supremacy does exist elsewhere in the West and could become more significant soon, too. Beyond that, many states outside the West have recently adopted immigration restrictions, and a passionate racial or ethnic concern may develop, too, which would be necessary for a global wave. If we do not experience a Fifth Wave of global terrorism soon, local terrorism will persist. Like crime, local terrorism is not likely to disappear, though the two have very different geographic patterns and durations. Crime is present in every state, but terrorist activity is intermittent in various countries depending on the character of the local political scene. In the United States, the unwillingness of many Republicans to accept the legitimacy of the 2020 election, and the fact that many Republican state legislatures are restricting voting, which may affect African Americans more than other demographics, could strengthen white supremacy movements.

NOTES

INTRODUCTION

1. On occasion before the global form developed, terrorism took on an international dimension, but that included only two states and one group. Irish immigrants in the United States, for example, created the Fenians, which after the American Civil War struck targets in Canada, hoping to provoke a war between the United States and the United Kingdom that the Irish could exploit to create the state of Ireland. When that failed, Fenians from the United States bombed targets in the England with the same purpose and futile end. But only Irish groups participated, and the actions involved a limited number of states. Global terrorism involves many states in various capacities and groups that cooperate in various ways.

2. Marc Lallanilla, "The Dark Side of the Nobel Prizes," *Live Science*, October 4, 2013, https://www.livescience.com/40188-dark-history-alfred-nobel-prizes.html.

3. Michael P. Carter provides an interesting discussion of the problem in "The French Revolution: Jacobin Terror," in *Morality of Terrorism*, 2nd ed., ed. David C. Rapoport and Yonah Alexander (New York: Columbia University Press, 1989), 133–51. See also my "Introduction to State Terror," in the same volume, 127–32.

4. Terrorism is defined in Title 22 Chapter 38 U.S. Code § 2656f as "premeditated, politically motivated violence perpetrated against noncombatant targets by subnational groups or clandestine agents." Often the term is misused. One can create terror without being a terrorist. Note, for example, the 2017 Las Vegas shooting, when a shooter opened fire on a crowd of concertgoers at a music festival, killing fifty-eight people and injuring 851.

The act was not associated with a political or religious objective, but virtually everyone described the shooter as a terrorist instead of a mass murderer. Scott Shane, "The Shocking Tragedy That Terrorizes, but Without an Obvious Terrorist Motive," *New York Times*, October 1, 2017.

5. See South Asian Terrorism Portal, Communist Party of Nepal-Maoist," updated through December 31, 2017, https://www.satp.org/satporgtp/countries/nepal/terroristoutfits/index .html.

6. The notion that terrorism has been embedded in modern culture is unfamiliar, and I will develop the contention more thoroughly as the book develops. Responses to the Fourth Wave suggest the view that the contemporary scene is really a byproduct of another culture. In discussing the Islamic element in the Fourth Wave, for example, the notion that a clash of civilizations is involved is commonplace, and only a few writers see Islamic violence as having an important global ingredient. See, however, John Grey, *Al Qaeda and What It Means to Be Modern* (London: Faber and Faber, 2003); and Marc Sageman, *Understanding Terrorist Networks* (Philadelphia: University of Pennsylvania Press, 2004).

7. J. B. S. Hardman, "Terrorism," in the *Encyclopaedia of the Social Sciences*, ed. Edwin Robert Anderson Seligman and Alvin Saunders Johnson (New York: Macmillan, 1930)

8. The social science of the period was committed to a theory of modernization, a theory that presumed that the present events in the "developing" world resembled those in the previous history of the developed portion. Another example in the period to illustrate the tendency to believe that terrorism becomes history and irrelevant to contemporary concerns when a wave ends is that after the Cold War ended, government funds for the RAND Corporation's terrorist studies dried up, and a promising program of studies was abandoned for a while.

9. Editors of successive volumes in a series of encyclopedias published at different times, of course, do not generally explain why they decide to omit some articles.

10. Richard Hofstadter, "Reflections on Violence in the United States," in *American Violence: A Documentary History*, ed. Richard Hofstadter and Michael Wallace (New York: Knopf, 1970), 3–4. The National Commission on the Causes and Prevention of Violence, established after the assassinations of Reverend Martin Luther King Jr. and Senator Robert Kennedy in 1968, introduced the term "historical amnesia." In the 1990s, I discovered that students in the classes I taught had no sense of what those in the 1960s had experienced.

11. Scott Stewart, "The Myth of the End of Terrorism," *Stratford Security Weekly*, February 23, 2012, 2.

12. Several friends working at the RAND Corporation told me about the decision.

13. Carl von Clausewitz, *On War* (Carlisle, PA: U.S. Army War College, 1991), 231.

14. Alexis de Tocqueville, *Democracy in America*, trans. Gerald E. Bevan (London: Penguin, 2003), book 1, chap. 13.

15. John Stuart Mill, A *System of Logic* (New York: Longmans,1949), Green Book 6, chapter 10, 3.

16. Karl Mannheim, *Essays on Sociology and Social Psychology* (New York: Routledge, 1952), 276–322.

17. Jose Ortega y Gasset, "The Concept of Generation," in *The Modern Theme* (New York: Norton, 1961), 14–15.

18. Stanley Rothman and S. Robert Lichter, *Roots of Radicalism: Jews, Christians, and the Left* (Oxford: Oxford University Press, 1982), 354.

19. Maria Hohn and Seungsook Moon, *Over There: Living with the U.S. Military Empire from World War Two to the Present* (Durham, NC: Duke University Press, 2010), 275.

20. Arthur Schlesinger, *The Cycles of American History* (Boston: Houghton Mifflin, 1986), 27. Schlesinger develops the concept of generation in chapter 2.

21. It should be emphasized that in the United States references to generations often appear in popular discourse. "Baby Boomers" were born after World War II, a wealthy and optimistic generation that produced a striking increase in birth rates partly because the previous generation had had serious economic problems and was less interested in having children. The "Lost Generation" refers to those who fought in World War I, and the "Greatest Generation" fought in World War II. The last two terms were employed by the public before the 1960s, when the generation concept became widespread.

22. *Merriam-Webster's Learner's Dictionary.*

23. Democratic states "overreacted," too. President Theodore Roosevelt in 1901 proposed sending all anarchists back to Europe. But Congress was more restrained and simply barred foreign anarchists from entering the county. More than a decade later, President Wilson's attorney general, Alexander Mitchell Palmer, implemented a proposal similar to Roosevelt's and rounded up all anarchists to ship them back "home," regardless of whether they had committed crimes. That event produced the 1920 Wall Street Bombing, which in turn became the justification for an immigration quota law, making it much more difficult for people from Southern and Eastern European states (the original home of most anarchists) to immigrate for decades—a law that Adolf Hitler praised highly. The very first reactions to 9/11 suggested that we had learned from past mistakes. The federal government made special efforts to show that the United States was not at war with Islam, and it curbed the first expressions of vigilante passions. The significance of subsequent measures seems more problematic. A policy of secret detentions was implemented, a common reaction to serious terrorist activities in many countries. Extensive revisions of immigration regulations have been instituted. Prisoners taken in Afghanistan were not prosecuted under criminal law, reversing a long-standing policy in virtually all nations, including the United States.

24. "President Trump, Please Read the Constitution," *New York Times*, editorial, November 23, 2015.

1. TERRORISM BEFORE THE GLOBAL FORM: FROM THE FIRST CENTURY TO THE TWENTIETH

1. David C. Rapoport, "Fear and Trembling: Terrorism in Three Religious Traditions," *American Political Science Review* 78, no. 3 (1984): 658–77, discusses religious terror in the Hindu, Islamic, and Jewish traditions. In the discussion here I added the Christian

example and eliminated the Hindu one, the Thugs who strangled victims for the goddess Kali but had no political objective. Messianic beliefs have frequently stimulated Christians to embrace terror a number of times. David C. Rapoport, "Messianic Sanctions for Terror," *Comparative Politics* 20, no. 2 (1988): 195–211.

2. "General Dwight D. Eisenhower (Ike) D-Day Message," Kansas History Gateway, http://www.kansasheritage.org/abilene/ikespeech.html.

3. These statements will be discussed in the chapters dealing with the First Wave and Fourth Wave.

4. Cited by Nazar Ul Islam Wani, "Impact of Crusades on Islam and Christianity," *International Journal of Humanities and Social Science Invention* 2, no. 3 (2013): 43.

5. John M. B. Porter, "Osama Bin-Laden, Jihad, and the Sources of International Terrorism," *Indiana International and Comparative Law Review* 13, no. 3 (2003): 871–86. One special reason Bin Laden was consumed with the "Crusader" experience was that he believed understanding how Islam had been removed from the Holy Land but fought its way back eventually provided an important strategic lesson for today's struggle against the Crusaders, a matter discussed in chapter 7.

6. Porter, "Osama Bin-Laden, Jihad, and the Sources of International Terrorism."

7. Hugh Schonfield, *The Passover Plot* (New York: Bernard Geis, 1965), 19.

8. Numbers 25:11.

9. For a convenient discussion of the *herem* and its revival by Zealots and the Sicarii as reflected in the Dead Sea Scrolls, see Roland de Vaux, *Ancient Israel* (New York: McGraw-Hill, 1972), 258–67. The later conception had new elements, namely, that the war would be a war to end all wars, that it would involve all men, and that the enemy would be under Satan's influence.

10. Josephus, *The Jewish War*, in *Works*, Loeb Classical Library (London: Heinemann, 1926), 2:254–57.

11. Josephus, *The Jewish War*, 451.

12. Keith Hunt, "The Forgotten Parthian/Israel Empire," http://www.keithhhunt.com /Part1html.

13. Flavius Josephus, *Antiquities of the Jews*, book 18 (Project Gutenberg, 2017), 256, http:// www.gutenberg.org/files/2848/2848-8.txt.

14. Guglielmo Ferrero, *Principles of Power* (New York: Ayer, 1972).

15. For the sake of convenience, we shall refer to the Nizari by their more familiar name, Assassins. When I speak of sympathetic Islam elements, I have in mind the Shi'a and especially the Ismaili, the two religious communities from which the Assassins spawned. Few Assassin documents have survived, and our picture of the sect is reconstructed mostly from bitterly hostile orthodox chroniclers who could not pierce the sect's veil of secrecy. Ismail K. Poonawala, *Bibliography of Ismaili Literature: Studies in Near Eastern Culture and Society* (Malibu: Undena, 1977), provides the most recent bibliography of primary and secondary sources; many items are annotated. The difficulties of the contemporary historian are described by Marshall G. S. Hodgson, *The Order of Assassins: The Struggle of the Early Nizârî Ismâ'ilis Against the Islamic World* (Gravenhage:

Mouton, 1955). Universally recognized as the best source, Hodgson's work was later sharpened in 1968. My discussion is based largely on these accounts and on Bernard Lewis, *The Assassins: A Radical Sect in Islam* (London: Orion, 2001).

16. Lewis, *The Assassins*. Initially, I was convinced that there probably was an element in the Islamic tradition pointing specifically to the dagger as a sacred weapon, but no such reference was cited in the secondary literature. A student (an army officer) in my class some forty years ago said that the dagger was the most efficient weapon available and there was no reason to think that the Assassins did not realize this obvious point.

17. Thomas Hodgkin, "Mahdism, Messianism, and Marxism in the African Setting," in *African Social Studies: A Radical Reader*, ed. Peter C. Gutkind and Peter Waterman (New York: Monthly Review Press, 1977), 307.

18. Denis MacEoin, "The Babi Concept of the Holy War," *Religion* 12, no. 2 (1982): 121.

19. Israel Friedlander, "The Heterodoxies of the Shiites Ibn Hazm," *Journal of the American Oriental Society* 28, no. 1 (1907): 80. Montgomery W. Watt, *The Formative Period of Islamic Thought* (Edinburgh: Edinburgh University Press, 1973), 48.

20. This campaign depended upon establishing murder as a measure necessary to protect summoners. One professional soldier likened the *fedayeen* to armed naval escorts, which never engage the enemy unless the convoy itself is attacked. Victims of the campaign were orthodox religious or political leaders who refused to heed warnings and remained scornful of the New Preaching. They even attempted to prevent it from being heard and acted in ways that demonstrated complicity in Islam's corruption.

21. Hodgkin, "Mahdism, Messianism, and Marxism in the African Setting," 99.

22. Lewis, *The Assassins*, 3.

23. Hodgkin, "Mahdism, Messianism, and Marxism in the African Setting," 84.

24. Hodgkin, "Mahdism, Messianism, and Marxism in the African Setting," 84.

25. "A state ought not during war to countenance such hostilities as would make mutual confidence in a subsequent peace impossible such as employing assassins, poisoners, breaches of capitulation, secret instigations to treachery and rebellion in the hostile state (for there must be) some kind of confidence in the disposition of the enemy even in the midst of war or otherwise . . . the hostilities will pass into a war of extermination. . . . Such a war . . . and all means which lead to it must be absolutely forbidden." Immanuel Kant, *Perpetual Peace*, trans. M. Campbell Smith, ed. A. Robert Caponigri (New York: Liberal Arts, 1948), 6; and Emmerich de Vattel, *The Law of Nations or the Principles of International Law* (London: Newbery et al., 1760), I, 19, 233.

26. Hodgkin, "Mahdism, Messianism, and Marxism in the African Setting," 76–77, 111–13.

27. The sect was the subject of many allegations, but it was never charged with instigating counteratrocities against groups or classes. Its targets were almost invariably individuals. The orthodox Sunni view was that the Nizari wanted to destroy Islam but not necessarily many Muslims. The Nizari apparently practiced indiscriminate slaughter, arguing that every member of a family of unbelievers was an unbeliever too. Watt, *The Formative Period of Islamic Thought*, 22.

28. Hodgson, *The Order of Assassins*, 79–80.

29. Hodgkin, "Mahdism, Messianism, and Marxism in the African Setting"; Saad Eddin Ibrahim, "Anatomy of Egypt's Militant Groups," *International Journal of Middle Eastern Studies* 12, no. 4 (1980): 23–53.

30. The deaths of these "hypocrites" released hitherto latent sympathies for Islam among their followers. Ultimately, Mohammed's question "Will no one rid me of her?" occasioned the original assassination. Henry II encouraged his knights in the same way when he grumbled about Becket. But how different the results were! Becket was martyred, the knights were punished, and the English king did penance. For a discussion of Christian and Graeco-Roman attitudes toward assassination, see David C. Rapoport, *Assassination and Terrorism* (Toronto: Canadian Broadcasting Corp., 1971), chap. 1. In the Koran the term "hypocrite" (*munafiqun*) refers to one whose fidelity and zeal Mohammed could not rely upon, persons "in whose hearts there is sickness, weakness, and doubt . . . who had joined Islam perhaps reluctantly . . . usually members of the aristocracy." Buhl Fr., "Munafiqun," *Encyclopedia of Islam* (London: Luzac, 1913). Most of those assassinated were Jews, but Mohammed's Constitution of Medina clearly indicates that his original community included Jews and that initially he intended to bring Islam as close to Judaism as possible.

31. Gershon Scholem, *The Messianic Idea in Judaism* (New York: Schocken, 1971), 12.

32. David Nicolle, *The First Crusade, 1096–1099: Conquest of the Holy Land* (Oxford: Osprey, 2003), 21–31. European kings led all the following crusades.

33. Speech of Pope Urban II at Clermont, 1095, "Holy Wars," BBC, http://www.bbc.co.uk/ethics/war/religious/holywar.shtml.

34. St. Thomas Aquinas, "The Just War," in *The Summa Theologica*, Great Books of the Western World 20 (Chicago: Encyclopedia Britannica, Inc., 1952), https://www.catholiceducation.org/en/controversy/politics-and-the-church/the-just-war.html.

35. The term *herem* most often occurs in the Book of Joshua.

36. August C. Krey, *The First Crusade: The Accounts of Eyewitnesses and Participants* (Gloucester, MA: P. Smith, 1958), 28–30.

37. Revelation 19:11–21.

38. Because the Zealots and Sicarii were rebels, it is easy to understand their atrocities as acts of terror. But the definitions of terrorism in the introduction would include Crusader atrocities as terrorist activity.

39. Philippe Buc, *Holy War, Martyrdom, and Terror: Christianity, Violence and the West, ca. 70 C.E. to the Iraq War* (Philadelphia: University of Pennsylvania Press, 2015), 67. Buc's illuminating book shows how Christian violence of the West is reflected in our secular political violence and especially in terrorism.

40. Norman Cohn, *The Pursuit of the Millennium* (Oxford: Oxford University Press, 1970), 148–63.

41. Buc, *Holy War, Martyrdom, and Terror*, 53.

42. Michael D. Hull, "First Crusade: Siege of Jerusalem," *Military History*, June 1999.

43. Hans Eberhard Mayer, *The Crusades*, 2nd ed. (Oxford: Oxford University Press, 1988), 171–76.

44. Maher Abu-Munshar, *Islamic Jerusalem and Its Christianity: A History of Tolerance and Tensions* (London: I. B. Tauris, 2007), 152–58.

45. Thomas F. Madden, *Enrico Dandolo and the Rise of Venice* (Baltimore, MD: Johns Hopkins University Press, 2003).

46. Aleksandr Vasiliev, *History of the Byzantine Empire* (Madison: University of Wisconsin Press, 1958), 2:446.

47. Vryonis Speros, *Byzantium and Europe* (San Diego: Harcourt, Brace & World, 1967), 152. When Innocent III learned about the Byzantine attacks he was filled with shame and rage and strongly rebuked the Crusaders.

48. Norman Davies, *Europe: A History* (Oxford: Oxford University Press, 1996), 362. The term "Albigensian" comes from the fact that the city of Albi produced so many adherents.

49. Raphael Lemkin, *Lemkin on Genocide*, ed. Steven Jacobs (Lanham, MD: Rowman & Littlefield, 2012), 71.

50. Mark Gregory Pegg, *A Most Holy War: The Albigensian Crusade and the Battle for Christendom* (Oxford University Press, 2008), 188. The French nobility were also deeply involved in the Crusade, partly because the king offered the property of heretics to any noble who took up arms.

51. Edward Peters, *Inquisition* (Berkeley: University of California Press, 1989), 67.

52. Jordan Bishop, "Aquinas on Torture," *New Blackfriars Journal* 87, no. 1099 (2006): 229.

53. John Van Antwerp Fine Jr., *The Bosnian Church: Its Place in State and Society from the Thirteenth to the Fifteenth Century* (London: Saqi, 2007), 126–32. Crusades in the Iberian Peninsula (1212–1250) against Muslim inhabitants were authorized, too.

54. The "People's Crusade," a group of peasants and petty nobles, engaged in some of the most anti-Semitic violence during this period, partly because it wanted to take money from the Jews and use it to purchase weapons for its journey to Jerusalem. Four centuries before the Crusades, a comparable experience happened in the Christian Byzantine Empire. In 614, a Persian army, which was not Islamic, captured the Holy Land, aided by Jewish forces that had rebelled against the Byzantines, the last serious Jewish attempt to retake the area till modern times. In 630, the Byzantine emperor Heraclius captured Jerusalem and instigated a Jewish population massacre. Jews returned when Muslims conquered the Holy Land in 638. Rivkah Duker Fishman, "Perspectives: The Seventh-Century Christian Obsession with the Jews: A Historical Parallel for the Present?" *Jewish Political Studies Review* 17, no. 3/4 (2005).

55. Kenneth Stow and David Abulafia, "The Church and the Jews," in *The New Cambridge Medieval History* (Cambridge: Cambridge University Press, 1999), 5:204–19.

56. For my original discussion of the Sons of Liberty and the KKK, see David C. Rapoport, "Before the Bombs, There Were the Mobs: American Experiences with Terror," *Terrorism and Political Violence* 20, no. 2 (2008): 167–94. It was republished in my Festschrift: Jean E. Rosenfeld, ed., *Terrorism Identity and Legitimacy: The Four Waves Theory and Political Violence* (New York: Routledge, 2008).

57. Cited by Arthur M. Schlesinger, "Political Mobs and the American Revolution, 1765–1776," *Proceedings of the American Philosophical Society* 99, no. 4 (1955): 249.

58. Dirk Hoerder, *Crowd Action in Revolutionary Massachusetts* (Cambridge, MA: Academic Press, 1977), 374. Hoerder does not say whether the leaders really were strangers or only dressed to look like strangers.

59. Cited by Schlesinger, "Political Mobs and the American Revolution," 250. Franklin usually refers to riots, not mobs, though the term "mob" was more common then.

60. George Rude, *The Crowd in History*, rev. ed. (London: Lawrence and Wishart, 1981), 27. Rude describes crowd activities as lasting a few days normally, though in a few cases, such as the Gordon Riots of 1780, rioters were out on the streets for several weeks.

61. Schlesinger, "Political Mobs and the American Revolution," 249. Schlesinger provides an extraordinarily candid account of a very delicate subject.

62. Quoted by Paul Gilje, *Rioting in America* (Bloomington: Indiana University Press, 1996), 37. Gilje defines "riot" as "any group of twelve or more people attempting to assert their will immediately through the use of force outside the bounds of law" (4).

63. See L. L. Bernard's discussion in the 1933 edition of the *Encyclopaedia of the Social Sciences*. The subsequent issue of the *Encyclopedia* ignored the subject. The 1968 edition for no explained reason eliminated most articles on violence, including terrorism, which had been concerns of the first issue.

64. Each colony produced variations in the social mixture. An analysis of the available information is available in Pauline Meier, "The Sons of Liberty, 1765–1766," in *From Resistance to Revolution* (New York: Knopf, 1972), appendix.

65. John Miller, *Sam Adams* (Redwood City, CA: Stanford University Press, 1936), 79.

66. Miller, *Sam Adams*, 59–60. Hutchinson was the lieutenant governor of Massachusetts and then governor during the period.

67. Miller, *Sam Adams*, 53.

68. Schlesinger, "Political Mobs and the American Revolution," 246. To do justice to the experience, one would need a new more pertinent term than "mob." That task cannot be addressed here, but as long as one is clear about the limitations of conventional language, the word "mob" can be used. Many historians follow the convention of the period and refer to mobs; in recent years, more historians are likely to refer to mob activity instead as riots, demonstrations, or crowds. Charles Tilly argues that the term "mob" is used by "elites for actions of other people and often for actions, which threaten their own interests." Charles Tilly, *From Mobilization to Revolution* (Boston: Addison Wesley, 1978), 227. The term "crowd" may be most appropriate, especially as redefined by George Rude, *The Crowd in the French Revolution* (Oxford: Oxford University Press, 1959), when he stripped the concept of its more invidious and irrational connotations. For an interesting use of the crowd concept, see Hoerder, *Crowd Action in Revolutionary Massachusetts*. Other prominent historians speak of crowds without explaining why they think the term should be preferred and put the term "mob" in quotation marks, e.g., Gary Nash, *The Urban Crucible* (Cambridge, MA: Harvard University Press, 1979).

69. Quoted from a contemporary Massachusetts newspaper, *The Constitution Courant*.

70. Miller, *Sam Adams*. There is some evidence that merchants induced the mob to steal the papers so that smuggling charges against them would be dropped. Meier, *From*

Resistance to Revolution, 58. But several days after the event Hutchinson said that Sam Adams did not organize the second mob to do what it did. Robert Middlekauff, *The Glorious Cause* (Oxford: Oxford University Press, 1982), 92. Liquor was often supplied to mob participants. Hoerder, *Crowd Action in Revolutionary Massachusetts*, 349.

71. Hoerder, *Crowd Action in Revolutionary Massachusetts*, 66.

72. Gilje, *Rioting in America*, 38.

73. Phillip Davidson, *Propaganda and the American Revolution, 1763–85* (Chapel Hill: University of North Carolina Press, 1941), 41.

74. Schlesinger published his essay in 1955, when terrorism was not as conspicuous or odious as it is today. Would his language be different now?

75. Richard Hofstadter and Michael Wallace, eds., *American Violence: A Documentary History* (New York: Knopf, 1970), 76–79. Section 1, "Political Violence," contains a piece entitled "Terrorism Against Loyalists." Despite including the piece, Hofstadter's interesting introduction quotes Howard Mumford Jones's very different view. "American mobs were curiously lacking in furious, deep-seated and blood thirsty resentment. No royal governor was hanged or shot. . . . No stamp collector or custom official was summarily executed, although some of them suffered physical injury" (14). Hofstadter finds the description apt but does not explain the conflict between the two.

76. See the discussion of "imagination" in the editors' introduction to Hofstadter and Wallace, *American Violence*, n99.

77. Gary B. Nash, *The Unknown American Revolution* (New York: Viking, 1973), 45.

78. Quoted by Robert M. Calhoon, *The Loyalists in Revolutionary America* (San Diego: Harcourt Brace, 1973), 273–74.

79. Calhoon, *The Loyalists in Revolutionary America*, 240–43.

80. Middlekauff, *The Glorious Cause*, 105–6.

81. Calhoon, *The Loyalists in Revolutionary America*, 94.

82. Hoerder, *Crowd Action in Revolutionary Massachusetts*, 340.

83. Quoted by Hofstadter and Wallace, *American Violence*, 71.

84. Davidson, *Propaganda and the American Revolution*, 113.

85. See David C. Rapoport, "The Politics of Atrocity," in *Terrorism: Interdisciplinary Perspectives*, ed. Yonah Alexander and Seymore M. Finger (Brooklyn: John Jay, 1977), 46–63.

86. Schlesinger, "Political Mobs and the American Revolution," 244. An earlier, very comprehensive discussion can be found in Davidson, *Propaganda and the American Revolution*, esp. chaps. 1–12.

87. Miller, *Sam Adams*; Meier, *From Resistance to Revolution*.

88. Davidson, *Propaganda and the American Revolution*, 247.

89. Miller, *Sam Adams*, 50–51.

90. The first British professional police force was established in London in 1829 after Lord Wellington warned that the army would dissolve if it had to deal with mobs. Some U.S. cities established professional police forces in the 1840s.

91. Gordon Wood, "The Crowd in the American Revolution," in *The American Revolution: Whose Revolution?*, ed. James K Martin and K. Stubas (Malabar: Krieger, 1977), 60.

92. Miller, *Sam Adams*, 71.

93. David McCullough, *John Adams* (New York: Simon Schuster, 2001), 67.

94. McCullough, *John Adams*, 67.

95. McCullough, *John Adams*, 65. There were two trials. In the first the officer was acquitted of the charge that he ordered the men to fire. In the second, six soldiers were declared innocent by virtue of self-defense. Two were found guilty of manslaughter, and their punishment was tattoos printed on their hands to indicate that offense. The evidence presented at the trial indicates that there was a civilian conspiracy to make the soldiers fire. Miller, *Sam Adams*, 184–88.

96. Oddly, Sam Adams asked John to take the case!

97. Schlesinger, "Political Mobs and the American Revolution," 247.

98. Schlesinger, "Political Mobs and the American Revolution," 246.

99. Schlesinger, "Political Mobs and the American Revolution," 246.

100. The original Sons of Liberty lasted about a year. It was revived in three cities two years later for a short period, but even then there was a gradual tendency to drop the name. It was almost never used after 1773, and during the decade of resistance it did not refer to a society; it was simply another name for "patriot."

101. Gilje, *Rioting in America*, 94.

102. William Loren Katz, *The Invisible Empire* (Greensboro, NC: Open Hand, 1986), 17.

103. Gilje, *Rioting in America*, 96.

104. Gilje, *Rioting in America*, 96. George C. Rable, *But There Was No Peace: The Role of Violence in the Politics of Reconstruction* (Athens: University of Georgia Press, 1984), 59, says that forty-six were killed.

105. Hofstadter and Wallace, *American Violence*, 15. One reason that the Memphis riot went out of control was that the police were largely Irish immigrants who had a special hostility to Blacks. Fierce riots against conscription in cities like New York, which produced several hundred deaths, were linked to persistent hostilities between Blacks and Irish immigrants.

106. In the United States, the House of Representatives votes on the charges for impeachment, but conviction requires two-thirds of the Senate, and the Senate was one vote short. Under the succession law governing the process, the president of the Senate, a Radical Republican, would have replaced Johnson.

107. Quoted by Rable, *But There Was No Peace*, 8.

108. In the 1830s the rage against abolitionists created more mobs in the Northern states than in the South. But the rage that Southern antiabolitionist mobs ignited helped move the South to secede. Clement Eaton has an interesting essay on the mob violence against abolitionists: Clement Eaton, "Mob Violence in the Old South," *Mississippi Valley Historical Review* 29, no. 3 (2001): 351–70.

109. Everette Swinney, *Suppressing the Ku Klux Klan* (New York: Garland, 1987), 46–47. "Historians rightly differentiate between the KKK of the 1860s and the 1920s because the purpose and character of the two are very different. In the course of the last century there have been three different KKK. The third is left over from the mighty Klan

of the 20s." Carl N. Degler, "A Century of the Klans: A Review Article," *Journal of Southern History* 31, no. 4 (1965). Oddly, though the original KKK had a much greater political effect, the secondary literature dealing with it is slimmer than that discussing the two less significant experiences in the twentieth century. See the bibliographical listings in William Fisher, *The Invisible Empire* (Lanham, MD: Scarecrow, 1980). We are not concerned here with the four reincarnations later in American history, when the KKK became active outside the South, i.e., 1915–1921, during the 1930s Depression: during the 1960s Civil Rights Movement, and during the Fourth Wave in the 1980s. In these four phases, Jews, Catholics, and foreign immigrants were also victims.

110. Gilje, *Rioting in America*, 210. Estimates vary. Gilje's statistics are from secondary sources, but his book shows a deep concern with counting riots.

111. The organization originated in December 1865, in Pulaski, Tennessee, when "six young men decided to form a club. Mainly college men, they had been officers in the late War. Their problem was idleness; their purpose was amusement. They met in secret places, put on disguises, and had great fun galloping about town after dark. . . . They soon discovered that their nocturnal appearances had an unexpected effect and they capitalized upon it." David M. Chalmers, *Hooded Americanism* (New York: Doubleday, 1965), 8–9. Why they named themselves the Ku Klux Klan remains a mystery. *Ku* and *klux* are variants of the Greek word meaning "circle" or "band."

112. Forrest served two years only, resigning apparently because KKK elements became too difficult to control.

113. William Gillette, *Retreat from Reconstruction: 1869–1879* (Baton Rouge: Louisiana State University Press, 1982), 18.

114. Rable, *But There Was No Peace*, 71.

115. Initially, the KKK claimed to be vigilantes enforcing the law, merging police and judiciary functions.

116. "Scalawags" are venomous, shabby, scabby cattle. "Carpetbagger" refers to the common belief that the immigrants brought all their belongings in a "carpetbag." Some carpetbaggers were Blacks from the North. The Klan's most important political purpose was to make it impossible for Blacks to vote, but secondary discussions of the KKK only began to focus on that question a century later and after the Civil Rights Movement developed in the twentieth century. Four important works that do treat the question are Gillette, *Retreat from Reconstruction*, chaps. 2 and 6; Allan Trelease, *White Terror: The Ku Klux Klan Conspiracy and Southern Reconstruction* (New York: Harper's, 1971); and Rable, *But There Was No Peace*.

117. Swinney, *Suppressing the Ku Klux Klan*, 49.

118. Gillette, *Retreat from Reconstruction*, 47.

119. Chalmers, *Hooded Americanism*, 5.

120. The Radical Republicans organized secret societies too, e.g., the Lincoln Brotherhood in Florida, the Heroes of America in North Carolina etc., but their presence intensified sentiment supporting the KKK.

121. Gillette, *Retreat from Reconstruction*, 162. This description appears again and again when Gillette discusses particular elections. We do not know the number of casualties, but it must have numbered in the thousands. In Louisiana alone, two elections in 1868 reveals that 1,081 were killed; most were Blacks. See Gilje, *Rioting in America*, 99.
122. Gillette, *Retreat from Reconstruction*, 163.
123. Gillette, *Retreat from Reconstruction*, 163.
124. Gillette, *Retreat from Reconstruction*, 317–18.
125. For a general discussion of the ballot fraud problem, see David C. Rapoport and L. Weinberg, eds., "Elections and Violence," in *The Democratic Experience and Violence* (Frank Cass, 2001), 15–51.
126. Gillette, *Retreat from Reconstruction*, 154.
127. In the KKK's second phase, which began in the 1920s, it operated in many states outside the South. Indiana seemed to be the center of its activity; ironically, during Reconstruction the KKK had discouraged sympathetic efforts in Indiana for fear that they would create a backlash in the North.
128. Gillette, *Retreat from Reconstruction*, 274–75.
129. Gillette, *Retreat from Reconstruction*, 51.
130. David Annan, "The Ku Klux Klan," in *Secret Societies*, ed. Norman McKenzie (New York: Collier, 1967), 227.
131. Rable, *But There Was No Peace*, 109.
132. It is doubtful whether a terror campaign by Blacks in the 1960s would have achieved a victory comparable to that produced by the Civil Rights Movement. The problem is an interesting one but cannot be addressed here.
133. Stanley Horn reproduced the oath in 1969. Stanley Horn, *The Invisible Empire: The Story of the Ku Klux Klan, 1866–1871* (Coscob: John E. Edwards, 1969), 54.
134. In the last half-century (i.e., Watts, Detroit, Chicago in the 1960s, Paris in 2005), mobs burned the property of persons in their own neighborhoods, making it more difficult for the communities they wanted to represent to support them enthusiastically.
135. Dictionary definitions of mobs do not specify the minimum number, and certainly the common impression is that the number of participants would have to be greater than the numbers given for most KKK activities. But there is no alternative term.
136. "From November 1870 to September 1871, the Ku Klux Klan sallied forth virtually every evening and morning in York County, South Carolina, committing at least eleven murders and tallying approximately six hundred cases of whipping and assault." Gilje, *Rioting in America*, 99.
137. Annan, "The Ku Klux Klan," 225.
138. Hoerder, *Crowd Action in Revolutionary Massachusetts*, 233. The statistics are informed estimates. Sons of Liberty mob estimates are universally very much higher than those offered for KKK mobs.
139. Nash, *The Unknown American Revolution*, 53.
140. Trelease, *White Terror*, 53.

141. Hoerder, *Crowd Action in Revolutionary Massachusetts*, 374. It is unclear from Hoerder's account whether the leaders really were strangers or were merely dressed as strangers.

142. The observation about the change in meaning is made in J. E. Cutler's classic study *Lynch-Law: An Investigation Into the History of Lynching in the United States* (New York: Longmans, Green, 1905), 276. He also points out that "the sentiment frequently expressed in a community where a lynching has occurred is to the effect that the victims got what they deserved." There are no reliable statistics on the number of victims lynched during Reconstruction. But statistics were kept for the period immediately following Reconstruction. Cutler's statistics cover the period from 1882 to 1903. During that twenty-two-year period, 1,985 Blacks were lynched in the South, as opposed to six hundred whites and others. If the same proportion were lynched during the Reconstruction period, the number of Black victims would be 990. The general view is that lynching became more common after the Democrats took over, but previous figures are unavailable. Estimates are that some three thousand Blacks from the 1880s to the 1960s, when the practice stopped, were lynched. Lynching, of course, was also a problem in the states in the Far West before governments became fully established.

143. Ida B. Wells, *Crusade for Justice: The Autobiography of Ida B. Wells* (Chicago: University of Chicago Press, 1970), 61–66.

144. Hoerder, *Crowd Action in Revolutionary Massachusetts*, 340. King Richard I apparently introduced the tar and feathering practice during the Crusades, but studies of the KKK do not mention the origin of the activity.

145. Hoerder, *Crowd Action*, 81.

146. Hoerder, *Crowd Action*, 338.

147. Hoerder, *Crowd Action*. Secondary sources generally do not discuss the election issue as it relates to the Sons of Liberty. That suggests perhaps that it was not an important concern for the Sons of Liberty because the colonial assemblies supported the group and there was no danger of losing that support as long as the group remained restrained. Hoerder says crowd violence occasionally at election times prevented elected Tories sometimes from taking their seats.

148. "John Brown: In His Own Words—Prelude," Erden Zikibay, http://www.zikibay.com/brown/prelude.html.

149. David S. Reynolds, *John Brown, Abolitionist: The Man Who Killed Slavery, Sparked the Civil War, and Seeded Civil Rights* (New York: Vintage, 2005), 163–66.

150. Reynolds, *John Brown*, 201–2.

151. Reynolds, *John Brown*, 201–2.

152. Cited by "John Brown Trial (1859)," Professor Douglas O. Linder, University of Missouri–Kansas City Law School, https://www.famous-trials.com/johnbrown.

153. Lincoln argued: "John Brown's effort was peculiar. It was not a slave insurrection. It was an attempt by white men to get up a revolt among slaves, in which the slaves refused to participate. In fact, it was so absurd that the slaves, with all their ignorance, saw plainly enough it could not succeed. That affair, in its philosophy, corresponds with the many attempts, related in history, at the assassination of kings and emperors. An enthusiast

broods over the oppression of a people till he fancies himself commissioned by Heaven to liberate them. He ventures the attempt, which ends in little else than his own execution." "Abraham Lincoln on John Brown, February 27, 1860," Harvard University Press Blog, December 3, 2012, https://harvardpress.typepad.com/hup_publicity/2012/12/abraham-lincoln-on-john-brown-february-27-1860.html.

154. Fergus M. Bordewich, "John Brown's Day of Reckoning," *Smithsonian Magazine*, 2009, https://www.smithsonianmag.com/issue/archive/.

155. Kate Larson, *Bound for the Promised Land: Harriet Tubman, Portrait of an American Hero* (New York: Ballantine, 2004), 177.

156. Hans J. Massaquoi, "Mystery of Malcolm X," *Ebony*, September 1964.

157. Paul Finkelman and Clayton Cramer, "Analogies: Was Timothy McVeigh Our John Brown?" History News Network (HNN), http://hnn.us/articles/139.html.

158. Uprisings occurred in Belgium, Italy, France, Spain, Portugal, Russia, Austria, Hungary, Poland, Ireland, Romania, and Greece. A classic discussion of the events can be found in James Billington, *Fire in the Minds of Men: Origins of the Revolutionary Faith* (New York: Basic Books, 1980).

159. Russia mobilized its army to send troops to crush the rebellion, but a second insurrection broke out in the Polish area of the Russian Empire, and Russian forces became too preoccupied to move against the Belgians. In addition to the Belgian example, one could cite the Hungarian uprising in 1848 as a success, because it produced the dual monarchy, i.e., the Austro-Hungarian Empire. But that event did not change the international order.

160. Clive H. Church, *Europe in 1830* (Crows Nest: George Unwin, 1983), 31–32.

161. Roger Price, *The Revolutions of 1848* (London: Humanities, 1988), 39.

162. John Breuilly, "1848: Connected or Comparable Revolutions," in *1848: A European Revolution*, ed. Axel Korner (Stuttgart: Macmillan, 2000), 34.

163. William L. Langer, *Political and Social Upheaval: 1832–1852* (New York: Harper and Row, 1969), 393.

164. Langer, *Political and Social Upheaval*, 25.

165. John E. Rath, "The Carbonari: Their Origins, Initiation Rites, and Aims," *American Historical Association* 69, no 2 (1964): 353.

166. Nationalist rebellions in Austria and Italy were the most serious and most often repeated.

167. Carl Friedrich and Roland Pennock, eds., "Tocqueville's Contribution to the Theory of Revolution," in *Revolution* (New York: Atherton, 1967), 87.

168. M. Cherif Bassiouni, "The Political Offense Exception in Extradition Law and Practice," in *International Terrorism and Political Crimes* (Springfield, MA: Charles Thomas, 1975), 398. See also Bogdan Zlatric, "History of International Terrorism and Its Legal Control," in the same volume, 474–84.

169. Billington, *Fire in the Minds of Men*, 348. For other discussions of the Commune, see Johannes Willms, *Paris, Capital of Europe: From the Revolution to Belles Epoque* (Teaneck, NJ: Holmes and Meier, 1997).

170. Benedict Anderson, *Under Three Flags: Anarchism and the Anti-Colonial Imagination* (Brooklyn: Verso, 2005), 1967.

171. "It provided the Russian Revolution with holy relics. Lenin was buried with a Communard flag, and the spaceship *Voskhod* was equipped with a ribbon from the banner of the Commune. Myths of the Commune abounded among the anarchists as well as among Chinese cultural revolutionaries of the 1960s and the Russian [terrorists] fifty years earlier, among the New Left as well as the Old in the Western world. Insofar as all later revolutionaries were to find unity among themselves, it was in the singing of the great hymn that emerged from the martyrdom of 1871." Billington, *Fire in the Minds of Men*, 344.

172. Billington, *Fire in the Minds of Men*, 141, believes that "the Decembrist movement was the starting point of the contemporary Russian revolutionary tradition."

173. Quoted by Franco Venturi, *Roots of Revolution* (New York: Knopf, 1960), 3.

174. "Charles X (and) Louis Phillippe . . . never put to the test [the issue of] whether the common soldier would follow his general or swing back to his natural social place." Katharine Chorley, *Armies and the Art of Revolution* (Boston: Beacon, 1973), 246.

175. See John Newsinger, *Fenianism in Mid-Victorian Britain* (London: Pluto, 1994); and Leon O'Broin, *Fenian Fever* (London: Chatto and Windus, 1971), chap. 2. Irish revolts subsequently were usually timed to take advantage of British wars or serious threats abroad. Irish revolutionaries sometimes sought alliances with the enemy, e.g., in World War I and II.

176. Erick Rauchway, *Murdering McKinley, Making Theodore Roosevelt's America* (New York: Hill and Wang, 2003), 90. Oddly, Russia and the Ottoman Empire were the only two countries in Europe that required passports to travel within their countries.

177. The railroad was critical for émigrés who participated in terrorism when their bases were in foreign territories or when they had to cross the continent in two or three days. The railroad enhanced the significance of diaspora communities, but it certainly did not create those communities. Most Russians who moved west to settle traveled by horse and wagon; Martin Miller pointed this out in an email.

178. Jeffrey D. Simon, "Forgotten Lessons from the History of Terrorism: The Galleanists and Militant Anarchism in America," *Terrorism and Political Violence* 20, no. 2 (2008): 195–214.

179. Brian M. Jenkins, "The Terrorist Mindset and Terrorist Decision Making: Two Areas of Ignorance," *Terrorism* 3, no. 3 (1980): 249.

180. Ernest Vizetelly, *The Anarchists* (New York: John Lane, 1911), 77. Emphasis added.

181. Cited by Richard B. Jensen, "Daggers, Rifles, and Dynamite: Anarchist Terrorism in 19th Century Europe," *Terrorism and Political Violence* 16, no. 1 (2004): 116. Emphasis added.

182. From the anarchist journal *Alarm*, cited by Paul Avrich, *The Haymarket Tragedy* (Princeton, NJ: Princeton University Press, 1984), 166.

183. Avrich, *The Haymarket Tragedy*, 162–63.

184. From the anarchist journal *Nemesis*, cited by Avrich, *The Haymarket Tragedy*, 162–63.

2. THE FIRST WAVE: ANARCHIST, 1879–1920s

1. The first chapter of Menachem Begin's discussion of the uprising against the British contains a moving description of the necessity of hope. Menachem Begin, *The Revolt: Story of the Irgun* (Tel Aviv: Steimatzky, 1977).

2. Jeremy Popkin, *Facing Racial Revolution* (Chicago: University of Chicago Press, 2007), 1.

3. The struggle between generations was described in Ivan Turgenev's famous 1862 novel *Fathers and Sons*. Fathers were unwilling to accept the reforms proposed, which led their sons to aim to destroy the system altogether.

4. Barbara Jelavich, *Russia's Balkan Entanglements, 1806–1914* (Cambridge: Cambridge University Press, 2004), 118–22.

5. William C. Fuller, *Strategy and Power in Russia, 1600–1914* (New York: Free Press, 1992), 273.

6. Sergei Nechaev, "Revolutionary Catechism" (1869); reprinted in David C. Rapoport, *Assassination and Terrorism* (Toronto: Canadian Broadcasting Corporation, 1971), 79–84.

7. Norman N. Naimark, "Terrorism and the Fall of Imperial Russia," *Terrorism and Political Violence* 2, no. 2 (1990): 278.

8. Zasulich had spent several years in prison for radical activities, and she had no personal relationship with the abused prisoner. For the most comprehensive English account of the incident and the various commentaries it generated, see Jay Bergman, *Vera Zasulich: A Biography* (Palo Alto, CA: Stanford University Press, 1983). See also Jay Bergman, "Vera Zasulich, the Shooting of Trepov, and the Growth of Political Terrorism in Russia," in *Terrorism: Critical Concepts in Political Science*, ed. David C. Rapoport (London: Routledge, 2006), 1:215–36.

9. Bergman, "Vera Zasulich," 224.

10. Naimark, "Terrorism and the Fall of Imperial Russia," 278.

11. Adam Ulam, *In the Name of the People* (New York: Viking, 1977), 269.

12. Bergman, "Vera Zasulich," 239.

13. Peter Kropotkin, *Memoirs of a Revolutionist* (New York: International Publishers, 1927), 64.

14. Ulam, *In the Name of the People*, 273.

15. Twain and Kennan did not know Stepniak was an assassin.

16. Ironically, afterward Zasulich abandoned all contact with terrorist activity, condemned it, and became a Marxist.

17. Ulam, *In the Name of the People*, 289. Figner's observation occurred after Zasulich's trial. Earlier she shared the general view that the city members became "obsessed with fireworks . . . assassinations of generals and police chiefs . . . enchantments . . . pulling the youth away from the real task, that of working with the peasants who need their help so much."

18. Ulam, *In the Name of the People*, 90.

19. Ulam, *In the Name of the People*, 293.

20. Amy Knight, "Female Terrorists in the Russian Socialist Revolutionary Party," *Russian Review* 38, no. 2 (1974): 140.

21. Ulam, *In the Name of the People*, 327. There is no agreement on the group's size. James Billington says it contained between four and five thousand, which is a large number. But he does not specify how many were engaged in assassination activity normally confined to the executive committee of Narodnaya Volya or individuals it selected. James Billington, *Fire in the Minds of Men: Origins of the Revolutionary Faith* (New York: Transaction, 1998), 47.

22. Avraham Yarmolinsky, *Road to Revolution: A Century of Russian Radicalism* (Stuttgart: Macmillan, 1955), 234–35.

23. The most significant Russian weapon was the bomb, and other terrorist groups used it extensively, too. But the Irish "Skirmishers" of the 1880s were the only ones who confined themselves to the bomb. See Jonathan W. Gantt, "Irish-American Terrorism and Anglo-American Relations, 1881–1885," *Journal of the Gilded Age and Progressive Era* 5, no. 4 (2006): 325–57.

24. It is interesting to note that secondary commentary occasionally refers to this activity as "suicide bombing," well before suicide bombing become significant in the Fourth Wave. See Anna Geifman, *Thou Shalt Kill: Revolutionary Terrorism in Russia, 1894–1917* (Princeton, NJ: Princeton University Press, 1993).

25. See Ze'ev Ivianski, "Source of Inspiration for Revolutionary Terrorism—The Bakunin—Nechayev Alliance," *Journal of Conflict Studies* 8, no. 3 (1988).

26. P. A. Lavrov and Sergey Stepniak-Kravchinsky, *Underground Russia: Revolutionary Profiles and Sketches from Life* (New York: Scribners, 1883), 99.

27. Stepniak, *Underground Russia*, 39–40. "A mid-60s group named Hell committed to assassination sought martyrdom in another bizarre way. . . . Immediately prior to the [assassination] he was to disfigure his face beyond recognition; immediately after he was to take poison—leaving behind a manifesto from the 'organization' which could be assured thereby an impact that peaceful propaganda could never have." Billington, *Fire in the Minds of Men*, 356.

28. Ulam, *In the Name of the People*, 365.

29. The letter appears in Stepniak, *Underground Russia*, 313–15.

30. Jews suffered enormously during Nicholas I's reign. Jewish boys between the ages of twelve and eighteen were conscripted to serve in the army for twenty-five years. During that time efforts were made to convert them to Christianity. Given the horrendous conditions under which they were forced to serve, many didn't survive, and if they did, few continued to identify themselves as Jews. Some Jewish parents were so desperate they would cut off the right index finger of their sons with a butcher's knife—without an index finger you couldn't fire a gun and were exempt from service.

31. The number was around 5,189,401 (4.13 percent of the total population). No country had more Jews at that time. "Minorities and Ethnic Diversity in Russia," *Facts and Details*, http://factsanddetails.com/russia/Minorities/sub9_3a/entry-5093.html.

32. "Hamas Covenant 1988," Avalon Project, Yale Law School, Lillian Goldman Law Library, http://avalon.law.yale.edu/20th_century/hamas.asp.

33. Earlier Russian secret police were mainly concerned with coup d'etat possibilities.

34. "Intelligence and Policy Monographs," Center for the Study of Intelligence, Central Intelligence Agency, https://www.cia.gov/library/center-for-the-study-of-intelligence/csi -publications/books-and-monographs/index.html; Ben Fisher, "Okhrana: The Paris Operations of the Russian Imperial Police," History Staff Center for the Study of Intelligence, Central Intelligence Agency (1997), https://www.cia.gov/library/center-for-the -study-of-intelligence/csi-publications/books-and-monographs/okhrana-the-paris -operations-of-the-russian-imperial-police/5474-1.html.

35. Burtsev is cited by Ze'ev Iviansky, "Individual Terror: Concept and Typology," *Journal of Contemporary History* 12, no. 1 (1977): 48. Iviansky explains Burtsev was attempting to rejuvenate the fortunes of his group, but Iviansky does not tell us why the tactic was rejected. Burtsev earned the Sherlock Holmes title for his work in discovering the notorious "agent provocateur" Azev. See Rita Kronenbitter, "The Sherlock Holmes of the Revolution," CIA Historical Review Program, Central Intelligence Agency (1993), https://www.cia.gov/library/center-for-the-study-of-intelligence/kent-csi/vol11no4 /html/v11i4a07p_0001.htm.

36. States used it initially as part of the peacemaking process. One handed over individuals to another to guarantee that an agreement would be kept. But sometimes hostages were seized and held against their will to prevent anticipated hostile acts.

37. "Hostage," *Encyclopaedia Britannica*, 11th ed. (Cambridge: Cambridge University Press, 1911).

38. The Prussians also executed National Guard members in Paris who had taken up arms against them. "The government of Versailles has put itself outside the laws of war and of humanity: it will be necessary to use reprisals," one manifesto issued by the Commune proclaimed. See Edward S. Mason, *The Paris Commune* (Stuttgart: Macmillan, 1930), 180. The rebels' appeal seems ironic because it is usually the rebel and always the terrorist who violate the rules of war. But the Commune's revolutionary army initially observed this rule of war.

39. The action of the Commune had an important precedent in revolutionary history. One should mention too that during the first French Revolution (1789), the revolutionary government passed the "law of hostages" on June 18, 1799, in order to cope with the insurrection in La Vendee. Relatives of émigrés were taken from the disturbed areas and imprisoned and executed if they tried to escape. But the insurrection only intensified.

40. I have examined various secondary accounts of this period in Russia, and none refer to hostage incidents. See, for example Geifman, *Thou Shalt Kill*. The Armenians and Macedonians each generated an important hostage incident in the periods in what follows.

41. Paul Avrich, *The Russian Anarchists* (Princeton, NJ: Princeton University Press, 1967), 43–84.

42. Geifman, *Thou Shalt Kill*, 250.

43. Avrich, *The Russian Anarchists*, 64.

44. Ronald Hingley, *The Russian Secret Police* (London: Hutchinson, 1970), 101.

45. Hingley, *The Russian Secret Police*, 113.

46. Geifman, *Thou Shalt Kill*, 250.

47. Quoted by Avrich, *The Russian Anarchists*, 138.

48. The Terrorist Brigade was not revived, but those Socialist Revolutionaries who turned to terror followed its strategy.

49. The comment quoted is by Avrich, *The Russian Anarchists*, 190.

50. The play was based on an incident Boris Savinkov describes in his *Memoirs of a Terrorist* (New York: A. & C. Boni, 1931), chap. 2.

51. As suggested, only the better-known groups are mentioned. I don't know if anyone has systematically assessed the total number and average durability of the groups. My sense is that there were at least a dozen and possibly two dozen.

52. Geifman, *Thou Shalt Kill*, suggests that the perpetrators always used anarchist justifications despite their true intentions, but a precise category cannot be given because so few were caught.

53. Avrich, *The Russian Anarchists*, 46–47.

54. Avrich, *The Russian Anarchists*, 162.

55. Vera Figner, *Memoirs of a Revolutionist* (New York: International Publishers, 1927), 94–95.

56. Figner, *Memoirs of a Revolutionist*, 95–96.

57. James Joll, *The Anarchists* (Cambridge, MA: Harvard University Press, 1980), 12. The figure was given by Kropotkin, who attended. But historians think the number is greatly exaggerated. See Nunzio Pernicone, *Italian Anarchism* (Princeton, NJ: Princeton University Press, 1993); and Andrew Carlson, *Anarchism in Germany*, vol. 1 (Scarecrow, 1972), chap. 8.

58. Cited by Yves Termon, "Russian Terrorism, 1878–1908," in *The History of Terrorism from Antiquity to Al Qaeda*, ed. Gerard Chaliand and Arnaud Blin (Berkeley: University of California Press, 2007), 150.

59. Marx's letter to his daughter Jenny Longuet shortly after the assassins were executed was quite striking in view of his initial reluctance to encourage terrorism. "Have you been following the trial of the people who carried out the attacks? They are solidly honest people, striking no melodramatic poses, unassuming, realistic, and heroic. Shouting and doing are irreconcilably contradictory. The Petersburg Executive Committee which has acted so vigorously is publishing manifestos of refined moderation. . . . They are seeking to explain to Europe that their modus operandi is a specifically Russian and historically inevitable method; there is no more reason to moralize about it than about the [1881] Chios [Greece] earthquake." Cited by Termon, "Russian Terrorism," 151.

60. Termon, "Russian Terrorism," 151.

61. Termon, "Russian Terrorism," 151.

62. Termon, "Russian Terrorism," 151.

63. Savinkov, *Memoirs of a Terrorist*, 78. Francois-Claudius Ravachol, executed in France in 1892, committed several brutal murders for petty theft and some large-scale bombing

outrages. At his trial, he proclaimed himself to be an anarchist, and after his execution some anarchists accepted him. But his early career convinced many that he was not only a petty criminal but also a police informer.

64. Ben Fisher, "Okhrana: The Paris Operations of the Russian Imperial Police," History Staff Center for the Study of Intelligence, Central Intelligence Agency (1997), https://www.cia.gov/library/center-for-the-study-of-intelligence/csi-publications/books-and-monographs/okhrana-the-paris-operations-of-the-russian-imperial-police/5474-1.html.

65. Apparently, travel in Russia was easier for those carrying foreign passports than for native Russians.

66. Savinkov, *Memoirs of a Terrorist*, 72.

67. Peter Hees, *The Bomb in Bengal* (Oxford: Oxford University Press, 1993), 90. The laboratory was moved from Paris to Geneva after two years.

68. See Kronenbitter, "The Sherlock Holmes of the Revolution."

69. Geifman, *Thou Shalt Kill*, 201.

70. Savinkov, *Memoirs of a Terrorist*, 196.

71. Richard Bach Jensen, "Daggers, Rifles, Dynamite: Anarchist Terrorism in Nineteenth Century Europe," *Terrorism and Political Violence* 16, no. 1 (2004): 134.

72. Jensen, "Daggers, Rifles, Dynamite," 131.

73. Ulrich Linse, "'Propaganda by Deed' and 'Direct Action': Two Concepts of Anarchist Violence," in *Social Protest, Violence, and Terror in Nineteenth- and Twentieth-Century Europe*, ed. Wolfgang J. Mommsen and Gerhard Hirschfeld (London: Springer Nature, 2020), 205.

74. For Italian anarchist activity in the United States, see Nunzio Pernicone, "Luigi Galleani and Italian Anarchist Terrorism in the United States," *Studi Emigrazione/Etudes Migrations* 30 (1993): 469–89; Lowell Blaisdell, "The Assassination of Humbert I," *Prologue: The Quarterly of the National Archives* 27, no. 3 (1995): 241–47; Jeffrey Simon, "Forgotten Lessons from the History of Terrorism: The Galleanists and Militant Anarchism in America," *Terrorism and Political Violence* 20, no. 2 (2008); Paul Avrich, *The Russian Anarchists* (Chico, CA: AK, 2005), 43–84.

75. Richard Bach Jensen, "The International Campaign Against Anarchist Terrorism," *Terrorism and Political Violence* 21, no. 1 (2009): 89–109. Jensen discusses the tensions with Germany and Russia and the lack of a federal police force.

76. Roosevelt's antitrust policies in part were shaped by his concern the big firms were alienating workers and creating grievances anarchists would exploit.

77. Denmark, Sweden, Norway, Spain, Portugal, and Switzerland, later.

78. The Japanese offer to finance Russian terrorists during the Russo-Japanese War (1905) encouraged Indian terrorists to believe that the Japanese would help them too. See Peter Heehs, *Nationalism, Terrorism, and Communalism: Essays in Modern Indian History* (Oxford: Oxford University Press, 1998), 4. The Russian Socialist Revolutionary Party turned the Japanese offer down. Savinkov, *Memoirs of a Terrorist*, points out fearing that knowledge of such a transaction during a time of war would destroy their political credibility.

79. There were also three assassinations in "minor states": Alexander I of Serbia (1903), Carlos I of Portugal (1908), and George I of Greece (1913). But the assassins were not terrorists. The first case involved military officers bent on a coup, the second was the product of mob action, and the third assassin was a criminal.

80. Frederic Zuckerman, *The Tsarist Secret Police Abroad: Policing Europe in a Modernizing World* (Palgrave: Macmillan, 2003); and Richard Bach Jensen, *The Battle Against Anarchist Terrorism; An International History, 1878–1914* (Cambridge: Cambridge University Press, 2014), discuss the problem in detail.

81. A Black Hand element was also involved in the assassinations of the Serbian king Alexander I and his wife, Queen Draga, in 1903; their bodies were then mutilated and thrown out on the street. C. L. Sulzberger, *The Fall of Eagles* (New York: Crown, 1977), 202. One reason for the assassination was that the king had married a commoner whose brother was likely to inherit the throne.

82. For an interesting and thorough analysis of the situation that makes Germany responsible for Austria-Hungary's unwillingness to wait for all the details even though it knew that Russia was ready to support Serbia fully, see Bernadotte E. Schmitt, "July 14: Thirty Years After," *Journal of Modern History* 16, no. 3 (1944): 169–204.

83. Noel Malcolm, *Bosnia: A Short History* (New York: New York University Press, 1996), 153.

84. The house where Princip lived in Sarajevo was destroyed during World War I. Later it was rebuilt as a museum in the Kingdom of Yugoslavia. But after Yugoslavia was conquered by Germany in 1941, the house was destroyed again. After the establishment of communist Yugoslavia in 1944, it became a museum again, and another museum was dedicated to Princip in the city of Sarajevo. During the Yugoslav Wars of the 1990s, the house was destroyed a third time; no attempts to rebuild it have yet been announced. Before 1992, the site on the pavement on which Princip stood to fire the fatal shots was marked by embossed footprints. These were destroyed as a consequence of the 1992–1995 war in Bosnia. There is still a plaque in front of the museum at the spot where Gavrilo Princip stood when he fired the shots. A plan to reconstruct Princip's birth house in Obljaj was made in 2014, the centenary of the assassination in Sarajevo.

85. After the Germans occupied Denmark during World War II, Iceland became a republic.

86. IMRO, the Macedonian group, several years later became intrigued with the strategy but achieved only marginally better results.

87. The British had a special obligation through the Cyprus Convention, a product of that war. See Christopher J. Walker, *Armenia: The Survival of a Nation* (Kent: Croom Helm, 1980), 121–23.

88. Khachig Tololyan, "Cultural Narrative and the Terrorist," in *Inside Terrorist Organizations*, ed. David C. Rapoport (New York: Columbia University Press, 1988), 255. Tololyan describes the narrative and the various forms in which it is expressed in vivid detail. "This tradition is alive in the web of culture, not just for the learned, the books, the museums. It is inscribed in the mind of a certain proportion of Diaspora Armenians as they grow up; it partially but importantly constitutes their Armenianness."

89. Francis Hyland, *Armenian Terrorism: The Past, the Present, the Prospects* (Nashville, TN: Westview, 1991), chap. 1.

90. Benjamin C. Portna, "The Reign of Abdulhamid II," in *The Cambridge History of Turkey* (Cambridge: Cambridge University Press, 2006), 4:54.

91. Walker, *Armenia*, 103, 129.

92. Walker, *Armenia*, 103.

93. Walker, *Armenia*, chap. 5. Clearly, the figures are rough, probably exaggerated, estimates. "This incident began the series of disturbances or, as most authors call them, massacres, in Eastern Anatolia which lasted until 1896 and resulted in the death of an indeterminate number of Armenians. This paper unfortunately cannot correct the long series of exaggerations and propaganda statements concerning it." Stephen Duguid, "The Politics of Unity: Hamidian Policy in Eastern Anatolia," *Middle Eastern Studies* 9, no. 2 (1973): 148.

94. For a good discussion of why the Armenians miscalculated in thinking the British would be their most important ally, see Robert F. Zeidner, "Britain and the Launching of the Armenian Question," *International Journal of Middle East Studies* 7, no. 4 (1976): 465–83.

95. Walker, *Armenia*. Walker gives two other reasons for the bank seizure. The European powers would be concerned about their citizens in the bank, and the bank was a symbol of capitalism. It is not clear why those who took the bank ignored their own ultimatum of forty-eight hours and gave up after twelve even though the Europeans had not really met their demands.

96. Walker, *Armenia*, 164–73.

97. Joan Haslip, *The Sultan: The Life of Abdul Hamid II* (London: Weidenfeld, 1958), 224. Haslip emphasizes that in Constantinople the massacres "revolted every law-abiding citizen and there had been many instances of Moslems protecting Armenians. Even the Holy Mosque of Eyoub gave shelter to fugitives" (225). She argues the Turkish public's reactions had more influence on the decision to stop the massacres than the European powers did but that seven thousand Armenians died as opposed to the smaller number Walker provides.

98. Armenians resided in three empires, the Ottoman, Russian, and Persian, which made their struggle for independence particularly difficult.

99. Richard G. Hovannisian, *Armenia on the Road to Independence* (Berkeley: University of California Press, 1967), 18.

100. A Belgian anarchist was also involved, and the Belgian government, which did not sign the St. Petersburg protocol, wanted him released. The sultan refused but changed his mind two years later. Sahali Ramsden Sonyel, *The Ottoman Armenians: Victims of Great Power Diplomacy* (Nicosia: Rustem and Brother, 1987), 263.

101. Sonyel, *The Ottoman Armenians*, 269.

102. Taner Akcam, *A Shameful Act: The Armenian Genocide and the Question of Turkish Responsibility* (New York: Metropolitan, 2006), 69–70. Akcam says "fifteen to twenty thousand Armenians were killed," but most accounts in the West are higher, often as much as thirty thousand.

103. The last Polish nationalist rebellion in 1863 occurred in Russia, but Poles in Austria and Prussia committed to working through the parliamentary bodies ignored it.

104. Michal Targowski argues that socialism was more important than nationalism in "Against Colonialism or Social Inequities: Polish Terrorists in the Long 19th Century," *German Historical Institute Conference* (2008). He notes that although his argument clashes with that of Western scholars like Walter Laqueur and Anna Geifman, it depends on primary Polish sources, police reports, correspondence memoirs, and programs.

105. Targowski, "Against Colonialism or Social Inequities," 3.

106. A variety of other Balkan organizations existed, the most notable perhaps being Young Bosnia and the Serbian Black Hand.

107. Roland Gaucher, *The Terrorists* (London: Secker and Warburg, 1968), chap. 8.

108. See Duncan Perry, *The Politics of Terror: The Macedonian Liberation Movements, 1893–1903* (Durham, NC: Duke University Press, 1988), 4, 103–5, 171, 478–95; as well as Theresa Carpenter, *The Miss Stone Affair: America's First Hostage Crisis* (New York: Simon and Schuster, 2003). The Stone incident captured the attention of the Western world, receiving extensive media and academic coverage and inspiring a 1958 Yugoslavian film.

109. Theodore Roosevelt to Alvey Adee, in *The Letters of Theodore Roosevelt*, ed. Ellting E. Morison (Cambridge: Cambridge University Press, 1951), 157. The irony of Roosevelt's concern is that this was the period in which women were seeking equal rights, a concern expressed by their significant role in First Wave terrorist activity.

110. Cited in Randall B. Woods, "Terrorism in the Age of Roosevelt: The Miss Stone Affair, 1901–1902," *American Quarterly* 31 (1979). Earlier in the nineteenth century Congress paid $80,000 (more than the sum the kidnappers asked for) to release a hostage seized at sea and held on the Barbary Coast. A second hostage crisis at the time of the Stone kidnapping involving Morocco appeared to restore the U.S, government's determination to resist, but ultimately the secretary of state promised not to use force. Carpenter also discusses the Morocco crisis: Carpenter, *The Miss Stone Affair*, 210–11.

111. "Stockholm Syndrome" refers to the psychological process that occasionally binds captor and captive in an unexpectedly powerful positive emotional bond. The name comes from an incident in a 1973 Stockholm bank robbery where a female hostage formed a deep commitment to her captor and refused to cooperate with those trying to free her.

112. Andrew Rossos, "The British Foreign Office and Macedonian Identity, 1918–1941," *Slavic Review* 53, no. 22 (1994): 369–94.

113. The British inappropriately referred to Indian terrorists as "anarchists."

114. J. E. Armstrong, quoted by Michael Silvestri, "The Bomb, Bhadralok, Bhagavad Gita, and Dan Breen: Terrorism in Bengal and Its Relation to the European Experience," *Terrorism and Political Violence* 21, no. 1 (2009): 8.

115. Steven G. Marks, "'Bravo, Brave Tiger of the East!': The Russo-Japanese War and the Rise of Nationalism in British Egypt and India," in *The Russo-Japanese War in Global Perspective*, ed. John W. Steinberg et al. (Leiden: Brill, 2005), 618. Only in India did the Japanese triumph precipitate a terrorist effort.

116. Silvestri, "The Bomb, Bhadralok, Bhagavad Gita, and Dan Breen," 94.

117. Marks, "'Bravo, Brave Tiger of the East!'" provides the Gandhi and Nehru quotations. Marks also notes that in Egypt, the war was followed everywhere, which helped incite riots against the British. Egypt was nominally under Ottoman rule, but British forces were stationed there in significant numbers. Paul Rodell traces the influence of the war in other non-Western areas. Paul Rodell, "Inspiration for Nationalist Aspirations," in *The Russo-Japanese War in Global Perspective*, ed. John W. Steinberg et al. (Leiden: Brill, 2005), 629–54.

118. A very good study of the group is Asok Kumar Ray, *Party of Firebrand Revolutionaries: The Dacca Anushilan Samiti, 1906–1918* (London: Minerva, 1999). He dedicates the book to members of the organization "who sacrificed their lives for the freedom of the country."

119. Matthew Plowman, "Irish Republicans and the Indo-German Conspiracy of World War I," *New Hibernia Review* 7, no. 3 (2003): 81–105.

120. Silvestri, "The Bomb, Bhadralok, Bhagavad Gita and Dan Breen," 3.

121. Silvestri, "The Bomb, Bhadralok, Bhagavad Gita and Dan Breen," 37. "Gita" is the Bhagavad Gītā, "Song of God," a sacred scripture of Hinduism. Ray notes that "during the initiation ceremony . . . religious rituals were performed resulting in the growth of patriotism as a religious cult. This has hardly any parallel except in the legends of Joan of Arc." Ray, *Party of Firebrand Revolutionaries*, 134.

122. Silvestri, "The Bomb, Bhadralok, Bhagavad Gita and Dan Breen," 24.

123. Silvestri, "The Bomb, Bhadralok, Bhagavad Gita and Dan Breen," 17.

124. Peter Heehs, *Nationalism, Terrorism, and Communalism: Essays in Modern Indian History* (Oxford: Oxford University Press, 1998), chap. 2.

125. Quoted by Ray, *Party of Firebrand Revolutionaries*, 137.

126. Robert A. Scalapino and George T. Yu, *The Chinese Anarchist Movement* (Greenwood Press, 1961), 2. For additional useful material on the Chinese experience, see Henrietta Harrison, *China (Inventing the Nation)* (Oxford: Oxford University Press, 2001), 108; Gotelind Müller-Saini, "China and the Anarchist Wave of Assassinations: Politics, Violence and Modernity in East Asia around the Turn of the Twentieth Century," German Historical Institute Conference, New Orleans, 2008; Edward S. Krebs, *Shifu: Soul of Chinese Anarchism* (Washington, DC: Rowman and Littlefield, 1998); Arif Dirlik and Edward S. Krebs, "Socialism and Anarchism in Early Republican China," *Modern China* 7, no. 2 (1981): 117–51.

127. Beck Sanderson, "Qing Dynasty Fall 1875–1912," in *East Asia 1800–1949* (Norwood, CT: Beck, 2007), 21:8, https://www.san.beck.org/21-2-QingFall1875-1912.html. The secret society organizing the rebellion was called the Society of Righteous and Harmonious Fists, which is the source of the term "Boxer Rebellion."

128. The contemporary quoted and paraphrased is Lin Hsieh. See Edward S. Krebs's very useful study "Assassination in Republican Revolutionary Movement," *Ch'ing-shih wen-t'i* 4, no. 6 (December 1981): 45–80. Important anarchist writers emphasized the victims should have been responsible for evil deeds. Gotelind Müller-Saini, "Terrorists or Heroes? Liang Qichao and Early Chinese Perceptions of Anarchism (Prior to 1903)," in *Liang*

Qichao Yu Jindai Zhongguo Shehui Wenhua [Liang Qichao and modern Chinese society and culture], ed. Li Xisuo (Tianjin: Tianjin guji chubanshe, 2005), 449. For discussions of the Chinese tyrannicide tradition, see Lie Zehua and Liu Jianqing, "Civic Associations, Political Parties, and the Cultivation of Citizenship Consciousness in Modern China," *Chinese Studies in History* 29, no. 4 (1996): 8–35; and Ingo Schaefer, "The People's Rights and Rebellion Development of Tan Sitong's Political Thought," in *Chinese Intellectuals and the Concept of Citizenship, 1890–1927,* ed. Joshua A. Fogel and Peter Farrow (Armonk, NY: M. E. Sharpe, 1997).

129. In 1900, three years before the first phase, Shih Chien Ju, a member of the republican movement, acting on his own initiative made two unsuccessful attempts using explosives to assassinate a Manchu provincial governor.

130. Krebs, "Assassination in Republican Revolutionary Movement," 61.

131. "Tongmenghui," *New World Encyclopedia,* https://www.newworldencyclopedia.org/entry /Tongmenghui.

132. Krebs, "Assassination in Republican Revolutionary Movement," 68. The money helped create the Eastern Assassination Corps, which cooperated with the Chinese Assassination Corps in the assassination of General Feng-Shan. The republican journal that endorsed assassination was *Min Pao.*

133. Chün-tu Hsüeh, "The Life and Political Thought of Huang Hsing: Co-Founder of the Republic of China," *Australian Journal of Politics and History* 13 (2008): 21–33.

134. The Japanese situation has been discussed in English by various authors. The most useful is Ira Lev Plotkin, "A Question of Treason: The Great Treason Conspiracy of 1911," PhD diss., University of Michigan, 1974. Also see Thomas A. Stanley, *Osugi Sakae, Anarchist in Taisho Japan: The Creativity of the Ego* (Cambridge, MA: Harvard University Press, 1943).

135. Plotkin, "A Question of Treason."

136. Plotkin, "A Question of Treason," 6.

137. Plotkin, "A Question of Treason," 3.

138. Plotkin, "A Question of Treason," 7

139. Stanley, *Osugi Sakae,* 46.

140. James Billington, *Fire in the Minds of Men,* 474.

141. "Errico Malatesta: Violence as a Social Factor, 1895," Reddit post in r/Anarchism, 2017, https://www.reddit.com/r/Anarchism/comments/6drmys/errico_malatesta_violence _as_a_social_factor_1895/. Spain's Prime Minister Eduardo Dato in 1923 was the last head of state or government anarchists killed.

142. Robert Graham, *From Anarchy to Anarchism (300 CE to 1939)* (Montreal: Black Rose, 2005), vol. 1.

143. V. Damier, *Anarcho-Syndicalism in the 20th Century* (Los Angeles: Black Cat, 2009).

144. *A Rivista Anarchica,* trans. Paul Sharkey (Milan: Ingraf Industria Grafica, 2002), 279.

145. Gino Loretta, an anarchist, tried to assassinate Mussolini in 1926. The plot was hatched in antifascist Italian exile circles in France and included persons of different political persuasions.

146. H. M. Bock, "Anarcho-Syndicalism in the German Labour Movement: A Rediscovered Minority Tradition," in *Revolutionary Syndicalism: An International Perspective*, ed. Marcel van der Linden and Wayne Thorpe (New York: Scholar, 1990), 59–80.

147. A. Beevor, *The Spanish Civil War, 1936–1939* (Maryknoll: Orbis, 1982).

148. Nurit Schliefman, "The Challenge to the Police," in *Terrorism: Critical Concepts in Political Science*, ed. David C. Rapoport (London: Routledge, 2006), 1:401–33.

149. Ivianski, "Source of Inspiration for Revolutionary Terrorism."

150. Several similar cases were produced in Spain in the same decade.

151. The practice was normal in countries using Roman civil law, where conviction required two eyewitnesses to a murder and circumstantial proof was not admitted. England was the principal exception to this traditional practice; there the common law prevailed, utilizing the jury system and circumstantial evidence. J. H. Langbein, "The Legal History of Torture," in *Torture*, ed. Sanford Levinson (Oxford: Oxford University Press, 2004), 93–101.

152. H. B. Clarke, *Modern Spain* (Cambridge: Cambridge University Press, 1986).

153. Temma Kaplan, *Anarchists of Andalusia, 1868–1903* (Princeton, NJ: Princeton University Press, 1997), chap. 5.

154. Jensen, *The Battle Against Anarchist Terrorism*, 348.

3. THE SECOND WAVE: ANTICOLONIAL, 1919–1960s

1. Alan J. Ward, *Ireland and Anglo-American Relations* (London: Weidenfeld, 1969), 170. President Wilson justified U.S. World War I involvement as a "war to end all wars" and his "Fourteen Points" animated the peace plan. The principles embodied in the Fourteen Points, Walter R. Mead emphasizes, still guide world politics today: "self determination, democratic government, collective security, international law, and a League of Nations or UN." David M. Kennedy wrote, "Every American president since Wilson has embraced the core precepts of Wilsonianism. Nixon hung Wilson's portrait in the White House Cabinet Room. . . . In the aftermath of 9/11, they have . . . taken on higher vitality." David M. Kennedy, "What 'W' Owes to 'WW,'" *Atlantic Monthly* 295, no. 2 (2005): 36.

2. Wilson could not get much American support, and only some World War I Allies signed the 1920 Treaty of Sèvres to create an Armenian state. The Turkish war of independence forced a new Treaty of Lausanne in 1924, which annulled the Treaty of Sèvres and established Turkey's current boundaries.

3. David E. Cronon, ed., "Wilson's First Draft of the Covenant of the League of Nations," in *The Political Thought of Woodrow Wilson* (Indianapolis, IN: Bobbs Merrill, 1963), 453–59.

4. Previously undivided Ottoman Arab territories were separated (i.e., Syria, Lebanon, Palestine, and Iraq) and designated Class A Mandates, signifying they would soon govern themselves. The former German-ruled African colonies of Tanganyika, parts of

Togoland and the Cameroons, and Ruanda-Urundi were Class B Mandates. Tanganyika was assigned to Britain, France administered the Cameroons and Togoland, and Belgium Ruanda-Urundi (now Rwanda and Burundi). Class C Mandates were various former German-held territories that Mandatories subsequently administered as integral parts of their territory: South West Africa to South Africa, New Guinea to Australia, Western Samoa to New Zealand, the islands north of the Equator in the western Pacific to Japan, and Nauru to Australia, Britain, and New Zealand.

5. Shamir later became Israel's prime minister (1983–1984 and 1986–1992). The IRA is the only non-Jewish group Begin, the Irgun leader, mentions in his account of the Jewish campaign.

6. Quoted by Michael Silvestri, "The Bomb, *Bhadralok*, *Bhagavad Gita*, and Dan Breen: Terrorism in Bengal and Its Relationship to the European Experience," *Terrorism and Political Violence* 21, no. 1 (2009): 17.

7. Menachem Begin, *The Revolt: Story of the Irgun* (Steimatzky, 1977), 307; Georges Dighenis-Grivas and Charles Foley, *Memoirs* (New York: Longmans, 1964), 204.

8. Lehi members admired Russian and Polish revolutionary groups greatly. See Joseph Heller, *The Stern Gang* (London: Frank Cass, 1995).

9. As a child, Grivas was "fascinated by "the legends of Dighenis Akristas, the half-mythical guardian of the frontiers of Alexander's empire. Not far from Trikomo was a huge rock which the village elders assured me had been hurled by Dighenis, and my mother often sang folk-songs recounting his acts of heroism." Dighenis-Grivas and Foley, *Memoirs*, 3.

10. The irony of combining Christian vows and a pagan god is never explained. See Cheres Dimitriou, "Political Violence and Legitimation, the Episode of Colonial Cyprus," *Qualitative Sociology* 30, no. 2 (2007): 186.

11. Ann Matthews, *Renegades: Irish Republican Women 1900–1922* (Cork: Mercier, 2010), 129–30.

12. Chattri Sanga was the Hindu name for the female group. Females in the English Suffragette movement occasionally engaged in terrorist acts but did not form groups that only used that tactic. Silvestri estimates the number of female terrorists outside the Women's Society remained small, at the most 150. They committed some spectacular assassinations. Silvestri, "The Bomb, *Bhadralok*, *Bhagavad Gita* and Dan Breen."

13. Terrorist activity sometimes changed public opinion so much that an element rejecting terror was able to use different tactics to achieve the political aim sought. Indian terrorists in the 1920s put the independence issue on the table, making it easier for Gandhi's nonviolent resistance movement to succeed. See David M. Laushey, *Bengal Terrorism and the Marxist Left: Aspects of Regional Nationalism in India, 1905–1942* (Firma K. L. Mukhopadhyay, 1975), 136.

14. The nationalist problem persists in Europe today and is sometimes associated with terrorist activity, for example, Basques and Corsicans. In 1993, a peaceful solution was devised in Czechoslovakia when it split into two states. In 1991, when Yugoslavia began to disintegrate, the area exploded. Two decades later, the status of Kosovo, a breakaway province of Serbia occupied by NATO (1999), is still unclear and deeply divisive both on

the domestic and international levels. Ian Kershaw provides a good discussion of the various forms after the Versailles Treaty but does not address the issue of why the earlier terrorist movements did not reemerge. Ian Kershaw, "War and Political Violence in Twentieth-Century Europe," *Contemporary European History* 14, no. 1 (2005): 107–23.

15. The numbers appear in Ian Kershaw, *Hitler*, 2nd ed. (London: Longman, 2001), 59. Good descriptions also are found in Robert Gellately, "Rethinking the Nazi Terror System: A Historiographical Analysis," *German Studies Review* 14, no. 1 (1991): 23–38; Charles Townsend, "The Necessity of Political Violence: A Review Article," *Comparative Studies in Society and History* 29, no. 2 (1987): 314–19; Marla Stone, "Staging Fascism: The Exhibition of the Fascist Revolution," *History* 28, no. 2 (1993): 215–43. Similar movements existed elsewhere, e.g., the Romanian Iron Guard and Brazilian Integralism.

16. Quoted by Roland Gaucher, *The Terrorists* (London: Secker and Warburg, 1968), 138–39.

17. There are case studies on French, Nazi, Italian, and Soviet state terror in David C. Rapoport and Yonah Alexander, eds., *The Morality of Terrorism*, 2nd ed. (New York: Columbia University Press, 1989), 127–87.

18. Quoted by J. Bowyer Bell, *On Revolt: Strategies of National Liberation* (Harvard University Press, 1976), 27.

19. Normally, Irish-Americans supported Irish rebels extensively. The Fenian movement, the principal nineteenth-century rebel force, was an American Civil War product that tried to invade Canada and hold a portion of the country "hostage" for negotiations with the British government, in the hope that would increase tensions between the United States and Britain. When those efforts were aborted, the Fenians went to Ireland hoping to spark rebellions there.

20. "The priority of Woodrow Wilson was approval of the League of Nations by the U.S. Senate [and] to make the new world order he envisaged . . . a reality, Wilson needed Britain as a staunch ally. These reasons beyond Wilson's own Ulster Presbyterian background rendered either the US political recognition of the Irish Republic, or support for nationhood before the League of Nations extremely unlikely." Francis Costello, *The Irish Revolution and Its Aftermath 1916–1923: Years of Revolt* (Dublin: Irish Academic Press, 2003), 49. Reacting to Wilson's policy, Irish-Americans aided those who were against joining the League of Nations. The Easter Rebellion (1916) was attempted with the belief that German aid was forthcoming, but Germany was unable to help. The Easter Rebellion received initially little support from the Irish public, but the tide turned in 1917 when the rebels were executed. Arthur Griffith, an Irish leader who opposed the uprising, said, "I knew the British were brutal enough to do it; I did not think they would be stupid enough. Had I foreseen that, perhaps my views on the whole matter might have been different." Dorothy McCardle, *The Irish Republic* (London: Gollancz, 1951). One major reason for the turning of the tide was the popular belief that the rebellion had convinced Britain to exclude the Irish from the Conscription Act in that year. But the need for more troops in France intensified and the effort to extend conscription to Ireland in 1918 intensified separation activities.

21. J. Bowyer Bell, *The Secret Army* (Cambridge, MA: MIT Press, 1988), 37.

22. Bell, *The Secret Army*, 169.
23. Ulick O'Connor, *Michael Collins and the Troubles* (Mainstream, 2001), 124.
24. O'Connor, *Michael Collins and the Troubles*, 4.
25. See Michael Hopkinson, *Green Against Green: Irish Civil War* (Gill & MacMillan, 1988); Edward Purdon, *Irish Civil War, 1922–1923* (Mercier, 2000).
26. While in France in 1919, Ho Chi Minh tried to end the French empire in Vietnam by petitioning Woodrow Wilson with quotations from the Declaration of Independence. Unable to obtain consideration at Versailles, he then led the anticolonial movement in Vietnam. Kim Huynh Khánh, *Vietnamese Communism, 1925–1945* (Ithaca, NY: Cornell University Press, 1982), 60.
27. John Halsted, "Comparative Historical Study of Colonial Nationalism in Egypt and Morocco," *African Historical Studies* 2, no. 1 (1969): 94.
28. The monarchy was established "to heed British advice on all matters affecting British interests and on fiscal policy as long as Iraq was linked to Britain." Helen Chapin Metz, ed., *Iraq: A Country Study* (Washington: GPO for the Library of Congress, 1988), 4; Paul Hemphil, "The Formation of the Iraq Army, 1921–33," in *The Integration of Modern Iraq*, ed., Abbas Kalidar (London: Croom Helm, 1979). See also Toby Dodge, *Inventing Iraq: The Failure of Nation-Building and a History Denied* (New York: Columbia University Press, 2003).
29. Joyce Laverty Miller, "The Syrian Revolt of 1925," *International Journal of Middle East Studies* 8, no. 4 (1977): 545–63. Miller notes that the Permanent Mandates Commission refused to accept France's initial 1925 report and discussed recalling the French Commission.
30. Miller, "The Syrian Revolt of 1925," 547–49. An interesting discussion of the difficulties in getting the Balfour Declaration is contained in Jehuda Reinharz, *Chaim Weizmann: The Making of a Statesman* (Oxford: Oxford University Press, 1993).
31. The Orthodox Church had been the major political power under the Turkish millet system for four centuries before the British arrived. The British tried to separate the church and state, taking vital powers from the church, including the right to tax. Kyriacos C. Markides, "Social Change and the Rise and Decline of Social Movements: The Case of Cyprus," *American Ethnologist* 1, no. 2 (1974): 309–30. Earlier, Cyprus had been a British base, though it was in the Ottoman Empire. After World War I, Cyprus became a British Crown Colony, and its Greek population expected that the British would eventually reunite the island with Greece.
32. Foster, *Alienation and Cooperation*, 38–39. "Comintern" is an abbreviation for Communist International, which from 1919 to 1943 intended to fight "by all available means, including armed force, for the overthrow of the international bourgeoisie and the creation of an international Soviet republic as a transition stage to the complete abolition of the State. The Comintern had seven World Congresses between 1919 and 1935. Joseph Stalin abolished it in 1943 to strengthen ties with the U.S. and UK during World War II." See Ruth T. McVey, *The Rise of Indonesian Communism* (Ithaca, NY: Cornell University Press, 1995).

33. Foster, *Alienation and Cooperation*, 296.

34. Cecil Hobbs, "Nationalism in British Colonial Burma," *Far Eastern Quarterly* 6, no. 2 (1947): 115.

35. Andrew Selth, "Race and Resistance in Burma, 1942–1945," *Modern Asia Studies* 20, no. 3 (1986): 483. Burma tried to get Chinese help, but only the Japanese were interested and helped precipitate the 1938 race riots. Tensions between ethnic groups became much more violent when Burma became a state. The largest Muslim group in Myanmar is the Rohingya people; the Rohingyas have been the most persecuted group under Myanmar's military regime. The United Nations states that the Rohingyas are one of the most persecuted groups in the world. https://www.ohchr.org/EN/NewsEvents/Pages /ReportingBackToMyanmarsRohingya.aspx.

36. The bomb droppers were Bhagat Singh and B. K. Dutt. For an interesting discussion of this issue, see Neeti Nair, "Bhagat Singh as 'Satyagrahi': The Limits to Nonviolence in Late Colonial India," *Modern Asian Studies* 43, no. 3 (2009): 649–81.

37. Political prisoners, a status rarely given especially to those who had used violence, were separated from ordinary criminals and given different food and special privileges, i.e., no hard labor, access to newspapers, etc.

38. Nair, "Bhagat Singh as 'Satyagrahi,'" 656.

39. A century after Bhagat Singh's birth, the governor of Pakistan's Punjab province established a memorial to him as the "first martyr of the subcontinent." A variety of popular films have been made about Bhagat Singh; the first was *Shaheed* (1965), and the most recent is *Rand de Basanti* (2006).

40. Brian Lapping, *End of Empire* (New York: St. Martin's, 1985), 38.

41. Mahatma Gandhi, *Selected Political Writings*, ed. Dennis Dalton (Indianapolis, IN: Hackett, 1996), 72.

42. R. Johnson, *Gandhi's Experiments with Truth: Essential Writings by and About Mahatma Gandhi* (New York: Lexington, 2005), 37.

43. The revolt was described as Arab rather than Palestinian because Palestinians were not generally seen then as a distinct entity; the Ottomans governed Iraq, Syria, and Palestine as one unit, which is why Syrians and Iraqis were involved in the activities. Recently, it has become common to speak of a Palestinian uprising. The main sources used are William F. Jabber Quandt and Ann Lesch, *The Politics of Palestinian Nationalism* (Berkeley: University of California Press, 1973); Y. Porath, *The Palestinian Arab National Movement: From Riots to Rebellion*, vol. 2 (Frank Cass, 1977); Anita Shapera, *Land and Power: The Zionist Resort to Force, 1881–1948* (Stanford: Stanford University Press, 1999); Rashid Khalidi, *The Iron Cage: The Story of the Palestinian Struggle for Statehood* (Boston: Beacon, 2006); Simon Anglim, "Orde Wingate and the Special Night Squad: A Possible Policy of Counter-Terrorism," *Contemporary Security Policy* 28, no. 7 (2007): 28–41; Tom Bowden, "The Politics of the Arab Rebellion in Palestine, 1936–39," *Middle Eastern Studies* 11, no. 2 (1973): 147–54; Kenneth Stein, "The Intifada and the 1936–9 Uprising: A Comparison," *Journal of Palestine Studies* 19, no. 4 (199): 64–85. Wingate trained 19,000

Jewish volunteers. John Newsinger, *British Counterinsurgency from Palestine to Northern Ireland* (Anthony Rowe, 2002), 4.

44. Bowden, "The Politics of the Arab Rebellion in Palestine," 149.

45. Bowden, "The Politics of the Arab Rebellion in Palestine," 148. Arabs killed 494 Arabs and 547 Jews.

46. Porath, *The Palestinian Arab National Movement*, 201.

47. In fact, only the English were targets; the Celtic areas, Scotland and Wales, did not experience attacks.

48. Bell, *The Secret Army*; Michael Smith, *Fighting for Ireland? The Military Strategy of the Irish Republican Movement* (New York: Routledge, 1995).

49. Quoted by Stephan Enno, *Spies in Ireland* (Macdonald, 1963), 38.

50. Martin David Dubin, "Great Britain and the Anti-Terrorist Conventions of 1937," *Terrorism and Political Violence* 5, no. 1 (1993): 1–28. See also Charles Townsend, "Methods Which All Civilized Opinion Must End," in *An International History of Terrorism: Western and Non-Western Experiences*, ed. Jussi Hanhimäki and Bernhard Blumenau (New York: Routledge, 2013), 34–50.

51. In a UN declaration, World War II allies pledged adherence to the Charter's principles.

52. Matthew White, "Secondary Wars and Atrocities of the Twentieth Century: India," http://necrometrics.com/20c300k.htm#India. The figures are median estimates of eight accounts.

53. Stephen Hunter and John Bainbridge Jr., *American Gunfight: The Plot to Kill Harry Truman—and the Shoot-Out That Stopped It* (New York: Simon & Schuster, 2005).

54. In 1967, Puerto Rico's governor gave Canales a full pardon.

55. All other members of the group were released too, and a member declared he was willing to do it again and would use grenades instead of bullets!

56. Sam Garrett, "Political Status of Puerto Rico: Options for Congress," *Congressional Research Service*, May 7, 2011.

57. Michael J. Cohen and Martin Kolinsky describe the British reluctance to expand military and economic resources as the Labour Party's attempt to strengthen its support among the lower classes. Michael J. Cohen and Martin Kolinsky, *Demise of the British Middle East Empire 1943–55* (Frank Cass, 1987), 36.

58. The League's last official act was expelling the Soviet Union in 1939 for invading Finland; the League officially dissolved in 1946.

59. The West described Soviet domination of the sovereign states of Eastern Europe after World War II as an empire. But the Soviet Union itself was seen as a state, not an empire, even in the West, until its surprising disintegration into separate sovereign entities, some of which generated Fourth Wave terrorist activity. See Hans Kohn, "Some Reflection," *Review of Politics* 18, no. 3 (1956): 259–62; Stephen Bowers, "Ethnic Conflict in the Soviet Commonwealth," *Low Intensity Conflict and Law Enforcement* 1, no. 1 (1992): 42–56.

60. Begin, *Revolt*, suggests that those interactions generated Soviet support in the United Nations.

61. Algerian terrorism was reprehensible to Americans, but Soviet adventurism, the necessity to decolonize, and relations with the Arab world were more significant to American policy makers.

62. Alistair Horne, *A Savage War of Peace: Algeria, 1954–1962* (New York: Viking, 1977), 243.

63. Ruth Gavison, *The Two-State Solution: The UN Partition Resolution of Mandatory Palestine—Analysis and Sources* (New York: Bloomsbury, 2013).

64. Horne, *A Savage War of Peace*, 248. Horne notes Tunisia provided the most convenient and safest route for army supplies and for troop training, resting, and operations inside Algeria; the military headquarters of the organization; an articulate ally in the international forum; and a potential bridge for negotiations with the French.

65. M. R. D. Foot's useful volume refers to terror tactics very briefly and only when discussing partisan forces in Eastern Europe supported by the Soviets dealing with a population element hostile to partisans. M. R. D Foot, *Resistance* (Eyre Methuen, 1976), 7–92. He does not discuss the problem of using terrorism to describe resistance activity. Gerard Chaliand and Arnoud Blin speak of terror by a communist resistance movement in France in 1941 in response to the transfer of five thousand Jewish prisoners to a concentration camp by killing a naval cadet "chosen at random." Oddly, they say nothing else on World War II resistance movements. Gerard Chaliand and Arnoud Blin, *History of Terrorism from Antiquity to Al-Qaeda* (Berkeley: University of California Press, 2007), 211. See the detailed obituary of Irv Refkin, an American the British and U.S. governments used to aid resistance forces during the war. Sam Roberts, "Irv Refkin, Brash Accidental Spy in World War II, Dies at 96," *New York Times*, November 7, 2017, https://www.nytimes.com/2017/11/07/obituaries/irv-refkin-brash-accidental-spy-in -world-war-ii-dies-at-96.html.

66. For a discussion of the relationship of resistance movements to postwar Western contexts, see Gabriel Almond, "The Resistance and the Political Parties of Western Europe," *Political Science Quarterly* 62, no. 4 (1947): 27–51.

67. Robert Kumamoto, "Diplomacy from Below: International Terrorism and American Foreign Relations, 1945–1962," *Terrorism* 14, no. 1 (1991): 31–38. The British were more concerned with the Palestinian situation and British casualties than with the potentialities of Soviet involvement. Palestinians complained that American policies encouraged Jewish terrorism.

68. Michael Cohen, *Palestine, and the Great Powers* (Princeton, NJ: Princeton University Press, 1982), 292.

69. Dighenis-Grivas and Foley, *Memoirs*, 149.

70. Settlers invented the name "Mau-Mau"; Africans did not have name for the group. Mau-Mau may be an anagram of the Kikuyu words *uma uma*, which means "get out, get out." James Walton, *Reluctant Rebels: Comparative Studies on Revolution and Underdevelopment* (New York: Columbia University Press, 1984), 105–6. Members of the group, especially in its later phases, sometimes called the association the Land and Freedom Army.

71. The Mau-Mau had "no hope or momentum by 1954 but sporadic episodes occurred until 1958." Bell, *On Revolt*, 103. "The Emergency" ended in 1960. It is also uncertain when

the campaign began, but the date given is usually 1952, when the first crops and native huts were burned, and the first cattle slaughtered. Bell, *On Revolt*, 94–106.

72. Cited by C. J. Alpert, "Kenya's Answer to the Mau Mau Challenge," *African Affairs* 53, no. 212 (1954): 242.

73. John Newsinger, *British Counterinsurgency from Palestine to Northern Ireland* (Anthony Rowe, 2002), 69. He adds, "What was not so well publicized were the reprisals which followed in which hundreds of suspects were killed out of hand by the police and loyalist home guards." The savage response was attributed to racism. See Susan L. Carruthers, *Winning Hearts and Minds: British Government the Media and Colonial Counterinsurgency, 1940–1960* (Leicester: University of Leicester Press, 1995).

74. Authorities overestimated the threat. Bell, *On Revolt*, 192. 1,077,600 people resettled in 854 villages by 1955. Carl Rosberg and John Nottingham, *The Myth of Mau Mau, Nationalism in Kenya* (Stanford, CA: Stanford University Press, 1966), 293.

75. Julie DaVanzo and J. Haage, "Anatomy of a Fertility Decline, 1950–1976," *Population Studies* 36, no. 3 (1982): 363. The Chinese began arriving in the fifteenth century. Indians constituted over 10 percent of the population.

76. A. J. Stockwell, "Policing During the Malayan Emergency, 1948–60: Communism, Communalism, and Decolonization," in *Policing and Decolonization: Politics, Nationalism, and the Police, 1917–65*, ed. David M. Anderson and David Killingray (Manchester: Manchester University Press, 1992), 105–26.

77. Bell, *On Revolt*, 86.

78. Horne, *A Savage War of Peace*, 94–96.

79. Bell, *The Secret Army*, 284.

80. The statement was released by the Irish Republican Publicity Bureau and signed "J. McGarrity, Secretary." Quoted in Patrick Bishop and Eamonn Mallie, *The Provisional IRA* (London: Heinemann, 1987), 45.

81. Bell, *On Revolt*, chap. 6; Haim Gerber, *Islam, Guerrilla War, and Revolution* (Lynne Reiner, 1988), chap. 3.

82. Haim Gerber, *Islam, Guerrilla War, and Revolution*, 149–50.

83. The 1974 uprising in the Portuguese homeland also inspired several Third Wave New Left student terror groups. The most important was Armed Revolutionary Action, led by a female physician, Isabel del Carmo.

84. Donald J. Alberts, "Armed Struggle in Angola," in *Insurgency in the Modern World*, ed. Bard E. O'Neill, William R Heaton, and Donald J. Alberts (Boulder, CO: Westview, 1980), 240–41.

85. For a discussion of the relationship between military and political forms that notes the special character of colonial armies, see David C. Rapoport, "A Comparative Theory of Military and Political Types," in *Changing Patterns of Military Politics*, ed. Samuel P. Huntington (New York: Free Press, 1962), 71–101. Only very recently has the United States recognized that "foreign mercenaries" may be useful for "wars of choice."

86. Horne, *A Savage War of Peace*, 51–52, 231,457, 461. French conscripts were reservists called up for limited service.

87. See "Portugal Migration," *The Encyclopedia of the Nations*, Advameg, https://www
.nationsencyclopedia.com/Europe/Portugal-MIGRATION.html; "Flight from Angola,"
Economist, August 16, 1975, https://www.economist.com/middle-east-and-africa/1975/08
/16/flight-from-angola; "Mozambique: Dismantling the Portuguese Empire," *Time*, July 7,
1975, http://content.time.com/time/magazine/article/0,9171,913229,00.html; and Eric Sol-
sten, ed., *Portugal: A Country Study—Portugal Emigration* (Washington, DC: GPO, 1993).
88. Alberts, "Armed Struggle in Angola," 253.
89. Alberts, "Armed Struggle in Angola," 256.
90. Alberts, "Armed Struggle in Angola," 257.
91. Shaloma Gauthier discusses the United Nation's unwillingness to use any term to describe
the Namibian struggle but terrorist. Both the nonstate groups and the state employed
terror. Shaloma Gauthier, "SWAPO, the United Nations and the Struggle for National
Liberation" in Townsend, "Methods Which All Civilized Opinion Must End," 169–88.
92. Gauthier, "SWAPO, the United Nations and the Struggle for National Liberation."
93. Dighenis-Grivas and Foley, *Memoirs*, appendix 1.
94. Dighenis-Grivas and Foley, *Memoirs*, 47.
95. Horne, *A Savage War of Peace*, 95.
96. Horne, *A Savage War of Peace*, 200.
97. Begin, *The Revolt*, 55–56. The Greek example Begin refers to is the communist uprising
of 1946–1949.
98. The British called them murderers, but Irish rebels described themselves "soldiers" even
in the First Wave, when other groups called themselves "terrorists." See Richard L. Clut-
terbuck, *Guerrillas and Terrorists* (Athens: Ohio University Press, 1980).
99. Nair, "Bhagat Singh as 'Satyagrahi,'" 665. Before that special incident, Singh had been
engaged in terrorist activity and was hanged by the British. It is not clear from Nair's
account whether Singh considered his earlier acts terrorist ones or simply realized they
were counterproductive and adopted a new strategy and language.
100. Lehi admired Russian and Polish revolutionary groups. See Heller, *The Stern Gang*. The
Zionist Revisionism movement established in 1925 was at odds with the main Zionist
movement on a variety of issues. In the 1940s and afterward, the Irgun, in contrast to
the main Zionist movement, represented a right-wing political orientation and aimed at
reestablishing ancient biblical boundaries for Eretz Israel, which included the West Bank,
Gaza, and Jordan.
101. Cited by Ze'ev Iviansky, "Individual Terror: Concept and Typology," *Journal of Contemporary History* 12, no. 1 (1977): 46.
102. Begin, *The Revolt*, chaps. 9–10. Begin was not the first to recognize the political value of
appropriate language. Nineteenth-century Irish rebels changed their name from the Irish
Revolutionary Brotherhood to the Irish Republican Brotherhood. Lehi argued there was
no real difference between its methods and those the British used in attempting to deal
with terror. But Begin argues that British efforts were morally inferior because they were
indiscriminate, while the Irgun was not. The term "freedom fighter" was first used by
Karl Heinzen in 1881, but he did not use it to replace the term "terrorist." Daniel Bessner

and Michael Stauch, "Karl Heinzen and the Intellectual Origins of Modern Terror," *Terrorism and Political Violence* 22, no. 2 (2010): 143–76.

103. Begin, *The Revolt.*

104. Grivas does not discuss the issue but describes EOKA's activity always as "guerrilla war," linking it with his experiences in Greek underground movements during World War II. Dighenis-Grivas and Foley, *Memoirs*, 29.

105. John Dugard, "International Terrorism and the Just War," in *The Morality of Terrorism*, 2nd ed., ed. David C. Rapoport and Yonah Alexander (New York: Columbia University Press, 1989), 77–98. The Algerian FLN called its members *fedayeen*, which comes from the Arabic word meaning "sacrifice." The term became common throughout the Islamic world, though it developed different connotations in the Fourth Wave.

106. Heller, *The Stern Gang*, 115–18. Heller notes that the two major non-Jewish inspirations for Lehi were the Russian terrorists and the terrorist Polish Socialist Party (PSP), led by Joseph Pilsudski, who had also participated in the Terrorist Faction of Narodnaya Volya.

107. For a more detailed discussion of the definition problem, see David C. Rapoport, "The Politics of Atrocity," in *Terrorism: Interdisciplinary Perspectives*, ed. Yonah Alexander and S. Finger (New York: John Jay Press, 1987), 46.

108. Dighenis-Grivas and Foley, *Memoirs*, 106. Grivas says that if he had other financial sources he would have gone ahead with the plan because it would display the "strength of the Organization on an international scale." His comment indicates that he did not fully realize the potential adverse consequences of international terror activity.

109. Horne, *A Savage War of Peace*, 257–58. Horne devotes only two pages out of 563 to the campaign, which suggests how restrained the FLN was with respect to the French population. Unsuccessful terrorist groups in the wave did not attack homelands, so while the restraint is important, it is not decisive. We do not know whether the Kenyans, Malaysians, Adenese, Indians, etc. discussed the issue.

110. Martha Crenshaw Hutchinson, *Revolutionary Terrorism: The FLN in Algeria, 1954–1962* (Stanford: Stanford University Press, 1978), 241.

111. Some uncertainty exists about the assassination's purpose, but the academic consensus is that those opposed to the treaty carried it out. Rex Taylor, *Assassination: The Death of Sir Henry Wilson and the Tragedy of Ireland* (London: Hutchinson, 1961).

112. Margery Forester, *Michael Collins: The Lost Leader* (Sedgwick and Jackson, 1971), 346–47. A third assassination victim was Vice President Kevin O' Higgins, in 1927.

113. Begin, *The Revolt*, 60.

114. Lehi planned but never made three attacks against Ernest Bevin, British minister of foreign affairs. Nachman Ben Yehuda, *Political Assassinations by Jews* (Albany: SUNY Press, 1993), 214–15. The Irgun organized a few attacks on British targets in Italy and occupied Germany. Lehi did not know that Israel and the Arab states had decided to reject the treaty, each for different reasons.

115. See J. Bowyer Bell, *Assassin* (New York: St. Martin's, 1979).

116. The *Oxford English Dictionary* defines "assassination" as "murder by treachery, surprise, or deceit." One reason the term is most often linked to prominent victims is that the word comes from the practices of the Islamic Assassins (described in chapter 2), which always were aimed at high officials.

117. Lehi made an unknown attempt on Ernest Bevin, the foreign minister, and eight unsuccessful efforts against two major figures, including a chief secretary of the British Mandate Forces and a high commissioner of Palestine. See Ben Yehuda, *Political Assassinations by Jews*, 195–206. Altogether, Lehi made forty-two assassination attempts; twenty-three were successful. Fifteen of the successful strikes, or 65 percent, were against Jews.

118. Ezer Weizmann, who later became Israel's president in 1993, was the designated leader of the 1947 effort.

119. Aden produced many assassinations. The NLF began its campaign with an attempt against the Aden high commissioner, Sir Kennedy Trevaskis (1963), who survived, but fifty-two people were wounded, inducing the British to declare a "state of emergency." Other victims were the superintendent of the police and the speaker of the house.

120. Dighenis-Grivas and Foley, *Memoirs*, 37. Grivas says an unsuccessful grenade attack was made against General Keightley's house too but does not say that this was an assassination attempt. The strikes against Harding are described on 53–54 and 68–69. An EOKA member planned the initial assassination by himself, and it is not clear from Grivas's account whether the organization authorized it. J. Bowyer Bell says that Grivas was not consulted on the final plan and opposed it because the assailants could not use the weapons properly. Bell, *Assassin*, 248–49. Afterward, EOKA did authorize an effort. Harding authorized a ten-thousand-pound reward for "my head," Grivas said, and responded by issuing a declaration proclaiming that Harding's "execution was a duty of every patriotic Greek."

121. Hutchinson, *Revolutionary Terrorism*, 90. The FLN made unsuccessful efforts to assassinate Governor General Jacques Soustelle and two other Frenchmen.

122. Bell, *On Revolt*, 97. A second victim unmentioned by Bell was a Nairobi city council member.

123. Benny Morris, *Righteous Victims: A History of the Zionist-Arab Conflict, 1881–2001* (New York: Vintage, 2001). For Irgun's account of the incident, see "The Pathway to Victory," in Begin, *The Revolt*, chap. 24.

124. Dighenis-Grivas and Foley, *Memoirs*, 72, 85.

125. Dighenis-Grivas and Foley, *Memoirs*, 34. "I intended to turn the youth of Cyprus into the seedbed of EOKA . . . and issued orders that students in both sexes should be enrolled in the Organization to distribute leaflets, watch British agents and police, and take part in demonstrations. The liveliest and bravest boys would graduate later to the fighting groups." The British novelist Lawrence Durrell, who was then teaching school in Cyprus, has an insightful and moving description of student involvements. Lawrence Durrell, *Bitter Lemons* (London: Dutton, 1957).

126. Dighenis-Grivas and Foley, *Memoirs*, 62.

127. Dighenis-Grivas and Foley, *Memoirs*, 63.

128. Dighenis-Grivas and Foley, *Memoirs*, 38. The order was circulated in 1955 after student riots materialized as the campaign's first public activity.

129. In view of the Haganah's antagonism, it is unlikely that the Irgun could have initiated a demonstration even if it had wanted to do so. In any case, Begin does not discuss demonstrations as a tool.

130. Begin, *The Revolt*, 84–85.

131. Charles Smith, "Communal Conflict and Insurrection in Palestine, 1936–48," in *Policing and Decolonization*, ed. David Anderson and D. Killingray (Manchester: Manchester University Press, 1992).

132. Charles Townshend, "Policing Insurgency in Ireland, 1914–23," in *Policing and Decolonization*, ed. David Anderson and D. Killingray (Manchester: Manchester University Press, 1992), 35–36.

133. See Yacef Saadi, *Souveneirs de la bataille d'Algiers* (Paris: R. Jourliard, 1962); Horne, *A Savage War of Peace*, chap. 9.

134. Durell, *Bitter Lemons*.

135. Bell, *The Secret Army*.

136. Bell, *The Secret Army*.

137. Horne, *A Savage War of Peace*.

138. Horne, *A Savage War of Peace*, 232–38.

139. Roger Trinquier made the best case for the effectiveness of torture: Roger Trinquier, *Modern Warfare: A French View of Counterinsurgency* (New York: Praeger, 1964). See also Pierre Videl-Naquet, *Torture: The Cancer of Democracy* (New York: Penguin, 1963). "Speaking to his comrade Lukashevich, Ulyanov [Lenin's older brother] said 'when society's most vital interests are in jeopardy, in a situation of depressing inequality between the rival sides, then the weak side must take to desperate means. The Irish, too, were forced to resort to dynamite.'" Ze'ev Ivianski, "The Moral Issue: Some Neglected Aspects of Individual Terror," in *The Morality of Terrorism*, 2nd ed., eds. David C. Rapoport and Yonah Alexander (New York: Columbia University Press, 1989), 230.

140. Dighenis-Grivas and Foley, *Memoirs*, 3.

141. Horne, *A Savage War of Peace*, 221–22.

142. The assassination put the group on the political map, especially after the assassins affirmed their deed in court. "At last Lehi has martyrs of its own. It was the execution which gave the assassination its true meaning." Heller, *The Stern Gang*, 139. The assassination infuriated Winston Churchill, who had considerable sympathy for the Zionist cause. Curiously, the event did have a "positive" momentary effect for Lehi in Egypt.

143. Initially, Haganah cooperated with the British and handed over Lehi members, though it did not abuse them.

144. Beyond that, killing other Jews was wrong, and the Irgun lacked the strength to wage a successful struggle.

145. Quoted by Michael Ben-Zohar, *Ben-Gurion: A Biography* (London: Weidenfeld, 1979), 129. At a Paris press conference, Ben-Gurion defending the decision to abandon diplomacy, saying "the acts of the British Government are a continuation of an expression of Hitler's policy hostility."

146. Eric Silver, *Begin, the Haunted Prophet* (New York: Random House, 1984), 82. Lehi and Irgun had brought forty thousand refugees to Palestine between 1938 to 1944.

147. Irgun members wore British uniforms when attacking British troops and thus were not guerrillas.

148. Begin wrote that if he pursued the effort to reclaim all of Eretz Israel, a civil war among Jews would occur. Since by far most Jews supported the Israeli Labor Party's partition plan, the Irgun would probably have been decimated. Begin's argument, however, is historical; namely, Jews should not spill Jewish blood and risk repeating the disaster of the Zealots two thousand years before; Begin, *The Revolt*, 31. Although the book was written years after he made the decision, I find his explanation credible. In a 1972 interview I had with him, he vigorously repeated it.

149. Thirty thousand Palestinian Jews fought in World War II; virtually all were Haganah members, and many were trained in partisan warfare, adding to the Irgun's difficulties.

150. No one was charged with the deed, and the imprisoned received amnesty. Thirty years later, after the statute of limitations expired, some former Lehi members acknowledged involvement. The assassination created tensions between Sweden and Israel; the Swedes thought the Israeli government had authorized the assassination, which added to their revulsion because the Israelis knew Sweden had played a crucial role in giving refuge to many potential Holocaust victims and survivors. Beyond that, Count Bernadotte was the major figure in an attempt to get Germany to transfer concentration camp inmates to Sweden, but Lehi fraudulently described him as an anti-Semite. The Israeli government disbanded Lehi afterward. Yitzhak Shamir, who had helped organize the assassination and was imprisoned for a short time afterward, became Israel's prime minister thirty-five years later. The painful breach was partially healed in a Tel Aviv ceremony in May 1995 attended by the Swedish deputy prime minister. Israeli foreign minister Shimon Peres issued a "condemnation of terror, thanks for the rescue of the Jews and regret that Bernadotte was murdered in a terrorist way. We hope this ceremony will help in healing the wound." Donald Macintyre, "Israel's Forgotten Hero: The Assassination of Count Bernadotte—and the Death of Peace," *The Independent*, September 18, 2008, https://www.independent.co.uk/news/world/middle-east/israels-forgotten-hero-the -assassination-of-count-bernadotte-and-the-death-of-peace-934094.html.

151. "Use of Children in the War Since 1998," *Angola—Forgotten Fighters: Child Soldiers in Angola* 15, no. 10(A), Human Rights Watch, http://www.hrw.org/reports/2003 /angola0403/Angola0403-03.htm.

152. Irish rebels made overtures to the Russians during the Crimean War and again in 1870 when another war with Russia seemed imminent. They sought German help during World War I and in 1939, before World War II.

4. THE THIRD WAVE: NEW LEFT, 1960s–1990s

1. Alfred Sauvy, "Three Worlds One Planet," *L'Observateur* no. 118, August 14, 1952; Leslie Wolf-Phillips, "Why 'Third World'? Origin, Definition, and Usage," *Third World Quarterly* 9, no. 4 (October 1987): 1311–27. Wolf-Phillips provides a very interesting discussion of the term.

2. When West Germany joined NATO, the Soviet Union asked if it could become a member, but NATO refused, fearing the Soviets would undermine the alliance.

3. Roberta Goren, *The Soviet Union and Terrorism*, ed. Jillian Becker (London: George Allen & Unwin, 1985), 80–84.

4. Charles Wright Mills, a prominent sociologist, popularized the term in C. Wright Mills, "Letter to the New Left," *New Left Review* 5 (1960).

5. Direct action occurs when a group takes an action that is intended to reveal an existing problem, highlight an alternative, or demonstrate a possible solution to a social issue. The American anarchist Voltairine de Cleyre wrote an essay called "Direct Action" in 1912 that is widely cited. Voltairine de Cleyre, *The Voltairine De Cleyre Reader*, ed. A. J. Brigati (Chico, CA: AK, 2004).

6. "Students for a Democratic Society (SDS)," Public Broadcasting Service (PBS)—Oregon Public Broadcasting, http://www.pbs.org/opb/thesixties/topics/politics/newsmakers_1 .html.

7. "Students for a Democratic Society (SDS): Port Huron Statement," *The Sixties Project*, June 5, 1962, https://history.hanover.edu/courses/excerpts/111huron.html.

8. Bill Ayers, Mark Rudd, Bernardine Dohrn, Jeff Jones, Terry Robinson, Gerry Long, Steve Tappis, et al., "You Don't Need a Weatherman to Know Which Way the Wind Blows," *New Left Notes*, June 18, 1969, 8.

9. "Report of the Subcommittee to Investigate the Administration of the Security Act and Other Internal Security Laws of the Committee of the Judiciary," U.S. Senate Judiciary Committee (Government Printing Office, 1975), 5, 8–9, 13, 18, 137–47.

10. Castro's campaign was a guerrilla one and targeted the army. But there were some terrorist incidents. The most important occurred when Castro took around fifty American hostages to prevent the Cuban dictator Batista from bombing Castro's forces.

11. Louis A. Pérez, *Cuba and the United States: Ties of Singular Intimacy* (Athens: University of Georgia Press, 2003).

12. "Growth of Investments in Cuba, 1958," *Gente* 1, no. 1, American ed. (January 5, 1958), Cuban Information Archives, https://cuban-exile.com/doc_226-250/doc0234-22.html.

13. Edward George, *The Cuban Intervention in Angola, 1965–1991: From Che Guevara to Cuito Cuanavale* (London: Frank Cass, 2005), 18.

14. This part of the agreement was secret because the presence of the missiles had never been publicly revealed.

15. President Lyndon B. Johnson, "President's Message to Congress, August 5, 1964," in *U.S. Congress, Senate, Committee on Foreign Relations, 90th Congress, 1st Session, Background*

Information Relating to Southeast Asia and Vietnam, 3rd ed. (Washington, DC: U.S. Government Printing Office, 1967), 120–22.

16. It is interesting that while Castro's own uprising was a guerrilla war where only military targets were struck, he was now supporting terrorist campaigns. See Hugh Thomas, *Cuba, or The Pursuit of Freedom* (Boston: De Capo, 1998); Peter Bourne, *Fidel: A Biography of Fidel Castro* (New York: Dodd Mead, 1986); Leycester Coltman, *The Real Fidel Castro* (New Haven, CT: Yale University Press, 2003); and "Section 6: 'USA: The Main Target'" and "Section 7: 'The Basic Goal—More Vietnams or a Tricontinental Basis,'" in *The Tricontinental Conference of African, Asian and Latin American Peoples: A Staff Study Prepared for the Subcommittee to Investigate the Administration of the Internal Security Act and Other Internal Security Laws of the Committee on the Judiciary United States Senate*, U.S. Congress, Senate Committee on the Judiciary, Subcommittee to Investigate the Administration of the Internal Security Act and Other Internal Security Laws (Washington, DC: U.S. Government Printing Office, 1966).

17. "The 1966 Solidarity Conference of the Peoples of Africa, Asia and Latin America," *Legacies of the Tricontinental*, https://www.tricontinental50.net/tricontinental-conference.

18. George, *The Cuban Intervention in Angola*, 18.

19. Pamela Falk, "Cuba in Africa," *Foreign Affairs* 65, no. 3 (1987): 1077–96.

20. Goren, *The Soviet Union and Terrorism*, 80–84.

21. The Korean War (1950–1953) was bloodier than the Vietnam conflict. It ended with an armistice agreement that separated North and South Korea, but no peace treaty was ever created, and over 25,000 American troops have remained in South Korea ever since the violence stopped.

22. Bernard Greiner, *War Without Fronts: The USA in Vietnam* (New Haven, CT: Yale University Press, 2009).

23. Seth Jones and Martin Libicki, *How Terrorist Groups End: Lessons for Countering al-Qa'ida* (Santa Monica, CA: RAND Corporation, 2008), 19. I used the RAND-MIPT database presented by Jones and Libicki, which covers the period from 1968 to 2006. It lists only the 648 groups that are no longer in existence. The number includes many not in the Third Wave: government-sponsored, right-wing, single-issue, and Second Wave and Fourth Wave ones. I separated the Third Wave groups; there were 403 in the database. The wave began eight years earlier, but the groups in that period were not added to the total. A study of all the groups, including ones still active in the ITERATE database, was made by Karen Rasler and William R. Thompson, "Looking for Waves of Terrorism," *Terrorism and Political Violence* 21, no. 1 (2009): 28–41. The figure for the entire period included ones still active. The number altogether is 1,483, but we eliminated 216 Fourth Wave entities. Other groups are classified as having unknown purposes, as right-wing, as single issue, or as state-organized groups. The number of New Left groups is even greater than the number attributed to the secessionist category because the authors included Second Wave secessionist groups still in the field when calculating the secessionist number. The estimate is made by examining the number of acts described in Edward F. Mickolus et al., *International Terrorism: Attributes of Terrorist Events,*

1968–2014 (Dunn Loring: Vinyard Software, 2015), http://gsg.uottawa.ca/iterate /iterate-e.html.

24. Nicola Miller, "The Historiography on Nationalism and Nationalist Identity in Latin America," *Nations and Nationalism* 12, no. 2 (2006): 203.

25. Gabriela Martinez-Cortes, Joel Salazar-Flores, Laura Gabriela Fernandez-Rodriguez, et al., "Admixture and Population Structure in Mexican-Mestizos Based on Paternal Lineages," *Journal of Human Genetics* 57, no. 9 (2012): 568–74.

26. The Maoist Sendero Luminoso (Shining Path) had roots in Peru's indigenous populations but refused to make contacts with outsiders, even other terrorist groups. The Guatemalan National Revolutionary Unity had sanctuaries in neighboring states and got significant support from Castro's Cuba and foreign groups but made no effort to rouse indigenous populations elsewhere. The Zapatistas in Mexico's most southern state, Chiapas, whose population was one-third Mayan, with kinsmen in neighboring states, sought no outside help. It aimed to synthesize Mayan practices with Marxist principles, transforming Mexico in the process. Two years later, Mexico gave Chiapas, dominated by the Zapatistas, significant autonomy.

27. Guido Panvini, "The Legitimation of Latin American Guerrilla Warfare in the Italian Radical Catholicism and in the Extra Parliamentary Left Wing," in *Revolutionary Violence and the New Left*, ed. A. M. Alvarez and E. R. Tristan (London: Routledge, 2017).

28. The Peruvian priest Gutiérrez coined the term. Over time, liberation theology grew into an international and interdenominational movement. For discussions of liberation theology, see G. Gutierrez, *A Theology of Liberation* (New York: Orbis, 1973); D. Tombs, *Latin American Liberation Theology* (Leiden: Brill, 2003); Kruijt Berryman, A. M. Alvarez, and E. Cortina, "The Genesis and Internal Dynamics of El Salvador's People's Revolutionary Army, 1970–1976," *Journal of Latin American Studies* 46, no. 4 (2014): 663–89.

29. Kruijt Berryman, *Liberation Theology: Essential Facts About the Revolutionary Movement in Latin America and Beyond* (Philadelphia: Temple University Press, 1988), 22–24.

30. Panvini, "The Legitimation of Latin American Guerrilla Warfare."

31. V. Garrard-Burnett, *Terror in the Land of the Holy Spirit: Guatemala Under General Efrain Rios Montt, 1982–1983* (Oxford: Oxford University Press, 2011); Paul Bastrop and Steven Leonard Jacobs, eds., *Modern Genocide: The Definite Resources and Document Collections* (Santa Barbara, CA: AB-CLIO, 2015), 2:877–996.

32. Jane Alpert, *Growing Up Underground* (New York: William Morrow, 1975), 122.

33. Bob Woodward, *The Secret Wars of the CIA, 1981–87* (New York: Pocket Books, 1987), 470–71.

34. John Bowyer Bell, "The Profile of A Terrorist: a Cautionary Tale," In *International Terrorism*, ed. C. Bauman (New York: St. Martin's, 1974).

35. The name came from Kurt Held, *Die Rote Zora und hire Bande* (Aarau: Sauerlander, 2003), which tells the story of a red-haired Croatian girl called Red Zora who leads a gang of orphans committed to dealing with injustices.

36. Christopher Hewitt, *The Effectiveness of Anti-Terrorist Policies* (Lanham, MD: University Press of America, 1986); P. Arthur, "Reading Violence: Ireland," in *The Legitimation of Violence*, ed. David Apter (New York: New York University Press, 1997), 14.

37. Michel Wieviorka, "ETA and Basque Political Violence," in *The Legitimation of Violence*, ed. David Apter (New York: New York University Press, 1997), 336.

38. Carrie Hamilton, *Women and ETA: The Gender Politics of Radical Basque Nationalism* (Manchester: Manchester University Press, 2007).

39. The Kurdish community contains many different religions and creeds, probably more than any other Middle Eastern community.

40. Aliza Marcus, *Blood and Belief: The PKK and the Kurdish Fight for Independence* (New York: New York University Press, 2007), 172–78. Marcus provides a very interesting discussion of the role of women in the PKK. Despite the PKK example, when a rural group moved to urban areas, it rarely changed its recruiting pattern, as the Whites' discussion of PIRA shows: Robert White and Terry Falkenberg White, "Revolution in the City: Resources of the Urban Guerrilla," *Terrorism and Political Violence* 3, no. 4 (1991): 100–33.

41. "Eritrean Peoples Liberation Front (EPLF)," Terrorism Research and Analysis Consortium (TRAC), https://www.trackingterrorism.org/group/eritrean-peoples-liberation-front-eplf.

42. A. J. Jongman provides statistics from 1968 to 1988 from several data sources. A. J. Jongman, "Trends in International and Domestic Terrorism in Western Europe, 1968–1988," *Terrorism and Political Violence* 4, no. 4 (1992): 41.

43. The figures come from the RAND Database of Worldwide Terrorist Incidents. Most of the 8,008 incidents are unclaimed. Databases classify an event as a bombing when the attack is on facilities and buildings.

44. Robert White, "The Irish Republican Army: An Assessment of Sectarianism," *Terrorism and Political Violence* 9, no. 1 (1997): 36. For a brief discussion of the problem, see also White and White, "Revolution in the City," 130n27.

45. John Bowyer Bell, *The Gun in Politics: An Analysis of Irish Political Conflict, 1916–1986* (Piscataway, NJ: Transaction, 1987), 51.

46. Glenn Frankel, "Havel Details Sale of Explosive to Libya," *Washington Post*, March 23, 1990.

47. Gene Shanahan, ed., *Influence on RAF Marighella, Mini-Manual of the Urban Guerrilla* (Seattle: Documentary Publications, 1985), 15. For discussion of Marighella's organization and tactics, see J. Becker, *Hitler's Children: The Story of the Baader-Meinhof Gang* (St. Albans: Grenada, 1979), 214–15, 465–89. His influence on the Red Brigades is noted by Allison Jamieson, "Entry, Discipline, and Exit in the Italian Red Brigades," *Terrorism and Political Violence* 2, no. 1 (1990): 1–4. Marighella also founded Ação Libertadora Nacional (ALN, National Liberation Action) in Brazil in 1967. Abraham Guillen was another important contributor to the urban guerrilla literature. He was an intellectual mentor for the Tupamaros and wrote *The Strategy of the Urban Guerrilla*, which played an important role in the activities of urban guerrillas in Uruguay, Argentina, and Brazil.

48. The movement was named after the revolutionary Túpac Amaru II, who in 1780 led an indigenous revolt against the Viceroyalty of Peru.

49. Alexus G. Grynkewich, "Welfare as Warfare: How Violent Non-State Terrorists Use Social Services to Attack the State," *Studies in Conflict and Terrorism* 31 (2008): 359.

50. For a useful brief discussion of the Tupamaro social service efforts and how it compares with the more prominent social service efforts of Islamic Fourth Wave groups, see Arturo Porzecanski, *Uruguay's Tupamaros: The Urban Guerrilla* (New York: Praeger, 1973).

51. Mickolus, *International Terrorism*. The fourteen-year period Mickolus discusses includes incidents by religious groups in the first two years of the Fourth Wave, discussed in the next chapter. A hostage incident often involved a number of hostages.

52. Richard Gillespie, *Soldiers of Peron: Argentina's Montoneros* (Oxford: Clarendon, 1982), 212n8.

53. Brian Jenkins, *International Terrorism: A New Kind of Warfare* (Santa Monica, CA: Rand Corporation, 1974), 4.

54. James Adams, *The Financing of Terror* (New York: Simon & Schuster, 1989), 94. For a good discussion of various problems associated with allowing corporations to pay ransoms to get hostages released, see Brian M. Jenkins, "Should Corporations Be Prevented from Paying Ransoms?" RAND Paper Series, RAND Corporation, 1974.

55. One striking and profitable bank-robbing incident occurred. In 1976, the PLO together with its bitter enemy, the Christian Phalanges, hired safecrackers to loot major bank vaults in Beirut. Estimates of the funds stolen are between $50 and $100 million. "Whatever the truth the robbery was large enough to earn a place in the *Guinness Book of Records* as the biggest bank robbery of all time." Adams, *The Financing of Terror*, 192.

56. Andrew Alderson, "The Truth About Shergar Race Horse Kidnapping," *Telegraph*, January 27, 2008, https://www.telegraph.co.uk/news/uknews/1576718/The-truth-about-Shergar-racehorse-kidnapping.html.

57. Martha Crenshaw's analysis of the rational reasons for different terrorist tactics is a valuable contribution to the literature. Martha Crenshaw, "The Logic of Terrorism: Terrorist Behavior as a Product of Strategic Choice," in *Origins of Terrorism*, ed. Walter Reich (Cambridge: Cambridge University Press, 1990), 7–24.

58. For a very useful discussion of the negotiation process, see Guy Olivier Faure and I. William Zartman, eds., *Negotiating with Terrorists* (London: Routledge, 2010). For an interesting discussion of hostage taking during the 1970s that highlights political as opposed to economic demands, see Clive C. Aston, "Political Hostage Taking in Western Europe: A Statistical Analysis," in *Perspectives on Terrorism*, ed. Lawrence Freedman and Y. Alexander (Wilmington, DE: Scholarly Resources, 1983), 99–130. See also Todd Sandler, "Terrorist Success in Hostage Taking Incidents: An Empirical Study," *Journal of Conflict Resolution* 31, no. 1 (1987): 35–53; and Paul Wilkinson, "Hostage-Taking, Sieges and Problems of Response" in *Terrorism Versus Democracy* (London: Frank Cass, 2000), 137–56.

59. Sixty-five other Palestinians were released.

60. Reuven Pedatzur, "The Slippery Slope of Prisoner Swaps," *Haaretz*, October 19, 2011, https://www.haaretz.com/1.5201293.

61. Clive Aston, *A Contemporary Crisis* (Westport, CT: Greenwood, 1982), 49. Aston provides a very useful discussion of the Munich event.

62. Abu Iyad and Eric Rouleau, *My Home, My Land: A Narration of the Palestinian Struggle* (New York: Times Books, 1981), 106–11.

63. Bruce Hoffman, *Inside Terrorist Organizations* (New York: Columbia University Press, 1998), 75.

64. Mickolus, *International Terrorism*. The demand success ratio is 45.08 percent (international) to 4.8 percent (domestic). The international shootout percentage is 15.53 as opposed 7.06. In international situations, no demand is met 35.23 percent of the time, as opposed to 13.6 percent of the time in domestic ones. The fourteen-year period includes two in which religious groups participated.

65. Anthony Depalma, "Pierre Vallieres, 60, Angry Voice of Quebec Separatism, Dies," *New York Times*, December 28, 1998, http://www.nytimes.com/1998/12/26/world/pierre-vallieres-60-angry-voice-of-quebec-separatism-dies.html.

66. Jones and Libicki, *How Terrorist Groups End*, 109.

67. The description is based on the ANC account to the Truth and Reconciliation Commission established by the government after the struggle was completed: http://www.stanford.edu/class/history48q/Documents/EMBA.

68. Sean Anderson and Stephen Sloan, *Historical Dictionary of Terrorism* (Lanham, MD: Scarecrow, 1995), 136.

69. In 1800, President George Washington paid Barbary pirates 20 percent of the federal government's annual revenues!

70. Michael B. Oren, "The Middle East and the Making of the United States. 1776 to 1815," speech delivered at Columbia University, November 3, 2005. Pirates are considered *hostis humani generis* (enemies of humanity), an international norm. After the Cold War was concluded, piracy revived partly because the seas were not as closely patrolled as they had been earlier. For a discussion of the relationship between terrorism and piracy, see Mikkel Thorup, "Enemy of Humanity: The Anti-Piracy Discourse in Present-Day Anti-Terrorism," *Terrorism and Political Violence* 20, no. 3 (2009): 401–11. The French call an airplane hijacker an "air pirate," a term many used in the English-speaking world as well, largely in the Third Wave's earlier phase. See, for example, James Arey, *The Sky Pirates* (London: Ian Allan, 1973); Peter M. Jacobson, "Piracy on the High Seas to Piracy in the High Skies," *Cornell International Law Journal* 5, no. 2 (1972); Peter St. John, *Air Piracy, Airport Security, and International Terrorism* (Westport, CT: Quorum, 1991).

71. Anna Geifman, *Thou Shalt Kill: Revolutionary Terrorism in Russia, 1894–1917* (Princeton, NJ: Princeton University Press, 1993).

72. As indicated earlier, the attackers pocketed much money at this stage of the campaign.

73. Obviously, these hijackings were generated by political circumstances, but since their purpose was to enable individuals to travel out of the county, they are not considered hijackings for political purposes.

74. Jin-Tai Choi, *Aviation Terrorism: Historical Survey, Perspectives, and Responses* (Stuttgart: Macmillan, 1994), 24.

75. Robert Holden, "The Contagiousness of Aircraft Hijacking," *American Journal of Sociology* 91, no. 4 (1985): 874.

76. Choi, *Aviation Terrorism*, 12–13.

77. Peter St. John, "The Politics of Aviation Terrorism," *Terrorism and Political Violence* 10, no. 3 (1998): 32.

78. Choi, *Aviation Terrorism*, 44.

79. Holden, "The Contagiousness of Aircraft Hijacking," does not give precise statistics for political extortion in Europe, but his descriptions and my own sense of the scene justify the picture of contagiousness the text presents.

80. Holden, "The Contagiousness of Aircraft Hijacking," 47. The hijackers were unexpectedly held in custody.

81. Holden, "The Contagiousness of Aircraft Hijacking," 47.

82. Choi, *Aviation Terrorism*, 23.

83. Choi, *Aviation Terrorism*, 8. Choi's figures for airplanes bombed in flight are twenty-three for the period as opposed to seven for the four years before. However, the upsurge in sabotage bombings really began in 1967, and if one puts 1967 in the period of concern, the figure would be twenty-seven as opposed to three.

84. Choi, *Aviation Terrorism*, 42.

85. David Phillips, *Skyjack: The Story of Air Piracy* (London: Harrap, 1973), 130–31.

86. Phillips, *Skyjack*, 173.

87. The observer status allows one to participate in debates but not vote. At present, the Holy See (Vatican) and Palestine are the only observer states at the United Nations.

88. In the first seven years of Palestinian hijacking, forty-three planes were taken; in the next ten years after Arafat's declaration, twelve were seized. Choi, *Aviation Terrorism*, 43.

89. Jeffrey D. Simon, *The Terrorist Trap: America's Experience with Terrorism*, 2nd ed. (Bloomington: Indiana University Press, 2001), 110–19.

90. Elaine Sciolini, "U.N. Unanimously Condemns Hostage-Taking," *New York Times*, December 19, 1985, https://www.nytimes.com/1985/12/19/world/un-unanimously-condemns-hostage-taking.html. Two events two months earlier induced the Soviets to join in pushing the resolution: the PLF hijacking of the Italian ship *Achille Lauro* and a kidnapping of four Soviet diplomats in Beirut, a Fourth Wave incident. The Soviets then supported the UN denunciation of the *Achille Lauro* incident.

91. Michael K. Bohn, *The Achille Lauro Hijacking: Lessons in the Politics and Prejudice of Terrorism* (Sterling, VA: Potomac, 2004), 6–7.

92. The Syrians recovered the body and sent it to the United States, where eight hundred people attended his burial. At first the PLO claimed his wife killed Klinghoffer to collect insurance but twelve years later apologized and paid Klinghoffer's children for the murder. The *Achille Lauro* hijacking has inspired a number of dramatic retellings. There were two TV movie dramas in 1989 and 1990. A popular and controversial opera,

The Death of Klinghoffer, was composed by John Adams and Alice Goodman in 1991, which has been modified and cancelled several times. On June 2014, the New York Metropolitan Opera cancelled an international simulcast and radio broadcast of Adam's opera out of "an outpouring of concern" that it "might be used to fan global anti-Semitism." For an interesting discussion of the tensions the event generated, see David C. Wills, *The First War on Terrorism: Counter-Terrorism Policy During the Reagan Adminis-tration* (Lanham, MD: Rowman and Litchfield, 2003), chap. 5. See also Zachary Woolfe, "Opera Under Fire," *New York Times*, October 19, 2013, who explains why all the changes made did not convince many that the presentations were all justifications for terrorism.

93. Tore Bjerga, *Maritime Terrorism: A Threat to Shipping and the Oil Industry?* (Oslo: Norwegian Institute of International Affairs, 1991), 9. Bjerga discusses 145 cases of ships and oil installations attacked from 1970 to 1985.

94. Brian Jenkins, *Embassies Under Siege: A Review of Forty-Eight Embassy Takeovers, 1971–1980* (Santa Monica, CA: RAND Corporation, 1981). Jenkins's very interesting systematic discussion does not use wave categories. He includes three other embassy attacks made in 1979 by Iranian religious elements, incidents we excluded here but will discuss in the next chapter. Thirty-one assaults were made against embassies and ten against other diplomatic offices.

95. As indicated earlier, thirteen years later Kozo Okamoto was among 1,150 prisoners released in the Jibril Agreement for three soldiers captured in the First Lebanon War.

96. Faure and Zartman, *Negotiating with Terrorists*, 18.

97. Paul A. Jureidini, "Review of Assassination in Khartoum," *Middle East Quarterly* 1, no. 4 (1994). In all cases, the hostage takers demanded free passage out of the country, but when Sudan refused their request the individuals involved became the only ones to turn themselves in, probably because they knew that the Sudanese government was sympathetic to the Palestinian cause.

98. Carlos was prominent in seven novels: Frederick Forsyth's *The Day of the Jackal*, Charles Lichtman's *The Last Inauguration*; Robert Ludlum's Bourne Trilogy; Tom Clancy's *Rainbow Six*, and Aline Griffith's *The Well Mannered Assassin*. He was portrayed in several films, including Mexico's *Carlos el Terrorista* (1979), *True Lies* (1994), *The Assignment* (1997), *The Jackal* (1997), *Terror's Advocate* (2007), and Denmark's *Blekingegadebanden* (2009). He has also been a subject in numerous television series.

99. Jennifer G. Schirmer, *The Guatemalan Military Project: A Violence Called Democracy* (Philadelphia: University of Pennsylvania Press, 1998), chaps. 1 and 2. The government claimed a Molotov cocktail used by a hostage taker was responsible.

100. The tactic, however, retained some attraction when Fourth Wave groups came on the scene The total number for the two decades was thirty-eight; most were carried out by religious groups.

101. C. J. M. Drake, "The Role of Ideology in Terrorists' Target Selection," *Terrorism and Political Violence* 10, no. 2 (1998): 53–85.

102. Emphasis added. R. Catanzaro, ed., "Subjective Experiences and Objective Reality: An Account of Violence in the Words of the Protagonists," in *The Red Brigades and Left-Wing Terrorism in Italy* (London: Palgrave Macmillan, 1991), 190–91.

103. "Rote Armee Fraktion, RAF-Auflosungserklarung," *rafinfo.de*, March 1998, http://www.rafinfo.de/archiv/raf/raf/20-4-98/php.

104. Quoted by Yonah Alexander and Dennis Pluchinsky, *Europe's Red Terrorists: The Fighting Communist Organizations* (London: Routledge, 1991), 31n9. The businessmen assassinated were Ernst Zimmerman, head of an aero-engineering company (1985); Karl Beckurts, a manager at Siemens, an engineering company (1986); Detley Karsten Rohwedder, the chief of a powerful trust that controlled the state-owned assets from East Germany and charged with privatizing them (1991). The two hostage killings occurred in 1977: Jurgener Ponto, chairman of Dresdner Bank, was killed in a botched attempt to make him a hostage, and Hanns-Martin Schleyer, chairman of the German Employers' Organization and a former SS officer, was killed when the government would not negotiate, and the RAF prisoners were discovered dead in their cells.

105. Allison Jamieson, *The Heart Attacked: Terrorism and Conflict in the Italian State* (London: Marion Boyars, 1989), 108. An attempt was also made to assassinate General Alexander Haig, the NATO supreme commander, in 1979.

106. Jamieson, *The Heart Attacked*, 32.

107. "31 Turkish Diplomats Killed by Armenian Groups," *World Bulletin*, April 26, 2015, http://www.worldbulletin.net/headlines/158358/31-turkish. The most significant Armenian group, the Armenian Secret Army for the Liberation of Armenia (ASALA), sought to make Turkey surrender territory for an Armenian state.

108. Drake, C. J. M, "The Role of Ideology in Terrorists' Target Selection," *Terrorism and Political Violence* 10, no. 2 (1998): 10. Note the explanation of Gerry Adams, vice president of Sinn Fein: "The IRA gave clear reasons for the execution. I think it is unfortunate that anyone has to be killed, but the furor created by Mountbatten's death showed up the hypocritical attitude of the media establishment. As a member of the House of Lords, Mountbatten was an emotional figure in both British and Irish politics. What the IRA did to him is what Mountbatten had been doing all his life to other people; and with his war record I don't think he could have objected to dying in what was clearly a war situation. He knew the danger involved in coming to this country. In my opinion, the IRA achieved its objective: people started paying attention to what was happening in Ireland." Quoted by Louisa Wright, "Clearly a War Time Situation," *Time*, November 19, 1979.

109. John Bowyer Bell, *The Secret Army: A History of the IRA, 1916–79*, 4th ed. (Dublin: Revised Poolbeg, 1990), 248; Gerry Adams, *The Politics of Irish Freedom* (Dublin: Brandon, 1986), 128–36.

110. The British held PIRA captives as "political prisoners" but revoked that status in March 1976. William Whitelaw, who granted it in the first place, later ranked that act as one of his "most regrettable decisions."

111. Sheila Rule, "I.R.A. Says It Killed Tory M.P. in Britain," *New York Times*, August 1, 1990, https://www.nytimes.com/1990/08/01/world/ira-says-it-killed-tory-mp-in-britain .html.

112. See George Kassimeris, "Fighting for Revolution? The Life and Death of Greece's Revolutionary Organization, 1975–2002," *Journal of Southern Europe and the Balkans* 6, no. 3 (2004) 259–72; and George Kassimeris, *Europe's Last Red Terrorist: The Revolutionary Organization* (London: Hurst, 2001).

113. Two other Greek groups, even smaller than 17N, emerged in the period, with similar aims but different tactics: the Revolutionary People's Struggle (ELA) and Revolutionary Struggle (EA). They used bombing as their principal tactic. ELA lasted until 2003. EA began in 2003, and its last known act was a rocket fired at the U.S. embassy in Athens (2007). It has not yet caused fatalities.

114. In 1999 President Clinton apologized on the behalf of the U.S. government for supporting the military junta because of Cold War considerations.

115. As indicated in the discussion of the Cyprus case in the Second Wave, EOKA attempted to overturn the Cypriot government to reunite the island with Greece, which prompted the Turkish army to arrive to protect Turkish Cypriots.

116. Kassimeris, "Fighting for Revolution?," 261.

117. Douglas Frantz, "2004 Olympics Might Force Greece to Attack Terrorism. Games in Athens Could Become a Security Nightmare," *SFGate*, January 7, 2001, http://www .sfgate.com/news/article/2004-Olympics-Might-Force-Greece-to-Attack-2967090.php.

118. "Misc. English Newspapers, 11-12-1974," baader-meinhof.com, http://www.baader -meinhof.com/11-12-1974-germans-order-extra-security-ny-times/.

119. "Hunger Strikes 1980–1981," *BBC News*, https://www.bbc.co.uk/bitesize/guides/zx49cj6 /revision/6.

120. B. Lynn, "Sands, ('Bobby') Robert (b. 1954) Republican Activist; 1981 Hunger Strike; Anti-H-Block MP April 1981—May 1981," *CAIN Web Service—Conflict and Politics in Northern Ireland*, Ulster University, January 5, 2003, https://cain.ulster.ac.uk/othelem /people/biography/speople.htm.

121. Terrence O'Keeffe, "Suicide and Self-Starvation," *Philosophy* 59, no. 229 (1984): 349–63.

122. "Britain's Gift to Bobby Sands," *New York Times*, April 29, 1981, https://www.nytimes .com/1981/04/29/opinion/britain-s-gift-to-bobby-sands.html.

123. Peter H. Merkl, "West German Left-Wing Terrorism," in *Terrorism in Context*, ed. M. Crenshaw (University Park: Penn State University Press, 1995), 199–202. Merkl also emphasizes that West German terrorists saw American behavior in Vietnam as very similar to that of the Nazis.

124. Jeffrey Simon, *Revolutions Without Guerrillas* (Santa Monica, CA: RAND Corporation, 1989).

125. The term "Naxalite" derives from a village in West Bengal where the movement began. For an interesting discussion of its history, see Dipak Gupta, "The Naxalites and the Maoist Movement in India: Birth, Demise, and Reincarnation," *Democracy and Security* 3, no. 2 (2007): 157–88.

126. Bernhard Blumenau, "But We Have a Chance! West Germany's Efforts Against International Terrorism at the U.N. in the 1970s," in *An International History of Terrorism: Western and Non-Western Experiences*, ed. Jussi Hanhimäki and Bernhard Blumenau (London: Routledge, 2013). Blumenau has an interesting discussion of West Germany's role in helping transform UN attitudes.

127. The two anticolonial cases in Namibia and the Portuguese Empire also described as "freedom fighter" efforts are Second Wave cases even though they occurred in the Third Wave era.

128. In addition to four UN conventions, there are eight other major multilateral terrorism conventions, starting with the Tokyo Convention of 1963, dealing with the aircraft safety. UN Office of Counter-Terrorism, "International Legal Instruments," https//www.un.org /counterterrorism/international-legal-instruments.

129. The name TREVI alludes to the fountain in Rome where the committee founding the organization first met. But the French gave TREVI the name to illustrate its purpose.

130. Stephen D. Collins, "Dissuading State Support of Terrorism: Strikes or Sanctions? An Analysis of Dissuasion Measures Employed Against Libya," *Studies in Conflict and Terrorism* 27, no. 1 (2004): 1–18.

131. H. Brands, *Latin America's Cold War* (Cambridge, MA: Harvard University Press, 2010), 123.

132. Brands, *Latin America's Cold War*, 97.

133. Brands, *Latin America's Cold War*, 102.

134. Brands, *Latin America's Cold War*, 102.

135. Vladimir Hernandez, "Jose Mujica: The World's 'Poorest' President," *BBC News Magazine*, November 14, 2012, https://www.bbc.co.uk/news/magazine-20243493; Jonathan Watts, "Uruguay's President José Mujica: No Palace, No Motorcade, No Frills," *Guardian*, December 13, 2013, https://www.theguardian.com/world/2013/dec/13/uruguay -president-jose-mujica.

136. Jones and Libicki, *How Terrorist Groups End*.

137. D. Kruijt, *Guerrillas: War and Peace in Latin America* (London: Zed, 2009), 41.

138. Karim Hauser, "Nicaragua and Iran, 'Invincible Union,'" *BBC World News*, June 11, 2007, http://news.bbc.co.uk/hi/spanish/latin_america/newsid_6741000/6741829.stm.

139. "Amnesty International Documents Armed Attack on Students in Nicaragua," *Amnesty International*, May 28, 2018, https://www.amnestyusa.org/press-releases/amnesty -international-documents-armed-attack-on-students-in-nicaragua/; Delphine Schrank, "Rights Commission Condemns Abuses During Nicaragua Protests," Reuters, May 21, 2018, https://www.reuters.com/article/us-nicaragua-protests/rights-commission -condemns-abuses-during-nicaragua-protests-idUSKCN1IM267.

140. Daniel Silva Fernandez and Flora Charner, "Protests on Nicaragua's Mother's Day Turn Deadly," CNN, June 1, 2018, https://www.cnn.com/2018/05/31/americas/nicaragua -mothers-day-deadly-violence/index.html.

141. "Nicaragua llega a 100 días de conflicto con 448 muertos y una economía a la baja," *Agencia EFE*, July 28, 2018, https://www.efe.com/efe/espana/mundo/nicaragua-llega-a-100 -dias-de-conflicto-con-448-muertos-y-una-economia-la-baja/10001-3703089.

142. "Nicaraguan Leader Daniel Ortega's Brother Calls on Him to End Violence," *BBC News*, July 28, 2018, https://www.bbc.com/news/world-latin-america-44992306.

143. Frances Robles, "In Nicaragua, Protests Lead to Life on Run," *New York Times*, December 25, 2018.

144. S. J. Rosen, "Kuwait Expels Thousands of Palestinians," *Middle East Quarterly* 9, no. 4 (2012): 76–83.

145. Several years earlier, the *New York Times* described the ANC as "one of the least successful liberation movements."

146. Racial discrimination had been common for 250 years, since the Dutch began to settle in the area. But in 1948 it was institutionalized, when apartheid was established, touching every aspect of social life and designed inter alia to strip nonwhites of their South African citizenship. Gandhi developed his policy of nonviolent resistance known as Satyagraha (devotion to the truth) initially in South Africa to protest the treatment of Indian immigrants. Nelson Mandela, the ANC's most prominent leader and a Gandhi disciple, authorized a statue honoring Gandhi's achievements in 2003 in Johannesburg.

147. "African National Congress Timeline 1980–1989," *South Africa History Online*, https://www.sahistory.org.za/article/african-national-congress-timeline-1980-1989; Anthea Jeffery, *People's War: New Light on the Struggle for South Africa* (New York: Ballantine, 2010).

148. See Stephen Zunes, "The Role of Non-Violent Action in the Downfall of Apartheid," *Journal of Modern African Studies* 37, no. 1 (1999): 137–69; I. W. Wink, *Violence and Non-Violence in South Africa: Jesus' Third Way* (Gabriola: New Society, 1988); Robert Ross, *A Concise History of South Africa* (Cambridge: Cambridge University Press, 1999).

149. The historic ANC alliance with the South African Communist Party and the Congress of South African Trade Unions has special qualities. The communists and trade unions have not contested any election; they field candidates through the ANC and hold senior ANC positions affecting party policy and dialogue.

150. Norimitsu Onish, "$21 Million in Assets Seized in South African Corruption Inquiry," *New York Times*, April 16, 2018.

151. B. Sengupta, "Senior Guerrilla Leaders Tied to Acts of Persecution after Civil War," *New York Times*, July 29, 2014.

152. Oleg Yasinsky, "Sexual Revolution: Sputnik Exclusive on FARC's Female Fighters," *Sputnik News*, May 9, 2016, https://sputniknews.com/latam/201609051044995272-farc-female-fighters/.

153. Nicholas Casey, "Waging War from a Hotel Basement: Colombian Rebels Offer Hostages and Ask for Talk," *New York Times*, August 24, 2018.

154. Casey, "Waging War from a Hotel Basement."

155. Alanne Orjoux and Lauren Said-Moorhouse, "ELN Claims Responsibility for Bogota Car Bomb That Killed 20 at a Police Academy," CNN, January 21, 2019; Pablo Beltran, "Exclusive Interview with Pablo Beltrán, Chief Negotiator of Colombia's ELN," interview by Claudia Korol, *Peoples Dispatch*, February 9, 2019, https://peoplesdispatch.org/2019/02/09/exclusive-interview.

156. Stephanie Nohlen, "Colombia at Odds with Cuba Over Extradition of Leftist Group Leaders," *Globe and Mail*, April 28, 2019, https://www.theglobeandmail.com/world /article-colombias-eln-problem-threatens-a-return-to-full-blown-violence/.

157. On August 28, 2019, almost three years after the rebels signed a peace deal, Ivan Marquez, a former commander of FARC, issued in a video a new call to arms because of what he called the government's violations of the peace agreement. It is not clear yet whether the call will end the agreement. Nicholas Casey and Lara Jakes, "Colombia's Former FARC Guerrilla Leader Calls for Return to War," *New York Times*, August 29, 2019, https://www.nytimes.com/2019/08/29/world/americas/colombia-farc-rebel-war .html.

5. THE FOURTH WAVE: RELIGIOUS, 1979–2020s?

1. Daniel Politi, "Argentina Designates Hezbollah Terrorist Group on 25th Anniversary of Bombing," *New York Times*, July 18, 2019, https://www.nytimes.com/2019/07/ 18/world/americas/argentina-hezbollah-terrorist-group.html. Eighty-five people were killed in the two attacks in Buenos Aires. Hezbollah also struck Israeli embassies in Asia.

2. Kim Willsher, " 'Carlos the Jackal' Goes on Trial in France," *Los Angeles Times*, November 9, 2011, https://www.latimes.com/world/la-xpm-2011-nov-07-la-fg-francejackal-trial -20111108-story.html.

3. The major exception was the Jewish Defense League (JDL), which focused largely in the U.S. and Canada. Rabbi Meir Kahane its founder moved to Israel where the group operated for a few years before becoming Kach. The JDL began its operations before the Fourth Wave emerged.

4. Ministry of Defense, Democratic Socialist Republic of Sri Lanka, "Humanitarian Operation-Factual Analysis: July 2006–May 2009," July 2011, https://www.globalsecurity .org/military/library/report/2011/sri-lanka-mod-humanitarian-op_20110801.pdf.

5. The Sikh diaspora in Canada may have been involved. C. C. Fair, "Diaspora Involvement in Insurgencies: Insights from the Khalistan and Tamil Eelam Movements," *Nationalism and Ethnic Politics* 11, no. 1 (2005): 25–36. Although the circumstantial evidence seems clear that a Sikh group committed the act, no one has been convicted.

6. The Russian government never identified the gas employed, and foreign scientists generally think it was one of the two mentioned. Mia Bloom, *Bombshell* (London: Penguin, 2011), chap. 2, provides an interesting description of the incident.

7. "International Criminal Court: Situation in Uganda," https://www.icc-cpi.int/uganda, June 23, 2007.

8. Shaul Shay, *Islamic Terror Abductions in the Middle East* (Eastbourne: Sussex Academic Press, 2007).

9. Seth Mydans, "Kurilovo Journal: From Village Boy to Soldier, Martyr and, Many Say, Saint," *New York Times*, November 21, 2003.

10. The National Movement for the Restoration of Pakistani Sovereignty captured Pearl. A Pakistani court convicted Ahmed Omar Saeed Sheikh, an al-Qaeda member, for organizing the beheading.

11. My original articles on the four waves provide a general picture, which is developed in more detail here. The original thesis was tested and confirmed by scholars subsequently. See Kristopher K. Robison, Edward M. Crenshaw, and J. Craig Jenkins, "Ideologies of Violence: The Social Origins of Islamist and Leftist Transnational Terrorism," *Social Forces* 84, no. 4 (June, 2006): 2009–26; James J. F. Forrest, "Kidnapping by Terrorist Group: Ideology, Geography and Victims," International Studies Association Conference, San Diego, CA, April 3, 2012, states that my distinction between Third and Fourth Wave tactics is borne out by a detailed examination of the cases recorded in the Global Terrorism Data Base.

12. Forrest, "Kidnapping," 15.

13. "Heated Debate Over Palestinian Prisoners in Israel," *BBC News*, July 6, 2011, https://www.bbc.com/news/world-middle-east-13989989.

14. Shireen Khan Burki, "*Haram* or *Halal*? Islamists' Use of Suicide Attacks as *Jihad*," *Terrorism and Political Violence* 23, no. 4 (2011): 587.

15. The Abrahamic religions (Judaism, Christianity, and Islam) condemn suicide and exalt martyrdom for the same reason; i.e., your life does not belong to you. The decision to call the tactic "suicide bombing" is another example of the common tendency to reshape language when discussing terrorism.

16. Robert Pape, "The Strategic Logic of Suicide Terrorism," *American Political Science Review*, 97 no. 3 (2003): 343–61; Mia Bloom, *Dying to Kill: The Allure of Suicide Terror* (New York: Columbia University Press, 2005); Mohammad Hafez, "Martyrs Without Borders: The Puzzle of Transnational Suicide Bombers," in *The Ashgate Research Companion to Political Violence*, ed. Marie Breen-Smyth (London: Routledge, 2012).

17. Bloom, *Dying to Kill*, 21.

18. The suicide attack of September 11 highlights this fact and was an event in a class by itself; 2,996 were killed, including 372 foreign nationals from sixty-one countries. Sixty-seven UK citizens were killed, more than in any previous terrorist incident. "Countries That Lost Citizens on 9/11," *Brilliant Maps*, September 11, 2015, https://brilliantmaps.com/9-11-victims/.

19. U.S. Office of Technology Assessment, "Adjusting to a New Security Environment: The Defense Technology and Industrial Base Challenge," February 1991, http://www.princeton.edu/~ota/disk1/1991/9101_n.html, 57.

20. Alex Schmid, *Handbook of Terrorism Research* (London: Routledge, 2001), 461. See also Milton Leitenberg and Raymond A. Zilinskas, *The Soviet Biological Weapons Program* (Cambridge, MA: Harvard University Press, 2012).

21. Robert Kisala, "1999 and Beyond: The Use of Nostradamus' Prophecies by Japanese Religions," *Japanese Religions* 23, no. 1 (1998): 143–57; Ian Reader, *Religious Violence in Contemporary Japan: The Case of Aum Shinrikyo* (Honolulu: University of Hawai'i Press, 2000), 50–52.

22. Bruce Hoffman, *Inside Terrorist Organizations* (New York: Columbia University Press, 1999), 94–95. In the same year, I argued the view that "WMD would replace the bomb went wildly against the facts" and that "the bomb would remain the principal terrorist weapon." David C. Rapoport, "Terrorism and Weapons of the Apocalypse," *National Security Studies Quarterly* 5, no. 1 (1999): 49–67. Hoffman changed his mind a year later. Oliver Roy, Bruce Hoffman, Reuven Paz, Steven Simon, and Daniel Benjamin, "America and the New Terrorism: An Exchange," *Survival* 42, no. 2 (2000): 156–72.

23. Osama Bin Laden, "Conversations with Terror," interview by Rahimullah Yusufzai (December 24, 1998), *Time*, January 11, 1999. Rolf Mowatt-Larssen provides an interesting discussion of the issue in Rolf Mowatt-Larssen, "Al Qaeda's Pursuit of Weapons of Mass Destruction Threat: Hype or Reality?" Belfer Center for Science and International Affairs, Harvard Kennedy School, 2010, https://www.belfercenter.org/sites/default/files/legacy/files/al-qaeda-wmd-threat.pdf.

24. Yoni Fighel and Moshe Marzouk, "Saudi Cleric Issues *Fatwah* on the Use of Weapons of Mass Destruction," The International Institute for Counterterrorism Herzliya, May 7, 2003, https://www.ict.org.il/Article.aspx?ID=881#gsc.tab=0. A *fatwah* is a nonbinding but authoritative legal opinion or learned interpretation that a qualified jurist, or mufti, can give on issues pertaining to Islamic law.

25. Jonathan B. Tucker, "The Role of the Chemical Weapons Convention in Countering Chemical Terrorism," *Terrorism and Political Violence* 4, no. 1 (2012): 107.

26. Damien Cave and Ahmad Fadam, "Iraqi Militants Use Chlorine in 3 Bombings," *New York Times*, February 21, 2007, https://www.nytimes.com/2007/02/21/world/middleeast/21cnd-baghdad.html.

27. In the United States, over three thousand municipal water treatment plants were inspected to make sure that the chlorine was well protected. Charlie Savage, "Chlorine Attacks Spur Warnings in the U.S.," *Boston Globe*, July 24, 2007, http://archive.boston.com/news/nation/washington/articles/2007/07/24/chlorine_attacks_in_iraq_spur_warnings_in_us/.

28. Sammy Alama and Lydia Hansell, "Does Intent Equal Capability? Al Qaeda and Weapons of Mass Destruction," *Non-Proliferation Review* 12, no. 3 (2005): 615–53. The authors consulted scientific authorities at the Center for Non-Proliferation Studies of the Monterey Institute for International Studies.

29. The plot took place in the early 1990s, and the participants were the first people convicted under the Biological Weapons and Anti-Terrorism Act of 1989. A year later, the police entered the Covenant, Sword, and Arm of the Lord commune in Arkansas and discovered thirty-three gallons of cyanide there. It aimed to poison the water supplies of several cities to expedite the coming of the Messiah.

30. Much Christian Identity literature, including *The Turner Diaries*, was found at the site.

31. Rajneeshee, a Hindu commune in The Dalles, Oregon, launched the largest bioterrorist attack in American history in 1984. It used salmonella to poison restaurant salad bars, produce in grocery stores, and doorknobs. No one died, but 751 were injured. The object was to incapacitate many voters to enable Rajneeshee candidates to win a local election.

Jonathan B. Tucker, ed., *Toxic Terror: Assessing Terrorist Use of Chemical and Biological Weapons* (Cambridge, MA: MIT Press, 2000), 115–38.

32. If one looked at the history of states employing chemical and biological weapons, one ould conclude that so far they have not been as effective as conventional ones. Rapoport, "Terrorism and Weapons of the Apocalypse," n12. The argument was based on a study of the unproductive efforts states experienced in their efforts to employ chemical and biological weapons, matters that presented even more obstacles for terrorist groups making their efforts. The article does not deal with the nuclear issue. Anne Stenersen concludes the internet has no value for those aiming to use WMD. Anne Stenersen, "The Internet: A Virtual Training Camp," *Terrorism and Political Violence* 20, no. 2 (2008): 215–33.

33. See Rollie Lal and Brian A. Jackson, "Change and Continuity in Terrorism Revisited: Terrorist Tactics, 1980–2002," in Memorial Institute for the Prevention of Terrorism (MIPT) Terrorism Annual (Oklahoma City: National Memorial Institute for the Prevention of Terrorism, 2006), 3–18, http://web.archive.org/web/20090210144856 /http://www.mipt.org/pdf/2006-MIPT-Terrorism-Annual.pdf.

34. Initially, the government portrayed the abuses as isolated incidents, but the Red Cross, Amnesty International, and Human Rights Watch, after multiple investigations, con- cluded they were not. "Amnesty International Annual Report 2006: The State of the World's Human Rights," Amnesty International, https://www.amnesty.org/download /Documents/POL1000012006ENGLISH.PDF.

35. Dianne Feinstein, "Let's Finally Close Guantanamo," *New York Times*, November 4, 2015, https://www.nytimes.com/2015/11/05/opinion/lets-finally-close-guantanamo.html.

36. Bin Laden's dedication reads "Pledge, O Sister: To the sister believer whose clothes the criminals have stripped off. To the sister believer whose hair the oppressors have shaved. To the sister believer whose body has been abused by the human dogs. Covenant, O Sister . . . to make their women widows and their children orphans."

37. It took time for the desire to become more efficient by studying the tactics of groups outside one's own tradition. If one compares bin Laden's work with Faraj's *Neglected Duty*, a work written at the beginning of the Fourth Wave to justify the assassination of President Sadat of Egypt (1981), the two authors seem to be in different worlds. Al-Farida al-gha'iba Faraj, *The Neglected Duty*, trans. Johannes Jansen (New York, 1986). Faraj cites no experience outside the Islamic tradition, and his most recent historical reference is to Napoleon's invasion of Egypt. The first copy was found by police in an English home in 2000. An edited version is on the Department of Justice website. Osama bin Laden, "The al-Qaeda Manual," obtained by the U.S. Department of Justice in 2000, https://www .justice.gov/sites/default/files/ag/legacy/2002/10/08/manualpart1_1.pdf. David C. Rapo- port, "Sacred Terror: A Case from Contemporary Islam," in *Origins of Terrorism*, ed. Walter Reich (Cambridge: Cambridge University Press, 1990).

38. Alisa Stack-O'Connor, "Lions, Tigers, and Freedom Birds: How and Why the Liberation Tigers of Tamil Eelam Employ Women," *Terrorism and Political Violence* 19, no. 1 (2007): 43–63.

39. Bloom, *Bombshell*; Bloom, *Dying to Kill*, 23. The woman's real name was Samira Ahmed Jassim.

40. Courtney E. Martin, "(Female) Suicide Bombers," *Huffington Post*, August 12, 2008, https://www.huffpost.com/entry/female-suicide-bombers_b_116773.

41. The magazine was named after al-Khansaa Bint Omar, a female poet of the pre-Islamic period who converted to Islam during the time of Muhammad and is considered to be the "mother of the *Shahida* (martyrs)." When her four sons died in the battle of al-Qadisiyyah, she did not mourn but thanked Allah for honoring her with their deaths. The PKK had a series of female attacks starting in 1996 in Turkey, but it was a Third Wave group. The effort in France was thwarted, but the French gave no details about where the woman came from, how the plot was thwarted, or what happened to the woman afterward. TRISA, "Threat Tactics Report: Islamic State of Iraq and the Levant," https://info.publicintelligence.net/USArmy-TRISA-ISIL.pdf.

42. TRISA, "Threat Tactics Report."

43. Bassem Mroue, "Female Suicide Bomber in France One of Many Throughout History," *CTV News*, November 19, https://www.ctvnews.ca/world/female-suicide-bomber-in5 -france-one-of-many-roughout-history-1.2665462.

44. Ami Pedahzur, William Eubank, and Leonard Weinberg, "The War on Terrorism and the Decline of Terrorist Group Formation," *Terrorism and Political Violence* 14, no. 3 (2002): 141–47.

45. Nathan Gonzalez, *The Sunni-Shia Conflict* (Orange County, CA: Nortia, 2009).

46. Maryam Mazavy, "Sikh Militant Movements in Canada," *Terrorism and Political Violence* 18, no. 1 (2006): 79–93.

47. David C. Rapoport, "Comparing Militant Fundamentalist Movements and Groups," in *Fundamentalisms and the State*, ed. Martin Marty and Scott Appleby (Chicago: University of Chicago Press, 1993), 429–61.

48. The name was taken from an Indian terror group in the First Wave fighting for national independence.

49. "Scholars and historians on both sides . . . agree that from the late 1960s to the mid-1980s the [Muslim] Brotherhood benefited from the Israeli government's support of non-violent Islamist Palestinian factions, believing they would be a useful counterweight to the secular nationalist Palestinian groups." Matthew Levitt, *Hamas: Politics, Charity, and Terrorism in the Service of Jihad* (New Haven, CT: Yale University Press, 2006), 24.

50. George Michael, "The Revolutionary Model of Dr. William L. Pierce," *Terrorism and Political Violence* 15, no. 3 (2003): 76. Michael notes that "although the current 'war on terror' has had a chilling effect on far-right activists, who fear the government's campaign could turn inward against them, 9/11 seems to have emboldened the National Alliance which demonstrated a penchant for street activism, including demonstrations at the Israeli Embassy to protest American and Israeli policies in the Middle East and nationwide distribution of literature to coincide with Jewish holidays and 9/11."

51. Michael Durham, "The American Far Right and 9/11," *Terrorism and Political Violence* 15, no. 2 (2003): 99.

52. Henry Schuster, "An Unholy Alliance," CNN, March 29, 2005, https://www.cnn.com /2005/US/03/29/schuster.column/.

53. Mazavy, "Sikh Militant Movements in Canada," 85–86.

54. See David Wilkinson, *Deadly Quarrels: Lewis F. Richardson and the Statistical Studies of Wars* (Berkeley: University of California Press, 1980), 87–91, 112.

55. Rapoport, "Comparing Militant Fundamentalist Movements and Groups," 446. When secular wars involve identity issues or the survival of the contending parties, as in World War II, they exhibit a similar intensity.

56. Natalie Davis, "The Rites of Violence: Religious Riot in Sixteenth-Century France," *Past & Present* 59, no. 1 (1973): 51–91.

57. Salman al-Odeh, "Saudi Cleric Salman al-Odeh: Jews Use Human Blood for Passover Matzos, the Holocaust 'Has Been Turned Into a Myth of Tremendous Proportions,'" interview on Rotana Khalijiya TV, *Memri*, August 13, 2012, https://www.memri.org /reports/saudi-cleric-salman-al-odeh-jews-use-human-blood-passover-matzos -holocaust-has-been-turned.

58. Jereon Adam, Kristof Titeca, Bruno De Cordier, and Koen Vlassenroot, "In the Name of the Father? Christian Militantism in Tripura, Northern Uganda, and Ambon," *Studies in Conflict and Terrorism* 30, no. 11 (2007): 963–84. In Uganda the Lord's Resistance Army describes itself as Christian and is one of the most indiscriminate groups in the wave. But it has other native religious elements that seem more dominant and is not an underground group in the sense we have been using the term.

59. Ayaan Hirsi Ali, "The War Against Christians," *Newsweek*, February 13, 2012, https:// www.newsweek.com/ayaan-hirsi-alithe-global-war-christians-muslim-world-65817.

60. The first two are the acceptance of Muhammad and prayers five times daily; the fourth and fifth are fasting during Ramadan and a pilgrimage to Mecca..

61. James Adams, *The Financing of Terror* (New York: Simon and Schuster, 1986), 192. Adams mentions charitable financing only with respect to the PLO.

62. "The Charter of Allah: The Platform of the Islamic Resistance Movement," in *The 1988–1989 Annual on Terrorism*, trans. Raphael Israeli, ed. Y. Alexander and H. Foxman (Norwell: Kluwer Academic, 1990), https://fas.org/irp/world/para/docs/880818.htm.

63. Matthew Levitt, "Hamas from Cradle to Grave," *Middle East Quarterly* 11, 1 (2004): 3.

64. Levitt, "Hamas from Cradle to Grave," 9.

65. "No Cash For Terror: Convictions Returned in Holy Land Case," U.S. Federal Bureau of Investigation, November 25, 2008, https://archives.fbi.gov/archives/news/stories/2008 /november/hlf112508.

66. Fletcher Baldwin Jr., "Introduction: Organized Crime—Terrorism and Money Laundering in the Americas," *Florida Journal of International Law* 3, no. 4 (2002): 15.

67. Evan Kohlmann, "The Role of Islamic Charities in International Terrorist Recruitment and Financing," DIIS Working Paper no. 2006/7, Danish Institute for International Studies, 2006, 2–3.

68. Jennifer Lynn Bell, "Terrorist Abuse of Non-Profits and Charities: A Proactive Approach to Preventing Terrorist Financing," *Kansas Journal of Law and Public Policy* 17, no. 3 (2008): 451.

69. AQAP attempted at least three unsuccessful efforts to bomb airliners over U.S. cities. On May 22, 2012, it organized a suicide bomber attack in Yemen's capital, killing over one hundred Yemenites.

70. In the Iran-Iraq War, Shi'a forces were on both sides, but Sunni-led Iraq aimed to take advantage of Iran's turmoil.

71. Martin Marty and Scott Appleby, "Introduction," in *Fundamentalisms and the State*, ed. Martin Marty and Scott Appleby (Chicago: University of Chicago Press, 1993), 3.

72. John Bowyer Bell, *On Revolt* (Cambridge, MA: Harvard University Press, 1976), 108. See also Christina Harris, *Nationalism and Revolution in Egypt: The Role of the Muslim Brotherhood* (Leiden: The Hague, 1964), chaps. 5–6. Besides guerrilla activities, the Brotherhood, according to Bell, did engage in at least three acts of terror in the period, two assassinations and the slaughter of twenty Egyptian Jews after Israel gained its independence.

73. Z. Munson, "Islamic Mobilization, Social Movement Theory, and the Egyptian Muslim Brotherhood," *Sociological Quarterly* 42, no. 4 (2001): 487–510. Alexus Grynkewich, "Warfare as Welfare: How Violent Non-State Groups Use Social Services to Attack the State," *Studies in Conflict and Terrorism* 31, no. 4 (2008): 354. Eli Berman, "Hamas, Taliban and the Jewish Underground: An Economist's View of Radical Religious Militias," National Bureau of Economic Research Working Paper 10004 (2003), http://www.nber.org/papers/w10004.

74. See Mahdi Khalaji, "The Dilemmas of Pan-Islamic Unity," *Current Trends in Islamist Ideology* 9 (2009): 68–72. Ultra-Orthodox Jews in the period planted explosives at the Ministry of Education, protesting efforts to secularize North Africa immigrants, but that was an isolated incident, not part of a campaign.

75. David Lesch, *1979: The Year That Shaped the Modern Middle East* (Boulder, CO: Westview, 2001). In earlier discussions of the four waves, I neglected the importance of the Camp David Treaty.

76. The chief groups were the People's Mujahedin of Iran (MEK) and the Fida'iyan-I Khalq. See Evand Abrahamian, "The Guerrilla Movement in Iran, 1963–1977," *Meria Reports*, March–April 1986, 3–15.

77. Charles Kurzman, *The Unthinkable Revolution in Iran* (Cambridge, MA: Harvard University Press, 2004), 102.

78. The United States criticized the shah's government at the time for its poor human rights record and unwillingness to push for substantial democratic reform. Since the United States was the Iranian government's principal benefactor, this criticism probably meant the United States would not protect the regime in the event of a sustained uprising.

79. A number of studies discuss this misunderstanding of the crucial importance of religion. Robert Jervis, *Why Intelligence Fails: Lessons from the Iranian Revolution* (Ithaca, NY: Cornell University Press, 2010); William Sullivan, *Mission to Iran* (New York: Norton, 1981); George Sick, *All Fall Down: America's Tragic Encounter with Iran* (New York: Random House, 1985). Sullivan was the ambassador to Iran and Sick a National Security Council member.

80. Baqer Moin, *Khomeini: Life of the Ayatollah* (New York: St. Martin's, 2009), 228.

81. Robert F. Worth, "Death of Iranian Cleric Could Set Off New Protests," *New York Times*, December 21, 2009, https://www.nytimes.com/2009/12/21/world/middleeast/21cleric .html.

82. *Time* designated Khomeini as its Man of the Year. "Ayatullah Khomeini, Man of the Year," *Time*, January 7, 1980, http://content.time.com/time/covers/0,16641,19800107,00. html.

83. Rouhollah K. Ramazani, "Constitution of the Islamic Republic of Iran," *Middle East Journal* 34, no. 2 (1980): 181–4.

84. Rouhollah K. Ramazani, *Revolutionary Iran: Challenge and Response in the Middle East* (Baltimore, MD: John Hopkins University Press, 1986).

85. The fatwa was lifted in 1998 but restored in 2012 after a movie on the internet depicting the Prophet Muhammad unfavorably led to attacks on American embassies in the Islamic world. Salman Rushdie describes his experiences underground in Salman Rushdie, *Joseph Anton: A Memoir* (New York: Random House, 2012).

86. In the 1920s, the Shi'a, upset because the new arrangements did not give them equality, rebelled in Iraq, Saudi Arabia, Bahrain, Kuwait, etc. But the revolts were brief, and the Shi'a seemed resigned to their fate, especially in Saudi Arabia, where a virulently anti-Shi'a Wahhabi view inspired governments. Ibrahim Fouad, *The Shia of Saudi Arabia* (London: Saqi, 2006), 70–71, notes that intermarriage among Sunnis and Shi'as in Saudi Arabia is highly restricted; that the Shi'a developed their own sense of social solidarity, distinct from the Sunni community; and that Shi'a university students do not mingle with their sectarian counterparts on campus.

87. Joseph Kostiner, "Shia Unrest in the Gulf," in *Shiism, Revolution, and Revolution*, ed. Martin Kramer (Boulder, CO: Westview, 1987), 174. For an interesting discussion of the Iranian Revolution's effects on Sunni extremism in the Middle East, see Emmanuel Sivan, "Sunni Radicalism in the Middle East and the Iranian Revolution," *Journal of Middle East Studies* 21, no. 1(1994): 1–30.

88. James Piscatori, "Religion and *Realpolitik*: Islamic Responses to the Gulf War," in *Islamic Fundamentalisms and the Gulf Crisis*, ed. James Piscatori (Chicago: American Academy of Arts and Sciences, 1991), 1–28. For a discussion of the Hazara and the challenges they faced as a minority during the twentieth century, see Sayed Askar Mousavi, *The Hazaras of Afghanistan: An Historical, Cultural, Economic, and Political Study* (Surrey: Curzon, 1998).

89. Egypt's isolation ended when it joined Iraq in the Iran-Iraq War and transformed it into an Arab-Persian war.

90. Piscatori, "Religion and *Realpolitik*," 1–28. In the run-up to the Gulf War (1990), after Iraq invaded Kuwait, Hussein connected Israel's occupation of Palestine with Saudi-U.S. cooperation. His aim was to create a gap between the Arab governments and governments elsewhere that supported the UN resolution for a coalition against Iraq.

91. Chris P. Ioannides, "The PLO and the Islamic Revolution in Iran," in *The International Relations of the Palestine Liberation Organization*, ed. Augustus Richard Norton and Martin H. Greenberg (Carbondale: Southern Illinois University Press, 1989), 74.

92. The most familiar of these events to a Western audience was the Mahdi uprising in the Sudan in the late nineteenth century, resulting in the murder of the legendary British general "Chinese" Gordon. Not all Islamic millenarian movements begin at the moment of a new century. Some forty years before the Sudan uprising, the Babi movement emerged in Iran to employ terror at existing governments; when it failed to achieve its objective, it transformed itself into the Baha'i movement, which became pacifist. In a sense, the pattern has been repeated a number of times in Christian millenarian movements: the Anabaptists, Mennonites, etc. Ironically, terror and pacifism both reject the conventional standards for regulating or employing violence.

93. Yaroslav Trofimov, *The Siege of Mecca: Forgotten Uprising in Islam's Holiest Shrine and the Birth of Al Qaeda* (New York: Doubleday, 2007). The year 1979 was also when Abdallah Azam created the structure that later became al-Qaeda. For a discussion of the history of Islamic millenarianism, see Ali Shaukat, *Millenarian and Messianic Tendencies in Islamic History* (Hainesport: United, 1993).

94. The degree and nature of American help is unclear. Most commentators think that it was extremely significant. But *The 9/11 Commission Report* says the common view is mistaken because the United States supplied "little or no assistance." *Final Report of the National Commission on Terrorist Attacks Upon the United States*, National Commission on Terrorist Attacks Upon the United States, July 22, 2004, https://www.9-11commission .gov/report/911Report.pdf, 45. Marc Sageman reconciles the two conflicting claims, and as a foreign intelligence officer who served in Afghanistan when the Soviets were the chief enemy, his description seems authoritative. He says U.S. aid was "significant" but funneled through Pakistani intelligence (ISID) and that the United States had no direct contact with the foreign volunteers. Marc Sageman, *Understanding Terrorist Networks* (Philadelphia: University of Pennsylvania Press, 2004), 56.

95. Many causes contributed to the disintegration of the Soviet Union, a fascinating problem, but one we cannot discuss here. While the Islamic view alluded to here is an exaggeration, there can be little doubt that the humiliating defeat in Afghanistan was a significant element.

96. *The 9/11 Commission Report* discusses the problem, as does *The Crowe Commission Report* in 1999 that investigated al-Qaeda bombing attacks against American embassies in Kenya and Tanzania in 1998. Admiral William J. Crowe, "Press Briefing on the Report of the Accountability Review Boards on the Embassy Bombings in Nairobi and Dar es Salaam," January 8, 1999, https://fas.org/irp/threat/arb/990108_emb_rpt.html. I first became aware of the government policy when friends at RAND told me that contracts had been cancelled. Scott Stewart, a member of a commission investigating the 1993 World Trade Center bombing, said the State Department "abolished my office . . . since terrorism was over." Scott Stewart, "The Myth of the End of Terrorism," *Stratfor Worldview*, https://worldview.stratfor.com/article/myth-end-terrorism. The academic world exhibited a similar pattern. As discussed in the introduction to this volume, the terrorism article in the first edition of the *Encyclopedia of the Social Sciences* (1933) declared that terrorism was a feature of the past and unlikely ever to be revived,

convincing those who edited the next edition (1968) that another article on the subject was not needed.

97. See Martha Crenshaw, "Why America? The Globalization of Civil War," *Current History* 100, no. 650 (2001): 425–32. For a systematic discussion of the data relating to international targets, see Eric Neumayer and Thomas Plumper, "International Terror and the Clash of Civilizations," *British Journal of Politics* 39 (2016); Thomas Plumper and Eric Neumayer, "The Friend of My Enemy Is My Enemy: International Alliances and International Terrorism," *European Journal of Political Research* 49, no. 1 (2010): 75–96; Eric Neumayer and Thomas Plumper, "Foreign Terror on Americans," *Journal of Peace Research* 48, no. 1 (2011): 3–17.

98. Ian Reader, "Specters and Shadows: Aum Shinrikyo and the Road to Megiddo," *Terrorism and Political Violence* 14, no. 1 (2003): 47–168.

99. The World Islamic Front issued the declaration, and it was signed by five people associated with al-Qaeda representing different organizations.

100. Al-Zawahiri's group Islamic Jihad in Egypt conducted the attacks.

101. Michael Barletta, "Chemical Weapons in the Sudan: Allegations and Evidence," *Nonproliferation Review* 6, no. 1 (1998): 5–48.

102. Lawrence Wright, *Looming Tower* (New York: Knopf, 2006), 322–31. Seven years later, Sudan was deemed partly responsible, and Sudanese assets were seized to compensate the sailors and their families. Apprehending the assailants took over a decade.

103. Sometimes, as various Balkan movements illustrate, national identity involved members from different states. The same process is evident among the Kurds. The Kashmir case has a special quality in that Pakistani and Kashmir identities are both involved.

104. Strikes on American soil began in 1993 with a partially successful effort on the World Trade Center. A mission to strike on the millennial celebration night in 2000 was aborted, but these strikes were not clearly related to al-Qaeda.

105. Begin's Irgun in the Second Wave initially had the same territorial objective but did not visualize a land governed by religious law. He gave up territorial claims for fear of provoking a Jewish civil war.

106. Ami Pedahzur and Arie Perlinger, *Jewish Terrorism in Israel* (London: Routledge, 2011), 50. Emphasis added.

107. David C. Rapoport, "Fear and Trembling: Terrorism in Three Religious Traditions," *American Political Science Review* 78, no. 3 (1984): 658–77.

108. Richard Chasdi, *Serenade of Suffering: A Portrait of Middle East Terrorism, 1968–1993* (Washington, DC: Lexington, 1999).

109. See Ami Pedahzur and Arie Perlinger, "The Fourth Wave: Comparison of Jewish and Other Manifestations of Religious Terrorism" in *Terrorism, Legitimacy, and Identity*, ed. Jean Rosenfeld (London: Routledge, 2011), 104. A more extensive account appears in Pedahzur and Perlinger, *Jewish Terrorism in Israel*. See also Ehud Sprinzak, *Brother Against Brother: Violence and Extremism in Israeli Politics from Altalena to the Rabin Assassination* (New York: Simon & Schuster, 2000).

110. "I really loved Rabin, and he would have reached a final peace deal." Bill Clinton, interview with Israeli Channel 2, *Times of Israel*, June 2013, https://www.timesofisrael.com/clinton-i-really-loved-rabin-and-he-would-have-made-peace/.

111. Sikhs were particularly upset with Article 25 of India's constitution, which suggests Sikhs are Hindus.

112. Katherine Frank, *Indira: The Life of Indira Nehru Gandhi* (New York: HarperCollins, 2001), 55.

113. Many Indians described Bhindranwale as a "Sant Monster," with the Frankenstein model in their mind. Pranay Gupte, *Mother India* (New York: Charles Scribner's Sons, 1992), 319.

114. See R. A. Kapoor, *Sikh Separatism: The Politics of Faith* (London: Allen and Unwin, 1986); David C. Rapoport, "Comparing Militant Fundamentalist Movements," in *Fundamentalisms and the State*, ed. M. Marty and Scott Appleby (New York: Sage, 1993); Harjot Oberoi, "Sikh Fundamentalisms Translating History Into Theory," in *Fundamentalisms and the State*, ed. M. Marty and Scott Appleby (New York: Sage, 1993); Carl H. Haeger, "Sikh Terrorism in the Struggle for Khalistan," *Studies in Conflict and Terrorism* 14, no. 4 (1991): 221–31; Jugdep S. Chima, *The Sikh Separatist Insurgency in India: Political Leadership and Ethno-Nationalist Movements* (Thousand Oaks, CA: Sage, 2010).

115. Chima, "The Sikh Separatist Insurgency in India," 382; Marc Sageman, *Understanding Terrorist Networks* (Philadelphia: University of Pennsylvania Press, 2004), 483; Ved Marwah, *Uncivil Wars: Pathology of Terrorism in India* (New York: Harper Collins, 1995), 175.

116. Singh Harjinder Dilgeer, *Genocide of the Sikhs, 1978–1984* (Waremme: Sikh University Press, 2011), 196.

117. Mark Tully, "After Blue Star," BBC World Service, May 23, 2004, https://www.bbc.co.uk/programmes/p0344v41.

118. Paul Wallace, "Political Violence and Terrorism in India: A Crisis in Identity," in *Terrorism in Context*, ed. Martha Crenshaw (University Park: Penn State University Press, 1995), 307.

119. No real effort was made to punish those responsible for the pogroms.

120. The besieged in Operation Bluestar had a much larger and better armed force than those in Operation Black Thunder. But that does not entirely explain the very different results.

121. It developed out of a previous organization, the Tamil New Tigers, established four years earlier.

122. Neil De Votta, "The Liberation Tigers of Tamil Eelam and the Lost Quest for Separatism in Sri Lanka," *Asian Survey* 49, no. 6 (2009): 1021–51, is an interesting discussion of the background to the Tamil uprising.

123. De Votta, "The Liberation Tigers," contends that "linguistic nationalist" concerns were more important than religious ones in provoking the conflict. He may be right, but he does not explain how the two categories should be distinguished and does not develop his argument. The deep involvement of Buddhist monks throughout the struggle is the basis for my describing the opponent as a religious one. It is also true that Christian churches, especially the Catholic ones, supported the Tamil cause strongly.

124. Rajiv Gandhi's successor withdrew the troops, but there was some indication that if Gandhi's reelection effort succeeded, he might send them back, which seems to be the reason he was assassinated.

125. "Taming the Tamil Tiger: From Here in the U.S.," U.S. Federal Bureau of Investigation, January 10, 2008, https://archives.fbi.gov/archives/news/stories/2008/january/tamil_tigers011008.

126. Sharon Otterman, "Trapped Civilians Now Able to Flee, Sri Lanka Says," *New York Times*, May 1, 2009.

127. De Votta, "The Liberation Tigers," 1047. Sri Lankan figures for the total killed were over 100,000. The American study cited is probably more accurate in doubling the figures.

128. Hammerskin Nation attacked a Sikh temple in Oak Creek, Wisconsin in 2012, killing seven, including a police officer.

129. Mark Fisher and Paul McCombe, "Going by the Book of Hate," *Washington Post National Weekly*, May 1995, 9. The book was published in 1976 under the name Andrew McDonald.

130. Michael Barkun, "Religion, Militias, and Oklahoma City: The Mind of Conspiratorialists," *Terrorism and Political Violence.* 8, no. 1 (1996): 51.

131. David C. Rapoport, "Messianic Sanctions for Terror," *Comparative Politics* 20, no. 2 (1988): 195–213; Rapoport, "Terror and the Messiah."

132. A hate crime is an intentional violent attack inspired by the victim's race, color, religion, national origin, gender identity, disability, or sexual orientation The first hate crime prevention act was part of the 1964 Federal Civil Rights Law, and it was followed by a number of laws, the latest signed by President Obama in 2009. The statistics on hate crime incidents vary annually but are generally between 7,000 and 8,000; the FBI is required to publish them.

133. The order's goal included a homeland Northwest Territorial Imperative that would bar Jews and nonwhites.

134. Some residents did not have a legal right to possess guns, e.g., those with criminal convictions on probation or with court-documented mental illness.

135. Jessica Walter, *Every Knee Shall Bow* (New York: Harper, 1995), provides a fascinating discussion of the Ruby Ridge encounter.

136. Several of those conversations were recorded and later analyzed in Robert R. Agne and Karen Tracy, "Bible Babble: Naming the Interactional Trouble at Waco," *Discourse Studies* 3, no. 3 (2001): 269–94.

137. In the negotiations, the Branch Davidian leader repeatedly denied the charge he had such a plan, and people escaping the compound said they had not seen any such preparation. John Hall's interesting essay "From Jonestown to Waco" discusses the importance of the Jonestown issue, which Branch Davidian apostates got government forces to believe. "It seems incontrovertible that the efforts of the Davidian apostates against David Koresh were the animating force, and the sine qua non, without which the BATF raid would not have taken place in the ways it did and perhaps not at all." John

Hall, Phillip Schuyler, and Silvaine Trinh, *Apocalypse Observed* (London: Routledge, 2000), 72.

138. For a critical account of government tactics, Michael Barkun, "Reflections After Waco, Millennialists, and the State," in *From the Ashes: Making Sense of the Extreme Right*, ed. J. R. Lewis (Washington, DC: Rowman and Littlefield, 1994). In 1997, Dan Gifford and Amy Summer's documentary, *Waco: The Rules of Engagement*, was nominated for a 1997 Academy Award for Best Documentary. The film critically examines law enforcement's conduct, leading up to the raid and through the fire's aftermath. It features footage of the congressional hearings on Waco, evidence often contradicting government spokespeople.

139. Michael Barkun, "Appropriated Martyrs: The Branch Davidians and the Radical Right," *Terrorism and Political Violence* 19, no. 1 (2007): 117–21.

140. Chip Berlet and Matthew Lyons, "Militia Nation," *The Progressive* 9, no. 6 (1995): 22. The numbers given by different commentators vary from several hundred thousand to several million.

141. Arie Perliger, "Challenger from the Sidelines: Understanding America's Violent Far Right," Combating Terrorism Center at West Point, November 2012, https://ctc.usma .edu/wp-content/uploads/2013/01/ChallengersFromtheSidelines.pdf.

142 The chief conspirators, Timothy McVeigh and Terry Nichols, met in 1988 at Fort Benning during basic training. Their accomplice Michael Fortier was McVeigh's army roommate. April 19 was also the anniversary of the Battle of Lexington, the start of the American Revolution, and other militias planned to use that date for attacks.

143. David C. Rapoport, "The Celestial Connection," *San Diego Union Tribune*, April 7, 1997.

144. "Project Megiddo," U.S. Federal Bureau of Investigation, October 20, 1999, https://fas .org/irp/eprint/megiddo.pdf.

145. For over four thousand years, Megiddo, a hill in northern Israel, has been the site of many battles. Ancient cities were established there to serve as a fortress on the plain of Jezreel to guard a mountain pass. As Megiddo was built and rebuilt, one city upon the other, a mound or hill was formed. The Hebrew word "Armageddon" means "hill of Megiddo." In English, the word has come to represent the battle itself. The book of Revelation designates Armageddon as the assembly point in the apocalyptic setting of God's final and conclusive battle against evil. The name "Megiddo" is an apt title for a project that analyzes those who believe the year 2000 will usher in the end of the world and are willing to perpetrate acts of violence to bring that end about.

146. Only Canada and Israel joined the United States in publishing them. The Canadian Project was "Doomsday Religious Movements" and the Israeli one "Events at the End of the Millennium: Possible Implications for the Public Order in Jerusalem." All three appear in Jeffrey Kaplan, ed., *Millennial Violence: Past, Present, and Future* (London: Routledge, 2002). Project Megiddo is slightly redacted. The volume also contains eight essays by scholars largely critical of the reports, especially the American one. The criticism obviously had the advantage of hindsight, but most scholars involved did publish skeptical essays beforehand.

147. J. Taranto, "The Year 2003 Problem," *Wall Street Journal*, February 3, 2003.

148. There is no evidence that the act was planned to precipitate other acts of violence by American and Canadian millennial groups, though had it succeeded it might have had that effect.

149. Nimrod Raphaeli, "Ayman Muhammad Rabi al-Zawahiri: The Making of an Arch-Terrorist," *Terrorism and Political Violence* 14, no. 4 (2002): 1–22.

150. Mohammad Hafez, "Martyrs Without Borders: The Puzzle of Transnational Suicide Bombers," unpublished ISA paper, 2012, 113.

151. "Largest Anti-War Rally," Guinness World Records, https://web.archive.org/web/20040904214302/http://www.guinnessworldrecords.com/content_pages/record.asp?recordid=54365.

152. Spain had only 1,300 troops in Iraq. Initially there was considerable popular opposition to sending them. But the bombings in March preceded an election. The winner used the issue in its campaign but said it would keep supporting the Americans in Afghanistan.

153. Jane Mayer, *The Dark Side* (New York: Doubleday, 2008), 3.

154. John Mueller and Mark G. Stewart, "Terrorism and Counterterrorism Since 9/11," International Studies Association Conference, San Diego, CA, March 22, 2012, https://politicalscience.osu.edu/faculty/jmueller/ISA12ter.pdf.

155. Shaykh Ayman al-Zawahiri, "Realities of the Conflict Between Islam and Unbelief," As-Sahab Media, *Dhu Qa'dah 1427 AH*, December 2006, https://www.cia.gov/library/abbottabad-compound/67/67BD026383A5C82BEBB2AD11BB31A1E9_Dr_Aiman_Reality_of_the_Conflict_En.pdf.

156. The article was originally published Louis R. Beam, "Leaderless Resistance," *Seditionist* 12 (1992); and appears in Jeffrey Kaplan, *Encyclopedia of White Power: A Sourcebook on the Radical Racist Right* (Lanham, MD: Altamira, 2000), 503–11. See also Louis Beam, "Computers and Patriots," *Seditionist* 11 (1991). For interesting articles on Louis Beam, see Jeffrey Kaplan, "Leaderless Resistance," *Terrorism and Political Violence* 9, no. 3 (1997): 80–95; and Ehud Sprinzak, "Right Wing Terrorism in Comparative Perspective: The Case of Delegitimation," *Terrorism and Political Violence* 7, no. 1 (1995): 17–43. Beam may have been the first participant to see the importance of the internet for terrorism. But infiltration had always been a preeminent feature of counterterrorism, and while he is not persuasive in estimating the internet's value for governments, his argument that it is valuable for terrorists is better. In technologically advanced societies, electronic surveillance can often penetrate the structure, revealing its chain of command. Experience has revealed over and over again that antistate organizations committed to violence are easy prey for government infiltration, entrapment, and destruction of the personnel involved.

157. Beam attributes the term and concept to Lt. Colonel Ulius Amoss, a former OSS member who joined the John Birch Society upon retirement and founded the International Services of Information Foundation, a private intelligence firm. Amoss published two papers for the firm, both entitled "Leaderless Resistance" (1953, 1962), in which he recommends the tactic if the communists took over the government. Those papers are not

available to the public and were written too early to anticipate the significance of the internet. Beam does not use the term "lone wolf"; two white supremacist disciples, Tom Metzger and Alex Curtis, popularized it in the 1990s.

158. Zeev Iviansky, "Individual Terror: Concept and Typology," *Journal of Contemporary History* 12, no. 1 (1977): 43–63. Iviansky was the first terrorism scholar to use the term "lone wolf" as the term for a terrorist who acted alone and was not part of a group. The *OED* notes the term was first used in 1909 and referred to the activity of "panhandlers." In the wilderness, a "lone wolf" is normally pushed out of a wolf pack because it is not sufficiently aggressive. Subsequent life outside the pack may animate the wolf enough to create a new pack. See Cristen Conger, "What Is a Lone Wolf?," *How Stuff Works*, http://animals.howstuffworks.com/mammals/lone-wolf2.htm/printable.

159. See Peter Nesser, "Research Note: Single Actor Terrorism: Scope, Characteristics, and Explanations," *Perspectives on Terrorism* 6, no. 6 (2012): 61–73; Jeffrey Simon, *Lone Wolf Terrorism* (Amherst, MA: Prometheus, 2013).

160. Martha Crenshaw, "The Causes of Terrorism," *Comparative Politics* 13, no. 4 (1981): 390; Christopher Hewitt, *Understanding Terrorism in America: From the Klan to al-Qaeda* (London: Routledge, 2003), 80. Most terrorism scholars endorse Crenshaw's position. Christopher Hewitt also emphasizes the difference between lone wolves and terrorists who act on their own but belong to an organization. He doesn't discuss the earlier lone wolf.

161. There is no comprehensive discussion of the mental condition of the earlier lone wolves.

162. Louis Beam, "For Whom the Bell Tolls: The Bombing in Oklahoma City," *Christian Identity Journal Jubilee*, 1995, 55.

163. Beam, "For Whom the Bell Tolls."

164. Scott Stewart and Fred Burton, "Lone Wolf Lessons," *Stratfor*, June 3, 2009, https://worldview.stratfor.com/article/lone-wolf-lessons; Scott Stewart, "Cutting Through the Lone Wolf Hype," *Townhall Finance*, September 23, 2011, https://finance.townhall.com/columnists/stewartscott/2011/09/23/cutting-through-the-lone-wolf-hype-n785627. Environmental groups associated with other purposes employed the tactic too and so far have not caused any deaths. Paul Joose, "Leaderless Resistance and Ideological Inclusion: The Case of the Earth Liberation Front," *Terrorism and Political Violence* 19, no. 3 (2007): 351–68; Stefan Leader and Peter Probst, "The Earth Liberation Front and Environmental Terrorism," *Terrorism and Political Violence* 15, no. 4 (2003): 37–58. For an interesting discussion of the millenarian dimension of environmental movements, see Martha Lee, "Violence and the Environment: The Case of 'Earth First,'" *Terrorism and Political Violence* 7, no. 3 (1995): 109–27.

165. See Beau Seegmiller's discussion of the case and the general problem in his "Radicalized Margins: Eric Rudolph and Religious Violence," *Terrorism and Political Violence* 19, no. 4 (2007): 511–28.

166. John Buntin, "Security Preparations for the 1996 Centennial Games: Seeking a Structural Fix," Harvard Kennedy School of Government Case Program, November 1, 1999, https://case.hks.harvard.edu/security-preparations-for-the-1996-centennial-olympic

-games-a/. Those killed were abortion clinic security guards; the injured were a nurse and five gay persons. Rudolph also did not claim that it inspired the attack at the time of the Olympics. Perhaps he thought the attack counterproductive because the injured were not security force members.

167. "The wrath of God burns furiously against the USA, and we are poised for destruction. Why? It is not only for the rare satanic zeal which kills babies. It is because of the pervasive lukewarmness which kills babies." Quoted by Jeffrey Kaplan, "Absolute Rescue: Absolutism, Defensive Action, and the Resort to Force," *Terrorism and Political Violence* 7 (1995): 45.

168. Richard Kelly Hoskins introduced the "order." Richard Hoskins, *Vigilantes of Christendom: The Story of the Phineas Priesthood* (Lynchburg: Virginia Publishing, 1990). Phineas was used as an inspiration for the Zealot uprising against the Romans, perhaps the first terrorist group in history. But the lone wolf feature there was not emphasized; see Rapoport, "Fear and Trembling." The role of Phineas in the Jewish tradition is given much more attention in Gideon Aran and Ron E. Hassner, "Religious Violence in Judaism: Past and Present," *Terrorism and Political Violence* 25, no. 3, (2014): 355–405. Kaplan discusses "The Phineas Priests" in his *Encyclopedia of White Power*, 222–24.

169. "Incidence of Violence and Disruption Against Abortion Providers in the U.S. and Canada," National Abortion Federation. We have cited only the U.S. statistics. The first abortion clinic murderer was Michael Griffin, who killed Dr. David Gunn (1993) and was a lone wolf unconnected with any movement. But within several months lone wolves associated with the pro-life rescue movement emerged. In 1994, the former Presbyterian minister and Army of God member Paul Hill killed three and wounded one in the worst American abortion clinic attack.

170. Mark Potok, "The Year in Hate & Extremism 2010," Southern Poverty Law Center Spring Intelligence Report (2011), 141, https://www.splcenter.org/fighting-hate/intelligence-report/2011/year-hate-extremism-2010.

171. "FBI Reports on Extremists in the Military," Southern Poverty Law Center Fall Intelligence Report (2008), https://www.splcenter.org/fighting-hate/intelligence-report/2008/fbi-reports-extremists-military; "White Supremacist Recruitment of Military Personnel Since 9/11," U.S. Federal Bureau of Investigation Counterterrorism Division Intelligence Assessment, July 7, 2008, https://documents.law.yale.edu/sites/default/files/White%20Supremacist%20Recruitment%20of%20Military%20Personnel%20Since%209-11-ocr.pdf. The FBI report states that "military experience is found throughout the white supremacist extremist movement as the result of recruitment campaigns by extremist groups and self-recruitment by veterans sympathetic to white supremacist causes. . . . A review of FBI white supremacist extremist cases from October 2001 to May 2008 identified 203 individuals with confirmed or claimed military service active in the extremist group movement at some time during the reporting period."

172. "Right-wing Extremism: Current Economic and Political Climate Fueling Resurgence in Radicalization and Recruitment," U.S. Department of Homeland Security, Extremism

and Radicalization Branch, Homeland Environment Threat Analysis Division, April 7, 2009, http://www.fas.org/irp/eprint/rightwing.pdf.

173. Ginger Thompson, "Extremist Report Draws Criticism; Prompts Apology," *New York Times*, April 16, 2009.

174. 9/11 most probably reduced the religious right's appeal, a factor less significant by 2009, but the U.S. Department of Homeland Security Report does not mention that.

175. The Assault Weapons Ban passed only on the agreement that it would expire in ten years. The Supreme Court decision *District of Columbia v. Heller* on the federal government supplemented *McDonald v. Chicago* (2010), restricting states and local governments too.

176. Perliger, "Challenger from the Sidelines," 67, 86, compiled the statistics, the most comprehensive available. He consolidated various data sets but does not explain why 1980s data are not included.

177. Skinhead groups were the only ones that did not attack property.

178. Since governments have limited roles subsidizing some abortion clinics, one could include antiabortion strikes as antigovernment attacks.

179. Abu al-Suri, "The Call to Global Islamic Resistance," CENTRA Technology, Inc., trans. from the Arabic by the DCIA Counterterrorism Center, Office of Terrorism Analysis, 2004, 1387–1368, http://wwe.openscoure.gov/portal/server.pt/gateway/PTARGS-0-0 -6093-989-0-43//http%3B7011/opensource.gov/content/Display/67/6719634. This link no longer works. I was not able to find and an English copy of the text, but there is an Arabic one available at https://ia802700.us.archive.org/23/items/The-call-for-a-global Islamic-resistance-pdf. Al-Suri served in the Afghan Arab training camps from 1987 to 1992. He then spent several years in Spain and the United Kingdom before moving back to Afghanistan in 1998, where he ran a military training camp and a media center. He started discussing leaderless resistance in the 1990s, but his writings became popular only after al-Qaeda lost its Afghanistan base and the Iraq invasion. Al-Suri uses Beam's term "leaderless resistance" and follows Beam by including individuals and autonomous cells in the concept. Lawrence Wright, "Annals of Terrorism: The Master Plan," *New Yorker*, September 4, 2006, https://www.newyorker.com/magazine/2006/09/11/the -master-plan; Sarah Zabel, *The Military Strategy of Jihad* (Carlisle, PA: U.S. Army War College, 2007), 5–7. See a comprehensive discussion of Abu Misab al-Suri's work in Brynjar Lia, *Architect of Global Jihad: The Life of al-Qaida Strategist Abu Mus'ab al- Suri* (New York: Columbia University Press, 2008). Brynjar Lia, "Doctrines for Jihadi Training," *Terrorism and Political Violence* 20, no. 4 (2008): 518–42, compares al-Suri with other al-Qaeda theorists.

180. Anwar al-Awakli was the first American-born person ever assassinated by direct order. Gal Perl Finkel, "A New Strategy Against ISIS," *Jerusalem Post*, March 7, 2017, https:// www.jpost.com/opinion/a-new-strategy-against-isis-483521.

181. Charles Savage, "Plane Plot Detailed in Support of Life Term," *New York Times*, February 10, 2012, https://www.nytimes.com/2012/02/11/us/underwear-bomb-plot-detailed-in -court-filings.html.

182. "Intelligence Officials Warn Attempted al-Qaeda Attack Months Away," *Fox News*, February 2, 2010, https://www.foxnews.com/politics/intelligence-officials-warn-attempted-al-qaeda-attack-months-away.

183. "Obama Says, "Lone Wolf Terrorist' Biggest U.S. Threat," Reuters, August 16, 2011, https://www.reuters.com/article/us-usa-obama-security/obama-says-lone-wolf-terrorist-biggest-u-s-threat-idUSTRE77F6XI20110816.

184. Jerome P. Bjelopera, "American Jihadist Terrorism: Combating a Complex Threat," U.S. Congressional Research Service, November 15, 2011, R41416, https://www.refworld.org/docid/4f1ea1862.html.

185. "Right-Wing Extremism: Current Economic and Political Climate Fueling Resurgence in Radicalization and Recruitment," U.S. Department of Homeland Security, Extremism and Radicalization Branch, Homeland Environment Threat Analysis Division, lists fifty-three plots, but sixteen were efforts to go abroad to join various jihadist groups, and we have excluded them to focus on attacks in the United States and on those by Americans on Americans abroad. One plot has occurred since the study was issued. Joseph Goldstein and William K. Rashbaum, "City Bomb Plot Suspect Called Fan of Qaeda Cleric," *New York Times*, November 20, 2011, https://www.nytimes.com/2011/11/21/nyregion/jose-pimentel-is-charged-in-new-york-city-bomb-plot.html. Four of the sixteen efforts to go abroad overseas occurred before May 2009.

186. The figures for lone wolf attacks vary considerably because some use the term only when one person is involved while others use the definition for leaderless resistance, so the attack may be the act of an autonomous cell. Thus, John Avalon lists seventeen attacks as lone wolf. John Avalon, "9/11 Anniversary: 45 Terror Plots Foiled in the Last Ten Years," *Daily Beast*, September 8, 2011, https://www.thedailybeast.com/911-anniversary-45-terror-plots-foiled-in-last-10-years.

187. Bjelopera, "American Jihadist Terrorism," 74, discusses all of the cases.

188. Bjelopera, "American Jihadist Terrorism," 43. There were other uncounted cases, the Christmas Day underwear bomber and two Americans in Somalia, but the first was a foreigner, and the others were abroad, not striking Americans.

189. David K. Shipler, "Terrorist Plots Hatched by the FBI," *New York Times*, April 28, 2012, https://www.nytimes.com/2012/04/29/opinion/sunday/terrorist-plots-helped-along-by-the-fbi.html. Shipler points out that most of the sting-operation plots involved incompetent and wholly unprepared individuals with little sense of what they were doing. The efforts most probably would not have occurred if they were left alone to organize the attempts.

190. Shipler, "Terrorist Plots Hatched by the FBI."

191. Barak Mendelsohn, *The al-Qaeda Franchise: The Expansion of al-Qaeda and Its Consequences* (Oxford: Oxford University Press, 2016). For Muslim attitudes since the Jordanian bombings, see Pew Research Center, July 1, 2014, http://www.pewglobal.org/2014/07/01/concerns-about-islamic-extremism. Palestinians are the only people where a majority approves of suicide bombing attacks on civilians, according to the State Department's Bureau of Intelligence and Research in 2006.

192. Stig Jarle Hansen, *Al-Shabaab in Somalia: The History and Ideology of a Militant Islamist Group* (Oxford: Oxford University Press, 2013), 208.

193. James Merriman, *A History of Modern Europe: From the French Revolution to the Present* (New York: Norton, 1996), 715.

194. Mark Bracher, "Rationalising the Post-'Arab Spring' Salafi-Jihadist Boom: Looking Beyond Syria," March 17, 2015, https://rethinkingislamwithsultanshahin.wordpress.com /2015/03/17/rationalising-the-post-arab-spring-salafi-jihadist-boom-looking-beyond -syria/.

195. David Ignatius, "Al-Qaeda Affiliate Playing Larger Role in Syria Rebellion," *Washington Post*, August 30, 2012, https://www.washingtonpost.com/blogs/post-partisan/post/al -qaeda-affiliate-playing-larger-role-in-syria-rebellion/2012/11/30/203d06f4-3b2e-11e2 -9258-ac7c78d5c680_blog.html.

196. "The Capture of Mosul: Terror's New Headquarters," *Economist*, June 14 2014, https:// www.economist.com/leaders/2014/06/14/terrors-new-headquarters.

197. William McCants, *The ISIS Apocalypse: The History, Strategy, and Doomsday Vision of ISIS* (New York: St. Martin's, 2015).

198. Lara Logan, "Iraq's Christians Persecuted by ISIS," *60 Minutes*, March 22, 2015, https:// www.cbsnews.com/news/iraq-christians-persecuted-by-isis-60-minutes.

199. "Iraq Insurgents Use Water as Weapon After Seizing Dam," Reuters, April 11, 2014, https://www.reuters.com/article/us-iraq-security-idUSBREA3A0Q020140411.

200. Graeme Wood, "What ISIS Really Wants," *Atlantic*, March 2015, https://www.theatlantic .com/magazine/archive/2015/03/what-isis-really-wants/384980/.

201. Thomas Jocelyn, "Al-Qaeda Appears 'Moderate' Compared to Islamic State, Veteran Jihadist Says," *FDD's Long War Journal*, October 25, 2015, https://www.longwarjournal .org/archives/2015/10/al-qaeda-appears-moderate-compared-to-islamic-state-veteran -jihadist-says.php.

202. Ben Hubbard, "Al Qaeda Tries a New Tactic to Keep Power: Sharing It," *New York Times*, June 9, 2015, https://www.nytimes.com/2015/06/10/world/middleeast/qaeda-yemen-syria -houthis.html.

203. Charles Lister, "An Internal Struggle: Al Qaeda's Syrian Affiliate Is Grappling with Its Identity," *Huffington Post*, May 31, 2015, https://www.huffpost.com/entry/an-internal -struggle-al-q_b_7479730.

204. Scott Stewart, "Time Is Working Against ISIS," *Stratfor Worldview*, November 5, 2015, https://worldview.stratfor.com/article/time-working-against-islamic-state.

205. David C. Rapoport, "Why Has the Islamic State Changed Its Strategy and Mounted the Paris-Brussels Attacks?" *Perspectives on Terrorism* 10, no. 2 (2016): 24–30.

206. Abu Hurairah, companion to Muhammad, reported in his Hadith that Muhammad said: "The Last Hour would not come until the Romans land at ao-A'maq or in Dabiq. An army consisting of the best (soldiers) of the people of the earth at that time will come from Medina."

207. Suadad al-Salhy and Tim Arango, "Sunni Militants Drive Iraqi Army out of Mosul," *New York Times*, April 17, 2015, https://www.nytimes.com/2014/06/11/world/middleeast /militants-in-mosul.html.

208. For interesting discussion of the European network ISIS organized, see Rukmini Callimachi, "How ISIS Built the Machinery of Terror Under Europe's Gaze," *New York Times*, March 29, 2016, https://www.nytimes.com/2016/03/29/world/europe/isis-attacks-paris -brussels.html; and Christoph Reuter, "Activating the Sleepers: Islamic State Adopts a New Strategy in Europe," *Speigel International*, March 29, 2016, http://www.spiegel.de /international/world/islamic-state-adopts-a-new-approach-in-europe-a-1084489.html.

209. Rowan Scarborough, "Islamic State Finds Success Infiltrating Its Terrorists Into Refugee Flows to West," *Washington Times*, January 29, 2017, https://www.washingtontimes .com/news/2017/jan/29/isis-finds-success-infiltrating-terrorists-into-re/.

210. "Syria: Aleppo 'One of the Most Devastating Urban Conflicts in Modern Times,'" International Committee of the Red Cross, August 15, 2016, https://www.icrc.org/en/document /syria-news-cities-aleppo-one-most-devastating-urban-conflicts.

211. "Syria: Raqqa in Ruins and Civilians Devastated After US-Led 'War of Annihilation,'" Amnesty International, June 5, 2018, https://www.amnesty.org/en/latest/news/2018/06 /syria-raqqa-in-ruins-and-civilians-devastated-after-us-led-war-of-annihilation/.

212. Martin Chulov and Kareem Shaheen, "Isis Leader Abu Bakr al-Baghdadi 'Seriously Wounded in Air Strike,'" *Guardian*, April 21, 2015, https://www.theguardian.com/world /2015/apr/21/isis-leader-abu-bakr-al-baghdadi-wounded-air-strike.

213. There were doubts about whether the caliph was severely injured. Eric Schmitt and Ben Hubbard, "ISIS Leader Takes Steps to Ensure Group's Survival," *New York Times*, July 20, 2015, https://www.nytimes.com/2015/07/21/world/middleeast/isis-strategies-include-lines -of-succession-and-deadly-ring-tones.html.

214. "ISIS," *History.com*, July 10, 2017, https://www.history.com/topics/21st-century/isis.

215. "Review of the Terrorist Attacks on U.S. Facilities in Benghazi, Libya, September 11–12, 2012," U.S. Senate Select Committee on Intelligence, January 15, 2014, https://web .archive.org/web/20140116130132/http://www.intelligence.senate.gov/benghazi2014 /benghazi.pdf.

216. Two months later, ISIS released a video in which it killed thirty Ethiopian Christians in Libya. Fifteen were beheaded. Douglas Ernst, "Mass Grave of Christians Slain by Islamic State in 2015 Uncovered in Libya," *Washington Times*, December 28, 2018, https:// www.washingtontimes.com/news/2018/dec/28/mass-grave-of-christians-slain-by -islamic-state-in/; Scarborough, "Islamic State Finds Success."

217. For an interesting discussion of the problem, see Jason Park, Rhiannon Smith, and Karim Mezran, "The Origins and Evolution of ISIS in Libya," Atlantic Council, Rafik Hariri Center for the Middle East, June 2017, https://www.atlanticcouncil.org/wp-content /uploads/2017/06/The_Originsand_Evolution_of_ISIS_in_Libya_web_0705.pdf.

218. Borzou Daragahi, "ISIS Resurrection: Libya Attacks Foreshadow Terror to Come," *Daily Beast*, May 9, 2018, https://www.thedailybeast.com/isis-resurrection-libya-attacks-fore shadow-terror-to-come.

219. Sami Aboudi, "In Yemen Chaos, Islamic State Grows to Rival al-Qaeda," Reuters, June 30, 2015, https://www.reuters.com/article/us-yemen-security-islamicstate-insight/in -yemen-chaos-islamic-state-grows-to-rival-al-qaeda-idUSKCN0PA1T920150630.

220. Bill Roggio, "North Waziristan Taliban Threaten Pakistani," *FDD's Long War Journal*, January 31, 2010, https://www.longwarjournal.org/archives/2010/1. In 2015, AQAP mounted a spectacular Paris attack on the magazine *Charlie Hebdo*'s personnel, killing eleven, for republishing cartoons demeaning the Prophet Muhammad.

221. Shuaib Almosawa, "Wedding Is Hit by Airstrike in Yemen, Killing More Than 20," *New York Times*, April 23, 2018, https://www.nytimes.com/2018/04/23/world/middleeast /yemen-wedding-bombing.html.

222. Antonio Guterres, "Yemen the World's Worst Humanitarian Crisis, Says UN Chief," Inter Press Service, April 4, 2018, http://www.ipsnews.net/2018/04/yemen-worlds-worst -humanitarian-crisis-says-un-chief.

223. Nick Cumming-Bruce, "War Crimes Report on Yemen Accuses Saudi Arabia and U.A.E.," *New York Times*, August 28, 2018, https://www.nytimes.com/2018/08/28/world /middleeast/un-yemen-war-crimes.html.

224. UN officials intend to scrutinize the report before releasing it. The precise details will be available then.

225. Although Alshamrani filed a formal complaint against one of his instructors for repeat-edly mocking him with the nickname "Porn Stash," investigators believe that the attack was premeditated and not a result of this incident.

226. Colin Clarke, "The Pensacola Terrorist Attack: The Enduring Influence of al-Qa'ida and Its Affiliates," *CTC Sentinel* 13, no. 3 (March 2020), https://ctc.usma.edu/pensacola -terrorist-attack-enduring-influence-al-qaida-affiliates/; "Explaining Boko Haram, Nigeria's Islamist Insurgency," *New York Times*, November 10, 2014, https://www.nytimes .com/2014/11/11/world/africa/boko-haram-in-nigeria.html.

227. Declan Walsh and Nour Youssef, "Militants Kill 305 at Sufi Mosque in Egypt's Deadli-est Terrorist Attack," *New York Times*, November 24, 2017, https://www.nytimes.com /2017/11/24/world/middleeast/mosque-attack-egypt.html.

228. Harriet Sherwood, "Christians in Egypt Face Unprecedented Persecution, Report Says," *Guardian*, January 10, 2018, https://www.theguardian.com/world/2018/jan/10/christians -egypt-unprecedented-persecution-report.

229. Harsh V. Pant and Kabir Taneja, "ISIS's New Target: South Asia," *Foreign Policy*, May 2, 2019, https://foreignpolicy.com/2019/05/02/isiss-new-target-south-asia/.

230. Amy Romano, *A Historical Atlas of Afghanistan* (New York: Rosen, 2003), 28.

231. Stephen Losey, "Air Force: Afghanistan Airstrikes Spike While Anti-ISIS Bombings Decrease," *Air Force Times*, November 21, 2017, https://www.airforcetimes.com /flashpoints/2017/11/21/air-force-afghanistan-airstrikes-spike-while-anti-isis-bombings -decrease/. Aliza was killed in February 2015 and Khan in July 2016.

232. "Islamic State of Iraq and the Levant—Khorasan Province," Wikipedia, https://en .wikipedia.org/wiki/Islamic_State_of_Iraq_and_the_Levant_%E2%80%93_Khorasan _Province. The article gets its cases from newspaper sources, and there may be a few cases missed, but the general argument concerning Pakistan attacks would not be affected.

233. Akhilesh Pillalamarri, "Revealed: Why ISIS Hates the Taliban," *Diplomat*, January 29, 2016, https://thediplomat.com/2016/01/revealed-why-isis-hates-the-taliban/.

234. The reports were released in 2007 and cover the years before 2001. Barbara Elias, ed., "Pakistan: 'The Taliban's Godfather?,'" National Security Archive Electronic, Briefing Book 227, August 14, 2007, https://nsarchive2.gwu.edu/NSAEBB/NSAEBB227/index .htm#17. For an interesting discussion of why Pakistan continues to support the Afghan Taliban, see Vanda Felab-Brown, "Why Pakistan Supports Terrorist Groups, and Why the US Finds It So Hard to Induce Change," Brookings Institute, January 5, 2018, https:// www.brookings.edu/blog/order-from-chaos/2018/01/05/why-pakistan-supports -terrorist-groups-and-why-the-US-finds-it-so-hard-to-induce-change.

235. Carlotta Gall, "Pakistan and Afghan Taliban Close Ranks," New York Times, March 26, 2009, https://www.nytimes.com/2009/03/27/world/asia/27taliban.html.

236. Daud Khattak, "The Complicated Relationship Between the Afghan and Pakistani Taliban," CTC Sentinel 5, no. 2 (February 2012): 14–16.

237. Thomas Joscelyn, "Taliban and Islamic State Target Religious Opponents in Afghanistan," FDD's Long War Journal, May 31, 2018, https://www.longwarjournal.org/archives /2018/05/taliban-and-islamic-state-target-religious-opponents-in-afghanistan.php.

238. "Bomber Strikes Gathering of Mostly Taliban Members Celebrating Cease-Fire, Official Says," CBS News/Associated Press, June 16, 2018, https://www.cbsnews.com/news /afghanistan-bombing-gathering-mostly-taliban-celebrating-cease-fire-official-says/.

239. Emma Graham-Harrison, "Taliban Fears Over Young Recruits Attracted to ISIS in Afghanistan," Guardian, May 7, 2017, https://www.theguardian.com/world/2015/may/07 /taliban-young-recruits-isis-afghanistan-jihadis-islamic-state.

240. Lauren McNally, Alex Amiral, Marvin Weinbaum, and Antoun Issa, "The Islamic State in Afghanistan: Examining Its Threat to Stability," Middle East Institute MEI Policy Focus Report 11 (May 2016), http://www.mei.edu/sites/default/files/publications/PF12_McNally Amiral_ISISAfghan_web.pdf.

241. President Ashraf Ghani, "Afghan President Ashraf Ghani Address to Joint Meeting of Congress," CSPAN, March 25, 2015, https://www.c-span.org/video/?324977-2/afghan -president-ashraf-ghani-address-joint-meeting-congress.

242. Ben Brimelow, "ISIS Wants to Be as Dangerous as the Taliban—but It's Not Even Close," Business Insider, February 11, 2018, http://www.businessinsider.com/isis-taliban -afghanistan-terrorism-2018-2.

243. Mujib Mashal and Eric Schmitt, "White House Orders Direct Taliban Talks to Jump-Start Afghan Negotiations," New York Times, July 15, 2018, https://www.nytimes.com /2018/07/15/world/asia/afghanistan-taliban-direct-negotiations.html.

244. Thomas Gibbons-Neff and Cooper Helene, "New U.S. Tactic in Afghanistan Urges Retreat," New York Times, July 28, 2018, https://www.nytimes.com/2018/07/28/world/asia /trump-afghanistan-strategy-retreat.html.

245. Lawrence Sáez, "Bangladesh in 2016: Transition and Turmoil Intertwined," Asian Survey 57, no. 1 (February 2017): 43–49

246. Rohan Gunaratna, "Global Terrorism Mid-Year Review 2016," Counter Terrorist Trends and Analyses 8, no. 3 (2016): 8.

247. Hannah Beech and Jason Gutierrez, "ISIS Bombing of Cathedral in Philippines Shows Group's Reach Into Asia," *New York Times*, January 28, 2019, https://www.nytimes.com /2019/01/28/world/asia/isis-philippines-church-bombing.html.

248. Viraj Solanki, "The Increasing Presence of ISIS in South Asia," International Institute for Strategic Studies, June 1, 2019, https://www.iiss.org/blogs/analysis/2019/06/isis-south -asia.

249. One reason Israel gave Egypt permission was that the ISIS franchise made an unsuccessful attack on Israel.

250. "Israel's Villa in the Jungle," *Economist*, May 12, 2016, https://www.economist.com/special -report/2016/05/12/israels-villa-in-the-jungle.

251. Lt. Colonel (U.S. Army, Ret.) Jeffrey F. Addicott, "The 2020 Trump–Taliban 'Peace Agreement'—Time to End the War on Terror," *Nebraska Law Review*, March 29, 2021.

252. Lt. Colonel U.S. Army Ret. Jeffrey F. Addicott provides a comprehensive discussion of the agreement's details in "The 2020 Trump-Taliban 'Peace Agreement'—Time to End the War on Terror," *Nebraska Law Review*, March 29, 2021, https://lawreview.unl.edu /2020-trump-taliban-peace-agreement%E2%80%94time-end-war-terror.

253. "Remarks by President Biden on the Drawdown of U.S. Forces in Afghanistan," July 8, 2021, http://www.whitehouse.gov.

254. Lara Seligman, "Top Generals Contradict Biden, Say They Urged Him Not to Withdraw from Afghanistan," *Politico*, September 28, 2021, https://www.politico.com/news/2021 /09/28/top-generals-afghanistan-withdrawal-congress-hearing-514491.

255. "In about 93 months . . . about 560 thousand were killed in Syria since the day of claiming rights to the International Human Rights Day," *Syrian Observatory for Human Rights*, December 10, 2018, http://www.syriahr.com/en/?p=108723.

256. Philip Taubman, "Soviet Lists Afghan War Toll: 13,310 Dead, 35,478 Wounded," *New York Times*, May 26, 1988, https://www.nytimes.com/1988/05/26/world/soviet-lists-afghan -war-toll-13310-dead-35478-wounded.html.

257. Rafael Reuveny and Aseem Prakash, "The Afghanistan War and the Breakdown of the Soviet Union," *Review of International Studies* 25, no. 4 (1999): 693–708.

258. Tom O'Connor, "How Many Russian Troops in Syria? Military Reveals Full Count as U.S. Told to Leave," Newsweek, August 23, 2018, https://www.newsweek.com/how -many-russia-troops-syria-military-reveals-full-count-us-told-leave-1088409.

259. Eric Schmitt, "C.I.A. Said to Aid in Steering Arms to Syrian Opposition," *New York Times*, July 21, 2012, https://www.nytimes.com/2012/06/21/world/middleeast/cia-said-to -aid-in-steering-arms-to-syrian-rebels.html.

260. Laura Rozen, "US Authorizes Financial Support for the Free Syrian Army," *AL-Monitor*, July 27, 2012, http://www.al-monitor.com/pulse/originals/2012/al-monitor/us-authorizes -financial-support.html.

261. "Army Private from Southwest Detroit Dies in Syria in Noncombat Incident," *WXYZ Detroit–ABC*, April 29, 2019, https://www.wxyz.com/news/army-private-from-southwest -detroit-dies-in-syria-in-non-combat-incident.

262. "Ask the Experts: Has U.S. Foreign Policy Been Too Focused on Counterterrorism," *Foreign Affairs*, June 14, 2018, https://www.foreignaffairs.com/ask-the-experts/2018-06 -14/has-us-foreign-policy-been-too-focused-counterterrorism.

263. See Helene Cooper, Noah Schmitt and Mark Landle, "Trump to Withdraw U.S. Forces from Syria, Declaring 'We Have Won Against ISIS,'" *New York Times*, December 19, 2018, https://www.nytimes.com/2018/12/19/us/politics/trump-syria-turkey-troop -withdrawal.html.

264. David Sanger, Mark Weiland, and Eric Schmitt, "Bolton Puts Conditions on Syria Withdrawal, Suggesting a Delay of Months or Years," *New York Times*, January 6, 2019, https://www.nytimes.com/2019/01/06/world/middleeast/bolton-syria-pullout.html.

265. Peter Baker and Lara Jakes, "Trump Throws Middle East Policy into Turmoil Over Syria," New York Times, October 7, 2019, https://www.nytimes.com/2019/10/07/us /politics/turkey-syria-trump.html.

266. Sanger, Weiland, Schmitt, "Bolton Puts Conditions on Syria Withdrawal, Suggesting a Delay of Months or Years."

267. "Has U.S. Foreign Policy Been Too Focused on Counterterrorism? *Foreign Affairs* Asks the Experts," *Foreign Affairs*, June 14, 2018, https://www.foreignaffairs.com/ask-the -experts/2018-06-14/has-us-foreign-policy-been-too-focused-counterterrorism.

268. Dan Lamothe and Josh Dawsey, "Trump Wanted a Big Cut in Troops in Afghanistan. New U.S. Military Plans Fall Short," *Washington Post*, https://www.washingtonpost.com /world/national-security/new-plans-for-afghanistan-would-have-trump-withdrawing -fewer-troops/2019/01/08/ddf2858e-12a0-11e9-a896-f104373c7ffd_story.html.

269. Samirah Majumdar and Virginia Villa, "Globally, Social Hostilities Related to Religion Decline in 2019, While Government Restrictions Remain at Highest Levels," Pew Research Center, September 30, 2021, https://www.pewforum.org/2021/09/30/globally -social-hostilities-related-to-religion-decline-in-2019-while-government-restrictions -remain-at-highest-levels/.

270. We used the "Global Terrorism Index 2019: Measuring the Impact of Terrorism," Institute for Economics & Peace, Sydney, Australia, November 2019, http://visionofhumanity .org/reports; and the "Global Terrorism Database (GTD)," National Consortium for the Study of Terrorism and Responses to Terrorism (START), University of Maryland, 2019, https://www.start.umd.edu/gtd. The time periods of the two bases are different. GTI covers from 2002 to the end of 2018, while GTD goes from 2015 to end of 2019. There are no clashes in the statistics presented but sometimes the subjects treated are different. My discussion uses information from both but none of the information drawn from one source conflicts with any in the other source.

271. "Background Report: Global Terrorism in 2017," National Consortium for the Study of Terrorism and Responses to Terrorism (START), University of Maryland, August 2018, https://www.start.umd.edu/pubs/START_GTD_Overview2017_July2018.pdf.

272. "Global Terrorism Index: Measuring the Impact of Terrorism 2019," Institute for Economics & Peace, 2.

273. "Global Terrorism Index: Measuring the Impact of Terrorism 2019," Institute for Economics & Peace, 2.

274. "Global Terrorism Index: Measuring the Impact of Terrorism 2019," Institute for Economics & Peace, 31–33.

275. Seth G. Jones, Charles Vallee, et al., "The Evolution of the Salafi-Jihadist Threat: Current and Future Challenges from the Islamic State, al-Qaeda, and Other Groups," CSIS Transnational Threats Project, November 2018, https://csis-website-prod.s3.amazonaws.com/s3fs-public/publication/181221_EvolvingTerroristThreat.pdf.

276. Jones, Vallee, et al., "The Evolution of the Salafi-Jihadist Threat."

277. See Rapoport, "Terrorism and Weapons of the Apocalypse," 49–67.

278. John Mueller and Mark G. Stewart, *Chasing Ghosts: The Policing of Terrorism* (Oxford University Press, 2016); John Mueller, "Is There Still a Terrorist Threat? The Myth of the Omnipresent Enemy," *Foreign Affairs* 85, no. 5 (2006): 2.

279. "Has U.S. Foreign Policy Been Too Focused on Counterterrorism?"

280. Vivian Yee, "Lebanon's Prime Minister, Saad Hariri, Steps Down in Face of Protests," *New York Times*, October 29, 2019, https://www.nytimes.com/2019/10/29/world/middleeast/saad-hariri-stepping-down-lebanon.html.

281. "Gaza Strip," World Factbook, Central Intelligence Agency, October 6, 2021, https://www.cia.gov/the-world-factbook/countries/gaza-strip.

CONCLUSION: THE FIFTH WAVE?

1. The conclusion's epigraph is from an interview with Jean-Claude Chesnais, *Valeurs Actuelles*, October 6, 1996; Michel Gurfinkiel, "Islam in France: The French Way of Life Is in Danger," *Middle East Quarterly* 4, no. 1 (March 1997): 19–29. Jean-Claude Chesnais is a leading French demographer at the National Institute for the Study of Demographics. Jean-Claude Barreau, a former government official in charge of immigration, expresses similar opinions in books on Islam and the Middle East, e.g., Jean-Claude Barreau, *La France va-t-elle disparaitre?* (Paris: Bernard Grasset, 1997). "User Clip: Bush Addresses the War on Terror—9/20/01," George W. Bush Presidential Address, September 20, 2001, C-SPAN, https://www.c-span.org/video/?c4869508/user-clip-bush-addresses-war-terror-92001.

2. Vincent A. Auger, "Right-Wing Terror: A Fifth Global Wave?" *Perspectives on Terrorism* 14, no. 3 (June 2020): 88–97; Amber Hart, "Right-Wing Waves: Applying the Four Waves Theory to Transnational and Transhistorical Right-Wing Threat Trends," *Terrorism and Political Violence*, January 12, 2021, https://www.tandfonline.com/doi/full/10.1080/09546553.2020.1856818.

3. Auger, "Right-Wing Terror."

4. Jennifer Rankin and Daniel Boffey, "EU Leaders Defend Migration Deals as Doubts Emerge," *Guardian*, June 29, 2018, https://www.theguardian.com/world/2018/jun/29/eu-leaders-defend-migration-deal-as-snag-emerges.

5. Daniel Koehler provides an interesting and useful account of right-wing European movements and related violence in "Right Wing Extremism and Terrorism in Europe: Development and Issues for the Future," *PRISM* 6, no. 2 (2016): 85–105.

6. "Economic Crisis in Europe: Causes, Consequences, and Reponses," European Commission Directorate-General for Economic and Financial Affairs, July 2009, https://ec .europa.eu/economy_finance/publications/pages/publication15887_en.pdf.

7. Fabrizio Tassinari, "The Disintegration of European Security Lessons from the Refugee Crisis", *PRISM* 6, no. 2 (2016): 70–83, https://cco.ndu.edu/Portals/96/Documents /prism/prism_6-2/Prism%20Vol%206%20No%202.pdf?ver=2016-08-03-155946-023.

8. Patrick Kingsley, "Migration to Europe Is Down Sharply. So, Is It Still a 'Crisis'?," *New York Times*, June 27, 2018, https://www.nytimes.com/interactive/2018/06/27/world/europe /europe-migrant-crisis-change.html.

9. Jacob Aasland Ravndal and Tore Bjørgo, "Terrorism from the Extreme Right," *Perspectives on Terrorism* 12, no. 6 (2018): 5–22. The article appears in a special issue, and several articles focus on the United States. The volume also contains a useful bibliography on the "extreme right" but does not discuss the activity as a wave phenomenon.

10. Raphael Bossong and Tobias Etzold, "The Future of Schengen: Internal Border Controls as a Growing Challenge to the EU and the Nordics," *Stiftung Wissenschaft und Politik (German Institute for International and Security Affairs)* 44 (October 2018), https://www .swp-berlin.org/fileadmin/contents/products/comments/2018C44_Bsg_Etz.pdf.

11. "The Nobel Peace Prize for 2012," Nobel Committee, October 12, 2012, https://www .nobelprize.org/prizes/peace/2012/press-release/.

12. Matthew Goodwin and Caitlin Milazzo, "Taking Back Control? Investigating the Role of Immigration in the 2016 Vote for Brexit," *British Journal of Politics and International Relations* 19, no. 3 (2017): 450–64.

13. "How Did Young People Vote in the Brexit Referendum?," *Full Fact*, March 23, 2018, https://fullfact.org/europe/how-did-young-people-vote-brexit-referendum/.

14. The UN High Commissioner for Refugees (UNHCR) has the mandate to see that the 1951 Convention is implemented.

15. Ina Sokolska, "Fact Sheets on the European Union: Asylum Policy," European Parliament, January 2020, https://www.europarl.europa.eu/factsheets/en/sheet/151/asylum -policy.

16. "Temporary Reintroduction of Border Control," European Commission—Migration and Home Affairs, https://ec.europa.eu/home-affairs/what-we-do/policies/borders-and -visas/schengen/reintroduction-border-control_en.

17. Rocio Naranjo Sandalio, "Spain's Summary Returns to Morocco Violate the European Convention on Human Rights," *Forced Migration Forum*, October 15, 2017, https:// forcedmigrationforum.com/2017/10/15/spains-summary-returns-to-morocco-violate -the-echr/.

18. "EU-Turkey Refugee Deal a Historic Blow to Rights," Amnesty International, March 18, 2016, https://www.amnesty.org/en/latest/news/2016/03/eu-turkey-refugee-deal-a -historic-blow-to-rights/.

19. Hugo Gye, "Locked Out: Just One in Five Muslims Are in Work as Report Finds They Are Held Back by Racism," *Sun*, September 7, 2017, https://www.thesun.co.uk/news /4411913/just-one-in-five-muslims-are-in-work-as-report-finds-they-are-held-back-by -racism/.

20. Bruce Stokes, "The Immigration Crisis Is Tearing Europe Apart," *Foreign Policy*, July 22, 2016, https://foreignpolicy.com/2016/07/22/the-immigration-crisis-is-tearing-europe -apart/.

21. Beyond racism, one reason for this difference is that Muslim women are far more likely to be stay-at-home mothers; 18 percent of Muslim women are recorded as "looking after home and family," three times as many as in the rest of the population. Even when Muslims do work, they find it harder to rise through the ranks and get well-paid jobs. "Islamophobia in Europe," Open Society Foundations, May 2019, https://www .opensocietyfoundations.org/explainers/islamophobia-europe.

22. "Global Views of Immigration and the Refugee Crisis," Ipsos MORI, July 2016, https:// www.ipsos.com/sites/default/files/migrations/en-uk/files/Assets/Docs/Polls/ipsos -global-advisor-immigration-and-refugees-2016-charts.pdf.

23. "Europe's Growing Muslim Population," Pew Research Center, November 19, 2017, https://www.pewforum.org/2017/11/29/europes-growing-muslim-population/.

24. Seckin Baris Gulmez, "EU-Skepticism vs. Euroscepticism. Reassessing the Party Positions in the Accession Countries Towards EU Membership," in *EU Enlargement: Current Challenges and Strategic Choices*, ed. Finn Laursen (Bern: Peter Lang, 2013).

25. "Spring 2015 Standard Eurobarometer: Citizens See Immigration as Top Challenge for EU to Tackle," European Commission, July 31, 2015, https://ec.europa.eu/commission /presscorner/detail/en/IP_15_5451.

26. Uuriintuy Batsaikhan and Zsolt Darvas, "European Spring—Trust in the EU and Democracy Is Recovering," Bruegel, March 2017, https://www.bruegel.org/2017/03 /european-spring-trust-in-the-eu-and-democracy-is-recovering/.

27. Krisztina Thana and Gergely Szakacs, "Hungary's Strongman Viktor Orban Wins Third Term in Power," Reuters, April 7, 2018, https://www.reuters.com/article/us-hungary -election/hungarys-strongman-viktor-orban-wins-third-term-in-power-idUSKBN1 HE0UC.

28. Luke Waller, "Viktor Orban: The Conservative Subversive," *Politico*, 2018, https://www .politico.eu/list/politico-28/viktor-orban/; Tim King, "Ties That Bind: Hungary's Fidesz and European Parliament," *Politico*, April 7, 2017, https://www.politico.eu/article/ties -that-bind-hungarys-fidesz-and-european-parliament/.

29. "Polish Opposition Warns Refugees Could Spread Infectious Diseases," Reuters, October 15, 2015, https://www.reuters.com/article/us-Europe-migrants-poland-idUSKCN0 S918B20151015.

30. Enes Bayrakli and Farid Hafez, eds., "European Islamophobia," *SETA*, 2015, https://web .archive.org/web/20170921071914/http://www.islamophobiaeurope.com/reports/2015 /en/EIR_2015_POLAND.pdf.

31. Bernard Rorke, "Bulgaria: Roma Murdered in Racist Attack," European Roma Rights Center, May 18, 2018, http://www.errc.org/news/bulgaria-roma-murdered-in-racist-attack.

32. Krasen Nikolov, "Deputy Interior Minister from IMRO Likes to Solve Problems by Fighting," *Mediapool*, May 18, 2017, https://www.mediapool.bg/zam-vatreshen-ministar-ot-vmro-obicha-problemite-da-se-reshavat-s-boi-news264042.html.

33. John Warisham, "The Situation of Roma and Travelers in the Context of Rising Extremism, Xenophobia, and the Refugee Crisis in Europe," Congress of Local and Regional Authorities, Council of Europe, October 20, 2016, https://rm.coe.int/1680718bfd.

34. "Far-Right Reaches for New Extremes in the Czech Republic," *Conversation*, July 15, 2015, https://theconversation.com/far-right-reaches-for-new-extremes-in-the-czech-republic-44496.

35. "5 Facts About the Muslim Population in Europe," Pew Research Center, November 29, 2017, https://www.pewresearch.org/fact-tank/2017/11/29/5-facts-about-the-muslim-population-in-europe/.

36. "Religious Communities and Life Stance Communities," Statistics Norway, https://www.ssb.no/en/trosamf/.

37. Besheer Mohamed, "New Estimates Show U.S. Muslim Population Continues to Grow," Pew Research Center, FactTank, January 3, 2019, http://www.pewresearch.org/fact-tank/2018/01/03/new-estimates-show-U.S.-muslim-population-continues-to-grow/.

38. "Portugal, the European Country That Wants More Migrants," *Straits Times*, July 2, 2018, https://www.straitstimes.com/world/europe/portugal-the-european-country-that-wants-more-migrants.

39. Lorenz Trish, "As Europe Moves Right, Portugal's Government Veers Left—and Thrives," *World Politics Review*, January 2, 2018, https://www.worldpoliticsreview.com/insights/23899/as-europe-moves-right-portugals-government-veers-left-and-thrives. See also Rodrigo Quintas da Silva, "A Portuguese Exception to Right-Wing Populism," *Palgrave Communications* 4, no. 1 (January 2018), https://papers.ssrn.com/sol3/papers.cfm?abstract_id=3162118.

40. "Immigration in Spain Grows by 157,097 People," *Datos Macro*, https://datosmacro.expansion.com/demografia/migracion/inmigracion/espana.

41. Santiago Abascal, "Cadiz, Covadonga, and Brussels," *Libertad Digital*, November 11, 2018, https://www.libertaddigital.com/opinion/santiago-abascal/cadiz-covadonga-y-bruselas-77185/.

42. Martin Caparros, "Vox and the Rise of the Extreme Rights in Spain," *New York Times*, November 13, 2019, https://www.nytimes.com/2019/11/13/opinion/spain-election-vox.html.

43. LG, "Vox Appeals to 'Good Immigration' to Stop Depopulation in Zamora," *La Opinion*, January 21, 2019, https://www.laopiniondezamora.es/zamora/2019/01/21/vox-apela-inmigracion-buena-atajar-1341663.html.

44. Silvia Amaro, "Majority of French Voters Want an EU Referendum: Citi," CNBC, April 4, 2017, https://www.cnbc.com/2017/04/04/majority-of-french-voters-want-an-eu -referendum-citi.html.

45. "Denmark's Immigration Issue," *BBC News*, February 19, 2005, http://news.bbc.co.uk/2 /hi/europe/4276963.stm.

46. Catrin Nye, "Converting to Islam—the White Britons Becoming Muslims," *BBC News*, January 4, 2011, https://www.bbc.co.uk/news/uk-12075931.

47. Ami Sedghi, "UK Census: Religion by Age, Ethnicity and Country of Birth," *Guardian*, May 16, 2013, https://www.theguardian.com/news/datablog/2013/may/16/uk-census -religion-age-ethnicity-country-of-birth.

48. "Exclusive: UK Muslims Prominent in Labour Resurgence," *Muslim News*, June 9, 2017, http://muslimnews.co.uk/news/uk/exclusive-uk-muslim-mps-prominent-labour -resurgence/.

49. Michael R. Bloomberg, "Sadiq Khan," *Time*, 2018, http://time.com/collection/most -influential-people-2018/5217530/sadiq-khan/.

50. "Baroness Warsi Quits as Foreign Office Minister Over Gaza," *BBC News*, August 5, 2014, https://www.bbc.com/news/uk-politics-28656874.

51. "Registration Summary: Britain First [De-registered November 2, 2017]," Electoral Commission, http://search.electoralcommission.org.uk/English/Registrations/PP2214.

52. Simon Sherwood, "The UK Independence Party: The Dimensions of Mainstreaming," in *Radical Right-Wing Populist Parties in Western Europe: Into the Mainstream?*, ed. Tjitske Akkerman, Sarah L. de Lange and Matthijs Rooduijn (London: Routledge, 2016), 27.

53. Claudia Ciobanu, "Europe: Home to Roma, and No Place for Them," Inter Press Service, May 16, 2008, http://www.ipsnews.net/2008/05/europe-home-to-roma-and-no-place -for-them/.

54. Elisabeth Rosenthal, "Italy Cracks Down on Illegal Immigration," *Boston Globe*, May 16, 2008, http://archive.boston.com/news/world/europe/articles/2008/05/16/italy_cracks_ down_on_illegal_immigration/.

55. Ylenia Gostoli, "Italy's Muslims Uneasy After Election of Far-Right Government," *Al Jazeera*, September 26, 2018, https://www.aljazeera.com/indepth/features/italy-muslims -uneasy-election-government-180926101907611.html.

56. Jessica Phelan, "Less Than Half of Italians Think Italy Benefits from the EU: Survey," *Local IT*, October 17, 2008, https://www.thelocal.it/20181017/italy-eu-eurosceptic-italexit -brexit.

57. Miles Johnson, "Why Italians Are Souring on the European Union," *Ozzy*, January 5, 2019, https://www.ozy.com/around-the-world/why-italians-are-souring-on-the-euro pean-union/91357/.

58. Michael Lipka, "Europe's Muslim Population Will Continue to Grow—but How Much Depends on Migration," Pew Research Center, Fact Tank, December 4, 2017, https:// www.pewresearch.org/fact-tank/2017/12/04/europes-muslim-population-will-continue -to-grow-but-how-much-depends-on-migration/.

59. "#1 Angela Merkel," *Forbes*, December 5, 2018, https://www.forbes.com/profile/angela
-merkel/#3904454e22dd.

60. Katrin Bennhold, "Germans Unnerved by Political Turmoil That Echoes Nazi Era," *New
York Times*, February 7, 2020, https://www.nytimes.com/2020/02/07/world/europe
/germany-thuringia-afd.html.

61. Katrin Bennhold, "Germany Places Part of Far-Right Party Under Surveillance,"
New York Times, March 12, 2020, https://www.nytimes.com/2020/03/12/world/europe
/germany-afd.html.

62. Frederic Simon, "Traditional Parties Hammered in Belgian Local Election," *Euractiv*,
October 15, 2018, https://www.euractiv.com/section/elections/news/traditional-parties
-hammered-in-belgian-local-election/.

63. "Free Speech at Issue 10 Years After Muhammad Cartoons Controversy," *Deutsche Welle*,
https://www.dw.com/en/free-speech-at-issue-10-years-after-muhammad-cartoons
-controversy/a-18747856.

64. Christian Wienberg, "Denmark's Biggest Party Adopts Anti-Immigrant View,"
Bloomberg, June 6, 2018, https://www.bloomberg.com/news/articles/2018-06-06/anti
-immigrant-view-adopted-by-denmark-s-biggest-political-party.

65. "DF: Starthjælpen skal holde udlændinge ude" (The start-up aid must keep foreigners
out), *DR*, December 7, 2006, https://www.dr.dk/nyheder/politik/df-starthjaelpen-skal
-holde-udlaendinge-ude.

66. Jo Becker, "The Global Machine Behind the Rise of Far-Right Nationalism," *New York
Times*, August 10, 2019, https://www.nytimes.com/2019/08/10/world/europe/sweden
-immigration-nationalism.html.

67. Oliver Gee, "Sweden's Islamophobia Is Getting Stronger," *Local SE*, January 2, 2015,
https://www.thelocal.se/20150102/swedens-islamophobia-is-getting-stronger.

68. Magnus Ranstorp, "Swedish Foreign Fighters in Syria and Iraq," Swedish Defence University, 2017, 23–34.

69. "Integreringsbarometeret 2013/2014," *Integrers-og mangfoldsdirektoratet (IMDi)*, 2014,
https://www.imdi.no/contentassets/cd74d67fc3dc4cb89f389809dd718da9/integrerings
barometeret-2013-2014.pdf.

70. Bradford Hanson, "The Norwegian Defense League as a Trojan Horse," *National Van-
guard*, October 28, 2016, https://nationalvanguard.org/2016/10/the-norwegian-defence
-league-as-trojan-horse/.

71. "Rise of the Right: Austria's Election Results and Their Implications for Europe," *RT*,
October 16, 2017, https://www.rt.com/news/406796-austria-vote-results-europe/.

72. "Islam in Austria," *Muslim Population*, http://www.muslimpopulation.com/Europe
/Austria/Islam%20in%20Austria.php#cite_note-0.

73. Tom Barfield, "Leipzig Mosque Construction Site Targeted with Dead Pig," *Local DE*,
February 25, 2016, https://www.thelocal.de/20160225/leipzig-mosque-construction-site
-targeted-with-dead-pig.

74. Marc Herman, "Why Europe Needs More Mosques," *Takepart*, July 1, 2016, http://www
.takepart.com/feature/2016/07/01/europes-war-against-mosques/.

75. Jeffrey Stinson, "Mosques Increasingly Not Welcome," *USA Today*, July 16, 2008, http://www.islamicpluralism.org/736/mosques-increasingly-not-welcome.

76. Todd H. Green, "The Resistance to Minarets in Europe," *Journal of Church and State* 52, no. 4 (2010): 619–43.

77. Pinchas Goldschmidt, "With Anti-Muslim laws, Europe Enters New Dark Age," *Politico*, July 27, 2018, https://www.politico.eu/article/with-anti-muslim-laws-france-denmark-europe-enters-new-dark-age/.

78. Gostoli, "Italy's Muslims Uneasy After Election of Far-Right Government."

79. Gostoli, "Italy's Muslims Uneasy After Election of Far-Right Government."

80. Alina Polyakova, "Strange Bedfellows: Putin and Europe's Far Right," *World Affairs* 177, no. 3 (2014): 36–40.

81. Christopher Scheutz and Melissa Eddy, "Austrian President Calls for Elections in September," *New York Times*, May 19, 2019, https://www.nytimes.com/2019/05/19/world/europe/austria-elections-far-right.html.

82. Alison Smale, "Austria's Far Right Signs a Cooperation Pact with Putin's Party," *New York Times*, December 19, 2016, https://www.nytimes.com/2016/12/19/world/europe/austrias-far-right-signs-a-cooperation-pact-with-putins-party.html; Alina Polyakova, "You Can't Trust the Far Right; The Latest Scandal in Austria Shows That Extremists Can't Be Tempered," *New York Times*, May 20, 2019, https://www.nytimes.com/2019/05/20/opinion/austria-russia-far-right.html; Scheutz and Eddy, "Austrian President Calls for Elections in September."

83. Polyakova, "You Can't Trust the Far Right"; Scheutz and Eddy, "Austrian President Calls for Elections."

84. "Statement by the Foreign Affairs Council on the Salisbury Attack," Council of Europe, March 19, 2018, https://www.consilium.europa.eu/en/press/press-releases/2018/03/19/statement-by-the-foreign-affairs-council-on-the-salisbury-attack/.

85. "Norwegian IS Travelers Lose Residence Permits," Sveriges Radio, September 14, 2009, https//sverigesradio.se/sis/artikel.aspx?programid=83&artikel=7200474.

86. Alessandro Sala, "E Trump incorona Salvini: "Diventerai premier in Italia," *Corriere Della Sera*, April 26, 2016, https://www.corriere.it/politica/16_aprile_26/trump-incorona-salvini-1427cf18-0b7b-11e6-a8d3-4c904844517f.shtml.

87. Jo Becker and Christina Anderson, "How Nationalism Found a Home in Sweden," *New York Times*, August 11, 2019.

88. Matt Appuzo and Adam Satariano, "Russia Is Targeting Europe's Elections. So Are Far-Right Copycats," *New York Times*, May 12, 2019, https://www.nytimes.com/2019/05/12/world/europe/russian-propaganda-influence-campaign-european-elections-far-right.html.

89. Max Fisher and Amanda Taub, "Trump Wants to Make It Hard to Get Asylum. Other Countries Feel the Same," *New York Times*, November 2, 2018, https://www.nytimes.com/2018/11/02/world/europe/trump-asylum.html.

90. Damien Cave, "Australia Election Results: Prime Minister Scott Morrison Seizes a Stunning Win," *New York Times*, May 18, 2019, https://www.nytimes.com/2019/05/18/world/australia/election-results-scott-morrison.html.

91. The special character of BJP's right-wing character and the dangers it generates are described well in Duncan McDonnell and Luis Cabrera, "The Right-Wing Populism of India's Bharatiya Janata Party (and Why Comparativists Should Care)," *Democratization* 26, no. 3 (2019): 484–501.

92. Peter Smith, *An Introduction to the Baha'i Faith* (Cambridge: Cambridge University Press, 2008), 94.

93. Dexter Filkins, "Blood and Soil in Narendra Modi's India," *New Yorker*, December 2, 2019, https://www.newyorker.com/magazine/2019/12/09/blood-and-soil-in-narendra-modis-india.

94. Jeffrey Gettleman and Maria Abi-Habib, "In India, Modi's Policies Have Lit a Fuse," *New York Times*, March 1, 2020, https://www.nytimes.com/2020/03/01/world/asia/india-modi-hindus.html.

95. Aditya Sharma, ed., "Great Indian Elections 1951–2019: The Story of How 90 Crore Voters Make and Break History," *News 18*, May 12, 2019, https://www.news18.com/news/india/great-indian-elections-1951-2019-the-story-of-how-90-crore-voters-make-and-break-history-2062747.html.

96. Simon Tisdall, "Narendra Modi's US Visa Secure Despite Gujarat Riots Guilty Verdicts," *Guardian*, June 2, 2016, https://www.theguardian.com/world/2016/jun/02/narendra-modis-us-visa-secure-despite-gujarat-riots-guilty-verdicts.

97. Dov Levin, "A Vote for Freedom? The Effects of Partisan Electoral Interventions on Regime Type," *Journal of Conflict Resolution* 63, no. 4 (2018): 839–68.

98. Oren Dorell, "Alleged Russian Political Meddling Documented in 27 Countries Since 2004," *USA Today*, September 7, 2017, https://www.usatoday.com/story/news/world/2017/09/07/alleged-russian-political-meddling-documented-27-countries-since-2004/619056001/.

99. Lucan Ahmad Way and Adam Casey, "Is Russia a Threat to Western Democracy? Russian Intervention in Foreign Elections, 1991–2017," https://fsi-live.s3.us-west-1.amazonaws.com/s3fs-public/is_russia_a_threat_to_western_democracy_russian_intervention_in_foreign_elections_1991–2017_.pdf. This paper was produced for a Stanford University Conference titled "Global Populisms as a Threat to Democracy?" on November 3–4, 2017. It focuses on the extent that Russia has been successful in influencing foreign politics.

100. Severin Carrell, "Russian Cyber-Activists 'Tried to Discredit Scottish Independence Vote,'" *Guardian*, December 13, 2017, https://www.theguardian.com/politics/2017/dec/13/russian-cyber-activists-tried-to-discredit-scottish-independence-vote-says-analyst.

101. Mason, Rowena "Theresa May Accuses Russia of Interfering in Elections and Fake News," *Guardian*, November 14, 2017, https://www.theguardian.com/politics/2017/nov/13/theresa-may-accuses-russia-of-interfering-in-elections-and-fake-news.

102. "Putin's Asymmetric Assault on Democracy in Russia and Europe: Implications for U.S. National Security," U.S. Committee on Foreign Relations, Minority Staff Report, January 10, 2018, https://www.foreign.senate.gov/imo/media/doc/FinalRR.pdf.

103. Dan Sabbagh and Luke Harding, "PM Accused of Cover-up Over Report on Russian Meddling in UK Politics," *Guardian*, November 4, 2019, https://www.theguardian.com /politics/2019/nov/04/no-10-blocks-russia-eu-referendum-report-until-after-election.

104. Rachel Ellehuus and Donatienne Ruy, "Did Russia Influence Brexit?," CSIS, July 21, 2020, https://www.csis.org/blogs/brexit-bits-bobs-and-blogs/did-russia-influence-brexit.

105. Kevin Breuninger, "Mueller Probe Ends: Special Counsel Submits Russia Report to Attorney General William Barr," CNBC, March 22, 2019, https://www.cnbc.com/2019 /03/22/robert-mueller-submits-special-counsels-russia-probe-report-to-attorney -general-william-barr.html.

106. Renée DiResta, Dr. Kris Shaffer, Becky Ruppel, David Sullivan, Robert Matney, Ryan Fox (New Knowledge), Dr. Jonathan Albright (Tow Center for Digital Journalism, Columbia University), and Ben Johnson (Canfield Research, LLC), "The Tactics & Tropes of the Internet Research Agency," New Knowledge, December 18, 2018, https:// disinformationreport.blob.core.windows.net/disinformation-report/NewKnowledge -Disinformation-Report-Whitepaper.pdf.

107. Ninon Bulckaert, "How France Successfully Countered Russian Interference During the Presidential Election," *Euractiv*, July 17, 2018, https://www.euractiv.com/section/elections /news/how-france-successfully-countered-russian-interference-during-the-presidential -election.

108. Bulckaert, "How France Successfully Countered Russian Interference."

109. Simon Shuster, "How Russian Voters Fueled the Rise of Germany's Far-Right," *Time*, September 25, 2017, https://time.com/4955503/germany-elections-2017-far-right-russia -angela-merkel/.

110. Matina Stevis-Gridneff, "Virus Variants Deliver Fresh Blow to Europe's Open Borders," *New York Times*, February 21, 2021, https://www.nytimes.com/2021/02/21/world/europe /european-union-coronavirus-borders.html.

111. Mark Potok, "The Year in Hate & Extremism 2010," Southern Poverty Law Center Spring Intelligence Report, 2011, https://www.splcenter.org/fighting-hate/intelligence -report/2011/year-hate-extremism-2010.

112. Sarah Childress, "A Guide to the New Militia Movement," *Frontline*, May 17, 2017, http:// apps.frontline.org/militia-movement/.

113. "Anti-Government Movement," Southern Poverty Law Center, 2021, https://www .splcenter.org/fighting-hate/extremist-files/ideology/antigovernment.

114. Cas Mudde, *The Far Right Today* (London: Polity, 2019); David Neiwert, *Alt-America: The Rise of the Radical Right in the Age of Trump* (London: Verso, 2017).

115. Silvia Amaro, "Trump Is Making a 'Historical Mistake' with the EU, Former US Ambassador Says," CNBC, November 12, 2019, https://www.cnbc.com/2019/11/12/trump-making -a-historical-mistake-with-eu-former-us-diplomat-says.html.

116. Alastair Macdonald, "Bannon's EU Project Eyes Government Allies," Reuters, July 25, 2018, https://www.reuters.com/article/us-eu-parliament-bannon/bannons-eu-project -eyes-government-allies-idUSKBN1KF2BN.

117. Agence France-Presse, "German Far Right Rebuffs Steve Bannon's Effort to Forge Europewide Populist Movement," *Telegraph*, August 11, 2018, https://www.telegraph .co.uk/news/2018/08/11/german-far-right-rebuffs-steve-bannons-effort-forge-europe -wide/.

118. Agence France-Presse, "Austria's Far-Right Unwilling to Collaborate with Bannon," *Times of Israel*, September 12, 2018, https://www.timesofisrael.com/austrias-far -right-unwilling-to-collaborate-with-bannon/; William James, "UKIP Will Not Join Steve Bannon's Anti-EU Movement, Says Leader," Reuters, September 21, 2018, https:// www.reuters.com/article/us-britain-eu-ukip/ukip-will-not-join-steve-bannons-anti-eu -movement-says-leader-idUSKCN1M10Q8/.

119. Mike McIntire and Nicholas Confessore, "Trump's Twitter Presidency: 9 Key Takeaways," *New York Times*, November 2, 2019, https://www.nytimes.com/2019/11/02/us /trump-twitter-takeaways.html.

120. Glenn Thrush and HYPERLINK "http://www.nytimes.com/by/maggie-haberman" Maggie Haberman, "Trump Gives White Supremacists an Unequivocal Boost," *New York Times*, August 15, 2017, https://www.nytimes.com/2017/08/15/us/politics/trump -charlottesville-white-nationalists.html.

121. "Thousands More Children May Have Been Separated," *Watchdog*, January 18, 2019, https://www.usnews.com/news/politics/articles/2019-01-17/watchdog-many-more -migrant-families-may-have-been-separated.

122. "Child Separations by the Trump Administration," prepared for Chairman Elijah E. Cummings, Staff Report Committee on Oversight and Reform U.S. House of Representatives, July 2019, https://oversight.house.gov/sites/democrats.oversight.house.gov /files/2019-07-2019.%20Immigrant%20Child%20Separations-%20Staff%20Report.pdf.

123. "President Trump Uses Term 'Chinese Virus' to Describe Coronavirus, Prompting a Backlash," *CBS News*, March 19, 2020, https://www.cbsnews.com/news/president-trump -coronavirus-chinese-virus-backlash/.

124. Global Terrorism Index 2020 Measuring the Impact of Terrorism, http://visionof humanity.org/wp-content/uploads/2020/11/GTI-2020-web-2.pdf.

125. "Oath Keepers," ADL, https://www.adl.org/resources/backgrounders/oath-keepers.

126. "Read the Full Transcript from the First Presidential Debate Between Joe Biden and Donald Trump," *USA Today*, September 30, 2020, https://www.usatoday.com/story/news /politics/elections/2020/09/30/presidential-debate-read-full-transcript-first-debate /3587462001/.

127. Mark Bray, *Antifa: The Anti-Fascist Handbook* (New York: Melville House, 2017), 54.

128. "Council of Europe: Greece Could Ban Golden Dawn," *Times of Israel*, April 16, 2013, https://www.timesofisrael.com/council-of-Europe-greece-could-ban-golden-dawn/.

129. Ylenia Gostoli, "Activists, Experts Hope for Justice as Salvini Trial Resumes," *Aljazeera*, December 11, 2020, https://www.aljazeera.com/news/2020/12/11/salvini-to-appear-on -court-for-illegally-detaining-migrants.

130. Dinah Pulver, Rachel Axon, Katie Wedell, Erin Mansfield, Zshekinah Collier, and Tyreye Morris, "Capitol Riot Arrests: See Who's Been Charged Across the U.S.," *USA*

Today, September 29, 2021, https://www.usatoday.com/storytelling/capitol-riot-mob
-arrests/.

131. Ben Doherty, "Woman Shot and Killed in Storming of US Capitol Named as Ashli Babbitt," *Guardian*, January 7, 2021, https://www.theguardian.com/us-news/2021/jan/07/ashli-babbitt-woman-shot-and-killed-in-storming-of-us-capitol-named.

132. "Atlanta Shootings Live Updates: Suspect Had Visited Targeted Spas Before, Police Say," *New York Times*, March 18, 2021, https://www.nytimes.com/live/2021/03/18/us/atlanta-shootings-massage-spa.

133. Michael M. Grynbaum, Davey Alba, and Reid J. Epstein, "How Pro-Trump Forces Pushed a Lie About Antifa at the Capitol Riot," *New York Times*, March 1, 2021, https://www.nytimes.com/2021/03/01/us/politics/antifa-conspiracy-capitol-riot.html.

134. My article "The Capitol Attack and the 5th Terrorism Wave," *Terrorism and Political Violence* 33, no. 5 (2021), provides a much more detailed discussion of the attack's context.

135. Michael Robinson and Kori Schake, "The Military's Extremism Problem Is Our Problem," *New York Times*, March 2, 2021, https://www.nytimes.com/2021/03/02/opinion/veterans-capitol-attack.html.

136. Matthew S. Schwartz, "Up to 25,000 Troops Descend on Washington for Biden's Inauguration," NPR, January 16, 2021, https://www.npr.org/sections/insurrection-at-the-capitol/2021/01/16/957642610/unprecedented-number-of-troops-descend-on-washington-d-c-for-bidens-inauguration.

137. An illuminating and extensive account of both strikes is Asne Seierstad, *One of Us: The Story of Anders Breivik and the Massacre in Norway* (New York: Farrar, Straus and Giroux, 2013), 272–344. See also Stian Bromark, *Massacre in Norway: The Terror Attack on Oslo and the Utoya Youth Camp* (Sterling, VA: Potomac, 2014); and Aage Borchgrevink, *A Norwegian Tragedy: Anders Behring Breivik and the Massacre on Utoya* (Cambridge: Polity, 2013).

138. Josiane Kremer, Marianne Stigset, and Stephen Treloar, "Norway Shooting Suspect Breivik Is Ordered Into Isolation for Four Weeks," *Bloomberg*, July 25, 2011, https://www.bloomberg.com/news/articles/2011-07-24/norway-killing-suspect-may-explain-motives.

139. Two other Norwegian "cells" were to follow him, but they did not do what Breivik expected. See "Norway: Anders Behring Breivik Claims 'Two More Cells,'" *BBC News*, July 25, 2011, https://www.bbc.com/news/world-europe-14280210.

140. Åsne Seierstad, "The Anatomy of White Terror," *New York Times*, March 19, 2019, https://www.nytimes.com/2019/03/18/opinion/new-zealand-tarrant-white-supremacist-terror.html.

141. Anders Brevik, "2083—A European Declaration of Independence," *Public Intelligence*, July 28, 2011.

142. "Global Terrorism Index 2019: Measuring the Impact of Terrorism," Institute for Economics & Peace, November 2019, http://visionofhumaity.org/app/uploads/2019/11/GTI-2010web.pdf.

143. "Christchurch Attack: Brenton Tarrant Pleads Not Guilty to All Charges," *BBC News*, June 14, 2019, https://www.bbc.com/news/world-asia-48631488.

144. Tarrant only mentions Australia, but New Zealand, the United States, and Canada meet his standards for being part of Europe.

145. Katrine Bennhold, "As Far Right Rises, a Battle Over Security Agencies Grows," *New York Times*, May 7, 2019, https://www.nytimes.com/2019/05/07/world/europe/austria-far-right-freedom-party.html. Chancellor Kurz found the poem despicable. "The choice of words is disgusting, shows contempt for human beings and is deeply racist. The Freedom Party . . . must distance [itself] from this immediately and unequivocally and issue a clarification."

146. Vikram Dodd, "Anti-Muslim Hate Crimes Soar in UK After Christchurch Shootings," *Guardian*, March 22, 2019, https://www.theguardian.com/society/2019/mar/22/anti-muslim-hate-crimes-soar-in-uk-after-christchurch-shootings.

147. The manifesto appears in Brett Stevens, "Alleged El Paso Walmart Shooter Protests Hispanicization of Texas," *Amerika*, August 3, 2019, http://www.amerika.org/politics/alleged-el-paso-walmart-shooter-protests-hispanicization-of-texas/.

148. "El Paso, Texas Population 2020," World Population Review, https://worldpopulationreiew.com/us-cities/el-paso-tx-population.

149. The far-right terrors statistics come from the Global Terrorism Index 2020, https://kbb9z40cmb2apwafcho9v3j-wpengine.netdna-ssl.com/wp-content/uploads/2018/0.

150. Lizzie Dearden, "Hate-Crime Reports Rise by Almost a Third in Year as Home Office Figures Illustrate EU-Referendum Spike," *Independent*, October 17, 2017, https://www.independent.co.uk/news/uk/crime/hate-crimes-eu-referendum-spike-brexit-terror-attacks-police-home-office-europeans-xenophobia-islamophobia-a8004716.html.

151. Daniel Koehler, "Recent Trends in German Right-Wing Violence and Terrorism: What Are the Contextual Factors Behind 'Hive' Terrorism," *Perspectives on Terrorism* 12, no. 6 (2018): 79.

152. "Germany: Altena's Pro-Migrant Mayor Stabbed in Kebab Shop," *Deutsche Welle*, November 28, 2017, https://www.dw.com/en/germany-altenas-pro-migrant-mayor-stabbed-in-kebab-shop/a-ar41556872.

153. Katrin Bennhold, "Trump Emerges as Inspiration for Germany's Far Right," *New York Times*, September 7, 2020, https://www.nytimes.com/2020/09/07/world/europe/germany-trump-far-right.html.

154. There are no comprehensive statistics on the matter, but this seems to be accurate.

155. Koehler, "Recent Trends." There does not seem to be statistical analysis of this issue for other European states, though my impression is that there are many in this category. While Koehler emphasizes the importance of this new element, which he describes as "hybrid terrorists," he does not discuss the terrorism as a wave phenomenon.

156. Chris Hawkins, "Counter-Terrorism Operations Against Right Wing Extremism in Western Europe Increase 191% in 24 Months," *Jane's IHS Markit*, December 7, 2018, https://ihsmarkit.com/research-analysis/counterterrorism-operations-against-right-wing-extremism.html.

157. Initially, left-wing elements made the majority of the anti-Semitic attacks, citing Israel's treatment of Palestinians E. H. Kaplan and C. A. Small, "Anti-Israel Sentiment Predicts Anti-Semitism in Europe," *Journal of Conflict Resolution* 50, no. 4 (2006): 548–61.

158. Patrick Kingsley, "Anti-Semitism Is Back, from the Left, Right and Islamist Extremes. Why?" *New York Times*, April 4, 2019, https://www.nytimes.com/2019/04/04/world/europe/antisemitism-europe-united-states.html.

159. James Angelos, "The New German Anti-Semitism," *New York Times*, May 21, 2019, https://www.nytimes.com/2019/05/21/magazine/anti-semitism-germany.html.

160. "The Old Scourge of Anti-Semitism Rises Anew in Europe," *New York Times*, May 27, 2019, https://www.nytimes.com/2019/05/26/opinion/antisemitism-europe-germany.html.

161. Nick Thorpe, "Hungary Vilifies Financier Soros with Crude Poster Campaign," *BBC News*, July 10, 2017, https://www,bbc.com/news/world-europe4055484.

162. "Labour Split: Nine MPs Quit in Protest at the Party's Leadership," *BBC News*, February 22, 2019, https://www.bbc.co.uk/newsround/47277863.

163. Carla Bleiker, "Sharp Rise in Right-Wing Crime in Germany Just 'the Tip of the Iceberg,' " *Deutsche Welle*, February 11, 2016, https://www.dw.com/en/sharp-rise-in-right-wing-crime-in-germany-just-the-tip-of-the-iceberg/a-19041652.

164. Tim Hume, "A Lit Fuse: How a Far-Right Terror Group's Bombing Campaign Unleashed Something Sinister in a Small German Town," *Vice*, March 5, 2018, https://news.vice.com/en_us/article/zmwvb3/freital-group-far-right-terrorism-germany.

165. Frank Jordans, " 'Revolution Chemnitz': Germany Arrests Seven Suspected Far-Right Terrorists Over Alleged Plot in Troubled Eastern City," *National Post*, October 1, 2018, https://nationalpost.com/news/world/germany-arrests-6-suspected-far-right-extremists-in-chemnitz.

166. Katrin Bennhold, "Plan for German 'Day X' Show Revival of Far Right," *New York Times*, August 2, 2020. Bennhold' s piece was the headline article. She is the newspaper's Berlin bureau chief.

167. Thoralf Cleven, "More Than 25,000 People on Right-Wing Enemy Lists," *RND Kieler Nachrichten*, July 30, 2018.

168. Bari Weiss, "The Terrorist in Your Hometown," *New York Times*, November 4, 2012, https://www.nytimes.com/2018/11/02/opinion/pittsburgh-synagogue-shooting-bari-weiss.html.

169. "Sweden Sword Attack: Two Killed by Masked Attacker," *BBC News*, October 22, 2015, https://www.bbc.com/news/world-europe-34602621.

170. "New Report Highlights Attacks on 39 Swedish Mosques in 2017," *Shia Waves*, June 15, 2018, http://shiawaves.com/english/world/6010-new-report-highlights-attacks-on-39-swedish-mosques-in-2017.

171. "Combat 18," *Counter-Extremism Project*, https://www.counterextremism.com/supremac/combat-18.

172. "Combat 18."

173. Ian Cobain, Nazia Parveen, and Matthew Taylor, "The Slow-Burning Hatred That Led Thomas Mair to Murder Jo Cox," *Guardian*, November 23, 2016, https://www.theguardian.com/uk-news/2016/nov/23/thomas-mair-slow-burning-hatred-led-to-jo-cox-murder.

174. Graham Macklin, " 'Only Bullets Will Stop Us!'—the Banning of National Action in Britain," *Perspectives on Terrorism* 12, no. 6 (2018): 107. The most conspicuous neo-Nazi

and anti-Semite provocation "was a visit to Germany in May 2016 where several activists took and posted online, photographs of themselves Sieg Heiling inside an execution room at Buchenwald concentration camp."

175. Macklin, "'Only Bullets Will Stop Us!,'" 111.

176. Jonathan Hall, "The Terrorism Acts in 2019: Report of the Independent Reviewer of Terrorism Legislation on the Operation of the Terrorism Acts 2000 and 2006," https://assets.publishing.service.gov.uk/government/uploads/system/uploads/attachment_data/file/972261/THE_TERRORISM_ACTS_IN_2019_REPORT_Accessible.pdf.

177. Hall, "The Terrorism Acts in 2019," 104–18.

178. "Far-Right Group National Action to Be Banned Under Terror Laws," *BBC News*, December 12, 2016, https://www.bbc.com/news/uk-38286708.

179. Nadia Khomami, "Alleged Neo-Nazi Admits Plotting Murder of MP Rosie Cooper," *Guardian*, June 12, 2018, https://www.theguardian.com/uk-news/2018/jun/12/man-pleads-guilty-to-plot-to-labour-mp-rosie-cooper.

180. An interesting and comprehensive discussion of al-Muhajiroun that sustains Rowley's view is Michael Kenney, *The Islamic State in Britain: Radicalization and Resilience in an Activist Network* (Cambridge: Cambridge University Press, 2018).

181. Jamie Grierson, "Four Far-Right Plots Thwarted Last Year, Says Counter-Terrorism Chief," *Guardian*, February 26, 2018, https://www.theguardian.com/uk-news/2018/feb/26/four-far-right-plots-thwarted-last-year-says-counter-terrorism-chief-mark-rowley.

182. "FBI Releases 2017 Hate Crime Statistics," FBI National Press Office, November 13, 2018, https://www.fbi.gov/news/pressrel/press-releases/fbi-releases-2017-hate-crime-statistics; Erin Donaghue, "FBI Report Shows Spike in Hate-Crimes for 3rd Year in a Row," *CBS News*, November 13, 2018, https://www.cbsnews.com/news/fbi-hate-crimes-increase-report-today-2018-11-13/.

183. Frank Witsil, "Expert: Michigan 'a Hotbed for Militia Activity,' with Growing Potential for Violence," *Detroit Free Press*, October 8, 2020, https://www.freep.com/story/news/local/michigan/2020/10/08/michigan-militia-wolverine-watchmen-gretchen-whitmer/5924615002/.

184. Jacob Ware, "Siege: The Atomwaffen Division and Rising Far-Right Terrorism in the United States," International Centre for Counter-Terrorism, October 9, 2019, https://icct.nl/wp-content/uploads/2019/07/ICCT-Ware-Siege-July2019.pdf.

185. A. C. Thompson, Ali Watson, and Jake Hanrahan, "Inside Atomwaffen as It Celebrates a Member for Allegedly Killing a Gay Jewish College Student," *ProPublica*, February 23, 2018, https://www.propublica.org/article/atomwaffen-division-inside-white-hate-group.

186. "Donning the Mask: Presenting the 'Face of 21st Century Fascism,'" Southern Poverty Law Center, June 20, 2017, https://www.splcenter.org/hatewatch/2017/06/20/donning-mask-presenting-face-21st-century-fascism.

187. Max Blumenthal, "Blowback: How US-Funded Fascists in Ukraine Mentor American White Supremacists," *Grey Zone*, November 15, 2018, https://thegrayzone.com/2018/11/15/blowback-how-us-funded-fascists-in-ukraine-mentor-us-white-supremacists/.

188. "Armed Conflict Between French Right and Muslims—How Real Is the Threat?," *Sputnik News*, June 27, 2018, https://sptnkne.ws/hTxM; Donaghue, "FBI Report Shows Spike."

189. "Shadowy Cell in France Plotted to Kill Muslim Civilians, Authorities Say," *New York Times*, June 28, 2018, https://www.nytimes.com/2018/06/28/world/europe/france-far-right -plots-muslims.html.

190. Chris Hawkins, "Counter-Terrorism Operations Against Right Wing Extremism in Western Europe Increase 191% in 24 Months"; "Italian Man Who Shot Migrants Given 12-Year Prison Term," Reuters, October 3, 2018, https://www.reuters.com/article/us-italy-shooting -macerata/italian-man-who-shot-migrants-given-12-year-prison-term-idUSKCN1MD2IY.

191. Megan Trimble, "Globally, Terrorism Deaths Are on the Decline," *U.S. News & World Report*, December 5, 2018, https://www.usnews.com/news/best-countries/articles/2018-12 -05/global-terrorism-deaths-down-globally-right-wing-terror-on-rise.

192. "Deaths from Terrorism Down in 2020," Global Terrorism Index, https://www .visionofhumanity.org/global-terrorism-index-2020-deaths-from-terrorism-reach-five -year-low-but-new-risks-emerge/.

193. For an interesting discussion, see Johannes Due Enstad, "Right Wing Terrorism and Violence in Putin's Russia," *Perspectives on Terrorism* 12, no. 6 (2018): 88–103.

194. "Neo-Nazi Gang Jailed Over 27 Murders," *RT*, July 12, 2011, https://www.rt.com/russia /neo-nazi-gang-27-murders/.

195. Janet Reitman, "U.S. Law Enforcement Failed to See the Threat of White Nationalism, Now They Don't Know How to Stop It," *New York Times*, November 3, 2018, https://www .nytimes.com/2018/11/03/magazine/FBI-charlottesville-white-nationalism-far-right.html.

196. Nick Corasaniti, Richard Pérez-Peña, and Lizette Alvarez, "Church Massacre Suspect Held as Charleston Grieves," *New York Times*, June 18, 2015, https://www.nytimes.com /2015/06/19/us/charleston-church-shooting.html.

197. Morgan Winsor, "Anti-Semitic Attacks in the US Have Doubled: ADL," *ABC News*, April 30, 2019, https://abcnews.go.com/US/anti-semitic-attacks-us-doubled-adl/story ?id=62722230.

198. Miriam Jordan, "HIAS, the Jewish Agency Criticized by the Shooting Suspect, Has a History of Aiding Refugees," *New York Times*, October 28, 2018, https://www.nytimes .com/2018/10/28/us/hias-pittsburgh-robert-bowers.html. Mark Oppenheimer provides an excellent analysis of the Pittsburgh Jewish community's reaction in *Squirrel Hill: The Tree of Life Synagogue Shooting and the Soul of the Neighborhood* (New York: Knopf, 2021).

199. Jill Cowan, "What to Know About the Poway Synagogue Shooting," *New York Times*, April 29, 2019, https://www.nytimes.com/2019/04/29/us/synagogue-shooting.html.

200. "2018 Hate Crime Statistics Released," U.S. Federal Bureau of Investigation, November 12, 2019, https://www.fbi.gov/news/stories/2018-hate-crime-statistics-released-111219.

201. Ed Shanahan, "Kosher Market Attack in Jersey City: 'I Just Hope They're Safe,'" *New York Times*, December 10, 2019, https://www.nytimes.com/2019/12/10/nyregion/kosher -supermarket-jersey-city.html.

202. Ken Schwencke, "Confusion, Fear, Cynicism: Why People Don't Report Hate Incidents," *ProPublica*, July 31, 2017, https://www.propublica.org/article/confusion-fear-cynicism-why-people-dont-report-hate-incidents.

203. Ruth Graham and Liam Stack, "Anti-Semitism Surges in Wake of Gaza Clash," *New York Times*, May 27, 2021.

204. Mattia Caniglia, Linda Winkler, and Solene Metais, *The Rise of the Right-Wing Violent Extremism Threat in Germany and Its Transnational Character*, European Strategic Intelligence and Security Center (ESISC), February 27, 2020, http://www. esisc.org/upload /publications/analyses/the-rise-of-the-right-wing-violent-extremism-threat-in -germany-and-its-transnational character.

205. Bill Bostock, "The Mass Shooter Who Killed 9 in Germany Published a Racist Manifesto Where He Identified as an Incel and Accused Trump of Stealing His Populist Slogans," *Insider*, February 20, 2020, https://www.insider.com/hanau-terrorist-manifesto -shows-non-white-hatred-incel-trump-theft-2020-2.

206. "White Supremacist Is Sentenced to Life for Synagogue Attack" *New York Times*, December 21, 2020, https://www.nytimes.com/2020/12/21/world/europe/germany -synagogue-attack.html.

207. Melissa Eddy, "German White Supremacist Is Sentenced to Life for Synagogue Attack," *New York Times*, January 15, 2021.

208. Katrin Bennhold, "An Officer's Double Life Puts Germany on Trial," *HYPERLINK "https://longform.org/archive/publications/new-york-times" New York Times*, December 29, 2020, https://longform.org/posts/an-officer-s-double-life-puts-germany-on-trial.

INDEX